History May Be Searched in Vain

History May Be Searched in Vain

A Military History of the Mormon Battalion

by
Sherman L. Fleek

UNIVERSITY OF OKLAHOMA PRESS
NORMAN

LIBRARY OF CONGRESS CATALOG CARD NUMBER 2005030741

Library of Congress Cataloging-in-Publication Data

Fleek, Sherman L.
 History may be searched in vain : a military history of the Mormon Battalion / by Sherman L. Fleek.
   p. cm. — (Frontier military series ; 25)
 Includes bibliographical references and index.
 ISBN 978-0-8061-9298-7 (paper)
 1. United States. Army. Mormon Battalion. 2. Mexican War, 1846–1848—Regimental histories—United States. 3. Mexican War, 1846–1848—Participation, Mormon. 4. Mormons—Southwest, New—History—19th century. 5. Mexican War, 1846–1848—Campaigns—Southwest, New. 6. Southwest, New—History, Military--19th century. I. Title. II. Series.
 E409.5.I72F58 2006
 973.6'24—dc22
                               2005030741

Library of Congress Cataloging-in-Publication Data as is
Copyright © 2006 by Sherman L. Fleek

Originally published in hardcover in the Frontier Military Series by the Arthur H. Clark Company, Spokane, Washington. Paperback published 2023 by the University of Oklahoma Press, Norman, Publishing Division of the University. Manufactured in the U.S.A.

The paper in this book meets the guidelines for permanence and durability of the Committee on Production Guidelines for Book Longevity of the Council on Library Resources, Inc.

All rights reserved. No part of this publication may be reproduced, stored in a retrieval system, or transmitted, in any form or by any means, electronic, mechanical, photocopying, recording, or otherwise—except as permitted under Section 107 or 108 of the United States Copyright Act—without the prior written permission of the University of Oklahoma Press.

Table of Contents

Maps and Illustrations 6
Chronology 7
Preface 17
Acknowledgements 21
Introduction 25
Manifest Mexico: Mr. Polk's War? 37
A Nation and a People 51
War Aims and a "Little" Mission 65
The Army for Mexico 81
The Army of the West and the Camps of Israel . . . 101
Recruiting the Battalion 125
The March Begins 143
A Change in Command 171
"Tyrants and Oppressors" 189
Cooke in Command 221
Cooke's Wagon Road 247
A Near Battle 273
An Equal March of Infantry 301
Occupying California 319
"You Are Discharged" 345
Epilogue 373
Appendix A: Army Pay Scale, 1846 385
Appendix B: Mormon Battalion Command and Staff . . 387
Bibliography 391
Index 403

Maps and Illustrations

First Lieutenant Andrew Jackson "AJ" Smith	85
Philip St. George Cooke	86
Captain James Allen	116
Melissa Coray	124
Map, Council Bluffs to Santa Fe and Pueblo	160
Map, The Mexica War, 1846–47	165
Captain James S. Brown	168
Second Lieutenant George Stoneman	216
Map, Cooke's Wagon Road	220
Philip St. George Cooke	224
Kit Carson	225
Tucson	286
Mission Church of San Xavier del Bac	291
Village of Pima Indians	296
Sergeant Major James Ferguson	369
Lieutenant Ruel Barrus	372

Chronology

1845

March 1	President John Tyler signs Texas annexation resolution. Texas will become the twenty-eighth state in December.
March 4	James K. Polk inaugurated as eleventh president of the United States.
July 25	Gen. Zachary Taylor and the Army of Occupation enter Corpus Cristi.
December 6	John Slidell reaches Mexico City and attempts to negotiate a peaceful resolution to the Texas boundary controversy. Slidell is also to attempt the purchase of New Mexico and Alta, or Upper, California from Mexico.
December 31	Gen. Mariano Paredes leads a bloodless coup against the Herrera government and becomes president of Mexico. He refuses any negotiations with the United States.

1846

January 13	President Polk orders General Taylor's Army of Occupation to the Rio Grande.
January 20	Brigham Young and Council of Twelve Apostles in Nauvoo, Illinois, publishes circular stating their intentions to send a pioneer company to the Rocky Mountains in the spring. He also sends a letter to Jesse Little of the Eastern States Mission to solicit aid from the federal government to assist in the migration west.

February 4	Vanguard of Latter-day Saints begin crossing the Mississippi River and establishes camps in Iowa Territory.
	Samuel Brannan and 238 Mormons set sail from New York aboard the *Brooklyn* en route to California via Cape Horn.
March 8	General Taylor and his army departs Corpus Cristi for its new post at the mouth of the Rio Grande; they will reach the Rio Grande on March 28.
April 7	Word of Mexico's rejection of Slidell's mission reaches Washington.
April 23	The Joint Occupation of Oregon Territory with Great Britain is terminated with the vote of the Senate. Polk will sign the termination resolution the next day.
April 25	Capt. Seth Thornton's reconnaissance patrol is attacked by Mexican forces. Taylor writes dispatch that hostilities have begun.
May 8	Taylor's army of all regular regiments defeats the Mexicans at the Battle of Palo Alto and wins the Battle of Resaca de la Palma the next day.
May 13	The United States declares war on Mexico. Secretary of War William Marcy sends a dispatch to Col. Stephen W. Kearny at Fort Leavenworth. He is to organize the Army of the West to march on Santa Fe. Marcy asks western governors for volunteers. Later, more than six thousand Missourians will serve in the war.
May 18	Taylor occupies Matamoros across the Rio Grande.
May 23	Jesse Little meets Amos Kendall, former postmaster general under Andrew Jackson, and discusses the Mormon Church's situation in Washington. A few days later Kendall meets with Polk and offers the Mormon Church as a possible source for volunteers in the Army of the West.
June 2	Polk orders Kearny to expand his mission to include California and directs him to enlist 500 Mormons into the Army of the West. The next day Jesse Little meets with Polk and Kendall to discuss the enlistment of Mormon volunteers.

CHRONOLOGY

June 5	Little meets Polk for the last time and learns of Polk's decision to enlist 500 Mormon volunteers once they arrive in California. Little tries to convince Polk to recruit the Mormons while still on the plains, but Polk rejects the offer.
June 14	Mormon parties reach the Missouri River at Council Bluffs. Lt. John C. Frémont and American settlers in California raise the "Bear Flag" standard and proclaim a new republic.
June 15	United States signs the treaty with Great Britain to settle Oregon Territory boundary issue at the 49th parallel.
June 16	Several companies of Col. Alexander Doniphan's 1st Missouri Mounted Volunteers as lead elements of the Army of the West depart Fort Leavenworth for Bent's Fort along the Santa Fe Trail.
June 19	Kearny orders Capt. James Allen, 1st Dragoons, to the Mormon camps in Iowa to muster 500 volunteers into military service.
June 26	Captain Allen arrives at Mount Pisgah, Iowa Territory, and declares his intention to enlist 500 Mormon volunteers in the war against Mexico. He issues his "Circular to the Mormons."
June 29	Kearny and most of the Army of the West assembled at Fort Leavenworth depart. The Mormon Battalion and Price's 2nd Mounted Missouri have yet to be organized or depart.
June 30	Captain Allen arrives at the Mormon camps at Council Bluffs. Jesse Little leaves Nauvoo to join with the Saints along the Iowa portion of the Mormon Trail. Brigham Young and church leaders decide to accept the offer to form the battalion even before meeting Capt. Allen.
July 7	Commodore John Sloat takes Monterey, California.
July 16	Captain Allen musters the Mormon volunteers into service at Council Bluffs, assumes command of the Mormon Battalion, and becomes a lieutenant colonel in the volunteer service.

July 20–21	The Mormon Battalion begins marching south to Fort Leavenworth.
July 23	Pvt. Samuel Boley, B Company, dies and is buried along the Missouri River. He is the first death in the battalion.
	Commodore Sloat relinquishes command of the Pacific Squadron to Commodore Robert Stockton at Monterey.
July 29	Lieutenant Frémont and California "Volunteer" Battalion raise the American flag in San Diego. Most of California seems to be under American control.
July 31	Samuel Brannan and 238 Mormons arrive in San Francisco Bay aboard the *Brooklyn*.
	General Taylor takes Camargo, Mexico.
August 1	The Mormon Battalion arrives at Fort Leavenworth and begins receiving its issue of military equipment.
August 1–2	The lead portion of the Army of the West under Kearny begin leaving Bent's Fort. Capt. Philip St. George Cooke leaves August 1 with a detail of twelve dragoons to march quickly to Santa Fe to negotiate a peace. Accompanying Cooke is James Magoffin, a longtime friend to Santa Fe traders.
August 3	In Mexico, the Paredes regime falls in a coup led by his vice president, Nicolas Bravo, a follower of Santa Anna.
August 7	Mormons known as the "Mississippi Saints" arrive at Pueblo in present-day Colorado and establish a temporary settlement near the fur trading post called Fort Pueblo.
August 8	Santa Anna departs Cuba en route to Mexico, passing through the American blockade, arriving on August 16 at Vera Cruz.
August 13	A, B, and E Companies of the Mormon Battalion leave Fort Leavenworth for Santa Fe. C and D Companies depart two days later, marching to overtake the rest of the battalion.
August 14	Frémont and Commodore Stockton enter Los Angeles. President Polk sends orders to Kearny to establish civil government in California.

August 18	Kearny enters and occupies Santa Fe.
August 19	C and D Companies overtake the main body of the Mormon Battalion. A strong thunderstorm disrupts the camp near Walaroosa, Kansas.
August 21	Lt. George Dykes and the sick men in wagons arrive in camp at Council Grove. He brings word of Lt. Col. Allen's illness. After recuperating from the storm, the battalion resumed the march.
August 23	Lt. Col. James Allen, first commander of the Mormon Battalion, dies. He is the first officer buried at what becomes Fort Leavenworth National Military Cemetery.
August 27	The battalion reaches Council Grove, a major landmark along the Santa Fe Trail.
August 29	Maj. Jeremiah Cloud, paymaster department; Lt. Andrew Jackson Smith, 1st Dragoons; and Dr. George B. Sanderson reach the battalion. Smith convinces the Mormon officers that he should become acting commander of the battalion.
August 30	Lieutenant Smith assumes acting command of the Mormon Battalion, which resumes the march under the leadership of Lt. "AJ" Smith the next day.
September 5	Mountain man and Frémont's scout Kit Carson departs California for Washington with news of the United States's control of California.
September 16	Lieutenant Smith orders Capt. Nelson Higgins of D Company to Pueblo, escorting some of the women and children with a squad of ten soldiers. They are to return to the battalion once the families are established. The next day Lieutenant Smith leads the battalion over the Cimarron route of the Santa Fe Trail. The battle of Nauvoo ends with the last of the Mormons leaving their homes.
September 20–24	Battle of Monterrey is fought against a well-defended and determined enemy as a difficult American victory.
September 23	Gen. John Wool, commanding the Army of the Center, departs San Antonio for his invasion of Chihuahua. His army consists mostly of volunteers.

	Mormons cross the Missouri River and begin building Winter Quarters, north of Omaha, Nebraska where some 5,000 Saints will live.
September 25	Kearny departs Santa Fe on his march to California, leaving Col. Alexander Doniphan in command at Santa Fe and Charles Bent as civil governor.
September 29	Lt. Archibald Gillespie, United States Marine Corps, surrenders Los Angeles to the Californios.
October 2	Kearny learns of Colonel Allen's death and appoints Captain Cooke to return to Santa Fe and assume command of the Mormon Battalion. Lieutenant Smith receives a dispatch ordering him to have the battalion reach Santa Fe by October 10 or the battalion will be disbanded.
October 3	Smith decides to divide the battalion and lead the strongest 250 men to Santa Fe. The main body is under way mid-afternoon.
October 6	Kearny meets Kit Carson along the Rio Grande and learns that California is under American control. Kearny persuades Carson to lead his command back to California. He also leaves his wagons for Cooke to bring to California and sends 200 of his 300 dragoons back to Santa Fe. Kearny, with a light mobile force, strikes out for California.
October 9	Lieutenant Smith leads the main body of the battalion into Santa Fe. The rear detachment will arrive on October 11.
October 13	Cooke assumes command of the Mormon Battalion and is thus promoted to lieutenant colonel of volunteers.
October 18	Cooke orders a detachment of sick men and families to Pueblo under the command of Capt. James Brown. All but five of the women are sent off and many able-bodied men escort their families to Pueblo.
October 19	Battalion leaves Santa Fe for its march to California.
November 1	Cooke reorganizes the battalion, placing Lt. George Dykes, the battalion adjutant, in command of D Company. Lt. Philemon Merrill becomes adjutant.

CHRONOLOGY

November 10	Cooke sends the last sick detachment of 55 men and 1 woman under Lt. William Wesley Willis to Pueblo. Four women remain.
November 13	Cooke leads the battalion away from the Rio Grande and the Chihuahua Road. They commence what will be called Cooke's Wagon Road.
November 17	The sick detachment under Capt. Brown arrives at Pueblo.
November 19	Polk appoints Gen. Winfield Scott to command the invasion of central Mexico and the capture of Mexico City. He will leave Washington on November 23.
November 22	Kearny reaches the Colorado River junction with the Gila.
November 30	The battalion crosses over the continental divide in the Guadalupe Mountains.
December 6	Kearny fights the Battle of San Pasqual. Twenty-one Americans are killed, and Kearny moves toward San Diego, when he is blocked and then besieged by Mexican forces a few days later. American reinforcements relieve Kearny and his command arrives at San Diego on December 12.
December 9	Mormon Battalion reaches the San Pedro River. Cooke's Wagon Road ends.
December 11	Wild cattle charge into the battalion during a halt along the San Pedro River and cause a ruckus. The march continues later that day.
December 12	Col. Alexander Doniphan and his 1st Missouri Regiment begin their campaign into Chihuahua.
December 16	The Mormon Battalion reaches Tucson and nearly has a battle with Mexican forces. The battalion camps north of town.
December 21	The battalion reaches the Gila River after a very hard march across the desert from Tucson. Along the Gila they follow the Dragoon Trail towards California
December 25	Colonel Doniphan's 1st Missouri defeats Mexicans at the Battle of Brazito, then enters El Paso.

1847

January 1	Cooke and Lt. George Stoneman launch a pontoon boat to float supplies down the Gila River. This endeavor will ultimately fail.
January 8	The battalion camps near the confluence of the Colorado and Gila rivers.
	Kearny and Stockton defeat the Mexicans at San Gabriel River and La Mesa the next day. Armed Mexican resistance in California ends.
January 9–10	The battalion makes the river crossing over the Colorado River and enters California.
January 19	Mexican revolt in Taos, New Mexico, begins. Governor Charles Bent is murdered. Col. Sterling Price of the 2nd Missouri Mounted Volunteers moves against the revolt and will crush it by February 4.
January 21	Battalion reaches Warner's Ranch and rests for two days.
January 29	The Mormon Battalion reaches San Diego, bringing the long march to an end.
February 3	The battalion is posted to Mission San Luis Rey.
February 8	Cooke commences drilling and training the battalion, the first real training it received.
February 22 & 23	Taylor defeats Santa Anna at the Battle of Buena Vista with an army consisting mostly of untested volunteers.
February 28	Doniphan and the 1st Missouri Volunteers win the Battle of Sacramento, then occupies Chihuahua.
March 9	Gen. Winfield Scott lands over 11,000 men at Vera Cruz, which will fall on March 29.
March 15	Cooke orders B Company to San Diego for garrison duty.
March 19	Mormon Battalion ordered to Los Angeles.
April 4–7	First Mormon groups of the pioneer party under Brigham Young begin to organize and move out from Winter Quarters towards the Elkhorn River in present-day Nebraska.
April 8	General Scott begins his campaign eastward towards Mexico City.

CHRONOLOGY 15

April 17	Cooke begins sending patrols to Cajon Pass and other key places to safeguard ranches and commerce.
April 18	Scott defeats Santa Anna at the Battle of Cerro Gordo.
April 24	Cooke orders the construction of Fort Moore on a hill overlooking Los Angeles.
May 9	Lt. Samuel Thompson of C Company and his squad skirmish with Indians near the Isaac Williams ranch. Several Indians are killed and wounded, with two battalion soldiers wounded.
May 13	Lt. Col. Cooke relinquishes command of the Mormon Battalion in order to return east with General Kearny. Mormon Capt. Jefferson Hunt becomes acting commander. Fifteen Mormon soldiers will serve as escorts for Kearny.
May 14	Nicholas Trist, President Polk's peace emissary, reaches Jalapa, Mexico, following Scott's army to Mexico City.
May 22	Doniphan and the 1st Missouri Volunteers meet Gen. John Wool at Buena Vista. In a few days his regiment will reach the Gulf of Mexico, completing the longest overland campaign in American history.
June 1	Brigham Young's pioneer party reaches Fort John, future Fort Laramie, Wyoming.
June 16	Kearny begins his march from Sutter's Fort eastward towards Fort Leavenworth. Col. Richard Mason, commander of the 1st Dragoons, assumes command of the Tenth Military Department and military governorship of California.
June 20	Col. Alexander Doniphan and the 1st Missouri are discharged in New Orleans and paid for the first time during their year's military service.
July 4	Col. Stevenson dedicates Fort Moore, named in honor of Capt. Benjamin Moore of the 1st Dragoons, killed at San Pasqual.
July 15	B Company arrives at Los Angeles, relieved from its occupation duties at San Diego.
July 16	Capt. Andrew Jackson Smith, 1st Dragoons, discharges the Mormon Battalion from active military service at Los Angeles.

July 20	Eighty-one Mormon Battalion veterans re-enlist for six months' service and become a company-size unit designated as the Mormon Volunteers.
July 21	Mormons Orson Pratt and Erastus Snow enter the Valley of the Great Salt Lake. Most of the advance company will enter the next day. Brigham Young and the last group of the pioneer company enter the valley on July 24.
August 20	Scott wins the battles of Churubusco and Contreras, near Mexico City.
August 22	Kearny and party reaches Fort Leavenworth. John C. Frémont is arrested for insubordination and eventually will be court martialed.
September 8	Scott wins the Battle of Molino del Rey. A week later, on September 13, Scott attacks Chapultepec Castle and Mexico City falls. Scott enters the city and receives the surrender the next day. The final major battles of the war are over.
December 27	Brigham Young, who returned from the Great Basin, is sustained and ordained as second president of the church. This action occurs during a conference of the church at Council Bluffs, Iowa, after his return eastward.

1848

January 24	James Marshall discovers gold near Sutter's Fort in California. The next year the great gold rush begins, which will bring several hundred thousand Americans to California.
February 2	Nicholas Trist signs the peace treaty of Guadalupe Hildago with Mexico, ending the Mexican War. The United States pays $15 million for land it already controls.
March 14	The Mormon Volunteers are discharged from active service.
July 15	Last U.S. troops under Col. William Worth leave Mexico.
October 31	Brig. Gen. Stephen Watts Kearny dies in St. Louis at the age of fifty-four.

Preface

My first real experience with the route the Mormon Battalion followed was more accident than process. In the early spring of 1985, I was flying a training mission in an Army AH-1 "Cobra" attack helicopter gunship northwest of Fort Bliss, near El Paso, Texas. We came to a high hover out in the badlands of southwest New Mexico a few miles northeast of Deming, when my fellow pilot, a non-Mormon, explained that we were a few hundred feet above and away from the adobe ruins of Fort Cummings, which was established in 1863. As we hovered around he also said that, since I was a Latter-day Saint, I would appreciate the fact that the famous Mormon Battalion had camped at this exact location during its march to California. On the night of November 16, 1846, the Mormon Battalion found water and camped at what is known today as Cooke's Spring, below Cooke's Peak, at the tip of Cooke's Range, all named in honor of Lieutenant Colonel Philip St. George Cooke, the battalion's most prominent commander. Thus was my first introduction with the route of march of the Mormon Battalion.

Almost fifteen years later, in February 1999, I finally determined that it was time to make the trek following the entire route of the Mormon Battalion. On several occasions I had followed or visited some of the route, but not the entire course at one time. I packed the necessary gear, my faithful army cot that has served me for more than a decade, and all the appropriate books, notebooks, travel guides, and my own maps, and departed in my Ford Ranger pickup truck. I call it a route because the majority of the battalion's route followed existing roads or trails such as the Santa Fe Trail and other roads.

The main and most important road guide was Dr. Stanley Kimball's 1988 *Historic Sites and Markers along the Mormon and Other Great Western Trails*, which I found to be invaluable. I also had Dr. Charles Peterson's and associates' 1972 *The Mormon Battalion Trail Guide*, another invaluable source, which provided incredible period accounts and descriptions of the events, sites, and scenes. I read word for word again Dr. John Yurtinus's remarkable and in-depth study, *A Ram in the Thicket: The Mormon Battalion in the Mexican War*. This was my Bible and light for my personal discovery of the march of the Mormon Battalion.

The purpose of this study is not to be a survey or history of the route and march, but I honestly felt that I could not finish this book until I experienced the route—completely and all at one time—so I took the time to drive the route. I will never forget reaching Cooke's Spring just at dusk and sleeping under the very cold open sky. I lay in my army mountain sleeping bag, and since there was no light from large cities, I could see forever. The heavens were completely open before me. I wondered if the battalion men sleeping here over 152 years earlier thought of the same things as I did. I felt as if I were completely alone, out on this tough and forbidding but beautiful desert landscape. I was warm, comfortable, and off the cold ground, whereas on November 16, 1846, with perhaps only a blanket for shelter, the battalion was definitely roughing it.

The Mormon Battalion saga has always been an interesting story to me, captivating me more in recent years to the point that I used the battalion as the basis for my thesis in graduate school. I learned a few things about the battalion in my youth. As I began my military career I naturally took more interest in the Mormon Battalion and its history. But it was not until I was hopelessly involved as a serious historian and had a few articles published that the importance of the Mormon Battalion as a military entity took root in my soul. I think I have read almost every available work concerning the history of the battalion, most every article, book,

PREFACE 19

and official document that I know of, to include dozens of the journals and diaries written by the veterans. I may have missed a few obscure or difficult-to-find journals, or any that are held by private owners, but most of the published and collected information I have perused.

It was a glorious moment on July 13, 1996, to dress in a period uniform and act as first sergeant of E Company during the historical mustering re-enactment at Council Bluffs. Since I was on active duty and had had much training in drill and ceremony, I was happy to join the ranks. The experience was both gratifying and pleasurable to march men about who, whether LDS or not, honored the battalion so much that they would serve as modern representatives of ancestors and others.

Acknowledgements

Since that day during the summer of 1996 when I decided to take the basic research of my master's degree thesis and complete this book, there have been many institutions and people I need to thank. I spent many hours at the Department of Church and Family History of the Church of Jesus Christ of Latter-day Saints, the Harold B. Lee Library at Brigham Young University, the Joseph Fielding Smith Institute for LDS History, the Utah Historical Society in Salt Lake City, the Library at the United States Military Academy at West Point, and the Missouri Historical Society in St. Louis. In Washington, D.C., I made many frequent visits to the Library of Congress, the National Archives, the Pentagon Library, and the United States Army Center of Military History. The many remembered but unnamed staff members who were helpful with every request, great and small, even with looks of curiosity and at times bewilderment, I thank with all my heart.

Special thanks to reviewers and readers who gave me invaluable assistance in every possible way. Dr. Larry Porter, now retired from Brigham Young University, was my guiding light at every turn, a great mentor and patient critic. The late Dr. Stanley B. Kimball taught history at Southern Illinois University at Edwardsville, near where I was stationed for three years. Stan knew the American immigrant trails better than most and was equaled by only a few. William G. Hartley, at Brigham Young University's Smith Institute before it sadly closed in July 2005, having never served in the military, saw the great void in Mormon Battalion scholarship with no genuine study of the military perspective. Kayla Willey of the

Lee Library at Brigham Young University, word-smithed and corrected nearly every page in early stages of the manuscript.

Several military historians reviewed the manuscript and provided great guidance. Lieutenant Colonel Joseph Whitehorne, U.S. Army (ret.) and Ph.D., offered substantial and wonderful comments based on his vast knowledge of military history as former historian for the secretary of the army. Joe's contribution was invaluable and essential. Lieutenant Colonel Alan Huffines of the Texas Army National Guard and his perspective as a historian of the Mexican War, never let me forget that it was the Texas Rangers who single-handedly won the Mexican War; Major Les' Melnyk, Ph.D., my colleague in the historical office at National Guard Bureau, a WWII and European military historian, saw with detached distance many ways where I wandered in the forest of details. Lieutenant Colonel Dan Stoneking, read the manuscript with his keen and trained eye for language, diction, and usage. Major David Donohue, U.S. Army (ret.), a fine and well-read military historian, provided assistance, especially with his strong background in Jacksonian and frontier era military history. Steve Allie, director of Fort Leavenworth's Frontier Army Museum, reviewed my military and other chapters. Dr. Joseph Dawson, of Texas A & M University, provided incredible assistance and insight. Dr. Richard Bruce Winders, of the Alamo Historical Museum, taught me much concerning the Mexican War and the military period. I also thank Dr. Stephen Carney of the U.S. Army Center of Military History for his review, recommendations and expertise as a Mexican War historian.

As the manuscript evolved, perhaps no two people provided more assistance, editing, and guidance in the final stages and helped in the publication process than Will Bagley and Lavina Fielding Anderson, both of the Mormon History Association. Without Will's championing the project, I doubt I would be writing this now.

There were other very special readers who assisted in soldier life, firearms, frontier army topics, and primary sources, as well as editing, grammar, structure, and chapter organization. My good friends

ACKNOWLEDGEMENTS

Joe Benton of Layton, Utah, and John Roller of Stafford, Virginia, took the time to read my manuscript and gave me insight for the general reader, one of my primary audiences.

Lastly, but not least, a special colleague I would like to thank: Mr. Val John Halford, a re-enactor and student of the battalion, who, having read some of my early articles, after several years tracked me down as a detective would and soon became a fast friend. Val provided the most thorough comments and critique that I received, point by point, page by page. His great love of the Mormon Battalion and his enthusiasm for a military perspective of the battalion gave me hope that there would be readers who would find interest in the book. Val's involvement has been crucial and it is beyond my ability to thank him.

Thanks to publishers and editors Bob Clark and Ariane Smith of the Arthur H. Clark Company, for accepting the manuscript and making it into a beautiful product and worthy read. Their meticulous review, edit, their willingness to see things my way, and their professional acumen no historian would turn away.

My wife, Michel, and my five children were encouraging, helpful, and fun throughout.

> LT. COL. SHERMAN L. FLEEK, U.S. ARMY (RET.)
> near New Market, Virginia
> November 2005

Introduction

History loves incongruities, turnabouts, and reversals. When people or events shift and they who were at odds become allies, or they who were friends become enemies—this is one of the great ironies in the affairs of men. Such is the case with the history of the Mormon Battalion. Lieutenant Colonel Philip St. George Cooke, a regular army officer, commanded the battalion during most of its service in 1846–47 and most notably during its long march to California. Most of the Mormon men he commanded developed a great respect for him, and he certainly held them in great regard as soldiers. Just ten short years later, in 1857, Cooke, commanding the 2nd U.S. Dragoons, marched west to Utah Territory as part of a military force to suppress the alleged rebellion of the Mormon people against federal authority. The likelihood of fighting and bloodshed was very possible, and some of the Mormon men sworn to stop the army's advance had served under Cooke in the battalion. Thus, fellow soldiers who had served together through so much were now facing each other in a new and unusual conflict. Fortunately, the Utah Expedition did not engage in battle, and former comrades in arms did not shed each other's blood.

The Mormon Battalion was a volunteer unit of five companies of mostly Mormon men who enlisted to fight in the Mexican War. It served as part of General Stephen W. Kearny's Army of the West invading and occupying what would become New Mexico, Arizona, and California. The battalion formed in July 1846 in Council

Bluffs, Iowa, and marched to California, where it was discharged from federal service in July 1847, after exactly one year's service. The battalion did not experience combat, but made one of the most incredible and challenging marches in American military history. The Mormon Battalion's significance centers around its religious nature, a rarity in American history; through the service and direct support of this body of soldiers who enlisted for religious and not patriotic reasons—leaving their families on the plains of the West during a dangerous trek—the Mormon hegira moved on to their new promised land in the West.

The Mormon Battalion's story of a grueling march across wide prairies, mountains, and deserts is difficult for us in the modern era to appreciate. The march is central to the battalion's story. It symbolizes the very essence of the Mormon drama as a frontier epic, and proves more than anything else the men's loyalty, stamina, and sacrifice. It is the unifying bond that laces through the story and ties the chronology and action together. No matter the dramatic events, the delays en route, or the personal experiences that transpired, the story always returned to the epic march.

This book is a military history of the Mormon Battalion. This is but one of many ways to view its history. The most common portrayal has been to treat the battalion as a group of pioneers, rather than soldiers. This depiction explains the great assistance the battalion provided to the Mormon flight; the opening for settlement of that region of the West through which the battalion traveled; the conflict between military and religious authority; the combat effectiveness of a religious unit that never fought in battle; and many other topics, some of which will be touched upon in this study.

Strangely, the battalion's story has not been told from the perspective of the profession of arms. Since it did not engage in battle, military historians have paid little attention to it. One may wonder what military value and benefit studying the Mormon Battalion would provide. How does one assess a military organization's ability and potential to serve in combat when it never in fact saw action?

INTRODUCTION

As those who have served in the military know, the acid test comes from evaluating rigorous and realistic training, morale, *esprit de corps*, and discipline infractions. In the Mexican War, another facet of importance was the desertion rate of 8 percent, nearly double that of any other American war.[1] With only one desertion, the Mormon Battalion did not experience one of the debilitating problems that other volunteer and regular army units did during the Mexican War.

The Mormon Battalion was the only religious unit in American military history in federal service, having been recruited solely from one religious body and having a religious title as the unit designation. The religious quality makes the Mormon Battalion different from other volunteer regiments called to arms. Certain questions, therefore, must follow, especially for the military commander tasked with leading such an organization: What were the soldiers' loyalties? If the soldiers were more loyal to their religion, would they submit to military discipline and authority? Is it a good practice to marshal soldiers from one religion for military service?

The Mormon Battalion represented other important qualities not often experienced in American military history. Regular army officers commanded the battalion during most of its service, instead of volunteer officers. In fact, army officials went to great lengths to insure that regulars lead the Mormon soldiers. Of the scores of volunteer regiments and battalions, only a very few had officers from the regular establishment take command.

The common reasons that other men joined the army—individual or collective patriotism, adventure, boredom, or avoiding the law—did not apply to the Mormon men who enlisted because of the directives and desires of their ecclesiastical leader, Brigham Young. There is no doubt that without Brigham Young's acceptance of the offer to form the battalion, there would have been no Mormon Battalion. The men enlisted as a religious duty rather than as a call to arms, and their service was linked to the promise

---

[1] Miller, *The Shamrock and the Sword*, 174. The army sometimes experienced much higher rates during peacetime on the frontier.

that if they enlisted to support and help fund the Mormon trek across the plains, the church in turn would support their families. Some of the salaries and allowances that these soldiers earned were donated to representatives for church use. No other American military unit has been formed to forward the cause of a religious group. Religion was central to the men, and it shaped the battalion in many ways.

Few soldiers have faced the difficult circumstance that the Mormon soldiers experienced in 1846: their families were also crossing the plains, encountering hardships and dangers themselves rather than being comfortable and protected at home and hearth. This situation would cause tremendous anxiety for a soldier in war. One of the great comforts to a soldier of any era is the knowledge that should he survive the horror of war, he would soon return home to the safety of his loved ones. The members of the Mormon Battalion did not have that same reassurance since they did not have a traditional, stable family homestead to return to after their service. In fact, most of the soldiers not only made the march of some 1,900 miles to California, but they also had to make the return journey either to the Great Basin or back to the Missouri River to reunite with their families.

The battalion was also unusual in American history because several families accompanied it for a portion of the journey, creating an additional hardship with the safety and welfare of several large families and dozens of women and children. Many military campaigns have had their various camp-followers, but commanders discouraged the practice at times for sound military reasons. During American campaigns, commanders rarely allowed families and other non-combatants to accompany armies. However, army regulations did allow the service of company laundresses and cooks. Oftentimes personal servants, either slaves or hired help, accompanied the soldiers, especially officers. This was an accepted practice of campaigning. The Mormon Battalion, however, was encumbered with many additional non-combatants, a condition that is unacceptable for military operations during war. When the fami-

INTRODUCTION

lies and most of the women were detached from the battalion, there was great anxiety and frustration among the men, affecting morale and discipline. Some able-bodied men refused to continue the march while their families and wives departed for Pueblo, present-day Colorado. This situation is a burden to a commander and to the good order and discipline of a combat unit.

It is important to place the Mormon Battalion fully into the context of the Mexican War itself. Many authors have failed to adequately link the battalion's history with Brigadier General Stephen W. Kearny's Army of the West or the strategic political and military dramas unfolding in Washington, Texas, northern Mexico and Mexico City. Previous writers and historians of the battalion, for the most part, have been silent on the causes of the war and the campaigns in Texas and Mexico, and say little of the campaign for New Mexico and California, where the Mormon Battalion played a small but essential part.

The Mexican War (known now in some circles as the U.S.-Mexican War) has mostly been an unpopular war, and few have taken the time to really understand the dimensions of this conflict. Once the Treaty of Guadalupe Hildago, which ended the war in 1848, became a reality, the United States acquired territory that added some 25 percent more land than it had before the war started in 1846. This area comprised California, Nevada, Utah, most of Arizona and New Mexico, and some areas of Colorado, Wyoming, and Oklahoma. But what of the war that provided so much territory?

"Overshadowed by the cataclysmic Civil War only thirteen years later," wrote historian John S. D. Eisenhower, "the Mexican War has been practically forgotten in the United States."[2] Like the War of 1812, the Mexican War—including the firearms, military life, morale, rank structure, organization, medical methods, military terms, supply and logistics, and even the geography of it—is unknown to most people, especially in the present day. Some

---
[2]Eisenhower, *So Far from God: The U.S. War with Mexico, 1846–1848*, xvii.

Americans, such as Civil War historians and buffs, know that many future general officers of the Civil War, both Federal and Confederate, received their baptism of fire during the Mexican War. Future generals such as U. S. Grant, Robert E. Lee, George McClellan, George Meade, James Longstreet, and Thomas Jackson, to name a few, first tasted battle in the Mexican War.

The American armed forces performed brilliantly during the Mexican War. In twenty or so major battles Americans fought against superior numbers, usually in less than desirable tactical positions. The results were remarkable. The United States Army was not only victorious but was nearly always decisively so. American armies defeated Mexican army after army. Some have written concerning America's military might against a smaller and militarily weaker Mexico; even General U. S. Grant, in his celebrated memoirs, raised this point. Superficially, that may be what many believe at first consideration. However, the United States, as in nearly every war, was unprepared for combat operations. When General Zachary Taylor moved into the disputed land between the Nueces River and Rio Grande in the summer of 1845, he commanded nearly half of the regular soldiers of the U.S. Army, only some 3,500 troops. European experts, including the esteemed Duke of Wellington, one of the victors at Waterloo, spelled doom for American military might against a larger regular Mexican army.

The call to arms was spontaneous and overwhelming for recruiting quotas, and the United States was left to assemble, organize, outfit, and train some 72,000 volunteers and 42,000 new recruits that would fill the under-manned regular regiments, with Congress authorizing ten new regiments of regulars. The antiquated common or enrolled militia system, where men had mandatory service, was unprepared and unreliable for military operations. Therefore, President James K. Polk elected to augment the regular army with volunteer units from the states, which were different from the common militia. These units were organized from various cities and counties and became a nucleus for the new state regiments and battalions. These volunteer units would be officered by men elected from their own ranks, or in some cases were led by current or former regular army officers. The Mormon Battalion was a typical volunteer battalion in many ways, but with three main differences: first, and most profound, its unique religious character; second, the commanders were regular army officers; and lastly, all the other officers and noncommissioned officers were appointed by a religious leader, Brigham Young, and not elected by the men as in other volunteer units.

Religion played a significant part in Mexico's war effort, and Mexican leaders often portrayed the war as defending Catholicism against "Yankee" Protestant aggression. Polk, the clever politician, recognized the religious dimension and commissioned Roman Catholic priests as chaplains in the army and aggressively sought support from American bishops and clergy.[3] Polk and his advisors severely underestimated the Mexican resolve to wage war. It is an amazing feat that Mexico was able to organize, equip, and train an army, then fight and lose a battle, then reorganize, re-equip, and re-train, fighting time and time again only to meet more disaster and ruin. The true and astounding measure of Mexican War leadership does not lie only with the Americans, but also with Mexico. This devotion matches Washington and his honored heroes of Valley Forge.

The Mexican War was won by two primary factors. The first was leadership—the distinguished and outstanding ability of three extraordinary but very different generals: Winfield Scott, Stephen Kearny, and Zachary Taylor. To a large degree, leadership on the small unit level found in companies and platoons was also extraordinary due to the abilities of hundreds of West Point–trained junior officers. The Mexican War was not only the testing ground for leaders of the Civil War, but it was also the validation of fire for the United States Military Academy. Leaders in the volunteer ranks such as Colonels Alexander Doniphan and Jefferson Davis, are great examples of the time-honored American icon: the citizen soldier. The second winning factor was the superiority of Ameri-

---

[3]Norton, *Struggling for Recognition: The United States Army Chaplaincy, 1791–1865*, 66–69.

can artillery, which decimated Mexican formations before they were able to close on the American lines. By this time American artillery had few peers in the world, and the accomplishments of these artillerymen are legendary and have been unparalleled since the days of Bonaparte and his triumphs.

The Mormon Battalion is thus revealed, a little-known but important part of the Mexican War. For years after the conflict, battalion veterans lived normal lives in historical obscurity, as do most veterans of wars. As they aged, the men reflected on their unique and distinguished service; before long, journals, biographies, and histories began to appear. Under the direction of the First Presidency, the presiding body of the Church of Jesus Christ of Latter-day Saints, Daniel Tyler, former sergeant of C Company, wrote his 1881 classic, *A Concise History of the Mormon Battalion in the Mexican War: 1846–1848*. For generations Tyler's dated chronicle was the bible of the battalion for Utah historical societies, veterans groups, church members, and scholars. But because of Tyler, with all his personal reflections and myths given to legend, any new study of the battalion has suffered for decades. The renowned Mormon historian B. H. Roberts wrote a short monograph in 1919, *The Mormon Battalion: Its History and Achievements*. Though Roberts is one of the great Mormon historians, this work was one of his less noteworthy contributions, which he wrote quickly to assist the funding for a Mormon Battalion monument at the state capitol in Utah. It dispels many popular but incorrect views, but is lacking in scope and depth. Other less scholarly and more readily available books came forth from religious and pioneer associations that highlighted the pioneer contributions of the battalion. Thus, the men of the Mormon Battalion for decades have been viewed as pioneers and not soldiers.

In 1928 Frank Alfred Golder published the best to-date journal study of the battalion, *The March of the Mormon Battalion, From Council Bluffs to California: Taken from the Journal of Henry Standage*. This work established a thorough narrative of the battalion's service.

INTRODUCTION

In 1975 John F. Yurtinus completed the most detailed and exhaustive study of the battalion to date, entitled "A Ram in the Thicket: The Mormon Battalion in the Mexican War." He deserves the praise and thanks of all students investigating the battalion, including this author. Unfortunately, though it has shortcomings with the military topics and terminology, Dr. Yurtinus has not yet published this important dissertation as a book.

By the mid-1990s several works appeared, which, more or less, champion the battalion members as pioneers and celebrate Mormon heritage rather than concentrate on their military service. Perhaps the most noteworthy is Norma B. Ricketts's *The Mormon Battalion: U.S. Army of the West, 1846-1848*, published in 1996. It is an outstanding research tool but it is not a scholarly book.[4] Recently a new documentary history of the battalion appeared under the editorship of David Bigler and Will Bagley, *Army of Israel: Mormon Battalion Narratives*, the fourth volume in this book's publisher's Kingdom in the West series. As a documentary history, it is an important collection of many lengthy primary source documents with excellent, detailed commentaries by two accomplished historians.

Being a military professional and a historian, I decided to approach the battalion from the view of the profession of arms and answer some of the nagging questions that non-military historians have neglected. The first is the obvious question: was the Mormon Battalion combat effective—meaning, could the battalion perform during war as a military unit? Second, in our contemporary era where the separation of church and state is a hallmark, one would question if organizing a religious unit was a sound military decision. Coupled with questions of morale, loyalty, and discipline, it would be interesting to examine the conflict of military versus ecclesiastical authority. One must understand, however, that regular army officers such as Captains James Allen and Philip St.

---

[4]There was no such entity or designation as "U.S. Army of the West" as found in some books. It was the "Army of the West." The U.S. Army itself also encompasses field armies, theater armies, numbered armies, or other designations with the word army. In the Mexican War there were the Army of Observation, which became the Army of Occupation under General Taylor; the Army of the Center under General John Wool; and the Army of the West under General Stephen W. Kearny.

George Cooke, who commanded the battalion, and their superior, General Kearny, measured all things military by the regular army.

Many exaggerated stories and tales have risen to condemn the supposed cruelty and leadership of one of the temporary commanders of the battalion, Lieutenant Andrew Jackson Smith. During an era when branding, flogging (on rare occasions), and summary executions were still practiced, Smith's methods and discipline were no harsher than that of his peers. The main problem centered on Mormon attitudes and expectations of serving under benevolent Christian gentlemen as officers, and not the hardened frontier professionals that they were.

Some of the men had some limited military experience prior to joining the battalion. A few had served in state militia, and many had served in the Nauvoo Legion, an Illinois militia unit consisting mostly of Mormons in the early 1840s under the command of their prophet and leader, Lieutenant General Joseph Smith.[5] Some Mormon men who enlisted in the battalion had experienced a skirmish or two against mob elements or state militia in Missouri in 1838. Mormon Battalion service was the pinnacle of Mormon military involvement to the present.

To understand the Mormon Battalion, one must study the profession of arms because it is the story of soldiers serving during war. There are many obsolete terms, practices, and methods used in the 1840s that elude us today, which must be addressed for a full understanding. Wherever possible, old terms have been substituted with modern terms or usages for clarity. For example, the term "unit" was not in use in that era, but it is used freely as a modern military term, along with other terms such as unit designations of A Company, C Company, etc., instead of the nineteenth-century terminology of Company A, Company D, and so forth. The military world can be puzzling and difficult for some. Since the majority of Americans today have not served in the military as in previous generations and has little experience with military matters, this basic knowledge is even more important.

---

[5]Joseph Smith received a commission of lieutenant general (three star) from the state of Illinois. See Gardner, "The Nauvoo Legion, 1840–1845: A Unique Military Organization," 187–89.

INTRODUCTION

To capture the broad scope of the military and political events of the war, I have inserted short narrative summaries set off in italics near the chronological action of the story. These interpolations illustrate action in the larger war, events in Washington or Mexico, and other relative or defining events beyond the drama of the Mormon Battalion. They serve to place the battalion in proper historical context.

The Mormon Battalion probably holds the prize for the most journals and diaries per capita of any military unit in history: nearly eighty separate records coming from a body of just five hundred men. Over fifty diaries, journals, memoirs, and typed manuscript copies and accounts are available in public collections and another thirty or so are in private or family collections. I researched nearly all the accounts in public collections and used them as a solid basis for sampling, analysis, and interpretation. Many of the primary accounts, unfortunately, provided little substance for military history.

In the spring of 2003, the Mormon Battalion legacy received perhaps its greatest journal discovery in decades with the University of Utah acquisition of the journal of Dr. George B. Sanderson, a volunteer assistant surgeon assigned to the battalion. Joining the great accounts of Daniel Tyler, Levi Hancock, Henry Standage, William Coray, and others, this journal provides a window to the soul of one of the two most hated characters of the battalion. Dr. Sanderson, known in Mormon legend as "Dr. Death," kept a journal with a full sweep of personal and poignant observations of many facets of the battalion's legacy: military, medical, religious, and geographical descriptions of the land they marched through, accounts of the local populations and the suffering during the long and weary march to California, a few comical anecdotes, and many very stirring entries. Thus, I am honored to be the first historian to have a scholarly examination of Dr. George Sanderson's journal. I sense it may provide a completely new evaluation of an American physician serving during war, a man who has been unfairly labeled and held in contempt for generations. Along with Sanderson's journal, this book also includes a recently published letter by civilian Lewis Dent, brother-in-law of General and President Ulysess S. Grant, who also accompanied the battalion to California.

The journal entries have been used and copied just as they appear in the original or available typescript texts, without using editing techniques to announce misspellings and grammatical errors unless meaning or clarity are at stake. Brackets include important omissions of subjects or verbs to help clarify quoted passages.

There is no attempt to list all the battalion men, other than the officers and noncommissioned officers. In fact, the actual number of those who served in the Mormon Battalion is still under debate and probably always will be. Also, it is not in the scope of this work to offer analysis of the detachments that wintered at Pueblo and their winter sojourn, nor the many deeds and accomplishments of former battalion members on their journeys to Utah or to the Mormon camps in Iowa or Nebraska. Unlike the stories of the great poet Homer, this is the *Iliad* only and not the *Odyssey*, because once the men were discharged in Los Angeles in July 1847, they were no longer soldiers. The focus of this book is the military experience of the Mormon Battalion, which the government raised to wage war.

The Mormon Battalion is a story of service, duty, camaraderie, compassion, sacrifice, and suffering. Lieutenant Colonel Cooke's declaration of the battalion's march being unequaled in history does not necessarily mean a measure of distance, but one of performance and endurance under extremely difficult conditions. Cooke's leadership and the loyalty and duty of the Mormon men in helping to secure much of northern Mexico for the United States contributed to American expansionism. All wars have their "Mormon Battalions"—something to be proud of and honor despite the horrors and privations of war. War, with all its appalling violence and suffering, somehow creates or enables an outpouring of sacrifice and commitment that few human endeavors can. Selfless service for country and comrades can exalt and ennoble the soldier above the carnage.

CHAPTER ONE

Manifest Mexico: Mr. Polk's War?

Hostilities may now be considered as commenced.
—*General Zachary Taylor*

Captain Seth Thornton, 2nd United States Dragoons, led his mounted patrol of sixty-three dragoons up near a high-built corral of chaparral. Slowly and cautiously they inched towards the hacienda at the other end. His men were nervous and excited, but ready. For weeks in the spring of 1846 the tension of war was on their minds, and the last few days were especially difficult. The patrol arrived at the hacienda on April 25. Captain Thornton knew that a few days earlier some sixteen hundred mounted Mexican soldiers had reportedly crossed the Rio Grande into Texas and were possibly nearby. The Mexicans were under the command of General Anastasio Torrejón, a young and ambitious man who would prove to be a courageous soldier. Torrejón hungered to strike the Americans, and Thornton's men would be his first bite.

Thornton could not hope to engage such a large force; rather, his mission was to make a reconnaissance and report back to brevet Brigadier General Zachary Taylor. The Americans were facing a very difficult situation, serving as part of Taylor's Army of Occupation. They were in territory claimed both by Mexico and the former independent Republic of Texas, now the twenty-eighth state in the Union. Texas and Mexico had quarreled over this land between the Rio Grande and Nueces River for ten years—now it was America's quarrel.

Anxious and troubled, Thornton dismounted and approached the hacienda. To his rear were First Lieutenant William Hardee, a future general in the Confederacy, and the remainder of the patrol. Thornton knew the likely outcome if he encountered any Mexican forces. Just days earlier, Colonel Truman Cross, Taylor's quartermaster, had been murdered and left on the sun-baked Texas plains by Mexican guerrillas. Another patrol had also been attacked while searching for Colonel Cross.

Captain Thornton had been warned by some rancheros that Mexican soldiers were in the area but, wishing to confirm the report himself, he continued. A tense moment prevailed as he knocked on the door; it seemed like eternity. Suddenly, Mexican soldiers appeared. Shots rang out—ambush! Men yelled out the warning. Within moments scores of carbines and muskets fired at the surrounded Americans. More than a dozen dragoons were shot from their horses. Lieutenant Hardee led some of the soldiers away towards the river only to be captured there. Thornton was wounded and captured immediately. Sixteen dragoons lay dead or wounded in the dust; the rest were captured.[1]

On Sunday, April 26, 1846, General Taylor penned these cryptic words to the adjutant general, the official channel through the War Department to the president: "Hostilities may now be considered as commenced."[2]

By the time this message reached Washington, a declaration of war against Mexico was merely a formality. For months Americans had expected that war was the last and only remaining option to solve the question of Texas security, American rights, and property. After all, the United States had exhausted all reasonable diplomatic solutions to avoid war—or had it?

---

[1] Eisenhower, *So Far From God*, 65.
[2] Zachary Taylor to the Adjutant General, April 26, 1846, House Exec. Doc., No. 60, 30th Congress, 1st Session, 288; Bauer, *The Mexican War*, 48.

MANIFEST MEXICO: MR. POLK'S WAR?

President James Knox Polk, the eleventh president of the United States, faced a dilemma in the spring of 1846 that few presidents past or future faced: the real possibility of a two-front war, or more correctly, two separate wars against two belligerents. (In World War II, the United States fought a two-front war against allied nations Germany, Italy, and Japan.) Polk was facing wars against two separate non-allied countries, Great Britain and Mexico, thus, two separate wars. The realities of armed conflict centered on America's westward growth, which collided with Mexico to the southwest and Great Britain to the northwest. The two areas of land at the center of this turmoil were very appealing and experiencing increased American settlement: Texas and Oregon.

Texas, the more popular concern, had been in the forefront of American presidential, political, and diplomatic thought for ten years. In the 1844 presidential race it was a key issue that Democratic candidate Polk rode to a narrow victory over Whig challenger Henry Clay of Kentucky. When Clay refused to entertain the annexation of Texas as a possible state, his political dream of thirty years of becoming president ended. Martin Van Buren, former president and Democratic stalwart, was the leading choice in the Democratic circus show until, like Clay, he would not embrace Texas annexation, which sealed his fate at the convention.[3] Polk became the first "dark horse" nomination in American history.

Not as popular, but perhaps more serious, Oregon country was the target of perhaps the most powerful nation on earth, Great Britain. In the 1844 election the popular slogan of "Fifty-four Forty or Fight" demonstrated American resolve to withstand Britain's perceived encroachment on the latitudinal line that Americans understood as their territory from a previous joint occupation treaty of Oregon. (Oregon in the 1840s included parts of present-day British Columbia and Alberta in Canada, and Washington, Idaho, Oregon, western Wyoming, and Montana.) The great Oregon Trail saw its first serious traffic in 1843, hence the birth of a great emigrant trail. It would soon witness an explosion of emi-

---
[3] Schlesinger, *The Age of Jackson*, 431; DeVoto, *Year of Decision: 1846*, 7–8.

grant traffic as thousands of settlers made the trek of some 2,200 miles.[4]

Polk did not want war, especially war with two separate nations over territory that he envisioned as American domain. He hoped diplomatic coercion and monetary concessions could avoid war through a graduated level of pressure to achieve his goals with Mexico and Britain.

The macro view of the dispute was larger than the Texas problem. Overriding it was the nineteenth-century Americans' emotional and sentimental belief in manifest destiny. The foundation of this sentiment was an almost religious idea of the mission and purpose of the American people to settle, civilize, and gain as much of North America as possible for the United States. The telegraph and the railroads drove a technological revolution that made possible a continental nation, from sea to sea, as first explored by army officers Captain Meriwether Lewis and Second Lieutenant William Clark in 1803–6. There were also other important ingredients in the propaganda surrounding manifest destiny, which embodied the idea that "it was perhaps the American destiny to spread our free and admirable institutions by action as well as by example, by occupying territory as well as by practicing virtue."[5] Some expansionists saw more land for slavery with an eye to New Mexico and California.

In 1819 the United States signed the Transcontinental Treaty, or the Adams-Onis Treaty, authored by Secretary of State John Quincy Adams. This agreement gave the United States joint control with Great Britain of the loosely defined Oregon territory. The treaty involved Spain ceding Florida to the United States in exchange for any claims the U.S. had of east Texas following the Louisiana Purchase from France in 1803. Spain then had unchallenged control over Texas and its other western domains. It also established the present-day northern border of California along the 42nd parallel, thus forming the joint United States–and

---

[4]See Edwin A. Miles, "Fifty-four Forty or Fight—An American Political Legend," 291–301.
[5]DeVoto, *Year of Decision*, 9.

British-occupied Oregon territory. Each party had full rights to survey, fur-trap, settle, and improve the northwest realm of the continent. With one-year advance notice, either party could dissolve the joint occupation agreement.

In January 1846, Polk threatened to issue the dissolution notification when he became annoyed with Britain's overt interest in extending its influence south of Vancouver Island, even as far south as Yerba Buena (present-day San Francisco) and Monterey in Alta, or Upper, California, which was Mexican territory. Polk and most Americans, though slightly hypocritical, were very interested in California and wanted no interference from the British. Polk used the famous Monroe Doctrine, which sought to prohibit European imperialism in the Americas, to check Britain's ambition.

Polk's desire to dissolve the joint occupation treaty did nothing more than anger the British as a continuation of the rhetoric in the 1844 election. By late May 1846, however, Lord Aberdeen, the British Foreign Secretary, extended some willingness to negotiate privately, while publicly expressing stern criticism at Yankee aggressiveness. The main problem centered around the proposed boundary at the latitude line of the 49th parallel cutting across Vancouver Island, which was wholly unacceptable to the British. Americans clamored for the 54° 40′ north parallel as the border. Polk, not wanting to push the British too far, directed timid Secretary of State James Buchanan to offer the 49th parallel and British control of the entire island so long as the British left the rest of Oregon and California alone. By the end of June the British accepted, and Polk, already engaged in one war, cleverly avoided a second war.[6]

After many years of maneuvering and intrigue, Mexicans rebelled against the decaying empire of Spain culminating in Mexico's independence in 1821. Though blessed with freedom from Spain and

---

[6]Miles, "Fifty-four Forty or Fight," 292–94. There are several other works dealing with the British problem in Oregon during the Polk administration; see Eisenhower, *So Far from God*, 20–23, 34–35, 59–60; McPherson, *Battle Cry of Freedom: The Civil War Era*, 47–49; Howe, *The Political Culture of the American Whigs*, 67, 81.

nationhood, the Mexican people had no idea how to rule and manage a country so vast. They were totally unprepared for entering the political, industrial, and diplomatic complexities of the nineteenth century. Hundreds of years of austere colonial rule, with a people steeped in tradition from a scrupleless upper class and military dictators to a mostly uneducated and impoverished class of peasants and Indians, created a situation that proved to have no easy solution.[7]

Mexican authorities struggled against the enormity of a large country with little industry, no developed transportation systems, a backward economy, and a political system of no legitimate parties. Though there were factions, no party system emerged. "After the war of Independence [from Spain], Mexican governments replaced each other in bewildering succession. It was rare for a Mexican president to complete his allotted term in office."[8]

Though Mexican territory was vast and widely fertile, Mexico had already lost real control of much of it, especially the lands Polk and others envisioned as part of the United States. Historian Cecil Robinson wrote concerning Mexico's stability: "While chaos ruled Mexico City, the vast reaches of territory in the northern regions of Mexico were greatly underpopulated and almost completely neglected. Large desert areas were in reality ruled by Apaches. The situation was such that the northern areas . . . positively seemed to invite foreign intrusion."[9] In this unstable and chaotic situation was the distant and isolated province of Texas, within the state of Coahuila, hundreds of miles from the center of Mexican control and authority. Soon the solution for the Texas problem could be resolved in only one way—military occupation.

The dispute over Texas was perhaps the single major cause of the Mexican War. In the 1820–30s, thousands of Americans migrated to Texas with its appealing open, unsettled tracts of lands. Mexican authorities first welcomed the stream of Americans, then became

---

[7] Archer, "Fashioning a New Nation," in Meyer and Beezley, eds., *The Oxford History of Mexico*, 321; Bauer, *The Mexican War*, 4.

[8] For one fine study concerning the Mexican position as to Texas and the Mexican War, see Robinson, trans. and ed., *The View from Chapultepec: Mexican Writers on the Mexican-American War*, xiv.

[9] Ibid.

alarmed at this growing flood and enacted strict laws governing the province of Texas, including conversion to the Roman Catholic faith, payment of church taxes, and Mexican citizenship in order to own property. Also, Mexico had abolished slavery in 1829, but with the entry of hundreds of American slaves, the government did not enforce the law strictly, allowing the state of Coahuila y Texas an exemption.[10]

In 1834 a more centralized government determined to restrict colonization and enforce restrictions on Anglo-American immigration, slavery, and citizenship. Unwilling to accept these restrictions, Anglo-Texans began to revolt against Mexican authority. The majority of Americans in Texas dreamed some day of becoming part of the United States, with independence from Mexico as an acceptable consolation and first step. In late 1835 Mexico decided once and for all to crush Anglo resistance and reestablish absolute rule in Texas. Rebellion and civil war were nearly ubiquitous at this time in Mexico. Many small but serious revolts by extremely unhappy peasant and middle-class factions, some involving government officials, erupted in several parts of the country. The revolt in Texas was easier for Mexican authorities to distinguish because of the ethnic appearances of most Texans.[11]

In early 1836, Antonio López de Santa Anna, president and dictator of Mexico, organized a small army of perhaps five thousand soldiers, a substantial force considering Mexico's resources. In addition to the soldiers, he marched north with over two thousand men, women and children as new Mexican colonists for Texas. The Mexicans defeated Texan forces at the Alamo and then massacred some three hundred Texans at Goliad, deeming them pirates rather than prisoners of war. But the small and impoverished Texas army under Sam Houston won an unexpected victory against Santa Anna at San Jacinto in April 1836.[12]

---

[10]Vazuez, "War and Peace with the United States," in Meyer and Beezley, eds., *The Oxford History of Mexico*, 346; Winders, *Crisis in the Southwest: The United States, Mexico and the Struggle over Texas*, 81; Eisenhower, *So Far from God*, 13; Bauer, *The Mexican War*, 5.

[11]Winders, *Crisis in the Southwest*, 14.

[12]For one of the most comprehensive and classic studies of the Texas War of Independence, see Lord, *A Time to Stand*; and Vazuez, "War and Peace with the United States," 354.

The Rio Grande was claimed by Texas patriots as the southern border of the Republic of Texas, plus the lands bordering the Rio Grande all the way north into present-day Colorado. The Congress of the Republic of Texas passed a law defining the boundary between their republic and Mexico "beginning at the mouth of the Sabine river, and running west along the Gulf of Mexico three leagues from land, to the mouth of the Rio Grande, thence up the principle stream of said river to its source," which would place the boundary in modern-day Colorado.[13] This "treaty" would not be accepted by the Mexican Congress.

After the battle of San Jacinto, the captured Santa Anna agreed to the claims of the southern border of Texas as outlined in the presumptive agreement called the "treaty" of Velasco. Upon Santa Anna's return to Mexico (after visiting President Andrew Jackson in Washington), the Mexican congress rejected the treaty, and the liberals deposed Santa Anna and formed a new government. (Santa Anna would regain power again in 1843 and then suffer exile to Cuba a year later at the hands of José Joaquín Herrera and other liberals.)[14]

Since no formal, legal treaty or agreement was reached, Mexico haughtily refused to recognize Texas's independence, though the United States and some nations of Europe did.[15] For the next decade Texans and Mexicans raided and devastated each others' settlements in the disputed area between the Nueces River and Rio Grande and elsewhere. Few Anglo-Texans actually settled there, but their claim to this land was as fierce as the Mexican government's resolve to forbid it. Texans even attempted to invade and settle areas of present-day New Mexico, another Mexican state, with disaster in 1841, when some of the Texans were killed and most were captured and sent on a cruel and arduous march to imprisonment in Mexico City. Many Americans, even Texans, had a dim view of this filibustering expedition.[16]

Mexican troops also invaded Texas twice in 1842 and occupied San Antonio for short periods, trying to win back the disillusioned

---

[13]Cited in Winders, *Crisis in the Southwest*, 48.
[15]Smith, *The War with Mexico*, 1: 84.
[14]Eisenhower, *So Far from God*, 15.
[16]Winders, *Crisis in the Southwest*, 50.

MANIFEST MEXICO: MR. POLK'S WAR?

colony.[17] These invasions and many other raids across Texas and northern Mexico enflamed hostilities between both sides. Thus the groundwork was laid for a bitter, bloody, ten-year diplomatic contest that failed and resulted in violent war and conquest.[18]

Polk's inability to solve the Texas problem peacefully overshadowed his success in Oregon. "Mr. Polk's War," as some derisively call it, actually snowballed during President John Tyler's preceding administration (1841–45). The heir to the late William Henry Harrison's presidency, the first Whig elected president, Tyler turned out to champion Democratic causes more than those of his own party.[19]

Just days before his term ended, Congress passed a resolution by a simple majority and narrow margin of two votes offering statehood to Texas. Tyler signed the resolution just before Polk's inauguration in March 1845. Texas then had to form a convention, write a constitution, and accept statehood by vote of the convention. In July, a popular convention ratified the resolution for statehood, following which the Republic of Texas became the twenty-eighth state of the Union on December 29, 1845.

Though Mexico still considered Texas to be its possession, in reality Texas was a separate, independent nation and had won a war of independence to establish it as such, just as the American colonies had against Great Britain.[20] Since 1836 Mexico could either reconquer Texas by force or accept it as an independent country. Mexico elected to do neither. Furthermore, Mexico's refusal to acknowledge Texan independence meant that it refused Texas's boundary claim along the Rio Grande. "In addition to ... [European recognition of Texas independence and loans], many Texans undoubtedly hoped that success in Europe might induce Mexico to recognize their independence or the United States to reconsider annexation."[21]

---

[17]Ibid., 60–68. [18]Bauer, *The Mexican War*, 5–6.
[19]Howe, *The Political Culture of the American Whigs*, 66.
[20]Vazuez, "War and Peace with the United States," 356–57; also see Pletcher, *The Diplomacy of Annexation: Texas, Oregon and the Mexican War*, 72–74. [21]Ibid., 79.

Mexican attitude and reaction during the statehood process could best be described as extreme and open hostility. In November 1844 Mexico's foreign minister, General Juan N. Almonte, wrote to the United States government, "My country is resolved to declare war as soon as it receives information of such an act."[22] The day after Tyler signed the resolution for statehood in March 1845, General Almonte, then serving as the Mexican ambassador in Washington, went to the state department, demanded his passport, wrote a belligerent note severing diplomatic relations, and departed.[23]

War, however, did not come. Mexico and the United States watched and waited. For Polk this meant sending troops to Texas. Though it was initially called the Army of Observation, brevet Brigadier General Zachary Taylor (actually colonel of the 6th U.S. Infantry Regiment) assembled his force in Louisiana and then sailed down the Gulf of Mexico to the small village of Corpus Christi.

By the summer of 1845, half of the regiments of the regular army, some thirty-five hundred men, were en route to Texas to serve under "Old Rough and Ready," General Taylor's nickname. Taylor was the "GI General" of the 1800s—unpretentious and down-to-earth, he was an old campaigner whom the men loved because of his common sense and lack of sophistication.

Historians differ greatly on Polk's actual intentions and various attempts at diplomacy, but sending Taylor to Texas and his choice in emissaries, intentionally or not, provoked the Mexicans into war.[24] "Since this strategy called for a negotiated settlement, Mexican intransigence forced Polk to grab for nearly any opportunity, no matter how unlikely, which might lead to the start of the talks that were necessary if hostilities were to be avoided or ended. Polk wanted a peaceful, diplomatic settlement."[25] Polk's last attempt rested on Congressman John Slidell of Louisiana. A former pro-

---

[22] Smith, *The War with Mexico*, 1: 84.
[23] Eisenhower, *So Far from God*, 22.
[24] For a study of Polk's determination to start a war, see Schroeder, *Mr. Polk's War: American Opposition and Dissent, 1846–1848*.
[25] Bauer, *The Mexican War*, 11.

fessor of Spanish at Columbia College, Slidell seemed a promising choice and departed for Mexico. The native New Yorker had an assortment of proposals and cash incentives for all or some of the lands Polk envisioned being part of the United States. Polk also offered to pay several millions of dollars of debt that Mexico owed American businesses and foreign enterprises. (This debt had been arbitrated through international courts and Mexico acknowledged its obligation.)

Slidell was bombastic, arrogant, and a man with serious deficiencies for such a sensitive mission. His worst fault was his utter contempt for Mexico as a nation and the Mexicans as a people. Sending Slidell to Mexico as emissary was perhaps Polk's greatest failure as a president. His official status was that of an envoy extraordinaire and minister pleni-potentiary, meaning that he had full power to act in behalf of the United States to negotiate and sign treaties. Mexican officials would neither recognize nor accept Slidell as a minister or as an official with authority. They would accept a "commissioner" who would act as a messenger for a settlement of the existing problem: the boundary of Texas.[26]

As Slidell sailed to Mexico, Polk made another decision that has been used to portray him as the architect behind the war. In October 1845, upon Taylor's recommendation, Polk decided to send Taylor more regiments from the regular army and ordered him to the Rio Grande. This tactic was meant to apply more pressure on Mexico. Taylor now had most of the regular army under his command, but it took time to make the necessary preparations for the 120-mile march across a stark wilderness to the mouth of the Rio Grande. Crossing the Nueces and penetrating the disputed area to the Rio Grande infuriated the Mexicans beyond any possible diplomatic solution, and a formal declaration of war against the United States was only weeks away.

As all these events developed, the Mexican government was going through its own upheavals. The movement of United States troops to Corpus Christi was more than a mere unsettling event; it

---

[26]Ibid., 23–24.

was a national catastrophe. An American army in Texas was a threat to Mexican national pride and interests, which fueled Mexican outrage. The liberal government headed by José Joaquín de Herrera hung on tenuously, reacting to American developments rather than trying to control events.

Slidell and party landed at Vera Cruz on the last day of November 1845, and were coldly ignored by President Herrera. Slidell's arrival could not have come at a worst possible time for the Herrera government. Losing patience, Slidell moved on to Mexico City without permission. The ruling liberals, military officers, and other leaders in Herrera's government knew that it was political suicide for any faction to discuss the annexation of Texas with Slidell.[27]

On New Year's Day 1846, General Mariano Paredes, a conservative, staged a bloodless coup and gained control of the government with the exiled Santa Anna's blessings. He immediately broke off all contact with Slidell, who returned to Louisiana and forwarded messages about the failure in Mexico. He richly laid the blame on Mexico's unwillingness to negotiate and settle the Texas issue, or to discuss America's acquiring more Mexican territory.

"If America ever fought an unavoidable war," summarized Jack Bauer, "it was the conflict with Mexico over the delineation of the common boundary."[28] Historian David Pletcher summarized four possible options left to Polk: (1) military invasion and conquest; (2) establishing a temporary protectorate over Mexico while the United States annexed lands it desired; (3) a slow and passive military infiltration and occupation of California and New Mexico and perhaps other states until Mexico acquiesced; (4) patiently wait until American settlers in California, the Great Basin, and the Southwest had gained sufficient political power to either rebel as in Texas or peacefully secede from Mexico.[29] Of course, Polk and most Americans chose the first option once diplomatic, monetary concessions, and graduated pressure failed.

---

[27]Eisenhower, *So Far from God*, 47; Bauer, *The Mexican War*, 24.
[28]Bauer, *The Mexican War*, xxv.
[29]Pletcher, *The Diplomacy of Annexation*, 582; for another recent study of the conflict and causes, see Frazier, *The United States and Mexico at War: Nineteenth-Century Expansionism and Conflict*.

MANIFEST MEXICO: MR. POLK'S WAR? 49

Mexico lost Texas through rebellion and military defeat, and Texas then established itself as an independent nation recognized by many of the great powers. Texas became an object of American expansion, which Mexico resisted. Mexico proved unable to block American and Texas unification. Though California and New Mexico were remote and neglected possessions, Mexican leaders failed in their hope to expand eventually and fill these states with more settlers and develop their resources. Mexico ignored diplomatic and military reality and lost in its gamble to withstand American power. The United States achieved its political aims to safeguard Texas and to acquire California and New Mexico through war when diplomacy failed.

With war on the horizon, most Americans turned to support the effort. But one people had little in common with their fellow citizens when it came to supporting a war, for that same nation had too often ignored their pleas for justice.

CHAPTER TWO

A Nation and a People

I confess that I was glad to learn of war against the United States and was in hopes that it might never end until they [the United States] were entirely destroyed.
—Hosea Stout

The Polks were at dinner when a messenger arrived with alarming news on May 11, 1846. The president read General Taylor's dispatch concerning the Mexican attack on Captain Seth Thornton's patrol. With some anxiety, Polk left his dinner table and immediately called a cabinet meeting. Fortunately for Polk, the cabinet, and the nation, it was Saturday evening and not Sunday, the Sabbath for the Polks. Mrs. Sarah Childress Polk, the first lady, expressly forbade all official visits, meetings, and ceremonies on the Sabbath. No doubt Mr. Polk would have conducted his meeting, but he may have had to pay dearly for it later. Thus, the cabinet met in an urgent meeting, discussed the news of Captain Thornton's engagement, and unanimously voted for a recommendation to Congress for a declaration of war. James K. Polk had a busy evening—he traded dinner for war.

Attitudes among Americans about the war against Mexico were diverse and complex. Most Americans plainly saw the reasons for the war as being a solution to the Texas problem and a response to an assault against American sovereignty, once the attack on Captain Thornton was made public.

There was some protest against the war in America, but it was limited and weak. Dissenters against the war never organized as the Federalists did during the War of 1812, which contributed to the demise of their party. Not wanting to make the same mistake, dissenters knew they had to support American soldiers going to war. Their main criticism was the manner, speed, and aggressiveness of the continentalists and Polk's disregard for a slow, managed application of manifest destiny. Northern Whigs, especially in New England, opposed the annexation of Texas as a slave state. The small but vociferous abolitionist movement was making its dissent and disgust with Polk known.[1] The events leading up to the declaration of war against Mexico seemed to some a perversion of America's mission and ideals for westward expansion, where American superiority and vanity perverted cautious diplomacy.[2] Whatever opposition politicians, editors, and clergy fostered, it never grew into a legitimate antiwar movement. Polk's America was fractured and suspicious but still intact.

The majority of Americans considered the realities of westward expansion and not the abstract virtues and morals held up by minority idealists who opposed the war. To most Americans the reality was land, homesteads, commerce, rights, and liberty. Americans, brilliant or simple, envisioned their nation from sea to sea, and few worried about the means to accomplish it.

Some Americans did not oppose the war; they just did not want to serve in the army and go to war. One such critic voiced his concern, "No siree! As long as I can work, beg, or go to the poor house, I won't go to Mexico, to be lodged on the damp ground, half starved, half roasted, bitten by mosquetos and centipedes, stung by scorpions and tarantulas—marched, drilled, and flogged, and then stuck up to be shot at, for eight dollars a month and putrid rations."[3]

The war bill signed by Polk authorized a call to the states of some 50,000 volunteers for one-year enlistments. Eventually, over 72,000 volunteers would serve. The response across the country to this call to arms was immediate and overwhelming. The War Department directed various states to provide allocations for regi-

---

[1] Eisenhower, *So Far from God*, 67–68.   [2] Ibid., 161.
[3] Millett and Maslowski, *For the Common Defense: A Military History of the United States of America*, 150.

ments of infantry, mounted soldiers, or batteries of artillery, with the result that every state soon had more volunteers than its required levy—in fact, several times the requirement. Mississippi was called to provide one infantry regiment of 1,000 men, but by June 1846, some 17,000 were clamoring to enlist. In Pennsylvania state officials chose some 2,000 men from over 7,000 who came forward in just the first few days.[4]

As in all wars, propaganda was central to the administration's effort to sell the war as a patriotic and honorable venture. "Are you ready? Your country now demands your service," went one recruiting hand-bill. "She calls upon you to rush to her standard: to fulfill your obligation as true and noble souled Volunteers."[5] Most newspapers and other forms of mass media of the day, as well as schools, churches, clubs, and associations espoused the war effort. Some linked the war with the Monroe Doctrine, trying to protect the Americas from tyrannical oppression, even if it was non-European. As an effort to free tens of thousands of poor Mexicans from a Latin American–style of tyranny, the war was labeled as a crusade against "The Mexican monarchist and tyrant, through his tools, and having an ephemeral sway in Mexico, upon your own soil... and waged war against us without any just cause whatever."[6]

Enthusiasm for the war was especially high in the trans-Mississippi West, not only as a patriotic venture but one that was tied to the economic growth for the gateway of the American west: St. Louis. (By 1846, Independence, Missouri, and the towns nearby were the eastern trailhead of both the Santa Fe and Oregon trails. St. Louis, however, was still the dominant economic center.) One chronicler and veteran of Colonel Alexander Doniphan's invasion of northern Mexico, Frank Edwards, wrote, "Perhaps no place could be found which would so readily respond to such a call as St. Louis: for it being the point where the Santa Fe traders procure their goods... and the young men of all classes were eager to go."[7]

---

[4] Hackenburg, *Pennsylvania in the War with Mexico: The Volunteer Regiments*, 3; Chance, *Jefferson Davis's Mexican War Regiment*, 4.
[5] Smith, ed., *The Chronicles of the Gringos: The U.S. Army in the Mexican War, 1846–1848*, 14.
[6] Ibid. [7] Edwards, *A Campaign in New Mexico with Colonel Doniphan*, 20.

Most men joined for the seemingly honorable reasons of loyalty, American honor, and the belief that the war for America's manifest destiny was a justified endeavor. Some enlisted for other reasons: the adventure, the opportunity to travel, or the chance to experience combat. Others enlisted for less honorable reasons, such as running from the law, escaping the boredom of farm or factory life, or just taking advantage of the situation. Some enlisted to have the government transport them to a frontier, like California, where they could desert and start a new life.

But there was one group of people who had a completely different view of the war. As some Americans wrestled with the causes and justifications of the war, one people seemed mostly united in their attitude of the war against Mexico.

"I confess that I was glad to learn of war against the United States and was in hopes that it might never end until they [the United States] were entirely destroyed," wrote Hosea Stout, a Mormon stalwart trekking across Iowa Territory in late May 1846. The attitude among the Mormons toward the war mirrored some of the common attitudes of their countrymen, though there were also some profound differences. Perhaps Stout's commentary is one of the most extreme judgments by the Mormon people. He continued, "for they had driven us into the wilderness & was now laughing at our calamities."[8] John Steele also shared such feelings: "I will see them [meaning the whole United States] in hell before I will fire one shot against a foreigner for them those who have mobbed, robbed, plundered and destroyed us all the day long and now seek to enslave us to fight for them."[9]

Most Mormons had little confidence in their government. Despite the distrust, strangely, they still held extremely strong beliefs in pure American values and democracy. The Mormon founder and prophet, Joseph Smith, had declared that the Constitution of the United States was a divinely inspired instrument from

---

[8] Brooks, ed., *On the Mormon Frontier: The Diary of Hosea Stout, 1844–1861*, 1: 163–64.
[9] John Steele, "Extracts from the Journal of John Steele," 6–7.

God that fostered conditions that created the establishment of His earthly kingdom. Even after years of severe persecution and government indifference, Mormons always maintained their strong regard for the ideals of the United States, though some reminiscences and diaries indicate serious condemnations.

Joseph Smith was a true expansionist, though not for the reasons of wealth or slavery held by many other Americans. He nevertheless accepted the vision of a continental America. In very direct terms Joseph Smith offered the federal government the services of the church for a grandiose vision to police the West with a volunteer army of 100,000 men. In March 1844, just three months before his assassination, he proclaimed his "Ordinance for the Protection of the Citizens of the United States Emigrating to the Territories." This proclamation was an element of Smith's political soul. Politics was an avocation Smith was learning in the spring of 1844, especially since he had declared his candidacy for the presidency of the United States. He outlined that every Mormon was "to show his loyalty to our Confederate Union and the Constitution of our Republic; to prevent quarrel and bloodshed on our frontiers; to extend the arm of deliverance to Texas; to protect the inhabitants of Oregon from foreign aggressions and domestic broils... to open vast regions of the unpeopled west and south to our enlightened and enterprising yeomanry."[10]

The Mormon attitude toward the United States was strained; many were very bitter. It is important to understand the Mormon story to comprehend their feelings in the spring of 1846. It necessarily begins with Joseph Smith, one of the most significant characters in American religious experience. He was born in 1805 in Vermont. As a boy settling in New York with his family, Joseph Smith sought a religious conversion and membership as a youth. He soon rejected the accepted religious sects around him and announced that he had received divine communications of his own from God. Eventually, according to his story, Smith would translate an ancient scripture he received, the *Book of Mormon*, claim divine authority, establish a church, instigate a close-knit commu-

---

[10]Smith, *History of the Church of Jesus Christ of Latter-day Saints*, 6: 275–77.

nal society, commence a missionary program of devoted followers who would spread the new gospel across the country and to Europe, and become a prophet to thousands of people, all before his thirty-fifth birthday. By this time, Joseph Smith had been jailed a half-dozen times, tarred and feathered, lost three children—one of whom died from the consequences of mob action—and forced out of several states.[11]

By 1831 the Church of Jesus Christ of Latter-day Saints had established one center of gathering in Kirtland, Ohio, and a second in Jackson County, Missouri. In both locales the Saints built cities, churches, schools, and began their own form of communal capitalism, completely intertwined with their church. Eventually, both centers were abandoned because of the vicious persecution from without and bitter factional splintering from within.

During these heady days of Jacksonian democracy, the Mormons were not the only minority group to experience this type of "democracy." Catholic schools and churches, Masonic lodges, and Jewish businesses and homes all felt the same bitter flames of torches in the night and charcoal-smeared faces of terror and hatred.[12]

The people involved in these acts were not necessarily wild ruffians or backwoods desperadoes; surprisingly, at least in the Mormon experience, the persecution often revealed a pattern where civil leaders and the citizenry acted together. As with other minority and ethnic groups that faced such treatment, the Mormons were seen as a threat to the community, hence the drastic measures.[13] Citizens who opposed the Mormons saw their intrinsic American rights and values attacked by a close-knit, fanatical theocracy that seemed to trample the Constitution under their growing numbers and threatened to control local politics. The perception of Mormon hegemony caused great turmoil and distrust among American citizens who had often been settled for years in these regions and states.

The small western Missouri settlement of Independence was the scene of the Latter-day Saints' first real clash with direct official

---

[11]For one of the best studies of early Mormonism, see Bushman, *Joseph Smith and the Beginnings of Mormonism*.
[12]Davis, "Nativist Reform and the Fear of Subversive Conspiracies," 461–71.
[13]Van Orden, "Causes and Consequences: Conflict in Jackson County," 337–48.

A NATION AND A PEOPLE

government power. In 1833 the "old settlers" had their fill with these mostly Yankee, non-slave-holding Mormons from New England and other northern states. The Missourians looked upon the Mormons as religious fanatics because of their pronouncements and revelations that they declared were received directly from God; that angels were visiting them; that Joseph Smith claimed to be a prophet like Moses or Abraham; and that only they had the true gospel. The Mormons declared that Jackson County, Missouri, was the center place for the "New Jerusalem" or city of Zion, and that the Mormons would "inherit" this promised land from God, and all the Gentiles would have to leave or convert to Mormonism. The Mormons were also very clannish and in their business dealings usually associated only among themselves. Whether these views about the Mormons were absolutely true or exaggerated, many Missourians believed them and were determined to not allow Mormons to take their lands and liberties.

Through quasi-legal and extra-legal means, the residents of Jackson County demanded their expulsion. Missourians destroyed a printing press, tarred and feathered leaders, and beat others. Eventually, the dispute turned into a contest of arms and mob action disguised with legal façades. Powerless to withstand armed force, the Saints evacuated their homes and crossed the Missouri River into several northern counties. After peaceful and legal remedies and petitions failed, Joseph Smith launched the Saints' quasi-military quest, called Zion's Camp, to retake their lands in Jackson County by force if necessary. Beginning in the spring of 1834, some two hundred Mormon men marched by various groups and routes, eventually assembling in western Missouri. It was a trying march of over eight hundred miles by foot-sore and famished men. Reaching Jackson County, it became apparent that to use force was quixotic, and Smith aborted the military reconquest of Zion, soon disbanding the group.[14]

After the forced exodus from Jackson County in 1833, most of the Saints gathered in northwest Missouri. Smith sought redress from the state of Missouri but all pleas fell on uncaring ears. The expul-

---
[14]Baugh, "A Call to Arms: The 1838 Mormon Defense of Northern Missouri," 30.

sion from Jackson County and the lack of concern by state politicians caused many Mormons to distrust government authorities.

In Kirtland, Ohio, with its newly dedicated, majestic temple, the Mormons experienced increasing difficulties both internally and externally. Internally, apostates chaffed with dissension as a result of the collapse of the church-supported Kirtland bank, whose failure was probably doomed even before the Panic of 1837 occurred, which only assured the bank's demise. In addition, the Mormon communal economic pact, called the United Order, failed, causing serious problems. Externally, there was pressure from anti-Mormon elements determined to push the growing Mormon population from Ohio. The Saints faced abandoning their homes, farms, and businesses, as well as their sacred temple. Though Ohio state officials were not involved in the violence against the Mormons, they did little or nothing to curb their citizens from their vicious acts. The Kirtland Saints packed and loaded their goods, gathered their children, and commenced a trek to join the Missouri Saints.[15]

In 1836 some Missouri citizens, including notable political leaders Alexander Doniphan and David Atchinson, were able to convince their state government to establish a Mormon "homeland" in the mostly unsettled northern portions of Ray County. Thus, Caldwell and Davies counties became Mormon domains.[16] Smith laid out the central city, called Far West, and soon homes and schools went up. Yet even in the safety of these predominantly Mormon counties of northwest Missouri, their sojourn was doomed. By the summer of 1838 the tension and strife between the Mormons and the earlier Missouri settlers had reached the boiling point. A riot broke out on election day in the town of Gallatin, and soon barns and homes on both sides burned. Finally, county militia faced county militia in actual firefights and skirmishes. Governor Lilburn Boggs, an icon of disdain for Mormons, issued his infamous "extermination order," which seemingly authorized an "open season" on Mormons if they did not flee from the state.[17]

---

[15] Allen and Leonard, *The Story of the Latter-day Saints*, 112–13.
[16] LeSuer, *The 1838 Mormon War in Missouri*, 25.
[17] Baugh, "The Haun's Mill Massacre and the Extermination Order of Missouri Governor Lilburn W. Boggs," 1–5.

As Governor Boggs signed the expulsion order, fanatics were already plotting to take matters into their own hands. Ignoring Smith's pleas to come to Far West for security, some remote Mormon communities hunkered down, determined to defend their homes. On a cold autumn day, October 31, 1838, a blacken-faced militia force attacked a sleepy hamlet named Haun's Mill. By the time the shots stopped, seventeen Mormon men and boys lay dead in the blacksmith shop. Terrified Saints fled to Far West for protection and leadership, which they had been admonished to do earlier. Within days Smith and several colleagues were turned over to their enemy, the Missouri state militia. Joseph Smith, his brother Hyrum, and others were marched off to prison. The militia forced the Mormons to surrender their arms. Defenseless, they were summarily rounded up and forced from their homes and property. Thousands of Latter-day Saints faced a dreadful mid-winter exodus under a man who gained the mantel of leadership by default when other leaders above him deserted Joseph Smith and the Saints: Brigham Young. Young led this hungry and frozen throng from Missouri. Many Mormons subsequently perished, some apostatized, but most endured. They retained a bitter memory of Missouri and distrust for most man-made governments.[18]

Smith languished six months in a windowless, dank, and damp dungeon jail, ironically in the town of Liberty. Secretly freed by his captors, he made his way to the bosom of the church in Illinois. Later, Smith made a trip to Washington to present his case before federal officials, even President Martin Van Buren, to show that they had lost scores of people and several million dollars' worth of property.[19] Though many consoling words were offered, the federal government did nothing. There was no legal or political precedent by which the federal government could intervene.[20]

For the next five years the Saints built their first magnificent city: Nauvoo. Brigham Young had done a masterful job in gather-

---

[18]Baugh, "A Call to Arms," 266–85.
[19]For a complete study and listing of the hundreds of petitions, see Johnson, ed., *Mormon Redress Petitions: Documents of the 1833–1838 Missouri Conflict*.
[20]Hill, *Joseph Smith: The First Mormon*, 270–74.

ing the flock and herding them back eastward to the banks of the Mississippi River across to Illinois. Yet Joseph Smith was still the prophet; Young, his loyal lieutenant, would wait until his day. Sick, demoralized, and defeated, the Mormons languished in miserable makeshift camps on river bottom land, some of it disease-infested swamps on the Illinois side of the great waterway. With his great flare and action, Smith inspired the Saints to purchase lands and build a new city—the city of God. Homes rose from the marshes, streets spread out in a network of proper square city blocks, business flourished, and Joseph Smith gained even more renown and prominence. The Illinois legislature granted Nauvoo a wide-ranging charter allowing for a municipal court, a university, and a city militia. The Nauvoo Legion was a unique militia organization, Mormon (for the most part) and officered by the hierarchy of the church. The legion grew to be one of the largest militia forces in America after the regular U.S. Army.[21]

Many citizens of Illinois, and especially Hancock County, initially welcomed the Mormons but later became concerned when thousands of converts poured into their homeland. They felt threatened when Smith and his people gained economic and political power. They were infuriated when they learned of the Mormons' unusual religious practices and beliefs, especially the rumors surrounding polygamy, which the Mormons started practicing secretly in Nauvoo. The church did not officially announce the practice of polygamy or plural marriage until years later, in 1852, following their safe arrival in Utah. Many impoverished Mormon foreigners arriving from Europe evoked xenophobia among the local non-Mormon citizenry and real estate deals and failures caused dissension among some of Hancock County's leading businessmen. The Mormons' clannish nature and the great power and control that rested in the hands of one man, a self-proclaimed prophet of God, caused even more alarm. The tempo and tension increased until it exploded in June 1844.[22]

---

[21]Ibid., 285–86.

[22]For the most recent and comprehensive treatments of Nauvoo, see Leonard, *Nauvoo: A Place of Peace, a People of Promise*; see also Launius and Hallwas, eds., *Kingdom on the Mississippi Revisited: Nauvoo in Mormon History*.

A NATION AND A PEOPLE

A newspaper in Nauvoo printed a personal attack on Smith, the church, and the doctrine of plurality of wives. As mayor of Nauvoo (and with regrettably poor judgment), Smith authorized the destruction of the press. Tension rose to the point that Smith felt that he had to order martial law in Nauvoo to safeguard public well-being—a decision that was highly inflammatory to his enemies and state officials. Governor Thomas Ford, whose election was substantially supported by the Mormon vote in 1842, decided to take personal command of the crisis before civil war erupted. Smith felt threatened, even though he was in command of the Nauvoo Legion, and decided to flee. He did this to avoid what he considered illegal arrest and also to avoid endangering the Saints in a battle in Nauvoo.

He eventually submitted himself with reluctance to county authorities. Joseph Smith and his brother Hyrum, his most valued counselor, were placed under arrest and accompanied by other friends to jail some twenty miles away in Carthage, the county seat. Just after five o'clock P.M. on June 27, an organized group of undeniably disguised county militiamen, led by prominent citizens, stormed the jail and killed the Smith brothers. Five men were arrested and charged with the murders, but the state and county authorities insured that these "honorable men" would escape justice.[23]

The Saints were not fooled. The governor of Illinois and the justice system had betrayed them once again. The murderers were free and their prophet was dead. Mormon attitudes hardened as their situation exacerbated, and they again faced the prospect of leaving their beautiful city and comfortable homes to flee into the wilderness to rebuild and begin anew.

By direct succession of Mormon priesthood authority, Brigham Young, the senior member and president of the Quorum of the Twelve Apostles, became the presiding leader of the church. Though a small minority challenged his authority and established various splinter groups, the vast majority of the Latter-day Saints

---

[23]For the most thorough account of the assassination of Joseph Smith and the political and legal results of the trial, see Oaks and Hill, *Carthage Conspiracy: The Trial of the Accused Assassins of Joseph Smith*.

accepted Brigham Young's leadership. His developing vision for the church had two main elements of: first and foremost, they had to complete the Nauvoo Temple and receive their sacred ordinances and blessings performed therein; secondly, the church had to move west for its salvation. It was during the latter that the Mormon Battalion was both conceived and born.[24]

The Mormons' first real and legitimate military unit was a duly sanctioned Missouri county militia. By the fall of 1838 civil war in Missouri was imminent, and county militia were facing each other in battle. After several brawls and sporadic violence, a minor skirmish took place on October 25, 1838, at small stream called Crooked River. With some sixty men, Mormon apostle David W. Patten attacked an armed force of less than fifty Missouri militia and forced them to withdraw. The Battle of Crooked River had four battle deaths and several wounded. Patten himself succumbed to a wound in the abdomen. This victory buoyed up Mormon resolve to protect their lives and land, but it also forced the Missourians to more austere and ignominious measures, and led to the Mormons' eventual removal from Missouri.[25]

Once in Illinois, Joseph Smith had realized that temporal security depended upon both God and the sword. John C. Bennett, a crafty Illinois politician and general in the state militia, helped create the Mormon-controlled Nauvoo Legion. This was a city or municipal militia unlike the normal county and state militia of the era. Actually, the legion functioned under the authority of the state and governor, but its powers were derived from the Nauvoo Charter, a municipal document.[26] The legion was organized into "cohorts" based on Roman militarism, with one cohort of infantry and one mounted. The legion was extremely top-heavy with senior

---

[24]Historian D. Michael Quinn has written two extensive but critical studies of Mormon church government, authority, succession, and power. See *The Mormon Hierarchy: Origins of Power* and *The Mormon Hierarchy: Extension of Power.*

[25]Baugh, "The Battle between Mormon and Missouri Militia at Crooked River," 85–104.

[26]Carthage, Illinois, twenty miles away also had a city militia: the Carthage Greys.

A NATION AND A PEOPLE

officers, many of whom were the presiding authorities in the Mormon Church. The governor commissioned Joseph Smith as lieutenant general, and for his efforts, Bennett became second-in-command as major general. Records reveal that the legion drilled in parade often, participated in "mock" battles, and held many musters about Nauvoo. At its peak, the Nauvoo Legion may have had a total of approximately three thousand enrolled, a very impressive number for a western state of sparse population, let alone a militia from one city. There are dozens of idealized pieces of artwork of a well-uniformed and organized Nauvoo Legion in parade and formation. The truth, however, is much different due to the relative poverty of the Mormons and the lack of funds from the state for such costly appearances.[27] After the death of Joseph Smith, the legion disbanded when the Nauvoo charter was rescinded in 1845 prior to the Saints' exodus into Iowa. Many of the Nauvoo Legion soldiers would later serve in the Mormon Battalion.

Did the military experience prior to 1846 prepare the Mormon men to serve as soldiers? The answer is difficult to ascertain because the Mormons saw no real battle except for small skirmishes in Missouri. Their Nauvoo Legion service was limited because the Mormon officers had little formal military experience. With no experienced cadre to train and lead the Nauvoo Legion, their service was mostly ceremonial and symbolic. The legion was probably no more prepared than any other militia unit of the day. It was unprepared for combat without intensive training by competent professionals and the time necessary to do so.

The five hundred men of the Mormon Battalion were philosophically and mentally unprepared for the rigid discipline and extreme conditions they were about to face.

---

[27]Saunders, "Officers and Arms: The 1843 General Return of the Nauvoo Legion's Second Cohort," 138–51.

CHAPTER THREE

War Aims and a "Little" Mission

*To conciliate them ... & prevent them
from taking part against us.*
—*President James K. Polk*

At 8 p.m., May 14, 1846, the day after the official declaration of war, two visitors appeared at the president's mansion. This was their second visit in as many days. One was a towering giant of a man, well over six feet tall, weighing some 250 pounds or more, with graying hair that proved his age of nearly sixty years. The general-in-chief of the army, Major General Winfield Scott, was already an American military legend, an icon of conservative politics and the military class. Accepting a commission in 1808 as a captain, Scott fought in several major battles in the War of 1812. Promoted to brigadier general and commanding a brigade by his thirtieth birthday, he fell severely wounded at the Battle of Lundy's Lane. Scott survived the war as one of America's few military heroes. At one point he crossed purposes with President Andrew Jackson, who court-martialed him in an attempt to drive him from the army. Scott endured and garnered a reputation as one of the leading military theorists and tacticians of the era. Serving in many capacities over the next thirty years, Scott was the heart and soul of the professional army and became general-in-chief in 1841. Always dressed to suit his ostentatious personality,

Scott's blue uniform was bedecked with as much gold braid as possible, gold epaulets with the two stars of a major general hung off his shoulders, and a buff or white sash wound around his growing girth. With Scott was Secretary of War William Marcy, one of the most accomplished politicians of the day and a chief proponent of the spoils system. Their conference with President Polk was recorded in official records and private journals as a meeting on "war plans."[1]

This conference lasted four hours, an amazing achievement considering the fact that Polk and Scott were political opposites. Polk was suspicious of Scott's political desires. To put it mildly, they despised each other and only associated when absolutely necessary. This was one of several meetings held during the first weeks of the war to discuss strategy, which later proved to be insufficient. Several months later they would meet again to once again hammer out the national strategy after realizing that "little" Mexico was a tougher nut to crack than anticipated.

When the United States declared war on Mexico, President Polk, as the commander-in-chief of the armed forces, developed his war aims and then his national strategy. He desired first and foremost to defeat Mexico militarily, but he also determined to use "limited" means to produce this end. He did not intend to invade and completely subdue the entire country and occupy all of Mexico. Polk wished only to invade and occupy that territory necessary to force Mexico's surrender. American forces were to conquer only the Mexican territory he envisioned as American domain—west to the Pacific coast. This territory included the present states of Colorado, Utah, Nevada, and the northern parts of California, Arizona, and New Mexico.

Polk had defined four basic points of national strategy: first, secure the Texas border by defeating the Mexican army and forcing it back into the northern provinces; second, invade, conquer, occupy, and annex New Mexico under the United States' control, if practicable, with another column to invade Chihuahua to secure

---

[1]Eisenhower, *So Far From God*, 92.

Taylor's flank in Texas; third, establish a naval blockade to isolate Mexico commercially; lastly, as the military moved to accomplish these goals, Polk desired to once again open negotiations for an acceptable peace, which would ensure Texas annexation and guarantee American control of northern Mexico. (California, though a major incentive of the war, was not a publicly announced goal of the early war aims.)[2] This was the national strategy by the end of May 1846. It would change within the year.

President Polk proposed that Congress authorize fifty thousand volunteer soldiers, because he felt the state militia would be the least effective way to quickly mobilize a large force for war. The Founding Fathers had envisioned the militia as America's premier fighting force, but it had declined to such a condition that, by the time of the Mexican War, it was mostly ineffective. "Thus, with the militias of the various states in such deplorable condition, it was essential that volunteers carry the load."[3] Additionally, as demonstrated during the War of 1812, the state militia was resistant to serving outside their own states and especially upon foreign soil. "The federal government came to rely upon volunteers during national emergencies because their use evaded the two great problems associated with militia: volunteers would serve for extended periods and could leave their state boundaries"[4]—and United States boundaries for that matter.

Polk requested to increase the strength of infantry companies from forty-two privates to a hundred, which would double the regular army immediately. The new volunteer regiments would have the same wartime strength. He also recommended that Congress increase the number of general officers in the regular army: two new major generals (two star), for a total of three including Scott; and four new brigadier generals (one star), for a total six. Eventually, Congress authorized only one new major general and two brigadier general positions. The major generals were Winfield

---

[2]Millett and Maslowki, *For the Common Defense*, 149, 151; Eisenhower, *So Far from God*, 92; Bauer, *The Mexican War*, 71.
[3]McGaffrey, *Army of Manifest Destiny: The American Soldier in the Mexican War: 1846–1848*, 16.
[4]Winders, *Mr. Polk's Army*, 68.

Scott and Zachary Taylor; brigadier generals were Edmund Gaines, John Wool, Stephen W. Kearny, and David Twiggs.[5] Polk would eventually commission several major and brigadier generals of volunteers.[6]

With the national strategy understood, Polk, through Marcy, Scott, and Secretary of the Navy George Bancroft, would direct the forces necessary to achieve it. Immediate dispatches went forth to Commodore David Conner ordering his squadron to blockade key Mexican ports in the Gulf of Mexico, which Conner had already been doing since the commencement of hostilities. Dispatches also went to Commodore John D. Sloat, commander of the Pacific Squadron, temporarily anchored at Mazatlán, Mexico, to seize key ports in California. Polk had previously instructed Sloat to take California ports once hostilities had commenced; now that war was a reality, Polk was merely confirming earlier directives. Sloat, in fact, had already sailed from Mazatlán in June 1846, after learning from Mexican authorities that war was present. He also feared British interference in California. Sloat arrived in Monterey, California, on July 2, and had captured the port by July 7.[7]

Polk directed his national strategy to the army's land forces through Secretary Marcy. General Taylor was to penetrate beyond the Rio Grande and occupy the northern states of Mexico. Curiously, in some of the early dispatches, Marcy ordered Taylor to advance south through central Mexico and to take Mexico City. As Taylor advanced from his base on the Rio Grande, Brigadier General John Wool, a regular army officer, was to assemble a mostly volunteer force, the Army of the Center. From San Antonio he would proceed south into northern Mexico, supporting and securing Taylor's right flank.

---

[5]Eisenhower, *So Far From God*, 96–97; Winders, *Mr. Polk's Army*, 35–37.
[6]If Lieutenant General Joseph Smith, the Mormon prophet, had been alive when the Mexican War began and had he volunteered, would he have been the senior-ranking officer in the army? No. His commission was as a militia officer of the state of Illinois. Militia officers did not automatically retain their militia rank when mobilized for federal service. President Polk appointed all militia or volunteer officers in the ranks of brigadier and major general. See Gardner, "The Nauvoo Legion, 1840–1845: A Unique Military Organization," 168–69.
[7]Eisenhower, *So Far From God*, 212–14; DeVoto, *Year of Decision*, 199.

WAR AIMS AND A "LITTLE" MISSION 69

On May 16, 1846, Secretary of War Marcy wrote orders to Colonel Stephen Watts Kearny, commander of the famous 1st U.S. Dragoons at Fort Leavenworth in Indian Territory (later Kansas). Kearny was to organize a new army, the Army of the West, and conduct an overland campaign to capture and occupy Santa Fe and secure the important trade route between the city and Fort Leavenworth for American use. Polk and his administration, especially the military departments and bureaus, faced the problems associated with providing the means, logistical base, and troops necessary for several simultaneous campaigns—a daunting task. A couple of weeks later Polk amended Kearny's orders to include California in the campaign. It was this strategic decision, the invasion of California and operational need to create the Army of the West, that conceived and gave birth to the Mormon Battalion and its eventual march to the Pacific Ocean.

The conquest of the Southwest, a long cherished dream for many Americans, was now reasonable and obtainable. By the end of May both Polk and Scott foresaw an easy campaign requiring few forces to conquer New Mexico. With additional volunteers and supplies, the great beckoning Mexican territory of Alta California was also obtainable. American political, cultural, and economic forces already heavily influenced both of these Mexican provinces, thus changing the social spectrum and political-economic existence of these regions from the rest of Mexico. Polk was confident that a rapid and convincing military campaign would pull these satellite territories into the American orbit. He was essentially correct.

President Polk provided the soil in which the idea of a Mormon military unit germinated. In his first state of the union message to Congress on December 2, 1845, Polk declared his intention to erect forts and blockhouses along the growing Oregon Trail and establish a mail service connecting Oregon with Missouri.[8] Brigham

---
[8]Richardson, *A Compilation of Messages and Papers of the Presidents*, 4: 396–97.

Young learned of the message and sent a reply to Polk offering the services of the Latter-day Saints to erect the forts and blockhouses and thus, earn funds for their removal to the West.

During the winter of 1845–46, Brigham Young's entire energy was focused on the Mormons' preparation and migration west. Soon plans and organization took shape as the Saints once again united for another trek—perhaps their most difficult. Church leaders published a "circular" outlining the basic program for the church to follow. Rather prophetic, and also politically accurate, the circular expressed the leadership's desire to settle in the area of the Rocky Mountains unless another permanent location was found. It also directly committed the Saints to loyalty to the United States, especially "should hostilities arise between the Government of the United States and any other power" over Oregon. It further admonished, "we [the Saints] are on hand to sustain the claim of the United States Government to that Country."[9] By implication this circular and declaration could include the conflict with Mexico as well. The Mormons were thus prepared religiously and politically to remain loyal to the federal government, and by implication, they were also prepared for a call to arms if necessary.

Within weeks the Mormon emigration was well underway. Samuel Brannan, presiding elder of the eastern states, sailed from New York City on February 4, 1846, aboard the *Brooklyn* with 230 Saints who would eventually land at San Francisco Bay.[10] This same day the first wagons crossed the Mississippi River from Illinois into Iowa Territory, thus beginning the removal from Nauvoo, which would peak between April and June 1846 and end in September.

Just a few days before, January 20, was a busy day for the clerks and secretaries of church president Brigham Young. Not only did the circular come forth, but Young also dictated a letter appointing

---

[9] "A Circular of the High Council to the members of the Church of Jesus Christ of Latter-day Saints, and to all whom it concern," Nauvoo, January 20, 1846, Journal History. The Journal History of the LDS Church, located in the LDS Archives, is a day-by-day account of church events compiled from journals, letters, meeting notes, and other primary sources.

[10] Sonne, *Saints on the Seas: A Maritime History of Mormon Migration, 1830–1890*, 71–72.

WAR AIMS AND A "LITTLE" MISSION

a replacement for Samuel Brannan as the presiding elder or "president" of the branches of the church and its concerns in the eastern states. The presidency of the eastern states mission would go to Young's nephew—Jesse Little.

Thus, Jesse Carter Little, a man little recognized in history, would write a letter that is little remembered, but which caused one of the most important events in Mormon history, setting in motion a causal relationship that quite literally saved the Mormon Church from financial ruin and possible extinction.

Jesse Little was a New Hampshire Yankee, though he was born in 1815 in Maine. He became a Latter-day Saint as a young man and served his church faithfully the remainder of his life. He completed several missions in the eastern states, and at a general conference of the church in Utah in 1856, Brigham Young, his uncle, called him to be a counselor in the Presiding Bishopric of the church. Thus, Little became a general authority of the church, a position of great responsibility and status among the Mormons. A handsome man with a narrow nose and dark eyes, he would in later life grow a pure white beard, accenting his good features. He died in 1893 in Salt Lake City at the age of seventy-eight.

In his 1846 letter of appointment, Young admonished Little to be mindful of any opportunities the government might offer him and "embrace those facilities if possible. As a wise and faithful man, take every honorable advantage of the times you can."[11] Brigham Young and Jesse Little did not realize that the idea of approaching the government would materialize in a call to arms during war.

It was in Philadelphia, the birthplace of American independence, that the Mormon Church now gained one of its most trusted, loyal, and dependable friends at a most propitious time. After a conference presided over by Elder Little, a sober and earnest young man of twenty-four years approached him. He introduced himself as Thomas L. Kane of Philadelphia. He had attended the meetings

---

[11] Brigham Young to Jesse Little, January 20, 1846, Utah State Historical Society.

and was very impressed with what he had heard and offered his services to Little and the Mormons.

Thomas Lieper Kane was an illustrious minor character in American history, as were his father, Jacksonian Democrat Judge John Kane, and his brother, Dr. Elisha Kent Kane, who would gain fame a few years later as an Arctic explorer. (Later, Thomas Kane served as military aide to the governor of Pennsylvania and, as such, held the honorary rank of colonel in the militia.) He was a serious-minded young man with indomitable courage, keen intellect, a reformer's compassion, a splendid education, and a gift of pen and oratory. But he was tragically plagued by weak health and constant infirmities that always seemed to strike him at his moments of supreme glory. Seventeen years later, on the night of July 1, 1863, with the first day of Battle of Gettysburg fought, Kane, a brigadier general of a Pennsylvania volunteer brigade in the federal 12th Corps, rose from his sickbed barely able to stand. He had traveled by train and then by horse all night from Philadelphia to Gettysburg to resume command of his brigade. The next day on Culp's Hill he and his men withstood several violent Confederate assaults. With the battle over he returned to the sick list and his active service in the war ended.[12]

Thomas Kane was delighted to meet some Mormons, a people he had heard much about and for whom he had developed an altruistic compassion. Kane provided Little with letters of introduction and advice on making political contacts. From this simple beginning, non-Mormon Colonel Kane became perhaps the greatest friend and advocate that the Mormons had during their exodus and the early Utah period.

Jesse Little arrived in Washington, D.C., on Thursday, May 21, 1846. The capital was in a tumult with excitement over the recent declaration of war. He first sought out Amos Kendall, former postmaster general under President Andrew Jackson. Kendall had been

---

[12]See Zobell, *Sentinel of the East: A Biography of Thomas L. Kane*; see also Wert, *Gettysburg: Day Three*, 65–66.

WAR AIMS AND A "LITTLE" MISSION 73

an influential member of Andrew Jackson's "kitchen" cabinet. Kendall's desire to assist the Mormons was not completely altruistic. He had a connection with a business associate, Alfred O. Benson of New York City, who had sought a real estate contract with Brigham Young through Samuel Brannan to obtain land in California. The entire scheme eventually died, but in May and June 1846, Kendall still desired its success, and Little was a representative of the church who Kendall thought he could help.[13]

It was during this meeting with Amos Kendall on Saturday, May 23, that the idea of a military unit composed of Mormons first arose. That very day, Washington received news of Taylor's double victories at Palo Alto and Resaca de la Palma of the 8th and 9th of May, respectively. The city was aflame with the news. Zachary Taylor was an overnight hero. Writing later, Little recorded Kendall's suggestion that "arrangements could be made to assist our emigration by enlisting one thousand of our men, arming, equipping and establishing them in California to defend the country."[14]

On the evening of May 25, Governor Archibald Yell of Arkansas and Kendall met with Polk and discussed the idea of mounting a military expedition to invade California. As of May 16, Polk had already authorized Kearny to take Santa Fe and the territory of New Mexico. They all agreed on the feasibility of extending the campaign to invade California. Polk therefore put in motion the plans to take California and to raise the forces to do so. On May 26 the cabinet approved an overland expedition to California. Polk's vision of America became more clear, but it was his industry that propelled his dream.

One must take time to understand the very unusual character and attitudes of James Polk, the eleventh president of the United States. He was a consummate politician, brilliant in strategy, logical and crafty, with connections that would help him to achieve his goals—but affable, friendly, and open, he was not. Polk and his associates formed one of the most evasive, secretive, and seclusive administrations in history. Cunning, calculated, mysterious, and distrustful

---
[13]Yurtinus, "A Ram in the Thicket: The Mormon Battalion in the Mexican War," 13–14, 26.
[14]Journal History, July 6, 1846, LDS Archives.

were characteristics of the man from Tennessee. He had learned his political lessons and honed his skills. He took few into his confidence, believed few people, and trusted and admired no one. Polk detested more than he loved; he criticized more than he praised. The presidency under Polk was a cold, deliberate projection of his personality. He hosted few official parties and receptions. Polk had one or two guests to dinner a few days a week, but for political and not social reasons. Once dinner was over, the guests departed and Polk returned to his business for several more hours of labor. Historian Justin Smith has written that Polk was "cold, narrow, methodical, dogged, plodding, obstinate partisan, deeply convinced of his importance and responsibility, very wanting in humor, very wanting in ideality, very wanting in soulfulness, inclined to be sly, and quite incapable of seeing things in a great way."[15]

Despite Polk's nature and flawed character, most of the nation rallied around his cause and austere determination. He worked at a feverish pitch with a relentlessness that wearied clerks and assistants. He gave himself so completely to his four years in office that just months after his term ended, his life ended also. It was a difficult proposition to gain Polk's attention and a greater victory still to actually win his approval. Eventually, Jesse Little was able to achieve both.[16]

Several more days passed by with no word from Kendall, Polk, or anyone of authority. Jesse Little turned to the mightiest weapon in his personal arsenal—the pen. It is certain that the letter he now wrote to Polk either moved, shamed, or inspired the president, because within two days, Little had his first interview with Polk. This single letter of June 1, 1846, written before Secretary of War William Marcy amended his orders to Colonel Kearny to include a campaign to secure California, was the stroke that created the Mormon Battalion. In this letter he expressed many things from his heart: the reality of the Mormon situation beginning with the Saints' anticipated trek across the Great Plains, their persecution as

---

[15]Smith, *The War with Mexico*, 1: 128–29.
[16]See Sellers, *James K. Polk, Continentalist, 1843–1846*.

WAR AIMS AND A "LITTLE" MISSION

a religious people, and their desire to remain American citizens, loyal to their government and institutions.

Jesse Little wrote "not, sir, as an office-seeker actuated by a selfish motive, but as the representative of a noble and persecuted people." He rehearsed many of the persecutions that the Latter-day Saints had endured and their desire to worship God in a free land, free from persecution and want.[17] He then expressed, "Our determinations are fixed and cannot be changed. From twelve to fifteen thousand [Saints] have already left Nauvoo for California, and many others are making ready to go. Some have gone around Cape Horn," referring to Sam Brannan and the *Brooklyn* Saints, and "have landed at the bay of San Francisco."[18] He was wise to express to Polk numbers that suggested the scope of Mormonism, particularly when he explained that there were an estimated forty thousand Mormons in Great Britain! It was perhaps a slight overestimate, but effective.

Polk's interest in Great Britain was just as paramount at this time as was the war with Mexico. Polk had thrown down the gauntlet in April by dissolving the joint occupation treaty of Oregon. The British now would determine whether Oregon justified a third war with the United States. Sensing the political opportunity he could gain by winning the loyalty of thousands of British Mormons, he must have been keenly impressed by Little's argument and the Mormons' potential influence. Little was implying that these British Saints would accept American citizenship over their British nationality, all based upon their conversion to Mormonism. Little continued, "They [American and British Mormons], as well as myself, are true hearted Americans, true to our country, true to its laws, true to its glorious institutions and we have a desire to go under the outstretched wings of the American Eagle."[19]

---

[17]Golder, *March of the Mormon Battalion, From Council Bluffs to California: Taken from the Journal of Henry Standage*, 81–82; a version of this letter is found in Bagley and Bigler, *Army of Israel: Mormon Battalion Narratives*, 32–35. Bagley and Bigler explain there is no known original source of this letter, only transcribed copies; since Golder's copy duplicates other copies perfectly, it is used.

[18]Golder, *March of the Mormon Battalion*, 83.

[19]Ibid.

Little now delivered the *coup de grace*: "We would disdain to receive assistance from a foreign power, although it should be proffered, unless our government shall turn us off in this great crisis and will not help us, but compel us to be foreigners."[20]

This veiled threat prompts the question: Why did President Polk decide to offer an opportunity of military service through Jesse Little to the Church of Jesus Christ of Latter-day Saints? Was it a military or political decision?

The most reasonable answer must lie with manpower needs to conduct the war. Did Polk need to enlist Mormon men to fight and win the war? The state of Missouri provided some 6,739 volunteers, second only to Louisiana in total volunteers.[21] One entire regiment, the 3rd Missouri Mounted Volunteers, was organized at Fort Leavenworth, and then disbanded because it was not necessary. Missouri alone could have provided ten more regiments. Other midwestern states provided thousands of volunteers. Polk had ample volunteers to conduct and sustain the war effort. Bringing the Mormons under arms was not a military or manpower concern; it was political gain for Polk.[22]

Little thought it best to end his letter on a positive note and not offend the president too much. He wrote, "but when we are called into the battle field in defence of our country, and when the sword and sabre shall have been unsheathed, we declare before heaven and earth that they shall not return to their scabbard until the enemy of our country, or we, sleep with the pale sheeted nations of the dead, or until we obtain deliverance."[23]

Jesse Little had seemingly beaten Polk at his own game. President Polk summoned him for an interview.

※ ※ ※

During the first week of June 1846, Polk had already worked out most of his plan for what would become the Army of the West

---

[20]Ibid.
[21]Tutorow, *The Mexican-American War: An Annotated Bibliography*, 361.
[22]See Sanders, "In the 1846, During the War with Mexico, was President Polk's Decision to Employ a Battalion of Mormons a Military or Political Decision?"
[23]Golder, *The March of the Mormon Battalion*, 84.

under Colonel, later brigadier general, Kearny. He had spent much time with many associates and advisors, including Senator Thomas Hart Benton from Missouri, who assured Polk that a force from Fort Leavenworth could make the march to California within the season. Polk's journal for the week was full of comments concerning the campaign to take California, including mention of the Mormon question. "Col. Kearny was also authorized to receive into service," wrote Polk, "as volunteers a few hundred of the Mormons who are now on their way to California, with a view to conciliate them, attach them to our country & prevent them from taking part against us."[24] He did not want Mormons to make up the majority of the military force in California.[25]

On June 3, Jesse Little, Kendall, and Polk spent three hours discussing the Mormon situation and the war. Polk was polite, cordial, and attentive to the plight of the Mormon people and their sufferings and history. What appealed most to Polk was the fact that the Mormons were already on the frontier and in motion toward California, and some of their men could be used once they arrived there.

Brigham Young was in fact considering several locations in the West for possible settlement—the Great Basin (sometimes called the Bear River Valley—a general term for what is now northern Utah and southern Idaho) and also California. But he did not communicate his intentions clearly to the majority of the Saints. Even Jesse Little was ignorant of Young's design.[26]

Polk intended to win the Mormons' loyalty and insure that they did not turn against the United States or try to establish their own independent country. Though his political reasons to enlist the Mormons were several, his military purpose was singular: they were to serve as soldiers in a combat unit in war.

Polk explained that he had not yet decided on how many Mormons would be mustered, and that he would discuss the matter with the secretaries of war and navy the next day. Little would then

---

[24]Quaife, ed., *The Diary of James K. Polk during his Presidency, 1845–1848*, 1: 437–40.
[25]Ibid., 1: 449–50.
[26]Arrington, *Brigham Young: American Moses*, 123–24; Stegner, *The Gathering of Zion: The Story of the Mormon Trail*, 41–42.

learn his final answer. Here the president was not telling the truth. Polk had already directed Secretary of War Marcy to call up several hundred Mormons to active service once they arrived in California. Marcy's letter of June 3 to Kearny was ambiguous about when and where the Mormon enlistment would take place, but indicated that they would join the army readily.

Marcy's order to Kearny read,

> It is known that a large body of Mormon emigrants are en route to California.... It has been suggested here, that many of these Mormons would willingly enter into the service of the United States, and aid us in our expedition against California. You are hereby authorized to muster into service such as can be induced to volunteer; not, however, to a number exceeding one-third of your entire force.[27]

Curiously, Polk recorded a different proportion of the army that the Mormons would constitute in his journal: "The mormons if taken into service, will constitute not more than ¼ of Kearney's command, and the main object of taking them into service is to conciliate them." Polk finished his entry, "It was with the view to prevent this singular sect from becoming hostile to the U.S. that I held the conference with Mr. Little." Polk also wrote that the Mormons would serve "under the command of a U.S. Officer," meaning the battalion commander would be regular army officer and not a volunteer officer as in other volunteer units. This important detail was not in Marcy's communication to Kearny.[28]

On June 5 Polk offered to enlist five hundred Mormons who would serve as volunteers. Polk was direct with Little and gave his assurance "that we [the Mormons] should be protected in California." Little inquired about going immediately to the Mormon camps in Iowa to begin the recruiting. Polk declined; he wished to enlist them after they had arrived in California.[29] But orders

---

[27] William Marcy to Stephen W. Kearny, June 3, 1846, Kearny's Letter Book, Missouri Historical Society, published in von Sachsen-Altenburg, *Winning the West: General Stephen Watts Kearny's Letter Book 1846–1847*; hereafter, Kearny's Letter Book, 287–88.
[28] Quaife, *Polk Diary*, 1: 444–46.
[29] Luce, "The Mormon Battalion: A Historical Accident," 27–38. During all the confusion of May 1846, Polk dispatched Lt. Archibald Gillespie to take secret orders to Americans in California. He went by sea, crossed Panama, and saw many adventures in California. See Hussey, "The Origin of the Gillespie Mission," 43–58.

authorizing the Mormon Battalion, dated June 3, 1846, were already en route to Fort Leavenworth.

Jesse Little had accomplished what his prophet, leader and uncle had asked of him: to secure government support to assist the Mormons in their westward exodus. Whatever sense of success he felt, there was also disappointment due to the fact that as far as Little knew it would be possibly a year or so before the fruits of this arrangement would benefit the church. It was also very possible that the war might end prior to enlisting the Mormon volunteers.

CHAPTER FOUR

The Army for Mexico

General Taylor knows nothing of army movement.
—*Lieutenant Colonel Ethan Allen Hitchcock*

The United States government formed the Mormon Battalion, as other volunteer units, to augment the regular army in achieving military victory against Mexico. The battalion was conceived, recruited, and organized for only one military purpose: to serve as a combat unit in war. Yet many historians and students of the battalion, past and present, have instead focused on aspects of its service other than a military unit marshaled for war.

The unique aspects of military life, tactics, rank, and organization have caused confusion in previous histories of the Mormon Battalion. A fundamental grasp of the military practices of the era provides a clearer understanding of the essence of this unique organization.

The argument that the United States has been unprepared for most of the wars it has fought can be easily applied to the Mexican War. For a nation of some twenty-two million people in 1846, a standing army of less than eight thousand officers and men seems inadequate, especially for a nation so geographically vast and with a frontier so unsettled. One reason for this small military capability was the intrinsic American distrust of a large, professional standing army and the reliance on the patriotism of the citizen-soldier.[1] Since the days of the founding of the Republic, the standing, or regular, army had sometimes been as small as a company (roughly an authorized strength of a hundred men) and could not hope to safeguard United States interests, especially on a wide frontier. As the nation grew and spread westward, the regular army grew also, but not in direct proportion.

The United States military establishment in the 1840s was extremely different from the large, technologically sophisticated armies of the modern era. Americans of the Jeffersonian and Jacksonian eras held the militia concept in sacred regard, because from colonial and revolutionary days the militia was a major force in securing American independence. Based on English practice, the "common militia" in America developed during the early colonial period and was the basis for military strength and community protection. The concept was that all able-bodied men of military age, roughly between eighteen and forty-five years old, in a community were obligated to serve in the militia and drill on scheduled days on a regular basis.[2]

The common militia, also called the "enrolled" militia, served through the pre-revolutionary period with mixed results. During the early months of the Revolutionary War, General George Washington realized that the militia alone could never defeat the professional British armies arrayed against him. Washington, the realist, had also acquired a begrudging respect for professional armies, regular soldiers, and their capabilities. As the war progressed he developed disdain for the militia's ineptitude, poor morale, and inconsistent performance under combat conditions. As soon as he trained and disciplined his army to meet the British, the militia enlistments expired and most of his army melted away.[3]

Washington had to convince a reluctant Continental Congress to authorize a standing regular Continental Army of a few regiments. What resulted was the "Continental Line," which consisted

---

[1] Millett and Maslowski, *For the Common Defense*, 53.
[2] Doubler, *I Am the Guard: A History of the Army National Guard, 1636–2000*, 6–7, 20–21.
[3] Ibid., 67–68.

of regiments and battalions recruited by the states for continuous or extended duty in the Continental Army. In modern thinking the Continental Line is similar to a combination of national guardsmen, reservists, volunteers, and draftees on extended active duty for the duration of a war. These units under Washington became the genesis of the future regular army.

Washington used the Continental Army as the basis for his military strategy and augmented it with militia levies from the various states.[4] Even though Washington had sincere reservations about the militia, he never denied its critical role in winning the war. Without the militia, in its various forms, the War of Independence would have failed.

After the revolution the standing army was the target of neglect, and Congress reduced it significantly. As various political factions fought over the power and hegemony of a centralized federal government versus the supremacy of the individual states, this same power struggle rose in regard to a new United States military theory and structure. Congress passed two pieces of legislation in 1792 governing the militia system and concept in America. The Uniform Militia Act and the Calling Forth Act regulated and authorized the powers and controls for the militia. They defined the federal government's role in using state militia. Reliance on the militia with a small regular army became the accepted military concept.[5] Unfortunately, these laws were ineffective in organizing, regulating, and enforcing the militia as a reliable reserve force.

Just twenty years later, during the War of 1812, the militia, heralded as the nation's main military force, once again proved incapable of prolonged and arduous combat operations. Some militiamen refused to invade Canada, charging that it was unconstitutional for the militia to invade foreign lands—that the militia was only for domestic defense. Again military leaders badgered Congress to strengthen a regular army, augmented by the militia.

---

[4]For origins of the National Guard and its relationship with the U.S. Army, see Doubler, *I am the Guard*; also, Mahon, *History of the Militia and the National Guard*, 35–45.

[5]Act of the Second Congress of the United States, Statute I, Chapter 28, May 2, 1792, *The Public Statutes at Large of the United States of America*, 1: 264–65, National Archives.

Fortunately, the war was generally limited in scope, but Congress did provide over thirty additional regular regiments, besides the dozens of volunteer regiments that served during this conflict.[6]

During the Jacksonian era the militia concept changed from a "common" or mandatory militia to a "volunteer" or organized militia. Though all able-bodied men of the community were theoretically members of the militia, a new volunteer concept evolved in the form of county and state units. The volunteer militia idea had originated prior to the Revolutionary War, but it was neither universal nor well established. These new units tended to have better morale, and attendance at scheduled drills improved greatly. Yet, there was little improvement in training and discipline. Firearms and equipment were usually provided by state arsenals often from older federal stocks. Uniforms were often gaudy, non-standard, and ostentatious. Sometimes there were no uniforms at all.[7]

Some militia units of this era had unusual names and designations, such as Colonel Caleb Cushing's Massachusetts Volunteer Regiment, the Baltimore-Washington Volunteers, the LaClede Rangers of St. Louis, and, of course, one of the most famous military units ever formed in American history, the Texas Rangers. In Mormon history students are familiar with the Carthage Greys and the Nauvoo Legion of Illinois, both of which were militia units during this period.

One indication of the European brand of militarism in America was the establishment of the United States Military Academy in 1802 by Thomas Jefferson. Though Jefferson was a former Virginia militiaman, he was perhaps the least likely president to establish such an elitist, professional military institution. His theory of *laissez-faire* economics and popular sovereignty was in contrast to military traditions and elitist academies.

---

[6]Doubler, *I am the Guard*, 86–87; Millett and Maslowski, *For the Common Defense*, 107.

[7]There are many general studies that address the growth and development of the military in the United States; Millett and Maslowski, *For the Common Defense*, is one of the best; see also Hassler, *With Shield and Sword: American Military Affairs, Colonial Time to the Present*; Weigley, *History of the United States Army*.

First Lieutenant Andrew Jackson "AJ" Smith, acting commander of the Mormon Battalion, whom most of the Mormon soldiers detested. Shown here as a major general during the Civil War, during which he had a distinguished career serving under Generals Grant and Sherman in the west. *Massachusetts Commandery Military Order of the Loyal Legion and the U.S. Army Military History Institute.*

West Point, as part of the Corps of Engineers, developed a curriculum based on the French example, with a strong concentration on engineering, mathematics, fortifications, and the classical languages of Greek and Latin, as well as French, history, and philosophy. As for military training, the academy focused on marching, swordsmanship, horsemanship, and drilling in small unit tactics. Combined with the austere discipline of a completely regimented life, West Point offered one of the best and most sought-after educations in America.[8]

Over two hundred West Point graduates served in the Mexican War, and they heavily influenced the outcome of the war. The regular officers who served with the Mormon Battalion were all academy graduates: Captain Philip St. George Cooke (class of 1827), Captain James Allen (1829), First Lieutenant Andrew Jackson Smith (1838), and Second Lieutenant George Stoneman, who graduated in 1846 just as the war began.

The Mormon Battalion was commanded by regular army officers, and participated in war aims and strategy planned and executed by the national army. Supplies, requisitions, tables of organization

---

[8]Millett and Maslowski, *For the Common Defense*, 133–35.

Philip St. George Cooke, the solid and hardened regular officer who led the Mormon Battalion to California and one of the finest and most experienced frontier officers in the antebellum army. During the Civil War, shown here as a brigadier general, Cooke had an unfortunate and tragic service record that somewhat tarnished his career. *Massachusetts Commandery Military Order of the Loyal Legion and the U.S. Army Military History Institute.*

and manpower, order of battle, ranks and responsibilities, and the Articles of War (the laws that govern soldiers while in active service) were all from the regular establishment. Though it was a unique religious organization, its standards were set by commanders who were all from the regular army and not Mormons.

The majority of the officer corps of the army during the nineteenth century served essentially the same function: they were trained to lead men in combat. They were expected to know their profession thoroughly, train and lead their men, and fight as well as their men. The role of officers on the small, unit level was a very demanding responsibility, especially in combat. The importance of the officers—lieutenants and captains—in combat during that era was critical because army tactics relied more on officers to command and lead units than on the subordinate noncommissioned officers, or NCOs, filling that role on the battlefield.

Non-commissioned officers of the ranks of corporal, sergeant, first sergeant and, on the battalion and regimental level, sergeant major, were drill masters and trainers and also served in specialized

THE ARMY FOR MEXICO

staff responsibilities such as farriers, musicians, buglers, quartermasters, commissary stewards, clerks, and medical orderlies. Line sergeants, as opposed to staff NCOs, did not attend any formal training school or academy, and there was no formal professional development program other than the experience and unit training they gained from years of service. Few sergeants stayed in the army long enough to sustain a reasonable career. If disease or combat did not claim their lives, the appeal of an easier civilian life and starting a family were major considerations for leaving. The small and isolated frontier army was a difficult environment in which to raise a family. Yet, in war NCOs served courageously and with distinction—a tribute to these men because of their lack of formal training. As with soldiers in all ages, they knew what was necessary to fight on the battlefield, and they did it.[9]

The army of this period was an extremely rugged institution and the soldier's life was an existence of manual labor and routine duties, some tactical training, ruthless discipline, and continual privation. The frontier army faced three plagues that accounted for more problems in keeping and maintaining a quality fighting force than all other factors: drunkenness, desertion, and disease.

Alcohol and its abuses were as intrinsic and ubiquitous in the army as birth and death is to life. Soldiers received a ration of spirits every day. Drunkenness and its associated deplorable results caused many a commander and soldier grief. Although alcohol was one consolation from the dreariness and boredom of soldiering, when used to excess it was a problem that few commanders could deal with effectively.[10]

Desertion was a constant of military life in the frontier army annually averaging some 5 percent of the total force.[11] The average recruit of the period was a simple laborer, a rural bumpkin, or a for-

---

[9]For schools and the opportunity for officer and NCO professional development, see Coffman, *The Old Army: A Portrait of the American Army in Peacetime, 1784–1898*, 156–61; Winders, *Mr. Polk's Army*, 63.   [10]Ibid., 135–37.
[11]Millet and Maslowski, *For the Common Defense*, 140–41.

eigner newly arrived, many of whom could speak little English. Few could read or write, and fewer had a quality education of any degree. Some were criminals, thieves, drunkards, and other sorts of malcontents.[12] They certainly were not the cream of American society. A fair portion of the recruits during this period, over 40 percent, were foreign-born men, mostly Irish and German with mixed loyalties and motivations. When conditions became difficult or unbearable, desertion was often the answer—a result of rigid discipline, low pay, few promotions, the boredom and privations of frontier life, the harshness of extended campaigns, and the quality of the men.[13]

But the worst plague the soldier faced was disease; it was the soldier's greatest enemy. More soldiers in the Mexican War died of natural causes than from wounds in combat. This has been true from Cæsar to Napoleon to the Spanish-American War. Only since World War II has the disease mortality rate dropped below that of those killed in action. Another little noted and often ignored calamity of military service is fatal accidents. Deaths and mishaps were caused by accidental discharges of muskets, soldiers thrown from horses, men run over by wagons, and the all-too-common problem in winter, fatal fires.[14]

Medical science as practiced in the armies of the frontier and Mexican War is best summarized as inadequate and primitive by contemporary standards. Serious fractures and infections to the limbs were met with amputation. Poor water and waste disposal practices caused most of the sanitary problems of the day. Many of the fatalities were from diarrhea, typhoid, cholera, and dysentery. Medicines and treatments were a combination of actual proven methods and reliance upon folklore and country remedies. Physi-

---

[12]As for criminals and malcontents, see Winders, *Mr. Polk's Army*, 60. Historian Edward Coffman wrote, "The army offered a chance to escape from a disagreeable situation, to disappear, and start life anew. It was a haven for those who found it difficult to make a living as civilians." This statement could be interpreted as men with bad luck or bad conduct. Coffman also wrote, "The army provided not only shelter for those who wanted to vanish from their homes but also transportation to points far from the scene of their problems." Coffman, *The Old Army*, 145–46.

[13]Millett and Maslowski, *For the Common Defense*, 140.   [14]Ibid., 653.

THE ARMY FOR MEXICO

cians during this era were faced with diseases they either did not know or were totally ignorant of how to treat.

Historian David Nevin wrote of one disease that crippled armies, called "El Vomito" by the Mexicans, known to the rest of the world as yellow fever. "Though no one knew it was carried by mosquitoes," wrote Nevin, "American soldiers bitten by mosquitoes would fall ill within days. After another week, four of every ten men stricken would die."[15]

Though medical treatment was primitive by modern standards, the regular army surprisingly established very high standards for its medical corps, surpassing those of the civil sector. To become a medical officer, one had to pass a very difficult and thorough entrance examination. Less than half of the applicants passed this examination the first time. No matter what the needs of the army were, the standards were seldom waived. Medical historian Mary C. Gillet wrote, "A civilian physician, writing in 1848, pointed out that the Medical Department's entrance examination had always been strict and that incompetents had never been known to pass them. The department's system, he stated, 'has saved thousands of brave men from the knives and nostrums [dubious remedies] of professional bunglers.'"[16] If a doctor could pass the medical corps examination and serve in the regular army or volunteer service for a period of time, then his future for a secure lucrative private practice was probably assured.[17] It is reasonable to assume that these standards may have been relaxed during the increased needs of war, but apparently not by very much. The age requirements changed, but the same rigid examination continued during the war, with the pass and fail rates being nearly the same as before the war.[18] Dr. George Sanderson, a non-Mormon, served as a commissioned medical officer in the battalion and met these rigid qualifications though many thought him to be a quack, which will be addressed more fully later.

The army of Manifest Destiny lost the battle to disease, but it viciously fought to defeat desertion, drunkenness, undiscipline,

---
[15]Nevin, *The Mexican War*, 129.
[16]Gillet, *Army Historical Series: The Army Medical Department: 1818–1865*, 79.
[17]Ibid., 78.   [18]Ibid., 96.

boredom, cowardice, and incompetence. To discourage desertion and other infractions, the soldiers faced extremely harsh, sometimes brutal punishments. Buck-n-gagging was a common punishment. A soldier sat down on the ground and his arms were brought forward and tied in front of his knees, a rod or stick placed between his elbows and knees. A stick was placed between his teeth and tied behind his head. He would sit in this position for hours at a time. Other punishments had men drawn and spread-eagled on wagon wheels; a deserter often received a "D" branded on the cheek or the hip, and their heads were shaved. Those punished were forced to do strenuous and degrading labor, or faced weeks in the stockade on little rations. Flogging was a common practice for decades, especially in the naval service, but by the 1830s reformers and congressional leaders condemned the practice. By the 1840s flogging, though used infrequently, was still a possible method of punishment. It was seldom employed during the Mexican War and abolished in the army by the Civil War era. Summary execution was a common punishment for desertion, insubordination, murder, and other capital crimes, especially during war. These practices were often used in the volunteer units as well as the regular units.[19]

By the 1840s the army was separated into several main branches or corps of service, following the European style of organization. Aside from purely administrative and support departments, such as the medical corps, commissary, quartermaster, ordnance, and so forth, the main corps were the combat arms of infantry, artillery, and dragoons. The Corps of Engineers, the service that the military academy was based upon, was the elite corps of the army. When an officer graduated from West Point, he was assigned a branch of service according to his ranking in the class and sometimes his personal preference. The distinguished graduates normally went to the engineers or the artillery. The rest of the class received commissions into the other, less prestigious branches,

---

[19]Winders, *Mr. Polk's Army*, 62; Coffman, *The Old Army*, 196.

THE ARMY FOR MEXICO

which in fact constituted the majority of the army. Officers occasionally transferred from service to service to fill vacancies, gain promotions, or improve their situation.

The effectiveness of the U.S. Army's artillery was one of the key factors that led to decisive victories by American forces during the Mexican War. The cannons of the period were long-range guns, which were effective up to some 1,500 yards or just short of a mile. During the Mexican War brilliant artillerymen such as Sam Ringgold revolutionized the concept of "flying artillery." This new tactic dictated that artillery batteries of four guns be divided into two sections, rapidly galloped into key firing positions, unlimbered and were ready to fire within minutes. This concept was perfected by hours and hours of tough, intensive drill and training. Other artillerists such as John Duncan and Braxton Bragg, a future Confederate general, expertly used the standard tactics of artillery, a slower, more methodical employment, with lethal results.[20]

Perhaps the most romanticized branch in the army corps was the mounted service—the dragoons, later called the cavalry. A dragoon, a French term, is essentially a heavily armed mounted soldier who could fight mounted as well as dismounted. Dragoons carried either carbines or rifles and sabers and pistols. The dragoons were the "shock" corps of the army, producing considerable fear and panic as they charged upon the opposing ranks with sabers drawn. By 1846 there were three mounted regiments, the 1st and 2nd U.S. Dragoons and the Regiment of Mounted Riflemen established in that same year. In 1855, Secretary of War Jefferson Davis created two new cavalry regiments, and in 1861, at the beginning of the American Civil War, the dragoon regiments were redesignated as cavalry and the dragoon faded into history. All the commanders and regular army officers of the Mormon Battalion had many years of service in the dragoons and were veterans of Colonel Stephen W. Kearny's famous and elite 1st Dragoons.

The infantry corps has been the main arm of all armies in all ages—the foot soldier who slugs into battle marching and carrying his own means of fighting and survival. The lowly infantryman of

---

[20] Eisenhower, *So Far From God*, 80.

the Mexican War marched twenty to twenty-five miles a day and fought in linear formations for maximum firepower. Through volleyed fire from hundreds of muskets at once, the infantry regiment remained the most devastating and effective combat arm of the era. Drilled and trained soldiers could fire, reload, and fire again three times a minute. It was General Winfield Scott who oversaw the codification of one of the first doctrinal manuals for American infantry tactics in 1835. Tactics as defined in that era was the execution of drills and movements that would move formations of regiments, battalions, and companies to close with and engage the enemy. One of Scott's chief changes from earlier doctrine was to organize the standard volley formation from three ranks to two ranks, which allowed more speed and flexibility in forming firing ranks.[21]

Unlike the modern era, soldiers on the battlefields of the 1840s seldom fought from cover—behind rocks, trees, or trenches. Of course soldiers fought from fortifications and redoubts, and in city streets during some battles, but not often. Most battles were fought in open, wide-terrain fields, prairies, and hills. Soldiers were drilled and trained so that they could effectively march and move in formation, wheel about, and then close and engage the enemy. The most effective method of delivering the maximum amount of firepower was by massed formations, two ranks of soldiers standing shoulder-to-shoulder and all firing simultaneously or by rank. Firing from a formation was best achieved in this era by employing at least a battalion, or better yet, a regiment on line.

The goal was to inflict the most damage to the opposing enemy's formation. Massed volley fire was considered the most desirable and effective means of inflicting damage. This meant, however, that one's own soldiers were also vulnerable to the enemy's massed volley fire. It took great discipline and strong leadership to inspire men to withstand such a dreadful brush with mortality. This method of volley fire had been a standard tactic and practice for decades, and was devastating in the Napoleonic era.

---

[21]Weigley, *History of the United States Army*, 177.

THE ARMY FOR MEXICO

* * *

By 1846 the standard infantry firearm was the smoothbore, muzzle-loading, flintlock musket. It had been the basic arm of the infantry with little variation since the early eighteenth century. The range that a trained soldier could point his musket (not aim, because there were no sights) and hit a target was only 100 yards, whereas a rifle of the time was effective up to 200 or 300 yards. A spent ball may actually travel as far as 500 to 700 yards, but this is well beyond the maximum effective range and would rarely strike a target with lethal force. Ulysses S. Grant commented that with an old musket, "at a distance of a few hundred yards a man might fire at you all day without your finding it out."[22]

A rifle has spiral grooves or riflings in the bore, which causes the projectile to rotate for a flatter, more level trajectory. This produces better accuracy, faster velocity, and triples the range over a smoothbore musket. However, the main disadvantages of the rifle were the reloading time, which was longer than the musket. The higher expense and the conceptual impracticability to train the entire infantry corps in rifle marksmanship were disadvantages. Rifles of the era were often called yagers, the English spelling of the German word for hunter, *jäger*.

Regular army recruits and new regiments formed during the Mexican War received basically the same firearms as volunteer units. The U.S. Model 1835 flintlock musket was the last production flintlock musket, and the U.S. Model 1842 was the first production percussion-lock musket. However, General Scott decided to not issue the new, non-combat-tested percussion-lock musket, also called the cap-lock, during the Mexican War. He was not convinced that the new firing lock system would work; therefore, not all units received the percussion-lock musket. The U.S. Model 1841 rifle, a percussion-lock often called the "Mississippi" rifle, was issued to some soldiers serving as skirmishers. This rifle was made famous by Colonel Jefferson Davis's 1st Mississippi Volunteer Infantry, or the "Mississippi Rifles," who received these firearms.

---

[22]Grant, *Personal Memoirs of U. S. Grant*, 1: 95.

The most technologically advanced and expensive firearm was the Hall breech-loading carbine issued to the dragoons and mounted troops. The Hall carbine fired a paper cartridge that was cut open by the closing breech when the chamber was closed. All new or advanced firearms were returned to the government after the war ended.[23]

The standard issue firearm for many volunteer units, including the Mormon Battalion, was the U.S. Model 1816 smoothbore flintlock musket, or a variation of it.[24] It copied earlier versions first developed in 1790s. Later models came forth with small variations. Though this design was established in 1816, the musket was not mass-produced until years later, from 1822 to the mid-1830s, at the Springfield, Connecticut, and Harper's Ferry, Virginia, armories. Some historians refer to the Model 1816 in types or variations of the basic model. Others maintain that it was an all-together new musket, the U.S. Model 1822, by the time it went into production. Regardless, the Model 1816 was the standard infantry musket for next twenty-five years, and over a half-million of this firearm were manufactured.[25]

The Model 1816 weighed 9 pounds, 2 ounces and fired a .64 caliber, 1-ounce lead ball, and had a barrel of forty-two inches. The barrel had a lug that attached an eighteen-inch socket bayonet. There was also the U.S. Model 1817 rifle, known as the "common rifle," which was a flintlock, and a few were provided to units for hunting and skirmishing. It fired a .54 caliber ball and had a thirty-three-inch barrel. These old firearms were available in great numbers at the army arsenals and posts and were issued to volunteer units. Some of the men of the Mormon Battalion received rifles, either the Model 1841 "Mississippi" *jäger* or the Model 1817 common rifles; a few men received the Model 1803 rifle.

A flintlock musket was a firearm that had a small piece of "flint" secured in a vice on the cock, now commonly called the hammer.

---

[23]Dawson, *Doniphan's Epic March, The 1st Missouri Volunteers in the Mexican War*, 36–37.
[24]Gibson, "Frontier Arms of the Mormons," 12–13.
[25]Reilly, *United States Martial Flintlocks*, 97–99; Gluckman, *Identifying Old U.S. Muskets, Rifles and Carbines*, 115–22; Allie, *All He Could Carry: U.S. Army Infantry Equipment, 1839–1910*, 4; Urwin, *The United States Infantry: An Illustrated History, 1775–1918*, 46.

THE ARMY FOR MEXICO 95

When the cock went forward, the flint struck the frizzen, which was a small piece of metal that swung forward, opening the powder pan. The spark caused by the flint striking the frizzen ignited gun powder in the pan, which, in turn, caused a spark to go through a vent that ignited gun powder in the chamber and exploded, hurling the ball, or bullet down the muzzle. In the early nineteenth century gunsmiths had developed the "percussion lock," which used a small copper cap filled with sulfurous of mercury to provide the ignition. The cock struck the cap that fit on a nipple, which ignited more easily and more effectively, and was therefore more reliable and less vulnerable to water damage than a flintlock and its powder pan. A few men of the battalion received these modern percussion lock firearms.[26]

The army also issued soldiers accouterments along with their muskets, thus forming the "weapon system." The musket weapon system came from the Ordinance Department. Each soldier received a black leather cartridge box that carried some thirty-two paper cartridges suspended from a 2.25-inch wide, whitened buff leather shoulder belt. The cartridge box hung off the soldier's right hip with the belt over the left shoulder. A second 2.3-inch-wide, white leather shoulder belt suspended the bayonet scabbard off the left hip. On this belt there was a round metal plate with the American eagle stamped on it. These two belts crossed at the chest, forming an X. Around the waist was a 1.5-inch-wide buff-white waist belt with an oval *U.S.* plate. The waist belt overlapped the shoulder belts at the waist and held them close to the body so the cartridge box and bayonet would not flap.[27]

Uniforms, haversacks, knapsacks, canteens, blankets, mess equipment, and shoes were issued by the Quartermaster Department, one of the many departments under the secretary of war. Soldiers wore heavy blue wool uniforms that were distinctively identified by rank, branch of service, and position in the army. The

---

[26] Gluckman, *Identifying Old U.S. Muskets, Rifles and Carbines*, 135–41.

[27] Allie, *All He Could Carry*, 4–5; described above is the 1839 accouterments and weapon system. The 1845 system had the bayonet scabbard suspended from the waist belt with a leather strap called a frog. Thus, there was only one shoulder belt for the cartridge belt. "Buff" leather refers to either buffalo or deer hide as opposed to cowhide, used and tanned for this purpose.

blouse or fatigue jacket and the trousers in the infantry were sky-blue. (During summer months soldiers sometimes wore white cotton-duck uniforms.) The headgear was a forage or wheel cap, which had a floppy, dyed-blue wool crown and a leather visor. The Mormon Battalion men did not receive their issue uniforms, but in lieu received a uniform allowance. Regardless of allowance or not, the quartermaster department was short of uniforms nationwide.

Soldiers also carried a white linen haversack and black-painted canvas knapsack. Overcoats were tied to the top of the knapsack by leather straps. Canteens issued were either wooden or "Indian" rubber canteens that carried two to three pints of water; there were also metal canteens issued during this era.[28]

The battle tactics of this era used were designed mainly for the standard fighting unit in the army: the regiment, composed by ten companies, each of which were made up of approximately 100 soliders. Battalions, formed by specific mission, could be include anywhere from two to eight companies—in the case of the Mormon Battalion, it was five companies. In early 1845, the United States Army had only eight regiments of infantry, two regiments of dragoons, and four regiments of artillery. The regiments were all numbered conveniently from one through the total number; therefore, the 3rd Infantry Regiment, 1st Dragoons, 4th Artillery, and so on. The same year, Congress authorized an additional regiment to safeguard the growing number of emigrant trains along the Oregon Trail. This new regiment was unique, officially named the Regiment of Mounted Riflemen. It was considered a mounted unit, but it was actually a regiment of riflemen equipped with the U.S. Model 1841 rifle. These soldiers were also trained to fight mounted.

Volunteer regiments recruited from the various states were also numbered sequentially, such as the 1st and 2nd Indiana Volunteer Infantry Regiments, the 1st Arkansas Volunteer Cavalry Regiment, the 1st and 2nd New York, and so on. A colonel commanded

---

[28]Winders, *Mr. Polk's Army*, 101–2.

THE ARMY FOR MEXICO

a regiment and had two staff "field grade" officers of the ranks of lieutenant colonel and major. The staff also included other officers of the ranks of captain and first and second lieutenant (company grade) serving as adjutant, quartermaster, and so on. There were enlisted staff soldiers such as sergeant major, clerks or orderly sergeants, and buglers and other musicians. A regiment normally consisted of ten companies. Each company had forty-two privates in peacetime; during war companies could have as many as a hundred privates. Thus, a regiment could have an authorized strength of from five hundred to one thousand men. Companies were designated by an alphabetic system: A, B, C, and so on, through K, omitting the letter "J" because it could be confused with "I" Company.

A captain commanded an infantry company with the other company officers being first and second lieutenants. An infantry company had three platoons of some thirty to thirty-five men each, or patrols and squads of a dozen soldiers. In most histories of the Mormon Battalion a 3rd lieutenant is listed, which is incorrect and not a rank at all.[29]

An archaic military status existed in this era called the "brevet" rank, an honorary rank given to an officer for gallantry or faithful service, or in some cases as a temporary designation when no vacancy existed. Just as with a normal promotion, the president recommended and the Senate approved a brevet promotion. Brevet rank offered status, recognition, and the actual wearing of the rank on the uniform. Pay was based on actual rank, however.

Commanding and controlling ten separate companies in the field was usually a difficult proposition, especially with limited and primitive communication. Frontier army regiments seldom served as complete regiments and were invariably separated. Companies were garrisoned at various forts and posts designed to best serve the army's frontier needs. Sometimes "battalions" were formed and led by the other field grade officers, the lieutenant colonel or the major, or perhaps a senior captain. There was no established doctrine or practice of how many companies formed a battalion; it all depend-

---

[29]Tyler, *A Concise History of the Mormon Battalion in the Mexican War 1846–1848*, 119–24; Ricketts, *The Mormon Battalion, U.S. Army of the West, 1846–1848*, 21–27.

ed upon the nature of the mission. Battalions could be formed with as few as two companies or as many as six or more, and were organized temporarily for certain or specific operations. The companies would later be returned to the permanent regimental structure. Battalions in the mid-nineteenth century normally did not have numbered designations.

The antebellum regular army had been so dispersed along the frontier that most officers, especially the senior officers who had not attended West Point, knew nothing of commanding so many troops at one time. Lieutenant Colonel Ethan Allen Hitchcock, grandson of his namesake, commanded the 3rd U.S. Infantry and was one of the few commanders who could move and drill his regiment with little difficulty. After watching Taylor's army train and drill for combat, he quipped, "General Taylor knows nothing of army movement."[30] It must have been humorous to watch elderly colonels, drill manuals in hand, bark out orders and commands that they little understood with their young adjutants nearby correcting and directing nearly every command. U. S. Grant, as a young lieutenant with the 4th Infantry at New Orleans, recorded a particular drill that had fatal results. His commanding officer, an "old gentleman," Colonel Josiah Vose, decided that war with Mexico was soon at hand and wanted to brush up on his tactics, which he had not done for many years. Vose drilled his command, wrote Grant, and "only two or three evolutions had been gone through when he dismissed the Battalion, and turning to go to his own quarters, dropped dead."[31]

The army organization above the regiment was the brigade of three to five regiments, which was commanded by a brigadier general (one star). Two to three brigades formed a division, which was commanded by a major general (two star). General Taylor's army in Texas consisted of three divisions at one time, but he was one of only two major generals in the regular army, Scott being the other. Brigadier General Kearny's Army of the West was actually an under-strength brigade of two volunteer regiments from Missouri,

---

[30] DeVoto, *Year of Decision*, 110.   [31] Grant, *Personal Memoirs of U. S. Grant*, 1: 60.

THE ARMY FOR MEXICO

six companies of regular dragoons, a battalion of volunteer artillery, various other company and battalion-sized units, and the Mormon Battalion. Later, the 1st New York Volunteer Regiment would come to California by sea.

When war occurred during the nineteenth century, regular army officers could change their rank and position in the regulars and hold an equal or higher rank in the volunteer service. This is what Captain James Allen did in organizing the Mormon Battalion. He accepted a commission and promotion to a lieutenant colonel of infantry in the volunteers. He would receive the full pay, rations, and benefits of a lieutenant colonel as prescribed by regulations until such time that his volunteer service ended. There was no guarantee that when an officer returned to the regular army there would be a position remaining for him with his former rank. This practice was extremely common in the Civil War. Regular army officers accepted commissions in the expanding volunteer service and promotion to higher ranks and positions.

Officers were appointed and promoted by seniority in the regular army. Volunteer commissions were granted to the men serving in the state militia or the volunteer units. Governors normally commissioned colonels and below, after the men "elected" the officers by vote or ballot themselves. Alexander Doniphan had served in the Missouri militia as a brigadier general for years, and then he enlisted as an ordinary private in 1846. His comrades of the 1st Missouri Mounted Volunteers elected him as their colonel and regimental commander, he then received his state commission by Governor John Edwards of Missouri, and finally he received a federal commission in the volunteer service.[32] (Polk, however, upset the process by appointing officers in the rank of brigadier general and above.)

Militia service provided social status and privilege, so to be elected as an officer, whether involved in war or not, was very prestigious. Prior to an election for a captaincy in a volunteer regiment, one rambunctious candidate made an amazing campaign speech:

---

[32]Eisenhower, *So Far from God*, 206.

Fellow citizens! I am Peter Goff, the Butcher of Middletown! I am! I am the man that shot that sneaking, white livered Yankee abolitionist s—n of a b—h, Lovejoy! I did! I want to be your Captain, I do; and will serve the yellow bellied Mexicans the same. I will! I have treated you to fifty dollars worth of whiskey, I have, and when elected Captain I will spend fifty more, I will.

With such qualifications, the Mexican army had little chance of victory.[33]

The Mormon Battalion was also authorized by Kearny in his letter of orders to Captain Allen to include separate staff positions that were normally found on the regimental level, such as an adjutant, who served as the personnel officer responsible for all correspondence, muster rolls, official orders, and returns; and also the special assistant to the commander, who was responsible for much of daily routine. The quartermaster officer was the chief logistician dealing with ammunition, stores, and supplies and the means to move them by wagon trains. Also, most units had a commissariat and subsistence officer who was responsible for stock herds, acquiring foodstuffs, and rations under the commander's guidance. Often a capable officer served as both quartermaster officer and commissariat and subsistence officer. The battalion also had assistant surgeons, a sergeant major who assisted the adjutant, quartermaster sergeants, and corporals. The musicians of a company were drummers and fifers who employed music for rhythm to keep pace and cadence, and a marching tempo for company formations. There were a dozen or more daily routine "calls," such as first call, sick call, recall, and tattoo. Regiments were authorized to have complete and formal regimental bands for military ceremonies and combat operations.

The Mormon Battalion that marched off to war in 1846 was unique in many ways, but in the final conclusion it served as part of the United States Army. Often the battalion has been incorrectly viewed as a pioneer company of Mormons. It can be fully understood only within the context of its true military nature.

---

[33]Chance, *Jefferson Davis' Mexican War Regiment*, 13.

CHAPTER FIVE

The Army of the West and the Camps of Israel

*... to comply with the unjust
demand upon us for troops ...*
—Brigham Young

A bluff situated more than a hundred feet above the Missouri River in northeast Kansas was an ideal place for a settlement, a beautiful locale overlooking the river. The tall cottonwoods, maples, and natural prairie grass added color and life to the rolling stretches of hills and sandy bluffs. The area was so impressive that on July 1, 1804, army explorers Lewis and Clark recorded their impressions of the "high and butifull Prarie" that would prove to be a logical site for a future army post.[1] Nestled in this choice spot sits perhaps the most important and famous garrison of the old frontier army: Fort Leavenworth. Named after the less famous Henry Leavenworth, colonel of the 3rd U.S. Infantry and established in 1827, Fort Leavenworth was the military gateway to the American West during the frontier era.

Early frontier officers displayed sheer brilliance in selecting the site for Fort Leavenworth, but their stroke of genius was not apparent at the time. As the years passed and the frontier developed, Fort Leavenworth's key location was invaluable to the growing settlements along the Missouri River, especially the small settlement of

---

[1]Moulton, *The Journals of the Lewis and Clark Expedition*, 2: 338.

Independence, Missouri, only thirty miles away. Independence would become the staging area for most early travelers on the Oregon-California Trail and the commercial caravans venturing southwest along the Santa Fe Trail. St. Joseph, Missouri, also thirty miles away, would gain glory as one of the jumping-off points for many variant trails that crossed the Missouri River and went northwest to intercept the Platte River Road, the first leg of the trail west. St. Joseph was also the birthplace of the famous Pony Express of 1860–61.[2] Nearly every important expedition, campaign, war, or other operation involving military forces in the West commenced or was staged from Fort Leavenworth. Even the terrible turmoil of "Bleeding Kansas," arguably where the first real shots of the Civil War were fired, was another episode where soldiers from Fort Leavenworth would provide military intervention. The Utah War, or Expedition, of 1857–58 against the Mormons was also based out of Fort Leavenworth, as were several western campaigns during the Civil War. It is impossible to discuss frontier military history without highlighting this famous and vital post, especially anything connected to the western theater of the Mexican War.[3]

In May 1846 when the war against Mexico commenced, a hard-ridden, weather-beaten old veteran of more than thirty years' service resided there. The colonel was a man whose name now honors several towns, a historic fort, and several counties in western states. Stephen Watts Kearny is remembered for many things, but his service during the Mexican War—his brilliant campaign to take New Mexico and California—established his name forever in military history.[4] Kearny's ability and leadership enabled the conquest of New Mexico without a battle. He assisted in reconquering California, after the short-lived American occupation failed, through a

---

[2]Kimball, *Historic Sites and Markers Along the Mormon and Other Great Western Trails*, 108, 128–34.

[3]Today Fort Leavenworth is known for two things: the Command and General Staff College and the Combat Studies Institute; and the famous "DB" or Disciplinary Barracks, where military criminals from all four branches of the military serve their time.

[4]The correct spelling of the name is Kearny, though the county and city in Nebraska are spelled "Kearney," as is the spelling in a lot of other material. Kearny is pronounced as "Car-nee."

THE ARMY OF THE WEST AND THE CAMPS OF ISRAEL 103

series of small but decisive victories aided by naval forces employed on the ground, "bear-flag" revolutionaries, mountain men, and some Mexicans-turned-American-patriots. Kearny's legend and legacy span nearly four decades of military service, and his achievements include brief war-time governorships of New Mexico and California, with his last posting as military occupation governor of Mexico itself from Mexico City.[5] He brought more territory under the American flag than any other soldier in United States history.

Born in 1794 in New Jersey, young Kearny was attending college at what is now Columbia University in New York during the War of 1812 when he enlisted and was later commissioned an officer. He fought in several major battles of that war and was wounded and breveted for bravery. After the war he continued in his new profession and served in many capacities in the small regular army through the years of the early republic. In 1833 Congress organized a dragoon regiment and Kearny received his lieutenant colonelcy under Colonel Henry Dodge. When the army created the 2nd U.S. Dragoons in 1835, Kearny stayed with the original regiment, the 1st Dragoons. He served on many of the most important early campaigns and expeditions of the frontier army. Finally promoted to colonel and given command of the 1st Dragoons, Kearny honed it into one of the most famous and elite regiments to carry United States colors. In 1845 he departed Fort Leavenworth with several companies of the 1st Dragoons and made one of the most arduous and important military "reconnaissances" in the West. Moving up the Platte and North Platte rivers to South Pass, he then struck south to Bent's Fort and finally returned via the Santa Fe Trail to Fort Leavenworth, covering some 2,200 miles in three months. Little did he know that the very next year he would follow part of this route commanding a new army.[6]

Kearny's distinguished service, leadership, and contributions truly merit his status as one of many unsung heroes in American history. Writer Bernard DeVoto appraised Colonel Kearny and his

---
[5] After Kearny left Santa Fe, he appointed Charles Bent of Bent's Fort fame as governor of New Mexico.
[6] See Clarke, *Stephen Watts Kearny: Soldier of the West*.

1st Dragoons as "the crack regiment of the army.... Kearny was not only a practiced frontier commander but one of the most skillful and dependable officers in the army." In simple analogy, DeVoto wrote that "In the vaudeville show of swollen egoism, vanity, treachery, incompetence, rhetoric, stupidity, and electioneering which the general officers during the Mexican War display to the pensive mind, Kearny stands out as a gentleman, a soldier, a commander, a diplomat, a statesman, and a master of his job."[7]

As the events transpired in spring of 1846, soldiers of the regular army who were not along the Mexican border paid special attention to the news of the war in Texas and the diplomatic wrangling in Oregon. Both places seemed a world away from the simple garrison life at Fort Leavenworth. Since 1827 the fort had improved measurably and its living conditions were among the best of the posts in the antebellum army. Not as isolated as other garrisons, new and growing businesses, shops, and hotels were all available at Independence, St. Joseph, and Kansas City, just a day away. Fort Leavenworth was a stop for riverboats, so life was not bland on this bend of the Missouri River.

Colonel Kearny probably knew that it was just a matter of time before he and his remaining six companies of the 1st Dragoons would be off to Texas, Oregon, or perhaps elsewhere to fulfill the strategic designs of the politicians who controlled the soldier's life.[8]

News of Taylor's fracas on the Rio Grande took two to three weeks to arrive in the States, and even longer to reach the Kansas post on the Missouri River. The telegraph was more of a curiosity than a tool in 1846—connecting only Washington and Baltimore—and had little practical use. Fate arrived on May 27, 1846, containing Kearny's expected orders. A letter from the War Department ordered him forward, to proceed along the Santa Fe Trail to protect the trade route full of American caravans and to invade New Mexico. He was directed to prepare his own regiment and

---

[7] DeVoto, *Year of Decision*, 234.
[8] Kearny had already lost four companies of ten to Taylor. Eventually these companies would accompany General Winfield Scott's invasion and campaign through central Mexico to the capital. See Eisenhower, *So Far from God*, 205 and 257.

THE ARMY OF THE WEST AND THE CAMPS OF ISRAEL 105

organize and equip a regiment of Missouri volunteers. Polk had requested that Governor John Edwards of Missouri form a mounted regiment (only eight companies) whose muster date bore the same date as Kearny's dispatch.[9]

Wasting no time, Kearny sent word to his two far-flung companies, K and G, to quickly report at Fort Leavenworth. When these two companies were added, Kearny's dragoons would number more than three hundred soldiers. Using riverboats down the Mississippi, Captain Philip St. George Cooke and K Company departed Fort Crawford, in present-day Wisconsin, and steamed down to meet Captain Edwin Vose Sumner commanding G Company at Fort Atkinson, in present-day Nebraska. They eventually arrived at Fort Leavenworth three days after their regiment had departed.[10] Cooke would play the most significant role of any regular army officer in the service of the Mormon Battalion.

As most Americans watched with curiosity the developments and news from Texas, many Missourians became so anxious that hundreds of men had already gathered at both Fort Leavenworth and Jefferson Barracks near St. Louis, hoping for a chance to fight if it came to war. Many of them enlisted in the regular army, filling the many vacancies in the regiments not already in Texas. Some were sent to Texas to fill the openings there. Now that Kearny had the authority to enlist and organize volunteers, he commenced immediately. During the first two weeks of June 1846, the shape of his campaign took form. He organized eight companies of more than eight hundred men into the 1st Regiment of Missouri Mounted Volunteers.

This regiment was a collection of some of the roughest, least disciplined, and most unlikely soldiers to ever serve in American history. Though unmilitary as these Missouri farmers, frontiersmen, teamsters, muleskinners, and misfits were, they were also adventurous, daring, wild, fearless, and tough. These were the kind of volunteers Kearny wanted. To command and lead these men would

---

[9] Kearny's Letter Book, 131–33, 286–88.
[10] Gardner, "The Command and Staff of the Mormon Battalion in the Mexican War," 337.

take a special leader, one tough as leather and hard as iron. Fortunately, with little pomp and ceremony these Missouri rascals were wise enough to elect one of their own to be their regimental commander. He was a man who had the ability, courage, and grit to control them but not break their wild spirit with undue military discipline and customs. Thus, Alexander Doniphan became commander and colonel of the 1st Missouri Mounted Volunteers.[11]

Of all the various commanders and personalities of the Mexican War era, none equaled Doniphan in natural, unschooled ability and frontier finesse. A man of varied talent, education, and accomplishments, he once stood eye-to-eye with Abraham Lincoln and proved to be the same height.[12] Standing at six feet, four inches and well over 250 pounds, red-haired and light-complected Doniphan was a soldier, lawyer, statesman, and farmer. When the Civil War came, he was caught in a dilemma of conscience and principle. He was a slave owner and supporter of the institution but, as a strong Unionist, he was against secession. Therefore, he would take no active military or political role for either side during the conflict.[13]

One of Doniphan's bravest deeds occurred in the fall of 1838, when he commanded a militia brigade from his hometown of Liberty, Clay County, Missouri. He refused to follow what he considered an illegal order from his superior: to take Joseph Smith, founder and first prophet of the Mormons, and several others to the Far West town square and execute them as enemies and traitors to the state. Joseph Smith had been turned over into the hands of the Missouri militia at Far West. It was not Doniphan's loyalty and friendship to Joseph Smith, a client of his law practice, that drove Doniphan to disobey the order; it was his love of justice and the law. In characteristic nineteenth-century prose, Doniphan retorted, "It is cold-blooded murder. I will not obey your order. My Brigade shall march for Liberty tomorrow morning, at 8 o'clock;

---

[11]Dawson, *Doniphan's Epic March*, 33.

[12]Ibid., 1. There is an oft-reported legend in many works that Lincoln and Doniphan stood back to back in the White House with Doniphan being a half-inch taller. See Niven, *The Mexican War*, 109.

[13]Dawson, *Doniphan's Epic March*, the last chapter. For the most recent biography of Doniphan see Launius, *Alexander William Doniphan: Portrait of a Missouri Moderate*.

and if you execute these men, I will hold you responsible before an earthly tribunal, so help me God."[14] This act of defiance by Doniphan was brave indeed; it would have been better if he remained behind and ensured that Joseph Smith and the others were not executed by illegal means. Nevertheless, Doniphan's bravery probably saved Joseph Smith from execution, but not incarceration. To this day Doniphan has been a hero and deliverer in Mormon history.

Along with Doniphan's regiment, Kearny was able to amass several hundred other supporting units of volunteers. Chief among them was a St. Louis artillery battery, which became an artillery battalion of 250 men under the command of Major Meriwether Lewis Clark. To add to the distinguished quality of frontier favorites in the Army of the West, Major Clark was the son of no less than William Clark, the great American explorer, and the namesake of Captain Meriwether Lewis, the other half of the greatest American exploration team.[15] Another battalion, one of makeshift qualities, was formed into two companies of infantry that demanded to march the entire way to Santa Fe. Rounding out this unusual army were 107 mounted cavalrymen, the LaClede Rangers, named after a ship landing in St. Louis. This company also included fifty Delaware and Shawnee Indian scouts. Not to ignore the opportunity for scientific advancement, Kearny also attached a small party of topographical engineers under First Lieutenant William Emory, one of the most distinguished army explorers and scientists of the era. Emory's appointment almost seemed an afterthought, as Kearny notified Emory of his decision just twenty-four hours before the march, giving Emory little time to gather his scientific instruments, other party members, and necessary equipment.[16]

By mid-June 1846 the Army of the West numbered approximately 1,600 to 1,700 soldiers. Why is it important to enumerate

---

[14] Smith, *History of the Church*, 3: 446; for a discussion of the Mormon conflict in Missouri, see Baugh, "A Call to Arms"; LeSueur, *The 1838 Mormon War in Missouri*, 182; and Launius, *Alexander William Doniphan*, 64–65.
[15] Eisenhower, *So Far from God*, 206n; DeVoto, *Year of Decision*, 267.
[16] Goetzmann, *Army Exploration in the American West, 1803–1863*, 130.

this small army? Secretary of War William Marcy had written to Kearny on June 3, 1846, authorizing the service of Mormon soldiers. As mentioned, there was an ambiguity in the orders that led Kearny to muster Mormon volunteers into service while they were still in the Midwest and not later in California as Polk had intended. Nevertheless, the important fact to remember is that Kearny was to have no more than one-third of his force comprised of Mormons. The actual size of the army was nebulous through most of June, and it was not until they were actually underway to Santa Fe that Kearny had consolidated his command. Also, the 2nd Missouri Mounted Volunteers and other units numbering nearly a thousand men would assemble later and proceed to Santa Fe. By late June, the Mormon contingent was considered part of the Army of the West. Following Polk's directive, Kearny limited the Mormon recruitment to a battalion-sized unit of some 400 to 500 soldiers, which was less than one-third of the Army of the West.

With all the haste, urgency, and efficiency Kearny could muster, June 16, 1846, was the red-letter day for the Army of the West.[17] The advance elements of the Army of the West began its arduous trek across the wide plains of Kansas along the Santa Fe Trail, seeming more of a typical caravan than the spearhead of a military expedition. A detachment of Doniphan's 1st Missouri was in the lead guarding one hundred wagons of provisions and over eight hundred head of cattle. Some of these provisions were allocated to the Mormon Battalion, but never reached them. Within a week, two companies of the 1st Dragoons and two more companies of Missouri volunteers ventured forth. By the end of June the majority of the Army of the West at Fort Leavenworth would be underway, while the Mormon Battalion was just drawing its first breath.[18]

※ ※ ※

The Mormon experience by 1846 included peaks of tremendous spiritual and religious manifestations, incredible growth, and glorious promises that, unfortunately, contrasted with valleys of some

---

[17]Bauer, *The Mexican War*, 130; Captain Benjamin Moore of the 1st Dragoons led two companies forward as the vanguard on June 5. [18]DeVoto, *Year of Decision*, 240.

THE ARMY OF THE WEST AND THE CAMPS OF ISRAEL 109

the most dreadful persecution and suffering ever experienced by an American religious group. The "victim" attitude that the Saints developed during this period resulted in their fear and distrust of local citizens and government officials. They saw the military in general as the agent that carried out the evil intentions of the citizens and officials. When United States Army representatives arrived in June 1846 at Council Bluffs, Iowa, to recruit the battalion, there was intense alarm that resulted in hysteria among many individuals. The news of the Mexican War was already known throughout many of the Mormon camps, and it was accepted with mixed emotions, ranging from patriotic fervor in support of the war to the war being a manifestation of God's judgment against the United States for the treatment of the Mormons. Because of the poor nature of communications of the day, rumors often arose, causing alarm and fear. One rumor that caught hold and endured is what I call the "prevention theory," the rumor that the government intended to prevent the Mormons from leaving the United States.

While in Iowa Territory some of the Saints believed the many rumors circulating about attempts to destroy the Saints, which now appear in journals and diaries. Stories circulated that volunteer regiments from Missouri, Illinois, or army regulars from Fort Leavenworth were forming to attack and destroy the defenseless Mormons. The United States soldiers' timely appearance excited these feelings even more. Some thought they were spies sent forth to gather intelligence concerning the strength and dispositions of the camps of Israel, or to orchestrate a plot to kidnap church leaders.[19] Two men, Jesse Martin and Henry Bigler, who would both later enlist in the battalion, met the soldiers in Iowa and, when asked, lied concerning Brigham Young's whereabouts.[20] Coincidentally, the same day the soldiers arrived at Mount Pisgah, some

---

[19] There is a letter from an army officer, William Prince, to a fellow officer, Richard B. Garnett, dated July 2, 1846, that explains that Prince dispatched another officer to observe the Mormons and their movements. This letter implies no other actions but just reports the general disposition of the Mormon camps. Prince was not instructed to do this by his superiors and there was no immediate consequence of his action. One could hardly construe this as a measure taken to prevent the Mormons from leaving the United States, or part of a conspiracy to destroy them. See Yurtinus, "A Ram in the Thicket," 42n 88.

[20] Henry W. Bigler, "Extracts from the Journal of Henry W. Bigler," June 30, 1846, 35.

of the members of the Quorum of the Twelve Apostles in camp on the Missouri River met to discuss a report that the governor of Missouri was dispatching an armed force to attack the Saints. They soon learned the report was false, but the fear and distrust the leading Mormons held against the United States is attested to by the fact that the rumors were considered important enough for those in authority to discuss them.

Scholarship has discovered some interesting points. The first mention, and perhaps the source concerning this theory, came from Illinois governor Thomas Ford in a letter to Sheriff Jacob B. Backenstos of Hancock County on December 29, 1845: "It is very likely that the Government at Washington will interfere to prevent the Mormons from going west of the Rocky Mountains. Many intelligent persons sincerely believe that they will join the British, if they go there [Oregon], and be more trouble than ever."[21] By spreading the rumor of military action, Ford perhaps hoped to hasten the Saints' departure. According to historian B. H. Roberts, "to prevent [by military means] the migration of the saints to the west, was wickedly put forth and fostered by Governor Ford (really to play upon the fears of the church and hasten its departure from Illinois)." Ford himself wrote in another letter, "But with a view to hasten their removal they were made to believe that the president [Polk] would order the regular army to Nauvoo as soon as the navigation opened in the spring [1846]."[22]

In President Polk's journal of January 13, 1846, he wrote that "as President of the US I possessed power to prevent or check their emigration," but he realized that he could not discriminate against the Mormons as a religious group any more than he could against any religious group. "By the constitution any citizen had a right to adopt his own religious faith," he wrote.[23] This was an important admission for a politician whose peers had seldom considered the religious freedom of the Mormons in the past.

Several letters written by non-Mormons expressed concern over

---

[21] Roberts, *A Comprehensive History of the Church of Jesus Christ of Latter-day Saints*, 2: 534.
[22] Ibid., 2: 532.
[23] Quaife, *Diary of James K. Polk during his Presidency, 1845 to 1848*, 1: 205–6.

THE ARMY OF THE WEST AND THE CAMPS OF ISRAEL

the Mormons settling on the frontier. One such letter spoke of many "Mormons hovering on our frontier, well armed ... depredating on our property."[24] The most prominent of these letters came from the pen of John C. Edwards, governor of Missouri, to Secretary of War Marcy. Edwards was not inciting any alarm concerning "well armed" Mormon pioneers "hovering on the frontier," but he challenged the logic of recruiting and arming five hundred Mormon men "as a most dangerous experiment on the part of General Kearney [*sic*]."[25] Edwards went on to explain that there was more hatred between the Mormons and the Missourians than either held against Mexicans. He thought it was insanity to mix these two antagonistic peoples into a military force. Governor Edwards ended his discussion on the Mormon question with this amazing—but for him, candid—statement, "They are a bad and deluded sect, and they have been harshly treated; but I suppose very correctly; yet they do not believe so, and under the treatment which they have received, if they are not enemies, both of our people and our government then they are better Christians and purer patriots than other denominations, a thing which no body in the west can believe."[26]

There is absolutely no truth, no evidence, and no historical record that the United States government, President Polk, or any other group, ever plotted or conspired to prevent the Mormons from leaving the United States or designed to destroy them. Much of the misinformation that forms the basis of this myth originated years after the Mexican War and the Mormon Battalion's service. Though there was alarm among some Missourians and other Americans in the Iowa vicinity, there is no evidence that there was a plot or plan to engage and destroy the Mormon people. Some Americans may have feared for their lives and property by the presence of the "vast throng" of Zion, but there was no attempt to prevent the Saints from leaving the United States or conduct a nineteenth-century version of genocide against them.

---

[24]L. Marshall to President of the United States, July 4, 1846, Putnam County, Missouri, National Archives; microfilm copy, Utah State Historical Society.
[25]John Edwards to William Marcy, August 11, 1846, Jefferson City, Missouri, National Archives; microfilm copy, Utah State Historical Society.
[26]Ibid.

The most important voice of the prevention theory was Brigham Young himself. Just one year and days after the battalion departed Council Bluffs, Brigham Young criticized President Polk and the United States for its tyranny against the Saints. In a sermon delivered in the valley of the Great Salt Lake on July 28, 1847, four days after his arrival, Young "damd Pres Polk, stated the numerous petitions to all the Governors & President—all refusing aid. that when the Saints were driven from Illinois, Polk's tyranny in drafting out five hundred men to form a Battalion, in order that the women & children might perish in the Prairies." Young said that "Missouri was ready 3[—] men to have swept the Saints out of existence."[27] Brigham Young "also established the myth that the Saints would be annihilated by the state militia of Missouri should they refuse the government's draft. Neither of these charges was grounded in fact." Aside from the incorrect term "draft," Brigham Young's echoing what Governor Ford wrote helped establish this myth found in so much Mormon literature.[28]

Years later, in February 1855, at the Social Hall in Salt Lake City, the battalion veterans held a reunion and a festival where President Young and his counselors spoke honoring the battalion's faithful service. During his speech Young extolled the men for their patriotism, valor, and service, and then said that the entire purpose for raising the Mormon Battalion was to test the loyalty of the Mormon people for the United States. Young was convinced that if the Saints had not raised the battalion, the United States and several state militia would have destroyed the church while on the plains:

> I was, and am fully persuaded that a senator [Thomas Hart Benton] from Missouri did actually apply for, and receive permission from President Polk, to call upon the militia of Iowa, Illinois and Missouri . . . to wipe this people out of existence, provided that those men [the Saints] who had been driven from their homes should refuse to comply with the unjust demand upon us for troops.[29]

Thus in one of the most interesting episodes of Mormon history, Brigham Young, the Mormon prophet and colonizer, after only

---

[27]Thomas Bullock, Journal, July 28, 1847, photocopy, LDS Archives.
[28]Yurtinus, "Ram in the Thicket," 332. [29]Tyler, *A Concise History*, 352.

THE ARMY OF THE WEST AND THE CAMPS OF ISRAEL   113

eight short years, specifically denied and castigated a program, a call to arms to form the battalion, that he gave sanction to, and which would have never occurred without his assistance and leadership.

President Young continued by not only condemning the Mormon Battalion's call but labeling it as evil:

> doubtless the spirits who surrounded the senator [Benton] alluded to, said that this people were hostile to the government; and the President gave him permission to call upon the governors of the States I have mentioned (if we did not fill the *tyrannical* requisition for five hundred of our men) and get troops enough to march against us, and massacre us all.[30]

Young was echoing the sentiments of his counselor, Jedediah M. Grant, who said, "You will all remember that I went to Washington, and I know from what I there *learned*, that the Hon. Thomas H. Benton advocated the necessity of raising troops and cutting off all the 'Mormons' from the face of the earth."[31] It would be interesting to discover how Jedediah M. Grant had *learned* about this conspiracy. Of course, there is neither record nor evidence to support any of these claims.

Historian John Yurtinus has categorized the prevention theory, along with other myths and legends, into a classification of "accepted interpretations to many nineteenth-century Latter-day Saints."[32] These myths and legends are "perpetuated history." Many other subsequent sermons and pronouncements concerning the battalion's recruitment, damning Senator Benton and President Polk over the next few years, occurred during a very precarious time for the Latter-day Saints. In 1855 when the Mormon Battalion reunion took place, Young was governor of Utah Territory and was under vicious attack by federal government officials because of the church's recent official announcement on plural marriage. His governorship was in question due to the combination of church and state under one person and the oligarchy of church leaders—something considered by many non-Mormons as most un-American. This was a period of severe civil and political unrest and conflict between federal and territorial authorities in Utah, which gave

---

[30]Ibid., italics added.   [31]Ibid., 348, italics added.
[32]Yurtinus, "A Ram in the Thicket," 658.

Young the opportunity to cast a few stones at the United States.[33] One of his favorite methods was to remind the Saints of their religious duties and evoke the memories of the persecution of the Mormons in Missouri and Illinois, thus further developing an attitude of victimization. The military recruitment of the battalion became just one of many in a litany of federal offenses.

The paradoxical nature of Young's about-face is most interesting. As we will see, if there is one man who was the symbol of the service and success of the Mormon Battalion, it was Brigham Young. He was the chief recruiter and father of the Mormon Battalion. He had a following of men who were already military-minded from the experiences that many had already witnessed and endured. For Brigham Young to denounce the program he helped establish seems rather hypocritical.

Yet for Young, with all worries of leading thousands of Saints through a frontier wilderness, the absence of some five hundred men was an enormous sacrifice. While crossing the plains of Iowa to assist in the recruitment, Young personally counted some eighteen hundred wagons among the displaced Mormons. Though this number may not be precisely accurate, it reflected the fact that if there was at least one able-bodied man per wagon, then five hundred men out of some eighteen hundred or more was indeed a tremendous cost to the Mormons.[34]

The weather in Iowa in June 1846 was hot and humid, described by some as oppressive and intolerable. The countryside had cast off its stern, cold winter. The rain came and the snow and ice melted into a wet and muddy spring, causing many problems and delays for the Mormon pioneers. With summer, the warm temperature brought abundant grass, flowers, and a landscape of immense beauty. Wildlife was plentiful and water was fresh and cool. The heat began in May and was miserable by June. Americans on the plains in the 1840s often complained of the terrible heat in their journals,

---

[33]Ibid., 650–51; see also Furniss, *The Mormon Conflict 1850–1859*.
[34]Brigham Young Manuscript History, July 7, 1846, LDS Archives.

but they were also accustomed to it—it was an irritant, but tolerable. The beauty of the Iowa plains and the ubiquitous rich farm lands around them caused some anxiety among the Saints. They feared they could never reside permanently in such a beautiful place. Their course with destiny them pushed them west and with faith they moved on.

Along the developing Mormon Trail lay Mount Pisgah, a settlement that had evolved into one of the staging areas between Nauvoo and the Missouri River. Hundreds of Mormons gathered there to raise crops, make repairs to wagons, and prepare for the next leg of the journey. One day in late June, in the camps around Mount Pisgah, an alarm went forth that caused an unusual excitement. A small party of soldiers with a wagon had arrived in camp.

One of the famous days in Mormon Battalion history was June 19, 1846, when Colonel Kearny penned an order to Captain James Allen, commander of I Company, 1st U.S. Dragoons, which began, "It is understood that there is a large body of Mormons who are desirous of emigrating to California, for the purpose of settling in that country, & I have therefore to direct, that you will proceed to their camps & endeavor to raise from amongst them 4 or 5 companies of volunteers to join me in my expedition to that country." From the void, the Mormon Battalion took form.[35]

The Mormon Battalion was one of only very few volunteer units in the Mexican War to have regular army officers assigned to command it, a rare instance in American military history. In Secretary Marcy's letter to Kearny authorizing the battalion, there was no mention of appointing a regular army officer, but he wrote that "you can allow them to designate, so long as it can be properly done, the persons to act as officers thereof."[36] In Polk's journal he mentioned the idea that the Mormons should serve under a "U.S. Officer." Therefore, Kearny did not have to appoint Allen as commander. It was very common in this era for regular officers to

---
[35] Kearny's Letter Book, 148–49; Tyler, *A Concise History of the Mormon Battalion*, 113.
[36] Kearny's Letter Book, 288.

Captain James Allen.
*State Historical Society
of Iowa—Des Moines.*

recruit men into volunteer service and transport them to mustering points, either depots or forts for induction, but not to serve in the unit. Volunteer officers, not regular officers, commanded most other volunteer units, battalions, and regiments. But there were exceptions. After its volunteer commander was killed in battle, a regular army officer, Captain Robert C. Buchanan, took command of the Washington and Baltimore Battalion of volunteers. Later, Captain George W. Hughes, a regular, commanded a regiment of Maryland volunteers.[37]

Captain Allen's status changed from regular to volunteer status when he assumed command of the battalion. Why would Kearny, Polk, and brevet Brigadier General Roger Jones, the adjutant gen-

---

[37]Tutorow, *The Mexican-American War*, 360; Heitman, *Historical Register and Dictionary of the United States Army from its Organization, September 29, 1789, to March 2, 1903*, 1: 258 and 1: 552. One could argue that Lieutenant John C. Frémont, in organizing his California Battalion volunteers, was a regular army officer who assumed command of a volunteer unit. I do not accept this idea, because Frémont never had authority from the War Department to organize this battalion. General Kearny never recognized his claim to this authority. In some sources the Washington and Baltimore units are designated as the 1st and 2nd D.C. and Baltimore Battalions; see Winders, *Mr. Polk's Army*, 148.

THE ARMY OF THE WEST AND THE CAMPS OF ISRAEL 117

eral, insist that the Mormon Battalion have a regular army officer in command? The obvious answer is that the trust and loyalty of the Mormons were in question; perhaps the military training and ability of Mormon volunteer officers were suspect, but that would be true of most volunteer officers and commanders. Even after Allen died, as will be shown, the War Department and General Kearny went to great lengths to ensure that a regular army officer commanded the battalion.[38]

With little understanding of the daunting task before him, Captain James Allen arrived at Mount Pisgah, June 26, 1846, to begin recruiting the Mormon Battalion. Allen wished to address the Mormon people and read a circular he had written and published for issue among the Mormons. It was an unusual sight to have a captain of dragoons—a regular army officer in full uniform—stand before a gathering of Mormon pioneers dressed in their worn clothes of poverty. These religious exiles stood and listened with tired and haggard faces. The camp was a collection of wagons, makeshift tents, and shelters. Some wondered why an army officer was there. What was he offering? From the beginning most Latter-day Saints were impressed with Allen's manners and sincerity. They would soon learn that Captain Allen was a man whom they could trust, and his influence, though brief, would have a great impact on the Mormons.

James Allen Jr. was a regular army officer who served for nearly twenty years on the frontier. Born in 1806 in Ohio, he later moved to Madison, Indiana, with his parents, James Allen Sr. and Jane Hethwood Allen. The family was Ulster, Scotch-Irish, first generation Americans and settled in the Ohio Valley by 1805. After living on a two hundred–acre farm in Kentucky, the Allens soon moved across the Ohio River to the new state of the same name. In

---

[38]In the Civil War there were many regular army officers who served in volunteer units or gained volunteer commissions and commands, but this was a consequence of the size of the army. In World Wars I and II, especially with National Guard, draftee, and federal reserve units—the modern-day equivalent of militia and volunteer service—the army would often assign regular army officers or former regulars in key leadership positions. This practice has often created discord or bitterness, especially where reserve component officers have served for years in peacetime only to be replaced in war by regulars. For a discussion of volunteer regimental commanders, especially political assessments during the Mexican War, see Dawson, *Doniphan's Epic March*, 32–35.

West Union, Adams County, the family rented a stone house on twenty acres. By the time he became a young man, James Jr. had moved back to Madison, Indiana, along the Ohio.[39]

James Sr. desired that young James seek a formal education.[40] Mr. Allen wrote letters to influential officials soliciting them to nominate his son for one of the best educations in America at the time. Congressman Jonathan Jennings, a member of the House of Representatives from Indiana, wrote Secretary of War John C. Calhoun on December 21, 1824, on young James Allen's behalf to seek his appointment to the United States Military Academy at West Point. "He is a young man of good character," Jennings wrote, "and ... we have no doubt he would be found worthy of such appointment."[41] James Allen received the coveted appointment and arrived at West Point in the early summer of 1825. Writing to Secretary Calhoun, Allen expressed gratitude for his appointment: "Sir: Your letter of 21st of Febry [1825] has been received, informing me that the president had on that day conditionally appointed me a cadet in the service of the united States."[42] Eighty-seven young men joined Allen the summer of 1825 on the hot and humid plain at West Point; forty-six would graduate four years later. Cadet Allen's academy career was undistinguished, graduating thirty-fifth in a class of forty-six that included some of the great future officers of the era. Among his peers were Robert E. Lee and Joseph E. Johnston, who would rise to be senior generals in the Confederate Army. In the classes just before and after his own, Allen rubbed shoulders with Jefferson Davis, Albert Sidney Johnston, Philip St. George Cooke, Leonidas Polk, and dozens of other classmates who would have profound influence during both the Mexican and Civil Wars.

Commissioned in the infantry, James Allen spent his first few years serving with the 5th Infantry at Fort Brady in Michigan. In 1832 Allen served on the famous Henry Schoolcraft expedition

---

[39]Wiggins, *The Rise of the Allens: Two Soldiers and the Master of Terrace Hill*, 12–13, 16–17.

[40]Appointment and Cadet Records of James Allen Jr., cadet number 575, class of 1829, United States Military Academy.

[41]Letter, Jonathan Jennings to John C. Calhoun, December 21, 1824, cadet records of James Allen Jr., cadet number 575, United States Military Academy.

[42]Wiggins, *The Rise of the Allens*, 18.

THE ARMY OF THE WEST AND THE CAMPS OF ISRAEL

exploring the northwest territory of Minnesota and looking for the source of the Mississippi River. Lieutenant Allen's detailed and descriptive map and report are now part of the Congressional Record and did much to further his career as an army explorer.[43]

When the U.S. Army formed the Regiment of Dragoons in 1833, Allen transferred to this new arm of the service and became a dragoon officer. He served with this regiment as it evolved into the 1st Dragoons under Kearny and became a first lieutenant in 1835. Two years later he received his promotion to captain, some eight years after his commissioning—a rapid advancement during the frontier army era. It was not unusual for an officer to serve eight to ten years as a lieutenant, another eight to ten as a captain, and hopefully receive promotion to major before becoming too old to serve. Allen lived and served at a dozen frontier posts in Illinois, Michigan, and what is now Kansas, Indian Territory (Arkansas), and Iowa Territory. Captain Allen was garrisoned at and one of the founding investors in the 1830s of what became Chicago, and for an even more enduring legacy, James Allen built Fort Des Moines on the Raccoon Forks and thus became the founder of what became the capital and chief city of Iowa: Des Moines.[44]

Little is known of Allen's personal life from primary sources. A recently published triple biography by David Wiggins entitled *The Rise of the Allens* sheds a little more light. The biography deals with James, his younger brother and fellow West Point graduate Robert, and also their nephew, Ben Franklin Allen.[45] Other than his official reports on expeditions, no journal or records are known to exist. Two letters he wrote are known, but no other biographical information has surfaced.[46]

---

[43] *A Map and Report of Lieut. Allen and H. B. Schoolcraft's visit to the Northwest Indians in 1832*, April 12, 1834; 23d Congress [Doc. No. 323], House of Representatives, 1st Session, transmitted from the War Department.   [44] Wiggins, *The Rise of the Allens*, 56, 100–2.
[45] Ibid.
[46] The two surviving letters written by Captain James Allen are addressed to "R" Allen of New Market, Highland County, Ohio, on January 15, 1842, and to his sister Mary Ann on October 31, 1842. They dealt with family business and his description of life on the frontier. It appears from these letters and other information that Allen never married or had a family of his own. Both letters are in the archives at the United States Military Academy. For a biographical essay on Allen, see Gardner, "The Command and Staff of the Mormon Battalion in the Mexican War," 331–51.

Though a fine officer, Captain Allen had a serious problem at one point in his career. Allen's superiors charged him with certifying inaccurate company rolls and musters, and he received a mild punishment in 1845.[47] Allen served with Kearny on many of the expeditions and campaigns of the 1st Dragoons, including an important 1839 expedition through much of present-day Iowa. There he commanded a detachment at Fort Des Moines for a brief time, and during the summer of 1844 Allen made a 740-mile march across the plains over parts of the future states of Iowa, Minnesota, and South Dakota.[48] Kearny had great respect for and trust in Allen and his ability, or he would have never entrusted him with recruiting and leading a battalion of volunteers, especially such a unique unit as the Mormon Battalion. Thus, he was now taking on the most unusual and important military responsibility of his career. His comrades in arms would be Mormon emigrants with no formal military training and experience.

After receiving permission from William Huntington, the camp leader at Mount Pisgah, Captain Allen addressed the Mormons and announced his mission. On hand was Elder Wilford Woodruff of the Quorum of the Twelve Apostles who was passing through at the time. Wisely, Woodruff dispatched an express rider to Brigham Young, who was already encamped on the Missouri River, to announce Allen's arrival and purpose. Young was already aware of Allen's mission prior to his arrival at Council Bluffs a few days later.

Allen's circular began stiffly: "I have come among you . . . to accept the service, for twelve months, of four or five companies of Mormon men who may be willing to serve their country for that period in our present war with Mexico; this force to unite with the Army of the West at Santa Fe, and be marched thence to California, where they will be discharged." He outlined some of the particulars: he requested men between the ages of eighteen and

---
[47]Roger Jones to Stephen W. Kearny, dated October 8 and 10, 1845, and December 16, 1845; Adjutant General's Office Correspondence 1800–1890, National Archives.
[48]Prucha, *The Sword of the Republic: U.S. Army on the Frontier, 1783–1846*, 375, 384–85.

THE ARMY OF THE WEST AND THE CAMPS OF ISRAEL 121

forty-five. He discussed the arms, rations, and pay, and emphasized what Allen hoped would be persuasive—namely, that this service would provide "an opportunity of sending a portion of their young and intelligent men to the ultimate destination of their whole people, and entirely at the expense of the United States."[49] He closed the circular by saying that he hoped to have the enlistment complete within six days of meeting with the main body of the Saints on July 5, 1846. As it turned out, Allen's battalion began its active service nearly two weeks past this stated goal.

Captain Allen's initial effect on the Mormons was overwhelmingly negative. Though the Mormons were hospitable and cordial, Allen met with no success. Not one recruit came forward. He soon moved west to meet Brigham Young and the leading Saints encamped at Council Bluffs.[50]

It is important to realize that without the approval and help of Brigham Young and the official sanction of the church, there would have been no Mormon Battalion. Allen realized that he had to meet with the leading men of the church to have any success in recruiting his volunteers. Perhaps the most succinct and poignant commentary on the Saints' willingness to enlist came from Daniel Tyler, who enlisted and served first as a corporal and then as sergeant in C Company: "Though Captain Allen represented the call as an act of benevolence on the part of the government, and assured the Saints that [t]here were hundreds of thousands of volunteers in the States ready to enlist, it is doubtful whether he would have got one of the Saints to join him if had been left to his own influence."[51] This statement is perhaps the most accurate commentary concerning recruiting the men who joined the Mormon Battalion. These Mormon men joined as a result of a call from their church, and not so much as a call of duty from their country.

---

[49]Recorded in Journal History June 26, 1846, LDS Archives; Tyler, *A Concise History*, 114; Roberts, *A Comprehensive History of the Church*, 3: 86–87; also see Mormon Battalion papers, reports and muster rolls, Record Group 94, National Archives.
[50]Yurtinus, "'Here is One Man Who Will Not Go, Dam'um': Recruiting the Mormon Battalion in Iowa Territory," 476.   [51]Tyler, *A Concise History*, 116.

Council Bluffs was already an important site on the American frontier, having received its name in 1804 from Meriwether Lewis and William Clark.[52] By June 28, 1846, Brigham Young had received word from Wilford Woodruff's messengers announcing the arrival of Captain Allen and his mission. Young took this intelligence in stride as he continued to consider and develop his plans for the single-most important task at hand: the preservation of the church by its movement west to the Rocky Mountains and beyond.

Of course, the original plan in the spring of 1846 was to move out quickly across the plains and establish the new "Zion" by winter. Yet, as the days and weeks went by, Young realized that the Saints were not progressing across Iowa as he had planned. The spring rains and mud, lack of food and wagons, and the general health of his people were such that reaching the mountains by winter or even establishing an advance post on the Platte River was becoming impossible. His plans changed drastically when he realized that they could never make the long trek to the Rocky Mountains in just one year. For some time he had considered sending an advance party of five hundred to one thousand men to the Great Basin to establish the first settlements, writing, "It is for the salvation of the Church that a Pioneer company start immediately."[53] The men of the advance party could establish a base settlement in the Great Basin and await the arrival of larger groups of the Saints. One more year would allow the time to make necessary preparations for such a large undertaking, moving over ten thousand impoverished Mormons across the wilderness of plains and mountains.[54]

Brigham Young needed a settlement to serve as a base camp in preparation for the next year's trek and the many years of immigration to follow. The Missouri River seemed the most likely place for such a settlement, since most of the Saints were already there or en route. Iowa in the summer of 1846 was still a territory, but would become the twenty-ninth state of the Union that December. It was

---

[52]Appleman, *Lewis and Clark's Transcontinental Expedition*, 90–92.
[53]Brigham Young to William Huntington, Camp of Israel, Missouri River, June 28, 1846; letter in William Huntington, Journal, Brigham Young University Library.
[54]Arrington, *Brigham Young: American Moses*, 128.

still very remote, uninhabited, and unsettled by white Americans. There were, however, several tribes on Indian lands in western Iowa, so the landscape was not unpopulated. He knew that the Missouri River afforded the best opportunities to establish temporary settlements, and he especially eyed the Indian territory across the Missouri River in modern-day Nebraska where few whites lived. They could not throw up settlements on Indian lands; Young would need government permission. Since leaving Mount Pisgah 130 miles to the east, the Mormons were crossing the river and living on Potawatomi Indian lands without official authority. It was crucial to receive government approval to reside on these lands for the next several years while the exodus continued. On June 30, the government authority that Brigham Young needed arrived at the Missouri, embodied in the form of a forty-year-old army captain, James Allen.[55]

---

[55] In the early 1830s the Mormons sent missionaries to the Indians in present-day Kansas, but the government's Indian authorities soon expelled them. Brigham Young knew he had to operate within government policy to remain on Indian lands.

Melissa Coray, eighteen-year-old wife
of William Coray, became one of these laundresses,
as did a dozen or so other women. She was one of four women
who would make the entire journey to California.
Courtesy of Norma Baldwin Ricketts.

CHAPTER SIX

Recruiting the Battalion

*It was against my feelings ... although
we were willing to obey counsel.*
—Henry W. Bigler

Brigham Young and the apostles on hand had already decided to accept the government's offer before they met Captain Allen. The leaders met and decided upon their course of action not in a sacred temple, a stately office, nor in a comfortable home, but in the most humble of surroundings—a tent with a dirt and sod floor. Orson Pratt's tent held the dubious honor of hosting a meeting where one of the most far-reaching and important decisions in Mormon history occurred.

There are many ways to look at the decision-making process Brigham Young employed. By complying with the offer, Young could transport several hundred able men to California and hence to the Great Basin at government expense. He could also request through Allen and the U.S. Army the authority to settle temporarily on Potawatomi lands in Iowa and across the Missouri River on Omaha lands. It is doubtful that Brigham Young knew on June 30, the day before he met Captain Allen, that in lieu of the men's uniform issue they could instead receive a clothing allowance of forty-two dollars.[1] This opportunity would provide more cash in the

---

[1] Both the journals of William Clayton and Willard Richards discuss that on July 13, 1846, Captain Allen explained the clothing allowance aspect to Brigham Young and his associates, though Allen was not aware of the exact allowances. The journals are in the LDS Archives.

enlistment contracts. He did realize that the church could possibly obtain some much-needed cash from the soldiers' salaries, which would help convey their families across the plains. But the offer also meant that five hundred men in their youth or prime of life would not be available to assist in the arduous task ahead. Many families would have to rely on others and the church for assistance. The aspects of loyalty and patriotism were also on Brigham Young's mind (though not so much on the mind of the ordinary Saint); he never intended for his followers to relinquish their rights as American citizens. Whatever his personal feelings and public pronouncements were, Brigham Young was a trueborn American. Heber C. Kimball, Willard Richards, and Orson Pratt agreed with Brigham. The decision is best expressed in these few words: "[it] was best to meet Captain Allen in the morning and raise the men."[2]

Captain Allen and his escort rode into the Council Bluffs camp at Mosquito Creek and formally met Brigham Young on July 1. They held a council and discussed the war, President Polk's offer, and recruiting the men. They held two or more meetings that day. Allen agreed that he would assist the Mormons in their most urgent need—the right to settle temporarily on Indian lands. At one point Brigham Young asked directly if Allen had the authority as an army officer to represent the president and decide policy. Allen returned "that he was the representative of President Polk and could act till he notified the President, who might ratify his engagements, or indemnify for damages."[3]

For several days rumors had buzzed through the various camps about the coming of the soldiers. Many were concerned and some frightened when the soldiers actually arrived. Others accepted the dragoons with guarded hospitality. Around noon on July 1, Allen stood on a wagon bed and addressed a large body of the Saints at Council Bluffs and explained the government's offer. He stated his purpose, read his circular, and distributed some copies. President Young followed and laid out the church's complete support to raise the volunteers. "I wished them [the Saints] to make a distinction

---
[2]Brigham Young Manuscript History, June 30, 1846, LDS Archives.
[3]Journal History, July 1, 1846, LDS Archives.

RECRUITING THE BATTALION

between this action by the general government and our former oppressions in Missouri and Illinois . . . ," he said. "Suppose we were admitted into the union as a state, and the government did not call on us, we would feel ourselves neglected. Let Mormons be the first to set their feet on the soil of California. . . . This is the first offer we have ever had from the government to benefit us."[4] In attendance at this gathering was Henry Bigler, who recorded that "President Young said, 'Captain Allen, you shall have your battalion if it has to be made up from our Elders,' and arose from his seat, walking out saying 'Come brethren, let us volunteer.'"[5]

The attitudes of the men who would enlist in the Mormon Battalion were disparate. Some readily accepted the call; others stated openly and defiantly that they would never serve, but then changed their minds and enlisted; some took the counsel of their leaders and enlisted on faith alone. From the beginning the project was encompassed by the calculating heart and soul of Brigham Young. Recruits began to come forth as he admonished them that "we want to conform to the requisition made upon us, and we will do nothing else till we have accomplished this thing." Recruiting the battalion became Young's highest priority, and he went after it with zeal. Until the battalion was filled and on its way, the great trek west was on hold. He declared, "If we want the privilege of going where we can worship God according to the dictates of our consciences, we must raise the Battalion."[6] Yet, the task was not an easy one, even for "Brother" Brigham.

Many still opposed and questioned the decision. A stern response came from one of the great Mormon pioneers, Hosea Stout. Upon learning about the military call for a battalion, he recorded, "We were all very indignant at this requisition and only looked upon it as a plot laid to bring trouble on us as a people."[7] He then commented on the prevention theory—that the enemies of the church would destroy them if they did not comply with federal

---

[4]Brigham Young Manuscript History, July 1, 1846, LDS Archives.
[5]Bigler, "Extracts from the Journal of Henry W. Bigler," 36. Young was called "President" because of his leading role in the presiding body of the LDS Church.
[6]Tyler, *A Concise History of the Mormon Battalion*, 117.
[7]Brooks, ed., *On the Mormon Frontier*, 1: 164–65.

demands. Again, though there was no proof for such an indictment, many among the Mormons believed it.[8] In the same vein, Abraham Day simply but forcibly said, "Here is one man who will not go, dam'um." Ironically, the next day after making this bold assertion, he volunteered to serve.[9]

Another man who held very strong feelings about the government's proposal was John Steele. Years later, Steele wrote, "Got to the Grand River, west of Pisgah, camped there until Colonel [Captain] Allen came along with his aide authorized to raise a Battalion of Mormons of 500 men. You can better imagine my feelings than I can describe them ... they [the United States] may all go to hell together." Yet once Steele arrived at the Missouri, he, like many others, had an amazing change of heart, due to one reason: the church leaders' influence.

> President Brigham Young, [Willard] Richards, [Heber C.] Kimball, [Ezra T.] Benson and others came to us on the Missouri.... They said it [the persecution] would all be overruled for the best, and the only thing left for us was to furnish 500 men and march against the Mexicans.... At last arrived at the Bluffs, as it was called Council Bluffs and agreed to enlist and enrolled myself in Company D under Captain Nelson Higgins.[10]

The day after the camp meeting at Council Bluffs, Elder John Taylor, one of the apostles, wrote a long entry in his journal that summarized his and many of the Mormons' sentiment. Taylor was in the jail at Carthage, Illinois, when Joseph and Hyrum Smith were murdered, and he himself received wounds by the assassins' hands. Taylor, an English emigrant, wrote,

> I have myself felt swearing mad at the government for the treatment we have received at the hands of those in authority.... If we come under Britain we have to be subjected to their provisions, if under the federal we have to be subject to them. The US are at war with Mexico and the US have a perfect right to march into California according to the laws of nations.... We would have a great story to tell that we fought for the liberties of the country and our children can say our fathers fought and bled for the country.[11]

---

[8] Ibid.
[9] Yurtinus, "'Here is One Man Who Will Not Go, Dam'um,'" 477.
[10] Steele, "Extracts from the Journal of John Steele," 6–7.
[11] John Taylor, Journal, July 2, 1846, LDS Archives.

RECRUITING THE BATTALION

Taylor, ironically, first expressed his anger at the United States, and then soon announced the loyalty that he actually felt. He then turned to the pride he had at the opportunity for the Saints to fight for their country. This is a very curious psychological twist for an intelligent man. Many of the men who served with the battalion went through this same process.

On July 3 Brigham Young, Captain Allen, and several of the leading Saints traveled east to Mount Pisgah to encourage others to volunteer. Along the way Young and Kimball preached, pleaded and exhorted men to enlist. Daniel Rawson's initial reaction to the call demonstrated perhaps better than any other example of the true nature of the church's influence. Rawson wrote:

> I felt indignant toward the Government that had suffered me to be raided and driven from my home. I made the uncouth remark that "I would see them all damned and in Hell." I would not enlist. On the way to the Bluffs we met President Brigham Young, Heber C. Kimball and W. Richards returning, calling for recruits. They said the salvation of Israel depended upon the raising of the army. When I heard this my mind changed. I felt that it was my duty to go.[12]

Jesse C. Little, with Colonel Thomas Kane, arrived in St. Louis from Washington, D.C., on June 21. From there Kane moved on to Fort Leavenworth while Little traveled up the Mississippi River to Nauvoo. He had no idea that an army officer was among the Saints recruiting the battalion.

Moving west, Jesse Little met Brigham Young's east-bound party west of Mount Pisgah on July 6. There is an interesting historical incongruity concerning this meeting. Little had left Washington with the full understanding that the Mormon volunteers would not be enlisted into the army until they arrived in California by their own means. He then met his prophet-uncle on the trail accompanied by a dragoon captain already at work recruiting the battalion. Did he ask about recruiting the men in California? Had

---

[12]Cited in Ricketts, *The Mormon Battalion*, 13.

Polk changed his mind? If Jesse Little questioned the new course of action or said anything at all, it is lost to history.[13]

Young and his recruiters, including Captain Allen, addressed the Saints at Mt. Pisgah. Sixty-six men came forward and enlisted after Brigham gave a stirring speech. One of the volunteers from Mount Pisgah was Robert Pixton, who wrote later in life, "The call was for 500 volunteers to go to Mexico or California and serve in the Mexican War. I was one to go. . . . If it had not been for the cause of God we never could have left our families on the wild prairie in an Indian country." Commenting on the church's promise to care for the families of the absent men, Pixton wrote, "We had a promise that they should be taken care of, but I am sorry to say many did not receive the attention they should have done."[14]

Dozens of others had already joined and were on the trail to Council Bluffs, where the mustering would take place. While at Mount Pisgah, Young wrote epistles to leaders at Garden Grove, another Mormon settlement east of Pisgah, and Nauvoo concerning the volunteer service and requested assistance in the endeavor. "There is war between Mexico and the United States," he wrote, "to whom California must fall a prey, and if we are the first settlers, the old citizens cannot have a Hancock (county) [Illinois] or Missouri pretext to mob the Saints. The thing [the Battalion] is from above, for our good."[15]

One young man, Zadock Judd, recorded a condition that the Mormon soldiers had to face that few soldiers who served in the Mexican War experienced:

> This was quite a hard pill to swallow—to leave wives and children on the wild prairie, destitute and almost helpless, having nothing to rely on only the kindness of neighbors, and go to fight the battles of a government that had allowed some of its citizens to drive us from our homes, but the word comes from the right source and seemed to bring the spirit of conviction of

---

[13] The Journal History, July 6, 1846, LDS Archives, only mentions that Brigham Young and Jesse Little met eleven miles east of Mount Pisgah, and that Little confirmed the government's offer in the vaguest of terms. Nothing else is recorded.
[14] Robert Pixton, "The Life of Robert Pixton," LDS Archives.
[15] Brigham Young to Samuel Bent, Mt. Pisgah, July 7, 1846, Journal History, LDS Archives.

its truth with it and there was quite a number of our company volunteered, myself and brother among them.[16]

The Mormon soldiers felt the pain and anxiety of leaving their families and loved ones on a difficult and dangerous trek west as victims of religious persecution. One of the great comforts a soldier has when he marches off to war is knowing that his family and loved ones are safe at home and hearth. This important assurance was missing with the men who served in the Mormon Battalion. They were asked to serve while their families were on a perilous trek across the American wilderness with no real idea as to where their final destination might be, and to fight for a nation that had neglected them or had done little to assist them. John H. Tippets wrote, "I started with heavy heart looking back on the condition of my family ... my feelings was wrought up to consider the uncomfortable situation of my family & the anxiety of my mind inexpressive."[17] Daniel Tyler wrote that "joining the army and leaving their families in such a condition was repugnant to their feelings," declaring that the Mormons were "loyal citizens, but they never expected such a sacrifice would be required of them to prove their loyalty to the government."[18] The tremendous allegiance that these men and their families displayed for their religion and their leaders, especially Brigham Young, is a great memorial to their religious faith. Few have been asked to sacrifice so much at the altar of devotion and duty. One thinks of Washington's destitute few in the frozen windswept reaches of Valley Forge.

As the Mormon Battalion took shape among the camps of Israel, the real war with Mexico had slowed to a crawl. General Zachary Taylor boiled under the Texas sun for three months after his glorious double victories. He now had over twelve thousand men under his command; more than

---

[16]Zadock Judd, "Autobiography of Zadock Knapp Judd (1827–1907)," Brigham Young University Library.
[17]John Henry Tippets, Journal, 6 and 9, Utah State University Library.
[18]Tyler, *A Concise History*, 116.

half were undisciplined and untrained volunteers with supplies and arms adequate for half that number. He finally determined to prosecute the war more aggressively and, on July 6, began moving men and supplies up the Rio Grande on a flotilla of riverboats. Taylor planned to move six thousand of the better trained and equipped regulars and volunteers upriver some 250 miles to Camargo, a small village where he would establish a base of operations for his invasion of northern Mexico. The remaining forces would follow once they were ready. The American invasion into Mexican territory had begun in earnest.[19]

Half a continent away, developments in California were accelerating at a quick pace. A few dozen expatriate American settlers and newcomers claimed control of the province of Upper California—or at least they thought they had. Using a flag with the image of a grizzly bear on all fours (some thought it looked more like a pig or a hog), this mostly undisciplined rabble of settlers, mountain men, and opportunists were able to oppose small and half-hearted attempts by Mexican officials to defeat them. For several weeks the "Republic of California" tried to establish a legitimate government, copying much of the American founding fathers' efforts. On July 4, with American symbolism at its best, the "Bear-Flaggers," now under the leadership of none other than brevet Captain John C. Frémont, Corps of Topographical Engineers, shifted their purpose and legitimatized their short-lived revolution by espousing United States authority at Sonoma, which they really did not have. They waited and hoped for intervention and reinforcements from the United States.

They did not have to wait long, for on July 7, 1846, Commodore John Sloat and his five-ship Pacific Squadron landed a party of U.S. Marines and sailors at Monterey and took control of one of the most important ports in California. Two days later, the Republic of California quietly melted like the morning fog when Sloat's forces and the Bear-Flaggers joined in the American military occupation of California. Military supremacy in California would totter back and forth for months between the American and Californio forces, until just before the Mormon Battalion arrived.[20]

---

[19] Eisenhower, *So Far from God*, 107–9.
[20] Neal Harlow, *California Conquered: The Annexation of a Mexican Province, 1846–1850*, 97–114. Seldom are the Californians referred to as Mexican, though that was their nationality.

One by one, group by group, Mormon men came forth to enlist. Captain Allen soon had his battalion. The party returned to Council Bluffs accompanied by dozens of new recruits. Many of the leading brethren were very active in promoting this new program. Another large assembly was held on July 13 to convince more Mormon men to enlist. According to Colonel Kearny's orders, Captain Allen was authorized to appoint an adjutant, a sergeant major, and a quartermaster sergeant. Also, Allen would then hold the rank commensurate with the responsibilities of a battalion commander of over four companies: "you will upon mustering into service the 4th company, be considered as having the rank, Pay & Emoluments of a Lt. Col of Infantry."[21] The phrase "be considered as having" is unique and seems a bit ambiguous, but the intent was very clear. Once Allen filled four full companies of infantry he became a lieutenant colonel effective that day—July 16, 1846. Allen would be a lieutenant colonel of volunteers and his actual status in the regular army changed. Though he retained his permanent rank in the regulars, there was no guarantee that he would retain his position in his old regiment after his volunteer service.

By July 16, enough volunteers had come forth to form four companies and part of a fifth. Allen organized the recruits into companies A through E and officially mustered them into United States service. With his commission to follow later, Lieutenant Colonel Allen read the oath of office and service to the men, and they swore that oath to an officer who held both regular and volunteer commissions in the United States Army. This ceremony was a very informal and simple affair. The men merely assembled in a square by companies as Allen officiated. They stood on the prairie grass, in the hot Iowa sun, dressed in their civilian clothing of home-spun or broad-cloth wear: broad-brimmed hats, calico and linen shirts and worn-for-wear trousers, and shoes and boots. The only thing military was Allen and his uniformed dragoons. As in many events

---

[21]Kearny's Letter Book, 149.

in history, though simple and insignificant at the moment, the passage of time would dictate otherwise.

Henry Bigler recorded as he enlisted,

> It was against my feelings, and against the feelings of my brethren although we were willing to obey counsel.... Still it looked hard when we called to mind the mobbings and drivings, the killing of our leaders, the burning of our homes and forcing us to leave the States.... To me it was an insult, but there was one consolation and that was [what] Brother Willard Richards... said, "If we were faithful in keeping the Commandments of God, that not a man shall fall by an enemy, no not as much blood shed as there was at Carthage jail."[22]

Another soldier came forth to enlist, but his decision and experience were very different than most. Sixteen-year-old William Hendricks had wanted for days to enlist, but his mother, Drusilla Hendricks, did not want to lose a son after nearly losing her husband, who was paralyzed by a bullet at the Haun's Mill massacre in 1838. While attending to breakfast the morning of the muster day, Drusilla heard an inward voice that touched her soul, saying her son William should enlist. Attempting to disregard the prompting, Drusilla sat down to breakfast with her family when a messenger announced that the battalion was still short of volunteers. Drusilla recorded, "William raised his eyes and looked me in the face. I knew then that he would go."[23]

The mustering of this volunteer battalion and Allen's official use of the designation "Mormon Battalion" in official orders and correspondence was unique in American military service. There has never been another military unit in American history that has had such a distinctive religious quality or had a religious name in its official designation. The soldiers who served were nearly all members in good standing from one church or denomination. The battalion came to be only because the presiding body of the church decided to support the enlistments and the men's service in war. Also, as time

---

[22]Bigler, "Extracts from the Journal of Henry W. Bigler," 36.
[23]Cited in Madsen, *Journey to Zion: Voices from the Mormon Trail*, 35–36.

RECRUITING THE BATTALION 135

will show, a large portion of the salaries and allowances the men earned became assets that the church would use for church purposes. The enlistment became a defined program of the LDS Church to assist in westward movement of the Saints. No other military unit in American history has had these unique features.

Some United States units have had a religious affiliation. For example, during the Civil War the famous "Irish Brigade" consisting of several New York, Pennsylvania, and Massachusetts volunteer regiments had a predominantly Catholic enrollment. The Irish Brigade originated with the 69th New York Volunteer Infantry, which had been a mostly Irish militia unit before the war, and the intention was to train Irish-Americans in military tactics to fight later for an independent Catholic Ireland. The Irish Brigade was not a religious unit though, nor did it have a religious designation. The title "Irish Brigade" was merely a nickname for what was actually the 2nd Brigade, then later the 3rd Brigade, 1st Division, II Corps, Army of the Potomac. The Catholic men of the Irish Brigade served for Union war aims, not for a program of the Catholic Church, whereas the Mormon men served to promote a defined program of their church and saw their service as a calling from God.[24]

In the modern era where the separation of government and religious association is an extremely sensitive issue, the Mormon Battalion's uniqueness is even more pronounced. Today, this association could never occur. Short of a general collapse of the federal government, it is impossible to foresee a situation where a religious unit would serve in the United States military again.

Allen and his men were very busy making arrangements for the pending departure. He soon issued General Orders Nos. 1, 2, and 3, "Head Quarters, Mormon Battalion, Council Bluffs, Iowa." These orders established that, first, Allen had assumed command; second, the appointments of the battalion staff were made as author-

---

[24]Faust, ed., *Historical Times Illustrated Encyclopedia of the Civil War*, 384.

ized by Kearny's orders; third, that Dr. William L. McIntire be appointed an assistant surgeon. The battalion staff as authorized by Kearny's orders of June 19 consisted of "an Adjutant, Sergeant Major & Qr Mr [quartermaster] Sergeant for the Battalion."[25] Allen selected First Lieutenant George P. Dykes as adjutant, Private James H. Glines as sergeant major, and Private Sebert C. Shelton as quartermaster-sergeant.[26]

Also included in the recruiting process were female laundresses, which army regulations authorized. Kearny's orders specifically addressed this subject: "Each Company will be allowed 4 women as laundresses, who will travel with the Comps, receiving rations & other allowances given to the laundresses of our Army!"[27] Many of the Mormon men saw a splendid opportunity to have their wives accompany them to California with government rations and allowances. However, transportation was a private matter for the laundresses, as was the compensation from the men for laundry services. Melissa Coray, eighteen-year-old wife of William Coray, became one of these laundresses, as did a dozen or so other women. She was one of four women who would make the entire journey to California. The Mormon Battalion experience would be one of the most defining events in her life, as it was for the men who served.[28]

Because of the unique nature of the Mormon Battalion as a religious/military unit, Allen allowed several concessions that were not consistent with traditional or accepted military practice. Along with the laundresses, he permitted several families to join the march; excluding the laundresses in their official capacity, a dozen or so other women and many children came along. Many of the officers brought their wives; Jefferson Hunt brought two polygamist wives, Celia and Matilda, and their various children. Even an elderly couple joined to assist Hunt's families, serving as a teamster and a camp helper. Some of the enlisted men's wives also accompanied their husbands. Along with these large and cumbersome families, there

---

[25] Kearny's Letter Book, 148–49.
[26] Tyler, *A Concise History*, 127–28.
[27] Kearny's Letter Book, 149.
[28] There are several books or articles that deal specifically with the women of the Mormon Battalion. See Larson and Maynes, *Women of the Mormon Battalion*; see also Ricketts, *Melissa's Journey with the Mormon Battalion: The Western Odyssey of Melissa Burton Coray, 1846–1848*.

RECRUITING THE BATTALION

were also several young teenage boys who came along as "servants or aides" to the officer-fathers, a very dubious distinction.[29]

Regrettably, the inclusion of so many women and children to accompany the battalion would prove to be a mistake by Lieutenant Colonel Allen. This decision soon haunted his successors and caused tremendous problems in morale, discipline, and unit cohesion. Eventually, most of the women and families left the battalion en route and traveled to Pueblo, Colorado, for the winter. A military campaign is no place for non-combatant women and children, especially a unit ordered to make a strenuous march under difficult conditions across more than a thousand miles of enemy territory.

Since the dawn of time, military campaigns have had camp followers, sometimes wives and families, children, concubines, mistresses, and such. They were about camp mostly in the "off-season" when campaigning and operations ceased during the winter months. There are examples of women and wives who served in many far-flung and dangerous campaigns, but that does not make it prudent. At times Alexander the Great had camp-followers of teamsters, herders, camp-helpers, wives and children of the men, entertainers, concubines, prostitutes, and so on, which often nearly outnumbered his fighting force. This severely affected his logistical base with the intrinsic inefficiencies of his era. Military leaders in history followed several courses with regard to camp followers when campaigning became intense or dangerous. They sent the people off, left them to their own fate, or had them slaughtered.

The practice of camp-followers was common in ancient history, particularly in the Middle East, but less common in European campaigns, especially through the modern age. But having large contingents of dependents and other people during an active campaign in America is rare.[30]

---

[29]For lists of the women and children who accompanied the battalion, see Tyler, *A Concise History*, 125–26; and Ricketts, *The Mormon Battalion*, 31–33.

[30]In searching American military history, there are few and rare instances that such non-combatants accompanied long and dangerous expeditions. Aside from the occasional wife or laundress, the practice is not common. During General Arthur St. Clair's disaster in 1791 against the old Northwest Indian tribes, there were a number of dependents that accompanied the army, some of whom actually died in combat. See Hassler, *With Shield and Sword*, 53–54.

Allen's decision, though championed by many of the men, was nevertheless unwise from a strictly military perspective. An experienced frontier line officer such as Allen was doubly wrong in consenting to such a proposition. The authorized laundress is one aspect of army tolerance, but wives, children, and elderly teamsters were beyond acceptable prudence. It is puzzling and absurd that Allen allowed so many dependents to go along.

A second regrettable effect of this decision was that the men who enlisted saw this venture more as a pioneering experience than as a military campaign. "From their frame of reference," historian John Yurtinus explained, "the Mormon Battalion was a 'Military Colony' en route to California at the expense of the American government."[31] Thus, through the years, and even into the present, many see the Mormon Battalion more as pioneers than as soldiers.

Efforts continued to recruit the final and fifth company of the battalion. Time was growing short and the church leaders doubled their efforts. At one point, when some of the Saints declined, President Young said, "Hundreds would eternally regret that they did not go, when they had the chance."[32] Unlike most volunteer units, the men did not directly appoint or elect their officers. This important responsibility was left to Brigham Young and the other apostles. Once the individuals were selected, the enlistees merely sustained the process. The officers chosen to be captains of the companies were Jefferson Hunt, A Company; Jesse Hunter, B Company; James Brown, C Company; Nelson Higgins, D Company; and Daniel Davis, E Company.

After receiving the oath of enlistment on July 16, the battalion formed by companies and marched eight miles south along the Missouri River to Sarpy's small trading post. Since 1824, Peter A. Sarpy had operated two trading posts, one of which consisted of some twenty or so log cabins with whitewashed walls called Bellevue on the Nebraska side of the Missouri River.[33] His second post, on the Iowa side, was a much smaller venture. There, the men received a few government-issued items such as blankets, utensils,

---

[31]Yurtinus, "A Ram in the Thicket," 196.   [32]Journal History, July 17, 1846, LDS Archives.
[33]Kimball, *Historic Sites and Markers along the Mormon and Other Great Western Trails*, 72.

plates, and provisions. They also purchased other items, which the paymaster would deduct from their pay.[34]

During the time that Young and Colonel Allen were working together to recruit the battalion, Young exacted from Allen several promises and conditions in return for his ecclesiastical assistance. Some of these promises later would have great impact upon the men's morale and combat efficiency. First, in the event that Allen died, or became unfit for duty, the senior ranking captain, a Mormon, would assume command.[35] Next, the battalion should not be divided, but serve as a whole.[36] Lastly, the wives and families accompanying the battalion were to remain with them and travel at government expense to California.[37] Allen's successors would eventually break all of these promises for justifiable military reasons.

It is difficult to imagine that a military unit mustered for service would be combat effective and able to operate under such conditions. Volunteer units by nature were at times very difficult to command, discipline, and develop into a cohesive fighting force. But with sufficient leadership and training, a volunteer unit could perform as well as the regulars. The Mormon Battalion made this challenge even more difficult by the unique and unusual conditions that Colonel Allen had to accept. This difficult quality of the Mormon Battalion arose from the obvious great influence and control that Young as a religious, rather than military, leader maintained over the men throughout their service. His influence was evident even after the battalion had reached California, half a continent away.

Brigham Young held a special council on July 18 with the newly appointed officers and NCOs in a grove of cottonwood and poplar trees near the Missouri River. There he instructed the men on several points. First and foremost, the officers and leaders were to be "fathers" to the men in their companies and conduct themselves by the power and authority of their ordained positions in the priesthood. Young challenged them to live according to Christian virtues of civility and gentleness and prohibit swearing, card playing, and gambling. He also cautioned the men to "have no conversation

---

[34]Guy M. Keysor, Journal, July 17, 1846, Utah State Historical Society.
[35]Tyler, *A Concise History*, 156.   [36]Ibid., 163.   [37]Ibid., 157.

with the Missourians, Mexicans or any other class of people, do not even preach unless the people desire it."[38] This was a very curious statement by President Young: to avoid contact with Missourians, which would exclude most of the Army of the West. But considering the miserable treatment the Saints received in Missouri less than a decade earlier, it again proves the bitter animosity that the Mormons still harbored and would harbor for years to come. Perhaps Brigham merely wanted them to avoid any confrontations that might arise, which was wise counsel.

Some of the other leaders counseled against the use of common medicines, but "if they [the men] were sick, they had the privilege of calling Elders and rebuking all manner of disease."[39] At various times over the next few weeks, Brigham Young's counsel challenged the men to refrain from using then-modern medical practices, rather to rely on divine intervention, administrations by the power of the lay priesthood that most of the men held, and proven home remedies of natural herbs and concoctions. This particular directive concerning medicine and treatment caused some great conflicts within the battalion.

Young directed that the men send a portion of their salaries back by church agents to the main body to assist with the general exodus. The issue of wages and cash became an important concern for Young, and he took great measures to ensure that the soldiers should donate as much as they could for church purposes.[40] Sergeant William Hyde recorded that the church authorities "met in private council with the commissioned and noncommissioned officers . . . and there gave us their last charge and blessing, with a firm promise that on condition of faithfulness on our part, our lives should be spared and our expedition result in great good and our names be handed down in honorable remembrance to all generations."[41]

This meeting and the counsel given to the new military leaders of the Mormon Battalion set the stage for many of the troubles later experienced in the battalion. It was also wise and benevolent

---

[38]Willard Richards, Journal, July 18, 1846, LDS Archives.
[39]Journal History, July 18, 1846, LDS Archives.
[40]Willard Richards, Journal, July 18, 1846, LDS Archives.
[41]William Hyde, Private Journal, July 18, 1846, Brigham Young University Library.

guidance from a man of God speaking to his flock. Brigham Young's words and religious points established in his followers' minds that ecclesiastical authority was more important than military discipline and authority, though he may not have realized it. His comments to these new, unschooled, and untrained military leaders caused duplicity in authority and loyalty. The pronouncement or prophecy by Brigham Young, that the men would not encounter combat if they obeyed counsel and performed their religious duties, was one of the unique qualities of the Mormon Battalion. The men understood this prophecy and lived to see it fulfilled. Though intended for good, and probably inspired and sincere counsel, from a military perspective this promise convinced the men that they would not see combat. The importance of training, drilling, strict discipline, and martial order became secondary or subservient to other priorities, such as getting to California and obeying the church leaders in the battalion. It also undermined legal and proper military authority. From a strictly military point of view, it is chaotic and unwise to confuse soldiers' loyalties with ideas that may conflict with the potential realities of military service. One has to remember that the Mormon Battalion was a religious/military unit. It would necessarily involve unique qualities such as the guidance that Brigham Young gave. The real question is whether it is good military practice to organize a unit for war that has a dual nature, with separate and conflicting loyalties and lines of authority. The history of the Mormon Battalion is a well-documented record of constant conflict with authority.[42]

In the evening after President Young's special meeting, the Saints held a farewell dance under the most primitive but festive conditions. William Pitt's brass band played several numbers, and the men, their wives, and others had a pleasant time together. It was the last public gathering that many of the battalion members would enjoy with their friends for nearly two years. On hand was Colonel Thomas Kane, recently arrived from Fort Leavenworth. He took

---

[42]See Campbell, "Authority Conflicts in the Mormon Battalion," 127–42; Black, "The Mormon Battalion: Conflict Between Religious and Military Authority," 313–28; and Christiansen, "The Struggle for Power in the Mormon Battalion," 51–69.

keen interest in the Saints and was soon accepted as a trusted friend. His poignant observations as a young bachelor recorded that "a well cultivated messo-soprano voice, belonging to a young lady with fair face and dark eyes, gave . . . a little song. . . 'By the rivers of Babylon we sat down and wept, We wept when we remembered Zion.'"[43]

By July 20, 1846, most of the fifth company had been recruited and all necessary preparations were complete. Lieutenant Colonel Allen formed his command of over five hundred Mormon men and the Mormon Battalion began an epic march that would end at the shores of the Pacific Ocean in California. They departed singing "The Girl I Left Behind Me." Some would die before seeing the vast ocean; many others would be forced to turn back during the journey. With the rising morning sun and the climbing heat of the day, these Mormon soldiers marched off to war—one in which they would not fight.

The monumental moment did not escape the shrewd eye of Brigham Young. A year and a half later he mused, "It must ever remain a truth on the page of history that while the flower of Israel's camp were sustaining the wings of the American eagle, by their influence and arms in a foreign country, their brothers, sisters, fathers, mothers, and children, were driven by mob violence from a free and independent state of the same national Republic."[44] This comment summarizes very well the attitudes of Young and most of the Saints regarding the sacrifice they provided and the irony of the situation.

Years later, Margaret Phelps, the wife of Private Alva Phelps of E Company, wrote,

> I was very ill at the time, my children all small, my babe also extremely sick; but the call [to enlist] was pressing; there was no time for any provision to be made for wife or children; no time for tears; regret was unavailing. He started in the morning. I watched him from my wagon-bed till his loved form was lost in the distance; it was my last sight of him.[45]

Private Alva Phelps died less than two months later.

---

[43] Tyler, *A Concise History*, 81.
[44] Recorded in the *Millennial Star*, 10 (March 15, 1848): 82; cited in Madsen, *Journey to Zion: Voices from the Mormon Trail*, 35.   [45] Tyler, *A Concise History*, 129–30.

CHAPTER SEVEN

The March Begins

*I have forsaken ... My possessions My family
and at the risk of life started for Mexico.*
—Private George Washington Taggart

The farmers along the rout thought we were a rough sett," wrote Private Abner Blackburn. "Chickens, ducks, pigs, and all kind of vegetables suffered without price. Some of those fellows would steal anny thing. One set of thieves carried [away] several bee hives while the oners were at dinner. One soldier drove off a cow and milked her to the fort and then sold her for whiskey."[1] This passage seems more appropriate for Missouri guerrillas during the Civil War who ravaged the countryside with vicious bushwhacking and wholesale plundering than soldiers of the Mormon Battalion. Private Henry Sanderson of D Company approached a farmer in his garden and helped himself to an armfull of produce with a glaring farmer looking on.[2]

The 150-mile march along the Missouri River from Council Bluffs to Fort Leavenworth was an uneventful beginning to the Mormon Battalion's long march across the Southwest. The fourth day out, less than forty miles along the trail, Private Samuel Boley died. His comrades buried him in a blanket and rough-hewn coffin. Boley would be the first of some two dozen deaths, all of them from natural causes.[3]

At this point in the battalion's service, the unit could hardly be

---

[1]Bagley, *Frontiersman: Abner Blackburn's Narrative*, 39.
[2]Henry W. Sanderson, "Diary of Henry Weeks Sanderson," Brigham Young University Library, 37. [3]Tyler, *A Concise History of the Mormon Battalion*, 131.

called a military force. Though Colonel Allen had mustered them into service, organized them into companies, and established a simple battalion staff, they were actually just a group of raw recruits marching together to Fort Leavenworth. In a modern analogy, it would be like a group of inductees boarding a bus to basic training, out of uniform with no military training and experience. They were without issue firearms or equipment and few had any shelter besides blankets. The men endured several thunderstorms that drenched them and caused some misery, a normal consequence of soldiering. Military discipline, drill and training, camp routine, march discipline, picket duty, and other tasks were still foreign to them. Fortunately, they had hundreds of miles and several months before the danger and possibility of combat would come.

The heat was oppressive, and the men suffered from want of supplies and proper food. At times the men were very low on flour to make bread or biscuits. A Missouri farmer who had contracted to deliver a wagonload of flour refused to provide it when he learned that the volunteers were Mormons. Allen learned of the problem and immediately ordered the man to deliver the flour or be arrested. This incident impressed the Mormon men, and they were convinced that Allen had their best interests at heart. Some of the men praised Allen with "Good for the Colonel" and "God bless the Colonel."[4]

Passing through St. Joseph, Missouri, many of the inhabitants were surprised that so many Mormon men had volunteered to serve in the war. At some locations the battalion tried to march in a proper formation to impress upon the locals that these Mormons were indeed soldiers and ready to serve. Some locals called the Mormon Battalion "a disgrace and a shame to the Government."[5]

Private John Steele recorded another riotous instance during this short march. Some of the men had "such a thirst for it [whiskey] I never saw, some of the men were so bad for it that they pulled [it] out of the hands of the owners and drank."[6] The tenets of the Mormon faith teach the total abstinence from alcohol. Though the doctrine that established this principle originated

---

[4]Ibid., 132.   [5]Ibid., 133–34.
[6]John Steele, Diary of John Steele, July 23, 1846, Brigham Young University Library.

with Joseph Smith in 1832, it was not until the twentieth century that church leaders stressed this doctrine in its present interpretation. The Mormons of the nineteenth century were sometimes given to drink, though drunkenness and its abuses were viewed as an evil and thoroughly condemned.[7]

The battalion arrived across the river from Fort Leavenworth the last day of July 1846. That night Allen sat down and completed a full roster of the battalion by name. Allen listed 496 effectives: 22 officers and 474 enlisted men.[8] He included the 3 Mormons who served on staff that were still on the company rolls. In the days before the army developed the Headquarters and Headquarters Company concept, commanders usually did not account for headquarters staff officers and NCOs on the company rosters. Another simple reason was that during this era, the staff was not considered part of the fighting force, therefore they were often omitted, including the commanding officer. Allen did not list Dr. William McIntire, appointed as assistant surgeon awaiting a commission in the volunteer medical corps. Among the soldiers who were on Allen's roster were several men who apparently enlisted at Council Bluffs and, for reasons not entirely clear, did not march with the battalion but joined it later at Fort Leavenworth. Other men enlisted at Fort Leavenworth. Some of these men were non-Mormons—two were teenaged Englishmen Robert Whitworth and William Beddome. Lewis Dent, a civilian probably going to California on personal business, accompanied the battalion during its march as a paymaster clerk.[9] Some of his letters were reprinted in

---

[7] Allen and Leonard, *The Story of the Latter-day Saints*, 524.

[8] James Allen, Return for July 31, 1846, Mormon Battalion Muster Rolls, Record Group 94, National Archives.

[9] Another non-Mormon who accompanied the battalion to California proved to have relation by marriage to one of the great characters of American history. Lewis Dent was the older brother of Julia Boggs Dent, who married a young second lieutenant in the 4th U.S. Infantry in 1848: Ulysses S. Grant. Lewis Dent to George Wrenshall Dent, February 1, 1847, San Diego, California, published in the St. Louis periodical, *The Daily Reveille*, June 12, 1847, and the St. Louis *The Weekly Reveille*; reprinted in *Nauvoo Journal* 11, no. 1 (Spring 1999). In this newspaper account, Lewis Dent is referred as "an officer in the pay department," but there is no record that he was ever commissioned in the regular or volunteer service. Yet, in Dr. George B. Sanderson's journal of January 1, 1847, Sanderson refers to Lewis Dent as a clerk to the paymaster Major Jeremiah Cloud; see "Journal kept by Dr. Geo[rge] B. Sanderson," January 1, 1847, typescript 55, Special Collections, Marriott Library, University of Utah; hereafter, George B. Sanderson, Journal, University of Utah Library.

contemporary newspapers. Also, a rogue named John Allen joined both the LDS Church and the battalion at Fort Leavenworth.[10] There may have been other non-Mormons with the battalion who are lost to history.

The records also show a couple dozen names that have lines drawn through them, and careful examination has determined that these men may have offered their names as recruits but did not actually serve. Through the year of the battalion's service, the unit strength would vary. Also, many contemporary rosters and listings do not include the regular army officers and those who joined or were attached at Santa Fe.[11]

The important military principle reflected by the roster is that a commander, through his adjutant (who serves as the administrative officer and military secretary—a sort of nineteenth-century operations officer) must have a complete and accurate roster or report of the unit's strength at all times. Since some of the men used aliases or variations of their actual names, it has been almost impossible to piece together a complete and accurate list of the men who served.[12] It is not important in this study to determine each soldier by name, but an accurate accounting of the strength of any unit was critical to combat operations. The military procedure even in the Mexican War era broke down unit strength into several

---

[10]Tyler, *A Concise History*, 210; see Bagley and Bigler, *Army of Israel*, 76–77.

[11]At Santa Fe, Willard Preble Hall, a prominent Missouri lawyer and later congressman, joined with the Mormon Battalion, as did Second Lieutenant George Stoneman, regular army, and Lieutenant Andrew Jackson Smith, who continued with the battalion. Cooke's escort party of several dragoons possibly joined the command, but not as members of the battalion. Whether all these soldiers were officially attached is not known because monthly returns do not list these dragoons. They were reassigned from Cooke's control to Captain John H. Burgwin's 1st Dragoons, along with the wagons Cooke left along the Rio Grande. Burgwin, along with some two hundred dragoons, remained behind with Colonel Alexander Doniphan in New Mexico. Captain Burgwin was later killed in the revolt at Taos in February 1847. See Bauer, *The Mexican War*, 140.

[12]Virtually every book or history of the Mormon Battalion has a listing or roster of the battalion. The most recent attempts to name and list the Mormon Battalion come from two sources: Ricketts, *The Mormon Battalion*, and Larson, *A Database of the Mormon Battalion: An Identification of the Original Members of the Mormon Battalion*. Though thorough and detailed, these lists do not agree on the same number, nor do they substantiate former lists. One of the problems with all of the lists is they include individuals who were not members of the battalion and exclude others such as the battalion staff. They are normally based only on the company rosters.

THE MARCH BEGINS

categories. First, there is the muster strength, or the assigned unit strength. The category of "attached" was not a procedure used often at this time in military units. A soldier was either a member of a unit or not. Then comes the detachments, such as sick list, detached service, details, authorized absence, guard duty, desertions, and various special duties that would take a soldier away from his normal duty with his unit. With all these detachments subtracted, the adjutant has a "present for duty" list. In that era the final total was sometimes called "effectives," though other terms were used also.[13] In the days before computers and personnel management systems, the manual methods were full of errors. The debate continues as to the final number of the men who served—over five hundred men. It is sufficient to say that the regular army commanders knew their unit strength at all times and that, for them, was critical.

In California, an aging and reluctant Commodore John Sloat relinquished command of his Pacific Squadron and the port of Monterey to Commodore Robert F. Stockton on July 23, 1846. Immediately, Stockton met and collaborated with John C. Frémont, commander of the "California Volunteer Battalion" to complete the conquest of California. No one really had the authority to raise a volunteer battalion or appoint Frémont as commander at the rank of lieutenant colonel, but that is what Stockton did. The Bear-Flaggers had joined with Frémont as volunteers. California, though without official sanction, was considered a United States possession by Americans there.

Just up the coast at San Francisco Bay, the ship Brooklyn *reached port with 238 Mormons on board under the leadership of Samuel Brannan. They had sailed from New York in February 1846 and arrived in California on July 31. Brannan and his followers would make one of the most important contributions to the history of early American California.*

Colonel Kearny (news of his promotion to brigadier general had not

---
[13]In the modern military there is one more category: "authorized" personnel strength dictated by manning documents and doctrine. Today the order is: authorized, assigned, attached, detached and absent (all the various reasons), then last, present for duty.

caught up with him yet) and his Army of the West gathered at Bent's Fort on the Arkansas River. The advance units arrived on July 28 and the entire forward element closed there by the 30th. At Bent's Fort, Kearny issued a proclamation declaring New Mexico a United States possession. He dispatched Captain Philip St. George Cooke with copies of the proclamation along with an escort of twelve dragoons and hired an agent, the mysterious James Magoffin. A well-established Santa Fe merchant, Magoffin convinced Mexican authorities there to submit peacefully to American control. After only a few days to rest and recuperate the animals, the entire army, minus the Mormon Battalion and Price's 2nd Missouri Volunteers still at Fort Leavenworth, pushed on to Santa Fe.[14]

After the departure of most of the Army of the West, Fort Leavenworth had only seventy or so regulars remaining for garrison duty under the command of Major Clifton Wharton of the 1st Dragoons. There also were several hundred Missouri volunteers forming the 2nd Regiment of Missouri Mounted Volunteers under Colonel Sterling Price. He had already dispatched some companies of his 845-man regiment, while the remainder and other units of artillery and cavalry were organizing and receiving equipment and arms.[15] Like Colonel Alexander Doniphan commanding the 1st Missouri Volunteers, Price was also a veteran of the Mormon civil war in Missouri in 1838.

Price served as a colonel in the state militia from Keytesville, Missouri, during the Mormon years. He later commanded a guard detail that guarded Joseph Smith and other Mormon leaders after their apprehension. Guards under Price's command became extremely offensive and profane toward their Mormon prisoners at Richmond, Missouri. After taking much degrading abuse to his ultimate limit, Joseph Smith stood forth, while shackled and chained, and rebuked Price's men. He commanded them: "SILENCE, ye fiends of the infernal pit. . . . Cease such talk, or you or

---

[14]Bauer, *The Mexican War*, 131–34.
[15]Shalhope, *Sterling Price: Portrait of a Southerner*, 59.

I die THIS INSTANT!" This episode has become legend in Mormon history.[16]

Colonel Price served commendably during the Mexican War as war governor of New Mexico, defeating a bloody Mexican uprising. Polk commissioned him a brigadier general of volunteers before the war ended.[17] A tough, austere, and inflexible man, Price was the embodiment of rural Missouri's slave-owning aristocracy. He was a large, barrel-chested man with premature silver-gray hair, a beautiful singing voice, and a dominating appearance. Price would have several encounters with the Mormon Battalion.[18]

Upon arriving at Fort Leavenworth the men of the battalion received their "A" or "wedge" tents designed to house six men. Kearny had allocated sufficient arms, equipment, tents, and provisions to outfit the battalion prior to his departure for New Mexico. All was ready when they arrived. Thus, they were issued their mess equipment for the six men as a "mess." Having endured several torrential thunderstorms with inadequate shelter on the march, the men now had proper military tents. Many were very sick with chills and fevers, probably malaria, from the combination of the march, the poor food, and no shelter. With rest, better rations, and new shelters, the men gained a sense of newfound camaraderie and their morale improved immediately. Sergeant William Hyde of B Company reported that "All was quiet and in good order" and that the singing and music reminded him of being "in a Methodist camp meeting."[19]

The weather during the day was still oppressively hot and humid, and some men gave exaggerated and outlandish estimates of 135 degrees at mid-day. Yet, with the shade of the trees and tents, conditions and life improved. Some recognized the distinct quality of Mormon soldiers serving together. Private John Steele wrote, "It

---

[16]Pratt, *Autobiography of Parley Parker Pratt*, 211; Shalhope, *Sterling Price*, 27.
[17]Winders, *Mr. Polk's Army*, 38.
[18]After serving as United States congressman, governor of Missouri, and commander of the state militia, Price fought during the Civil War for the Confederacy. He would have key roles in several major battles and campaigns in the western theater, especially his 1864 raid into Missouri, and became a major general. DeVoto, *Year of Decision*, 312; see Shalhope, *Sterling Price*.   [19]William Hyde, Journal, August 2, 1846, Brigham Young University Library.

looked well to see about 100 tents all filled with the Elders of Israel."[20]

The tents not only seemed like ancient Israel, but were an attraction to sixteen-year-old British emigrant Robert Whitworth and his traveling partner, William Beddome. "There was a large camp of little white tents on the outside of the fort . . . ," he wrote. "We were informed that they were part of the [Mormon] Battalion that lay encamped before us. We had never thought of volunteering before, but we were almost immediately seized with a desire to live in one of the little white tents." Learning of the pay and the mission to march to California, the two young non-Mormon Englishmen enlisted. The allure of military life attracts people in many different ways.[21]

The first official order Colonel Allen gave at Fort Leavenworth was the appointment of Dr. George B. Sanderson—soon to be a controversial figure in the battalion—"a surgeon in the United States Army, to serve with the Mormon Battalion of volunteers," adding, "This appointment is subject to the approval of the President of the United States."[22] Allen issued this order on August 1, 1846, the day the battalion crossed the Missouri River and arrived in garrison. On the same day, Allen wrote a letter to the adjutant general informing him of his desire that both medical doctors, McIntire and Sanderson, be commissioned medical officers in the volunteer service. "I consider both of these officers necessary in the service of my Battalion," wrote Allen. "Doctor McIntire is a Mormon and though[t] it my duty to appoint him inasmuch as he was recommended for the place by the Elders of the Mormon Church." Though McIntire was "a regular graduate of a Medical School," recorded Allen, "I do not deem him qualified to perform all the duties of his profession that are now and will be required in the Battalion."[23]

---

[20] John Steele, Diary, August 1, 1846, Brigham Young University Library.
[21] Gracy and Rugeley, "From the Mississippi to the Pacific: An Englishman in the Mormon Battalion," 134.
[22] General Order, No. 4, Headquarters, Mormon Battalion, dated August 1, 1846. National Archives, microfiche copy, # A-139, Utah State Historical Society.
[23] Ibid.

THE MARCH BEGINS

Colonel Allen did not explain why McIntire was not qualified, though it was probably due to the fact he had not passed the rigid entrance examinations mentioned earlier. It may have been because Allen did not want all his key posts filled by Mormons, or that he made the appointment to appease the church leaders. Allen did, however, explain his high regard for Dr. Sanderson, who "is known to me as a gentleman of the first respectability and of accomplished skill and attainments in his profession." Both physicians were to serve as assistant surgeons; however, Sanderson's appointment order contains the language "subject to the president's approval," whereas Dr. McIntire's order does not. This was, at least in Dr. Sanderson's case, a commissioning process, though Allen desired both officers to serve as military surgeons.[24]

In the army of this era there were three levels of medical officers: senior surgeon, surgeon, and assistant surgeon. These positions equated to ranks: a senior surgeon rank was achieved normally after ten years of service with the rank equivalent to major and served with units of regiment or above; a surgeon normally, but not always, was a regimental position and held the rank equivalent of captain; and an assistant surgeon had the status of a lieutenant and served normally under the tutelage of a surgeon, if possible, in a line regiment. Army physicians were almost always referred to by no other title than "doctor" or "surgeon." Historian Francis Heitman in his register of army officers listed Dr. George B. Sanderson as "an assistant surgeon of volunteers" and did not list McIntire.[25]

The battalion was not authorized to have a surgeon, and Dr. Sanderson probably did not qualify to be a surgeon because of his lack of military experience. It is also interesting that Allen appointed Dr. McIntire assistant surgeon two weeks earlier at Council Bluffs and then appointed Sanderson surgeon immediately upon arriving at Fort Leavenworth. Allen either knew of him previously or Dr. Sanderson came highly recommended through official channels.

---

[24]Letter from Lieutenant Colonel James Allen to brevet Brigadier General Roger Jones, Adjutant General, dated August 1, 1846, copy in Utah State Historical Society. A copy of the volunteer commission of Dr. George B. Sanderson as assistant surgeon is on microfilm reel #A-139.   [25]Heitman, *Historical Register and Dictionary of the United States Army*, 1: 858.

Dr. George Sanderson served as a commissioned medical officer; thus his directives and authority were of more importance than a contract civilian. Still, the commanding officer is professionally obligated to adhere to and enforce recommendations from government surgeons, commissioned or contract. Little is known of Sanderson as a historical character, other than that he served with the battalion and that he kept a poignant and descriptive journal.[26] George Sanderson resided in Platte County, Missouri, not far from Fort Leavenworth, and he was British by birth. He married Ellen Johnson on November 25, 1844, and owned a large farm named "Hazlewood," where he owned as many as fifteen slaves.[27]

With great anticipation the men awaited the issue of arms, equipment, and provisions, which they received by companies.[28] In a letter from Captain Henry S. Turner, acting adjutant to Colonel Kearny, addressed to Captain William H. Bell, an ordnance officer at the St. Louis arsenal, dated June 26, 1846, Kearny requested the arms and accouterments for the battalion. Turner outlined that "For Capt Allens Battalion of Volunteers 400 Muskets with Bayonets & accoutrements complete including slings & 200 rounds of ammunition in cartridges for each with requiste number of flints—100 Carbines with accoutrements ... 200 rounds of ammunition in cartridges for each with requisite number of Percussion caps" would be issued. Turner also ordered the additional equipment requested for the battalion: "100 Cavalry Sabers with Belts Plates & complete—100 Dragoon Pistols with requisite number of flints. 100 Holsters (pair of) No ammunition for Pistols."[29]

This letter clearly identifies the numbers of firearms and accou-

---

[26]As mentioned in the introduction, in the spring of 2003 a journal of George B. Sanderson was made public and obtained by the Marriot Library Special Collections at the University of Utah. Another window into the life and deeds of this major character in the Mormon Battalion story is now available for study.

[27]Hamilton Gardner, a former military officer and historian, concluded that Dr. George B. Sanderson was a contract surgeon; of course this is not the case. See Gardner, "The Command and Staff of the Mormon Battalion," 349; notes 24 and 25 above reference Dr. Sanderson's commission; county tax and other vital records regarding Sanderson are found in Paxton, *Annals of Platte County, Missouri*, 62, 65, 124.

[28]Kearny's Letter Book, 152.

[29]Captain Henry S. Turner to Captain William H. Bell, June 26, 1846, Kearny's Letter Book, 153.

THE MARCH BEGINS 153

terments that were requested for the battalion. The muskets, of course, were smoothbore flintlocks. The "carbines" mentioned were not issued to the battalion, but caplock and perhaps flintlock rifles were. Many journals record that the men also had "yagers" (German *jägers*), which are not carbines or cavalry firearms as Turner ordered, but a type of rifle. The "Dragoon Pistols" were the U.S. Model 1836 single-shot, muzzle-loading, flintlock pistol. The "Cavalry Saber" was either the U.S. Model 1840 Cavalry Saber or U.S. Model 1840 Infantry Sword. Whether they actually received the exact type, amount, and description of firearms and equipment that Captain Turner ordered is not important. Supply requisitions are seldom filled exactly. The men would have received what was available.

The most modern standard issue firearm available was the U.S. Model 1842 musket, which had the new percussion caplock system. But General Winfield Scott had little confidence in the musket's new ignition system, the percussion or cap-lock, and decided to rely on the proven flintlocks. Some of the regulars were reissued flintlocks, as were the volunteer units. One of the conditions of enlistment that Colonel Allen offered the Mormons was that they were to retain their firearms upon honorable discharge from the Army. The United States Army was not about to give away new and expensive firearms to one-year volunteers, yet the army was willing to empty the arsenals and posts of old, antiquated pieces.[30]

The men of the battalion were issued several different firearms. Most of the men carried the Model 1816 smoothbore flintlock; a few received either the 1817 Common flintlock rifle and the newer Model 1841 percussion lock, "Mississippi Rifle" or *jäger*. On the official Ordinance Department returns for the Mormon Battalion, there is listed the "half-stock" rifle. This was a version of the U.S. Model 1803 Rifle, similar to a later design, the Model 1814. The

---

[30] The 1st New York Volunteer Regiment mustered in New York City in August 1846. Many of the men joined especially for the opportunity to travel to California at government expense and then remain to settle in California. These men were also allowed to retain their firearms; see Captain Jim Balance, "Stevenson's Regiment: First Regiment of New York Volunteers," 6. The battalion was not the only volunteer unit to receive their firearms upon discharge.

Model 1803 was originally designed for Captain Meriwether Lewis for his military expedition to the Pacific Ocean; however, the new model was not developed and manufactured in time for the Lewis and Clark venture. It was nicknamed the half-stock, because the stock ran only halfway along the normal length of the barrel.[31] The men who received these *jäger* rifles retained them as private firearms later.

Though the men were to retain their firearms after their service, the quartermasters still required the company officers to sign receipts of issue, because the men would be charged if they lost them while in service. The men received buff white leather waist and shoulder belts, canteens, blankets, linen haversacks, canvas knapsacks, leather cartridge boxes, and triangular eighteen-inch socket bayonets and scabbards. The officers also received sabers or swords and a few received singleshot, flintlock pistols as opposed to the new five- or six-shot revolvers just recently developed by "Colonel" Samuel Colt.

At one point as the men pressed forward to receive their muskets, Colonel Allen exclaimed, "Stand back, boys; don't be in a hurry to get your muskets; you will want to throw the d—d things away before you get to California."[32] Allen's words rang true. While at the fort, Allen apparently attempted to introduce his new volunteer battalion to some military training and tactics. This is one of the few times they received any formal training until much later in California. Allen also commended the Mormon soldiers on that, though they were inexperienced and lacked training, he "had not been under the necessity of giving the word of command the second time. The men, though unacquainted with military tactics, were willing to obey orders."[33]

One important item of military issue the men did not receive was their uniforms. Almost to the man, the Mormon volunteers accept-

---

[31]For a description of various firearms issued to the battalion, see Tyler, *A Concise History*, 136; for the weapons designed but not used on the Lewis and Clark Expedition, see Moore and Haynes, *Tailor Made, Trail Worn*, 258. The Ordnance Department records are also found in the LDS Archives; see also Mexican War Reports and Returns, Record Group 94, National Archives.   [32]Tyler, *A Concise History*, 136.
[33]Ibid., 137.

ed a cash clothing allowance of forty-two dollars in lieu of their regulation uniform. Private Christopher Layton wrote about an amusing character who wished to gain some recognition with a military uniform piece: "In the Battalion was a man whom we will call C., who had, by some means, procured a peculiar kind of hat belonging to an officer's uniform of the Nauvoo Legion. This lone hat was the only article of uniform in the Battalion, except that worn by the Colonel ... [his] messmates teased him about his hat."[34]

The battalion was not the only volunteer unit to not receive its uniform issue. The Missouri volunteers and others also declined their uniforms for various reasons, whether for the allowance or because of the fact that the typical Missouri volunteer was a nonconforming, free-spirited individualist.[35] There is also another reason for units not receiving uniforms. With the advent of the war, "[t]he Quartermaster Department did not have enough uniforms to clothe the volunteers at the start of the war, as its warehouses held only scant supplies needed to supply the small peacetime army." This may have been true with many volunteers at different military posts. In the case of the Mormon Battalion, the reasons for taking the clothing allowance in lieu of uniforms was certainly the fact that the men and the church needed ready cash. As for the other volunteers, individualism, money, or lack of uniforms were all possible alternatives.[36]

The clothing allowance was an important factor of service in the Mormon Battalion, which provided some $21,000 in cash for the soldiers, their families, and the use of the church. Brigham Young sent several prominent Latter-day Saints to Fort Leavenworth for the purpose of collecting funds from the men for general church use: apostles Parley P. Pratt, John Taylor, and Orson Hyde, and also Jesse Little. The apostles were en route to a mission in England and needed funds for their travel and proselytizing work. Little was

---

[34]Christopher Layton, Journal, LDS Archives; also there is another version edited and published by Barton and McIntyre, *Christopher Layton*, which is nearly a complete duplication of major portions of Daniel Tyler's, *A Concise History of the Mormon Battalion*.

[35]Nevin, *The Mexican War*, 112; for a depiction of the Missourians' undisciplined but fierce fighting acumen, see DeVoto, *Year of Decision*, 252–53.

[36]Winders, *Mr. Polk's Army*, 108.

returning to his duties in the eastern states, but would then go to Council Bluffs to join Brigham Young's advance party to Utah in 1847. The elders collected some $5,192, donated to Brigham Young and the Quorum of the Twelve Apostles. The remainder of the cash was either retained by the soldiers or sent to their families in Iowa.[37]

The donation of money for church purposes, as well as the fact that through Brigham Young's leadership the men enlisted, demonstrated that the battalion's purpose was to promote church programs; patriotism and national war aims were secondary. The men looked upon their service as a call from God and their church and not so much as a patriotic venture. They knew they were serving the church and complying with Brother Brigham's counsel. That does not mean that some of the men did not feel an intrinsic patriotic pride in their service and loyalty to the national government. Private George Washington Taggart, a musician in B Company, for one, wrote,

> I have forsaken for the time being My possessions My family and at the risk of life started for Mexico as a united States Soldier with 500 of My Brethren in order to show that the Blood of my grandfathers who fought and bled in the revolutionary war and the spirit of liberty and freedom still courses in the veins of some of their posterity that are called Mormons.[38]

At Fort Leavenworth the battalion experienced its first incidents of military discipline. On August 6 Colonel Allen relieved battalion quartermaster Sergeant Sebert Shelton and appointed Lieutenant Samuel Gully of E Company. Replacing a sergeant with a lieutenant was an unusual decision. Perhaps he felt the responsibility was too much for the authority of a sergeant. It is impossible to evaluate Gully against Shelton—neither had any real military experience. Gully may have had more natural ability, thus his selection by Brigham Young as a company officer. Some of the men complained about Shelton's incompetence.[39] This was not a pro-

---

[37]Yurtinus, "A Ram in the Thicket," 77.
[38]George Washington Taggart to Fanny Taggart, Fort Leavenworth, August 6, 1846, LDS Archives. [39]William Coray, Journal, August 2 and 6, 1846, LDS Archives.

THE MARCH BEGINS 157

motion for Gully; it was a change of duty—when Shelton returned to D Company, he was reduced to private.

While at Fort Leavenworth waiting for all the arrangements to be made, some of the men had time to reflect upon their difficult situation. Private John Tippets recorded, "I was waiting with the greatest anxiety of mind that a man could have that had a family that was near and dear to him ... they were left in the open prairie in a wagon exposed to the winds and storms."[40] Many others were concerned about their families and the future that lay ahead of them.

At Fort Leavenworth religious authority was first exerted in an effort to establish policy in the Mormon Battalion. After some of the men became intoxicated and one was actually placed in the guardhouse, Private David Pettegrew of E Company went forth exhorting the men to abide by their religious duties. His comrades held Pettegrew in fond regard. He was known as "Father Pettegrew" because he was an older, middle-aged man with a head of flowing silver-white hair that complimented his pious nature. He spoke firmly but sincerely of their sacred responsibilities and duties in the church.[41] Pettegrew condemned evil practices and often reminded the men of the promised blessings by the Lord's mouthpiece, Brigham Young, if they followed his counsel. He went from company to company, tent to tent, crossing company lines to admonish the men concerning their spiritual responsibilities.

Along with Pettegrew, another strong voice of religious responsibility came from Private Levi W. Hancock, a musician in E Company. Hancock was, by ordination, the presiding ecclesiastical authority in the Mormon Battalion. He served as a member of the church's First Council of Seventy and was a general authority of the church, a position of great religious significance then and now among Latter-day Saints. Hancock was a man of forty-three years at the time of his enlistment and had provided good and faithful service in his duties in the church. He was a serious-minded, devoted Mormon, and his obligation to serve his brethren as the

---
[40] John H. Tippets, Journal, August 6, 1846, Utah State University Library.
[41] David Pettegrew, Journal, August 9, 1846, Utah State Historical Society.

shepherd of the flock or congregation was not imagined; it was real. Hancock was not a mean or egotistical man thirsting for authority; he merely desired to obey counsel and serve the Lord. The religious nature of the battalion would cause conflict with authority as time went on.

After nearly two weeks at Fort Leavenworth, the unit was prepared to resume its march westward. The companies had received their wagons, equipment, and tents, and the men their firearms, personal equipment, and pay. The Army of the West had sent forward to Bent's Fort a wagon train of supplies for the battalion. Allen attempted to train his battalion, but his time was devoted mostly to the logistics of the campaign. The battalion received a very limited amount of drill and training at Fort Leavenworth. It would be impossible to state that the battalion was ready for combat at this point; it was still quite green, untrained and undisciplined for combat operations.

To ensure a regiment, the basic combat unit of this period, or in this case a battalion, was ready for combat operations, intensive drill and training were necessary. Many hours of daily drilling for several weeks was the standard program to instill in the officers, NCOs, and soldiers the discipline, confidence, coordination, and unit cohesion to stand face to face with an enemy formation a hundred yards away, trade lethal volleys, and not break, waver, or run. Not only were the mechanics of precision drill of firing and reloading under fire needed, but the ability to work as a unit and team to march in column, deploy, maneuver, wheel-about, change directions, and charge without flinching or breaking ranks had to be instilled. In this era this level of performance was achievable, but only after many long hours of drill and repetition under the eyes and hands of professional and experienced officers and NCOs. Volunteer units, when trained and drilled to standard, could perform and fight effectively. Unfortunately, because of the battalion's lengthy recruiting time and the lethargic march to California, the regular army officers did not have the time to train the battalion to standard until it was in California.

THE MARCH BEGINS

✳ ✳ ✳

General Kearny realized when he organized the Army of the West and ordered them along the Santa Fe that he had to disperse the units to conserve grass and forage for the hundreds of animals moving along this very arid trek.[42] Yet, in the Mormon Battalion's case, the delay at Fort Leavenworth had nothing to do with Kearny's march timetable. Colonel Allen wanted to recruit the men in just a few days and then travel the Missouri River by riverboat. But this did not happen as hoped, so he was well behind his desired schedule upon arriving at the fort. Allen obviously wanted to outfit the battalion and be on the trail as soon as possible. Sadly, as the departure time approached James Allen became very ill. Unable to perform his duties, he made the final arrangements for the march from his sickbed. With a sense of urgency, Allen ordered the battalion forward to attempt to overtake Kearny. Lieutenant George Dykes, battalion adjutant, remained behind with Allen, as did Lieutenant James Pace, Sergeant Major James Glines, and a few others.

The many families that had accompanied the battalion also made their final arrangements for provisions, tools, grain, wagon repairs, teams, and other tiresome details. The government was under no obligation to transport noncombatants halfway across the continent to California, and it was left to the husbands and families to find their own means of travel. Several soldiers combined resources to purchase wagons and teams for the journey. Some unaccompanied married men and bachelors provided funds to have some of these outfits carry their personal belongings. In the group, too, there were also the government wagons that would provide the logistics of provisions and equipment, as well as a large herd of beef for the standard ration of meat. The hired laundresses received government rations, but transportation was not a government responsibility. The women's laundry services were not paid by the government but by the men themselves.[43]

---

[42]Dawson, *Doniphan's Epic March*, 52; see Chalfant, *Dangerous Passage: The Santa Fe Trail and the Mexican War*.
[43]Ricketts, *The Mormon Battalion*, 37.

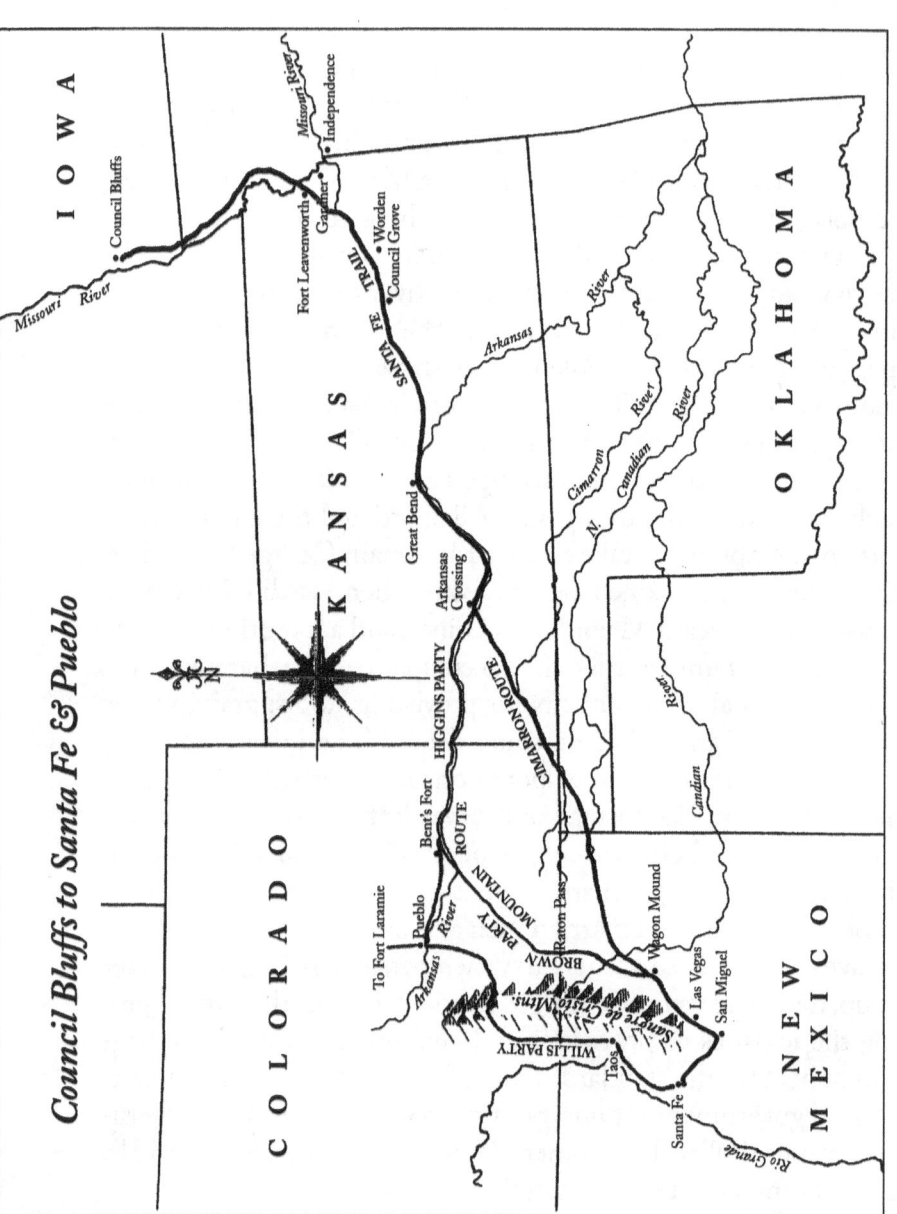

THE MARCH BEGINS 161

Regular army officers usually had their own mounts for which the army provided reimbursement for use and fodder on a daily rate. Whether the company Mormon officers rode or marched is unknown. They probably did some of both.

With no real military tactical training and just the basic issue of arms and equipment, the battalion was embarking on a journey that would end some seventeen hundred miles later on the shores of the Pacific Ocean. On August 13, the first companies—A, B, and E—commenced their march under the command of the senior company commander, Captain Jefferson Hunt. C and D companies remained behind to complete their preparations and clean up the camp. They departed on the 15th.[44] During this same period Price's 2nd Missouri Mounted Volunteers and some additional artillery began their march.

The route they followed was an established military road known as either the Fort Leavenworth Road, the Fort Scott Road, or the Military Road. Military caravans and other parties heading south to connect with the Santa Fe Trail near present-day Olathe, Kansas, had used the Fort Scott Road since 1842. After only a dozen or so miles the battalion turned off the Fort Scott Military Road and followed what is called the military branch of the Santa Fe Trail from Fort Leavenworth. This part of eastern Kansas has great historical significance since two major trails (Oregon and Santa Fe) and many variants of these trails criss-crossed and connected at several points. From Independence, Missouri, both the Oregon and Santa Fe trails were basically the same until separating at present-day Gardner, Kansas. The battalion followed Kearny's well-worn military route and intercepted the Santa Fe Trail near

---

[44]There are several outstanding studies of the Mormon Battalion Trail: Stanley Kimball's *Historic Sites Along the Mormon Trail and other Great Western Trails* is generally available, whereas, "The Mormon Battalion Trail Guide," a study by Charles S. Peterson and several associates, was never published but remains in a typeset format and is not easy to find. Kimball researched a study for the National Park Service on the battalion's trek on the Santa Fe Trail. See Kimball, "The Mormon Battalion on the Santa Fe Trail in 1846." Also, Dan Talbot's *A Historical Guide to the Mormon Battalion and Butterfield Trail* is available, but the maps only deal with the route in Arizona; see Kimball, "The Mormon Battalion Trail Guide," 5 and note 10.

present-day Worden, Kansas. For the next seven hundred long, dreary miles the men would eat the dust of the Santa Fe Trail, a major western route since 1822.[45]

The Mormon volunteers commenced the great trek without their commander and as a separate unit. (Other units of the Army of the West were yet to follow.) The march order and discipline of a five-company volunteer infantry battalion is not a very difficult logistical or leadership challenge. Even with an interval to control dust and tactical separation, the actual march column length could not have been very long, perhaps a half-mile at most. It was certainly not much over a mile, even with the wagon train and beef herd. Tactical separation between companies (the distance between units to safeguard against ambush and allow freedom of maneuver) during the frontier and Mexican War periods was not very long, perhaps a hundred to two hundred yards. One has to remember that the basic fighting unit of the period was the regiment (though frontier service seldom allowed a regiment to serve as a complete unit). A battalion, consisting of half the strength of a regiment of 1,000 or more soldiers, still had to deploy from the march column to a battleline formation with the companies close enough to form and fight together as a battalion. No one expected to encounter Mexican forces so far from the front or enemy territory, but military training dictates that "as one does in training, one does in battle." The best time for an untrained, undisciplined volunteer infantry battalion to learn march discipline is during the march. Though there were no standard march rates and distances established in manuals, from the standard quickstep pace one can deduce a typical or average march rate. For frontier infantry units a typical march rate was two to three miles an hour, which would make an average daily rate of twenty to twenty-five miles for sustained marches, with occasional rest and recuperation days.

Kearny marched his column anywhere from twenty to thirty miles a day. Of course, most of his soldiers were mounted, but he also had a small dismounted battalion of infantry, which often out-

---

[45]Kimball, *Historic Sites Along the Mormon Trail and other Great Western Trails*, 187.

marched the mounted units.[46] During its march to the Pacific the Mormon Battalion seldom met this rate. The records show that the battalion had approximately 160 march days from Council Bluffs to San Diego. It met or exceeded this typical or average distance of twenty miles a day on 35 days. On December 18 and 19, 1846, it marched thirty and thirty-two miles respectively. Frontier officers became masters of the art of pushing men and animals to their limits while still maintaining discipline and conserving water, food, and forage. They marched vast distances across difficult terrain, then deployed their force to engage and fight on little rest and poor rations.

A march column could vary, but columns of four or eight men abreast were the common practice. Straggler control was an afterthought, it seems. Even the main body of the Army of the West suffered from serious straggling. One seasoned frontier regular of the time commented on the straggling by volunteers: "If regulars were to straggle so[,] they would be considered as mutinizing."[47] Those men unable to keep pace in the battalion simply jumped aboard the wagons with the sick, of which there were many. Command and control of the march column, rate of march, march discipline, intervals, and camp and sanitary discipline was virtually non-existent in the battalion until officers of the Regular Army took command.

Hunt and his Mormon brethren were learning to be adequate pioneers at the time they enlisted in Iowa. They were not, however, experienced soldiers. Pioneers do not necessarily make good soldiers. Hunt's goal was merely to march the battalion to Santa Fe, expecting Colonel Allen to overtake the column. Crossing the American Southwest under such primitive conditions, coupled with the inability to always obtain sufficient water, forage, fuel, and adequate campsites for a battalion and, at least initially, a large number of camp followers, presented its challenges.

After a few days a camp and march routine evolved. Englishman Private Robert Whitworth wrote, "After tents are pitched, every

---

[46]DeVoto, *Year of Decision*, 253–54.   [47]Ibid., 270.

one drops the profession of arms and goes to cutting or carrying Wood or Water and cooking the evening meal, which being disposed of we gather around the fire and talk about almost everything, particularly California & Mexico, during which Smoking & chewing Tobacco is not forgot."[48]

☽ ☽ ☽

Commodore Robert Stockton with his confederate in arms, "Lieutenant Colonel" John C. Frémont, occupied Los Angeles with a collection of naval, marine, and volunteer forces on August 13, 1846. Earlier the Mexican authorities of Upper California, Pío Pico, the civil governor, and General José Castro, the commanding general, had met with American consul Thomas Larkin, Stockton, and Frémont in Monterey to discuss the avoidance of any combat and form an independent republic under United States protection. The Mexicans agreed to this compromise, but Stockton would not. The venture collapsed with Castro departing south to gather his military forces for war. Frémont embarked his "California volunteers" aboard one of Stockton's vessels and they sailed south to capture Los Angeles, San Diego, and other key cities. California was subdued, as far as Stockton and Frémont were concerned.[49]

Thousands of miles away, the "soldier of the people" landed at Vera Cruz. Passing with impunity through the American blockade on a British merchantman, Antonio López de Santa Anna disembarked at Vera Cruz on August 16. He had negotiated for months through agents with the Polk administration to plan his return to Mexico and lead his country to a peaceful resolution of the war, as well as the boundary problems over Texas and the purchase of California. Now on his home soil, Santa Anna, the ever-evasive, ever-scheming, self-centered survivor, had American support but his own plans in his head, which did not include appeasing America.

At the same time, General Kearny and his advance element of the Army of the West continued its march to Santa Fe. Organized Mexican resistance assembled in the treacherous canyons east of Santa Fe, but its

---

[48]Gracy and Rugeley, "From the Mississippi to the Pacific," 136.
[49]Eisenhower, *So Far from God*, 215–16; Harlow, *California Conquered*, 137–58.

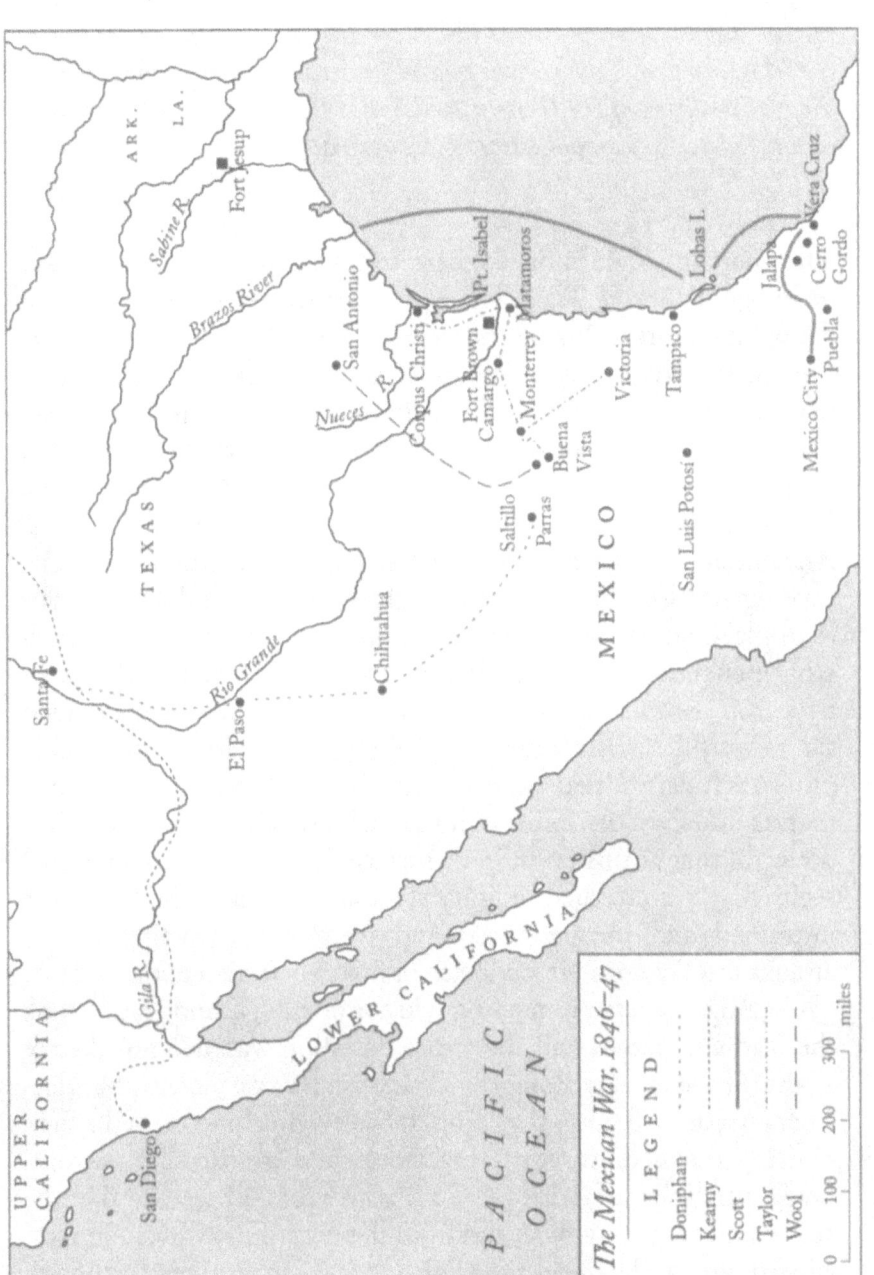

Map based on information provided by author.

resolve and leadership failed. The closer Kearny approached, the more the Mexican army, which was much larger than Kearny's force, melted away. The Army of the West entered Santa Fe on August 18, 1846, and conquered a Mexican possession without firing a shot.

The marching Mormon soldiers followed Kearny's main body down the Santa Fe Trail. Their progress was extremely slow and deliberate at first. During the first few days the companies sometimes marched only five or ten miles a day. Slowly the men and animals became accustomed to the routine. Camp, noise, light, and march discipline in the nineteenth century, and what is now called "operational security," were not as well defined as in modern times. In its primitive form, the practice had been around for ages. Ancient armies sometimes moved at night as silently as possible, making no fires and executing night maneuver and attacks. For example, General George Washington successfully saved his small Continental Army from annihilation when he extracted it in darkness from Brooklyn, New York, in 1776. (The Americans evaded the powerful British army at night, employing strict noise discipline such as muffled oars, no marching drums, no loud commands, and light discipline of no campfires, lights, or torches.) It is doubtful that at this point in its service the battalion's operational security was up to such military standards, because the men were untrained and inexperienced and were not expecting enemy attacks this far from New Mexico or possible Indian raids.

On August 19, the remaining two companies, C and D, overtook the lead companies and the entire battalion was assembled once again. The same day along the Wakarusa River a violent thunderstorm descended upon the camp in the evening and caused a fury, blowing down tents, scattering stock, and overturning wagons. Sergeant William Hyde of B Company wrote, "it seemed that the very elements were at war, and from the fury of the wind, connected with rain and hail, and the lightning which streaked forth with all its forked fury, followed by loud peals of thunder, it appeared

THE MARCH BEGINS

that the very prince and power of the air was coming in all his fury against us."[50] The battalion spent two days recovering from the storm. Besides enduring Mother Nature's wrath, the battalion faced the first of many storms unrelated to the weather.

At Hurricane Point—an appropriate name for the events that took place there—the first of several authority and personality conflicts that had been brewing for some time came to a head. Most of the problems resulted from the fact that the Mormon volunteers were not accustomed to military life and discipline. While C and D Companies remained at Fort Leavenworth with the responsibility to clean up the camp used by the battalion and burn excess brush, there were conflicts among the officers. Captain James Brown, commander of C Company, though very sick, directed two of his officers, Lieutenants George Rosecrans and Robert Clift, to comply with the orders from Lieutenant George Dykes, the battalion adjutant. Both lieutenants refused to do so. Both parties made insulting comments. Brown had threatened to shoot Clift after learning that Clift had tried to influence Brown's wife against him. The situation had become extremely nasty. Lieutenant Clift made a formal charge sheet against Captain Brown for threatening his life.

As the men recovered from the thunderstorm, the problems that had developed at Fort Leavenworth reached their peak. Because of Brown's threats against Clift, Rosecrans and Clift wanted to replace Brown as commander, and they involved the enlisted men in the attempt. Also, Lieutenant Cyrus Canfield of D Company under Captain Nelson Higgins wanted Higgins removed as commander as well. Lieutenant Dykes, accompanying the two companies forward to overtake the battalion, tried to settle the matter. If Brown would make a public apology to the company, Clift would then drop the charges of assault against his commander.

---

[50]This location has come to be known as Hurricane Point in many journals and some histories. One can hardly believe that a sudden, though violent, thunderstorm, or possibly part of a tornado-producing storm, on the plains of Kansas would be considered a hurricane: a tropical ocean phenomenon of titanic proportions whose direct effect and magnitude could not reach central Kansas. William Hyde, Journal, August 19, 1846, Brigham Young University Library.

James S. Brown, at about age thirty. *Courtesy Pioneer Memorial Museum, International Society, Daughters of Utah Pioneers.*

Captain Brown began to apologize, but it turned into a harangue against the two officers and the enlisted men, which offended them even more. The incident grew uglier as these lieutenants boasted and toasted with the men of the companies for Brown's and Higgin's removal. "Here is to Capt. Brown," went one toast, "that he may be discharged and sent back to the Bluff [Council Bluffs], having disgraced himself as an officer and that his place may be filled by Lieut Rosecrans who raised the co[mpany]."[51] Eventually, Captain Hunt, the acting commander of the battalion, intervened and chastised both parties and then directed that the men accept Brown and Higgins as their rightfully appointed commanders, actually meaning those sanctioned by Brigham Young and the church.

This incident has interesting military lessons. Even the regular army was plagued by personality conflicts and sometimes great misunderstandings; even duels resulted in the early years of the

---

[51]William Coray, Journal, August 20, 1846, LDS Archives.

American Republic. That several lieutenants tried to replace their commanding officers is a very serious offense, whether justified or not. To then involve the enlisted men was an intolerable action. The erring junior officers should have been relieved, perhaps even cashiered for the good of the service. Captain Brown's threat against Clift was foolhardy, and a formal military investigation should have solved that problem. The basic problem was that the battalion had no discipline and military standards. Though Hunt, the senior officer, seemingly settled the matter, he did not correct the problem. The feelings and anxieties continued to grow and eventually caused more problems for the battalion. Lieutenants do not question the orders and directives of their company commanders and directives from battalion headquarters. Allen's sickness and absence did not help the situation. This incident demonstrates the problems intrinsic to a new military unit comprised of volunteers who had not learned their duties. Volunteer units often perform exceedingly well, once they are trained, disciplined, and have learned their duties.

Just short of Council Grove on August 26, 1846, Lieutenant Samuel Gully and Private Sebert Shelton arrived from Fort Leavenworth with the news of Allen's tragic death. After nearly two weeks of illness, Allen succumbed on August 23. The news "struck a damper to our feelings," wrote Sergeant William Hyde, "we considered him a worthy man ... look upon him as our friend."[52]

Sergeant William Coray offered similar comments: "Suffice it to say that it [Allen's death] caused more lamentation from us than the loss of a Gentile ever did before. Capt. J. Allen was a good man; he stood up for our rights better than many of our brethren ... was never abusive or tyrannical, which is the case with nearly all the regulars. In short, he was an exception among officers of the U.S.A[rmy]."[53]

---

[52]William Hyde, Journal, August 26, 1846, Brigham Young University Library.
[53]William Coray, Journal, August 26, 1846, LDS Archives. Mormons commonly used the term "Gentile" in the nineteenth century to denote non-Mormons. Mormons believe they are the modern-day people of Israel; therefore, non-Mormons are gentiles.

Lieutenant Colonel James Allen, commander of the Mormon Battalion, was the first known army officer to die and be buried in the graveyard at Fort Leavenworth, which later became Fort Leavenworth National Military Cemetery.[54] His headstone reads:

> JAMES ALLEN
> LT COL
> MORMON BN
> MO VOLS
> INDIAN WAR
> MEXICAN WAR
> 1806–1846[55]

---

[54] Yurtinus, "A Ram in the Thicket," 97 n.160.

[55] The headstone has the error "MO VOLS," meaning Missouri Volunteers. Lieutenant Colonel James Allen was not a Missouri Volunteer.

CHAPTER EIGHT

A Change in Command

The appointment of Smith ... caused a greater gloom throughout the command than the death of Colonel Allen had.
       —Corporal Daniel Tyler

While the battalion was facing bad weather and internal stormy relations out on the plains of Kansas, its commander, Lieutenant Colonel James Allen, sank deeper and deeper into sickness, finally passing away on August 23, 1846. He died of what was called "congestive fever." Allen had been convalescing for some time, aided by his young niece, and when his condition worsened he was taken to the quarters of First Lieutenant Andrew Jackson Smith, an officer in the 1st Dragoons. On hand to assist him were several Mormon officers and members of the staff, Dr. George Sanderson, assistant surgeon; Lieutenant Samuel Gully, quartermaster officer; and Lieutenant James Pace of E Company.[1] (Lieutenant Dykes, the adjutant, and Sergeant Major Glines had departed Fort Leavenworth and overtook the battalion on August 21.) Prior to his death, Allen and Lieutenant Smith had discussed the proposition that Smith assume command if Allen should be unable to continue. Therefore, when Allen died,

---

[1] Samuel Gully to Brigham Young, August 23, 1846, Brigham Young Papers, LDS Archives; Captain Henry S. Turner, Kearny's adjutant and Allen's long-serving colleague, suggested that Allen, like many frontier officers and men of the time, indulged in habits and vices that my have exacerbated his health problems, namely alcoholism. See Clarke, *The Original Journals of Henry Smith Turner: With Stephen Watts Kearny to New Mexico and California 1846–1847*.

Major Clifton Wharton, the commanding officer at Fort Leavenworth, approved Smith's request to take temporary command of the Mormon Battalion until they could consult General Kearny. Wharton took several actions: first, he sent Smith forward to overtake the battalion; second, he recommended that a messenger inform Brigham Young of Allen's death; and last, he notified the War Department.

According to Lieutenant Pace, as soon as Allen died at Fort Leavenworth, Smith and Dr. Sanderson attempted to assume control of the battalion by ordering Lieutenant Gully, the quartermaster, to depart to overtake the column. Gully refused. Wharton explained his understanding of the impasse. Pace wrote,

> He [Wharton] said we now had a perfect right to elect our own Colonel, and that no one had the right to assume command.... He also added that we were a separate corps from all other soldiers in the service. He then suggested that one of us should return to Council Bluffs and inform our President of our situation, and return to the command as soon as possible.[2]

The messenger that Major Wharton sent to Brigham Young at the Camps of Israel was Pace himself. After three long days at a quick step, Pace arrived on August 26 and informed Young of Allen's death. Now came one of the most curious requests in American military history. Pace was carrying a letter from Lieutenant Smith, written the day Allen died, requesting the opportunity to command the battalion. "President Brigham Young: Sir—It is with the deepest regret that I have to inform you of the death of Lieutenant Colonel James Allen.... If it is the wish of your people that I should take charge of the battalion, and conduct it to General Kearney, I will do it with pleasure and feel proud of the command." Then Smith included an interesting comment that he could not later fulfill: "[I] will use my best endeavors to see all orders and promises heretofore given, carried into execution... Your obt. Servant, A. J. Smith."[3] Young answered Smith's request in two letters by quoting Allen's promise to him, that "on the subject of command we can only say Col. Allen settled that matter at

---

[2]Tyler, *A Concise History*, 151.   [3]Ibid., 154.

A CHANGE IN COMMAND

the organization of the Battalion," and with "Consequently the Command must devolve to Captain Jefferson Hunt."[4] Commenting on the change of command problem in the Mormon Battalion, historian Bernard DeVoto wrote,

> the prophet had acknowledged him [Allen] as commander of the expedition, which deputized him in the authority of the priesthood, the succession of which was broken by his death. The prime source of the trouble his successors experienced was the fact that they held commissions only from James K. Polk, not from Brigham Young.[5]

It is inconceivable that military authorities should have to consult a religious leader, or any private citizen, on military matters, especially on the question of a change in command of a combat unit during war. Wharton's answer, of course, was that he recognized that the battalion was a "separate" and unique unit, but that should not have mattered. Once the battalion was mustered, it should have operated as any other unit in military service, especially in the field during war. Brigham Young's purpose all along was for the battalion to benefit the church; its service to the nation was secondary at best, though it was important to him to prove that the Saints were loyal to the United States to some degree. He prophesied that the battalion would not see combat, so its military service was unimportant to him. Young saw the battalion as pioneers and settlers for the church, not as soldiers. He considered the entire affair a call of service from God, not a patriotic venture or a call to duty during war. Of course, the men echoed this sentiment and felt the same way.

The official dispatch notifying the War Department of Allen's untimely death was written by Lieutenant Smith. On August 25 Smith wrote a dispatch addressed to brevet Brigadier General Roger Jones, the adjutant general, just before Smith arrived at the battalion's camp at Council Grove. In the nineteenth-century army, all official correspondence from commanders, officers, military bureaus, and other government officials was addressed to the adjutant general, who would forward the message as necessary. Smith wrote,

---

[4]Ibid., 155–156.   [5]DeVoto, *Year of Decision*, 322.

I was requested by Lt Col Allen of the Mormon Battalion, a few days before his death, to take charge of & select such papers as were directed to the Adj. Genl. US A[rmy] & forward them to Washington.... The Battalion left the Fort a few days before the death of Lt. Col. Allen & are now encamped at Council Grove.... I am now on my way to report to Genl. Kearny.... I will therefore with the consent of the Mormons, take charge of the Battalion at Council Grove & conduct it to Genl. Kearny.... As no officer [regular army officer] has been assigned to the command of the Battallion I am in hopes that my course will be approved by the [War] department.[6]

When the War Department learned of Lieutenant Colonel Allen's death, officials in Washington, D.C., selected another officer, Captain Philip R. Thompson, stationed at Jefferson Barracks near St. Louis, to take command of the battalion. Thompson was an 1835 graduate of West Point, commissioned in the 1st Dragoons, and had just been promoted to captain in June 1846. Fate would have it that Captain Thompson would never overtake the battalion.[7] He would, however, receive his battle laurels serving as a regular army advisor to Colonel Alexander Doniphan, and earned a brevet promotion for valor at the battles of Brazito and Sacramento.[8]

There was a notation on the back cover of Smith's letter to the adjutant general, "It appears from the letter that Lt. Smith had undertaken this only Lt. S. has not sufficient rank to command the Mormons, but he can take charge of them very well until overtaken by Capt Thompson."[9] One can only assume that the writing was that of Brigadier General Jones, or at his direction. Thus, the War Department felt that Smith was not experienced or high enough in rank to command the battalion, which was not necessarily a condemnation of Smith as an officer.

The Mormon men have written much about Lieutenant Smith

---

[6]Andrew Jackson Smith to Roger Jones, August 25, 1846, Camp near Fort Leavenworth, National Archives; copy on microfilm, Utah State Historical Society.
[7]DeVoto named this officer Captain Jacob Thompson, whereas Joseph Dawson has the correct name: Philip R. Thompson. See DeVoto, *Year of Decision*, 322; Dawson, *Doniphan's Epic March*, 103–4.
[8]Heitman, *Historical Register and Dictionary of the United States Army*, 1: 957; Dawson, *Doniphan's Epic March*, 226.
[9]Andrew Jackson Smith to Roger Jones, August 25, 1846, Utah State Historical Society.

as a virtual tyrant and brutal officer. As mentioned earlier, in an era when the typical frontier army officer was a rigid disciplinarian in an extremely dangerous profession, Smith was no more severe than his peers.[10]

By all accounts Smith was an outstanding officer and does not deserve the severe treatment that many journals and diaries recount and, hence, some histories amplify. Born and raised in Pennsylvania, Smith graduated in 1838 from West Point, then joined Kearny on the frontier, serving in many antebellum campaigns or expeditions. After the Civil War, Smith assumed command of the newly organized 7th U.S. Cavalry with young George Armstrong Custer as his lieutenant colonel. Smith retired as a colonel of cavalry in 1869 and became head postmaster in St. Louis. Andrew Jackson Smith's father, Samuel Smith, a veteran of the Revolutionary War, named him in honor of the hero of the Battle of New Orleans, General Andrew Jackson, since Smith was born soon after the battle in 1815.[11]

President Young sent Lieutenant Pace on to Santa Fe with his reply that Captain Hunt must take command. Accompanying Pace were two notable Mormon frontiersmen and pioneers: John D. Lee and Howard Egan. Lee would later etch his own name into the annals of the American West surrounding events at Mountain

---

[10]Aside from the numerous comments in the journals and diaries recorded by the men about Lieutenant Smith, there are a few derisive comments by later historians. Daniel Tyler wrote, "It would have been difficult to select the same number of American citizens from any other community who would have submitted to the tyranny and abuse that the Battalion did from Smith and Sanderson"; see Tyler, *A Concise History*, 147. Russell C. Rich wrote, "the battalion were not acquainted with his [Smith's] character; nevertheless the choice for him to lead them was of their own doing. It was the privates, however, who suffered the most under his rather tyrannical command"; see Russell C. Rich, *Ensign to the Nations: A History of the LDS Church from 1846 to 1972*, 68.

[11]During the Civil War, A. J. Smith took a commission in the volunteer service, commanding cavalry and infantry brigades and divisions, then finally commanding a corps under Generals Grant and Sherman. He fought in the battles of Corinth, Vicksburg, Nashville, and several other major campaigns. In July 1864, Smith defeated Confederate General Nathan Bedford Forrest at the Battle of Tupelo, which was no small military task. Also in 1864, Smith, commanding a separate corps of about fifteen thousand troops, fought against Confederate General Sterling Price during Price's sweeping statewide raid, which failed to bring Missouri into the Confederacy. Gardner, "Command and Staff of the Mormon Battalion," 346–47; Faust, ed., *Historical Times Illustrated Encyclopedia of the Civil War*, 694.

Meadows in southern Utah. These two would serve as agents for the church to collect more pay at Santa Fe and return it to the church. With little fanfare the trio departed.

Out on the plains of Kansas the battalion remained at Council Grove, the first major stop along the Santa Fe Trail, to await guidance. With the news of Allen's death on August 26, they also learned that a regular army officer, Smith, was en route to take command. This development caused considerable consternation among the officers and men. They knew full well of Allen's promise to Young and the church that should Allen be unable to serve as battalion commander, then Captain Hunt would take command. With this situation in mind, Hunt called a council of officers and laid the matter before them. They discussed the issue at length, and then recommended that a "committee" be appointed to research the legal and proper military procedures relating to a change of command decision. At Council Grove, the committee reported that by military law, it was Captain Hunt's right to command. This is a very curious episode, because one would wonder how the research was conducted. None of these men had any military experience. Though they had had the Articles of War read to them, they were probably still unfamiliar with them and any other established code of military conduct. (It is doubtful that they even carried the official volumes of the Articles of War. Colonel Allen probably had a copy in his baggage, which, of course, would have remained behind with him.) They came to the decision from a democratic, quasi-religious, and common-sense perspective: Colonel Allen had made a promise to Brigham Young that Hunt should command, and that was that.[12]

This is another very curious aspect concerning the unmilitary nature and conduct of the Mormon Battalion. For a committee to research and approve a change of command appointment and to

---

[12]Jefferson Hunt to Brigham Young, Santa Fe, October 17, 1846, LDS Archives; see also Udall, *Captain Jefferson Hunt of the Mormon Battalion*, 69.

A CHANGE IN COMMAND 177

then have a council of officers decide the matter is foreign to military practice and procedure. It is true that a commander may defer a matter to his staff for their "recommendation" and approval, but the army does not operate by committee and make decisions by consensus-building. Often a senior officer may call his subordinate leaders together for their advice and input, but the final decision and responsibility always lies with the senior officer.

The root of the problem was that the officers and men of the Mormon Battalion had no experience or knowledge of the profession of arms. They relied more on their religious experience to settle matters. Also, the democratic process, committee organization, individual rights, independent action, and casting of votes are all intrinsic to American character and were a deeply held value during the early republic, especially on the frontier. So, as Mormons, they were extremely obedient to church directives and pronouncements; as Americans they were democratic and individualistic enough to appreciate group decisions.

On the hot and sultry afternoon of August 29, 1846, First Lieutenant Andrew Jackson Smith, Dr. George B. Sanderson (after having overtaken Major Jeremiah H. Cloud), and other troops of the Army of the West, and arrived at camp. According to Dr. Sanderson, "At Council Grove arrived there about one oclock found them apparently glad to see me. Myself and Lt. Smith held a council." Smith met with the volunteer officers of the Mormon Battalion and announced his desire to take command. One of the points he presented was that as a regular army officer, he was schooled in the proper procedures for the procurement of provisions, requisitions, manning rosters, pay and allowances, drill, tactics, and training. These were all strong points to consider, especially since the men were probably very concerned about rations and supplies, as most soldiers would be. Smith also explained that he was an experienced frontier officer. He had traveled the same route just the year before during Kearny's reconnaissance to South Pass and back along the Santa Fe Trail to Fort Leavenworth. These were all important and strong considerations.

Dr. Sanderson wrote, "Some of the [Mormon] officers appeared willing   others opposed."[13]

Some stood forth to recommend that Lieutenant Smith take command. The most prominent was Major Jeremiah Cloud of the paymaster department.[14] He supported Smith's proposal that a regular army officer was more able to complete the necessary requisitions for supplies, rations, and the muster rolls. Major Cloud probably exaggerated the importance of having a regular army officer to process supply requests. The battalion was a volunteer unit in the Army of the West, and the commissary, quartermaster, and other logistical officers of the Army would not allow it to go unsupplied. Perhaps with Smith in command, the task would be easier, but it was certainly not impossible without him. "But after some time deliberating and councelling," recorded Dr. Sanderson, "they offered the command to Lt. Smith of 1st Dragoons."[15]

But would the Mormon volunteer officers agree to it? Upon Smith's arrival several Mormon officers immediately accepted him; one of these was Lieutenant Dykes, the battalion adjutant. Captain Hunt asked Smith if, as the commander, he would accept the promises and conditions that Allen had accepted. Smith agreed. Hunt then discussed the change of command in an esoteric discussion with only the other Mormon officers. Using a simple democratic "town-hall" parliamentary formality, Captain Higgins moved and Captain Davis seconded that Smith take command. Hunt, the senior Mormon volunteer officer, affirmed also, and the decision was made. They then approached Smith with their deci-

---

[13] George B. Sanderson, Journal, August 29, 1846, 3, University of Utah Library.

[14] There is little information on Major Jeremiah H. Cloud, Paymaster Department. Cloud hailed from Tennessee and was appointed as a paymaster of volunteers on July 2, 1846. He undoubtedly was en route to California and was traveling with the Mormon Battalion for protection and convenience. Daniel Tyler wrote that Major Cloud was a regular army officer, which is incorrect; see Tyler, *A Concise History*, 368. He was not a member of the Mormon Battalion and not listed on the battalion staff. See Gardner, "The Command and Staff of the Mormon Battalion during the Mexican War." Major Cloud died on August 4, 1847. See Heitman, *Historical Register and Dictionary of the United States Army*, 1: 311. For a discussion of the permanent commissions and staff departments, see Utley, *Frontiersmen in Blue: The United States Army and the Indian, 1848–1865*, 49.

[15] George B. Sanderson, Journal, August 29, 1846, 3, University of Utah Library.

A CHANGE IN COMMAND 179

sion that he would assume command the next day, August 30. Several officers, however, demurred and were hostile to Smith's assumption of command.[16]

Smith's intention was to take command of the battalion, lead it to Santa Fe, and report to General Kearny. Whatever means he used to convince the Mormon officers otherwise were, in fact, ploys. He also realized that he needed to gain their approval because of their unique status in the volunteer service. This is not to say that "AJ" Smith was a dishonest or dishonorable officer and man; he merely entered a game of chance and used his best cards to win the hand and achieve his goal. He was indeed more qualified to take command than the Mormon officers and had the experience and knowledge to lead it to Santa Fe.

One problem was that the Mormon officers had not obtained their "commissions," a signed certificate of status, rank, and date. Without their commissions signed by either a governor or by President Polk, they had no official standing. Captain Hunt, aware of this official short-coming, later wrote to Brigham Young: "inasmuch as we had neither commissions nor certificates that we were officers," there was not much the Mormon officers could do to validate their actual authority.[17]

There was also the unsubstantiated rumor that if Smith did not assume command, then Colonel Sterling Price of the 2nd Missouri Mounted Volunteers would attach the battalion to his regiment.[18] This was as improbable as it was highly unlikely. One of the last things Price would want was to attach a dismounted battalion, especially five hundred Mormons, to his mounted regiment, thus slowing his march. As with many episodes in the Mormon Battalion drama, at times rumors seemed to rule.

In strict military protocol and procedures, Smith's assumption of command can only be viewed as temporary, or in an "acting" capacity. The key element that was missing was orders. Written orders were preferable, but verbal orders could be binding for an unusual

---

[16]Yurtinus, "A Ram in the Thicket," 105–6.
[17]Jefferson Hunt to Brigham Young, October 17, 1846, LDS Archives.

circumstance or a very brief period. Smith had neither. He was not acting under any authority whatsoever, though Major Wharton at Fort Leavenworth was aware of his actions, and his request was en route to Washington. An officer does not take command without orders. There were only two permanent commanders of the Mormon Battalion, Lieutenant Colonels James Allen and Philip St. George Cooke. The others, namely Hunt and Smith, were all temporary or acting commanders.

In a letter to Brigham Young from Santa Fe, Captain Hunt explained the situation, the decision, and the consequences of the change of command in great detail. "Now the question was," wrote Hunt, "whether I should go ahead as I had done" or relinquish command to Smith, "for there appeared to be some division [among the officers] in the matter." Hunt then mentioned the review of military law by Dykes and Hunter. Upon Smith's arrival, Hunt wrote, "I was made acquainted with him. He soon told me he desired to lead the battalion to Santa Fe, and referred to the benefits we should receive from having a United States officer at our head. I told him it might or it might not be so, but for myself I was willing to risk marching the Battalion myself to Gen. Kearney." Hunt then recalled all the items previously mentioned by Colonel Price desiring control of the battalion: the requisition forms and orders necessary for supplies, keeping Allen's promises, Major Cloud (he wrote the name Walker, for some reason), the paymaster's speech, and the Mormon officers' private council. Thus, Hunt ended, "The matter was talked over . . . that Lieut. Smith should lead us to Santa Fe. . . . Smith was apprised of this and took command the next morning." Hunt obviously knew that he was going against counsel of the prophet-to-be, and that he needed to explain himself as soon as possible.[19]

The unknown problem that the battalion officers, both regular and volunteer, soon faced was that the men felt betrayed by Smith's assumption of command. Corporal Daniel Tyler captured the

---

[18]Ibid.; also in Udall, *Captain Jefferson Hunt of the Mormon Battalion*, 69–70.
[19]Udall, *Captain Jefferson Hunt of the Mormon Battalion*, 69–70; Bagley and Bigler, *Army of Israel: Mormon Battalion Narratives*, 99–101.

extreme emotion and sense of betrayal that some felt: "When the command was given to Lieutenant Smith, the soldiers were not consulted. This caused ill feelings between them and the officers that many hold to this day." Of course, Tyler was one of the principals to hold a grudge over several decades. The enlisted men thought that they should have had a say in the change of command. Tyler was accurate in one aspect: "The appointment of Smith, even before his character was known, caused a greater gloom throughout the command than the death of Colonel Allen had."[20]

Thus, the infamous dual nemeses of the Mormon Battalion, Smith and Sanderson, began their experience with the Mormon soldiers. They gained so much infamy that legend and myth, and not the facts, often rule to the present.

Smith's assumption of command was the most difficult challenge from a leadership perspective that the battalion experienced during its year of service. The men were military novices and unaccustomed to military life. Colonel Allen had the uncanny ability to be both a kind and benevolent man while still being a tough frontier officer. "They lamented the death of Col. Allen very much," wrote Dr. Sanderson during his first day with the Mormons. "A eulogy or sermon was this day delivered by one" of the Saints.[21] Smith would make mistakes because he did not understand the nature of the Mormon soldiers and the basis of their unique enlistment. It was probably his first experience with volunteers, and both parties suffered because of it.

By the end of August the battalion was once again on its way to Santa Fe. It was crossing some of the most beautiful and bounteous land in America: the green rolling hills of east-central Kansas, with picturesque scenes of small, scattered forests, valleys with shimmering streams of fresh water, tall luxurious prairie grass, and abundant game. With all its entrancing beauty and scenery, the trail was also

---
[20]Tyler, *A Concise History*, 144.
[21]George B. Sanderson, Journal, August 29, 1846, 3, University of Utah Library.

entering Indian lands and the possibility of danger increased, causing some anxiety. The Indian removal policies of the earlier decades had given the lands west of the state of Missouri to the displaced eastern woodland tribes, along with the indigenous tribes. Comanches were probably the most feared Indian nation at the time. Smith ordered that each company have a detail of six soldiers with loaded muskets serving as advance and flank security during the march and as sentinels at night. It was a common march practice to not have muskets loaded unless contact with the enemy was likely. Only scouts, flankers, and skirmishers had loaded muskets.

One of Lieutenant Smith's first actions was to fill out the routine monthly muster roll of the battalion. On August 31, 1846, he listed 21 officers and 475 enlisted men.[22] As they continued, Smith began to take stock of the fitness and effectiveness of his temporary command. With his experienced eye, he realized there were many improvements to make. The battalion was not alone under Lieutenant Smith's command as they followed the Santa Fe Trail. "Our Command now consists of the following Mormon Battalion five companies rank and file ordinance train and provision train with company. Baggage waggons. Amounts to over fifty[wagons]. Beef cattle about one hundred and eighty," recorded Dr. Sanderson.[23] Groups, families, and commercial enterprises often traveled as caravans along the trail for protection and assistance. It is also true with military units on campaign.

Smith must have been immediately struck by the many extra baggage wagons and private vehicles, as well as the many lingering invalid men, real or imagined. In all likelihood, the dozens of women and children, camp followers, must have troubled him. Within days he took steps to improve the camp and march discipline.

One of the first measures Smith made was to get the sick and lame not accounted for on the sick list out of the wagons and given proper medical care through official means. He learned that many

---
[22] A. J. Smith return for August 1846, Mormon Battalion, Muster Rolls, National Archives.
[23] George B. Sanderson, Journal, August 31, 1846, 4, University of Utah Library.

A CHANGE IN COMMAND

of the men were avoiding sick call and simply riding on wagons because they were too sick to march. Many men were indeed very ill from "the ague"—malaria and fevers; several were nearly incapacitated from dysentery or other maladies. He instructed Dr. Sanderson to make a medical examination of the weak and infirm.

Dr. Sanderson began examining the sick men and treating them. It is interesting that even Sanderson had solicited Brigham Young's approval in a letter, saying, "everything that I have in my power shall be extended to them [the soldiers] for their comfort."[24] Yet Sanderson would become the victim, as was Smith, of Mormon malice and myth for generations. "I attended sick call this being the first morning it ever sounded in this camp," recalled Sanderson, "about fifty men reported themselves sick. but on this matter I doubted their judgement, and I thought some eight or ten out of that number was indisposed from eating quantities of grapes, peanuts, etc."[25] Thus, according to proper military and camp procedure, Lieutenant Smith and Dr. Sanderson began the routine process of sick call in the morning to ascertain the physical wellbeing of the men, which Captain Hunt had not been performing. This routine procedure, used by all armies for most of recorded history, soon aggravated the men.

On September 3, a noteworthy incident that took place over this sick call problem began the troubles between Smith, Sanderson, and the Mormon volunteers. It was one of many incidents resulting in a conflict between ecclesiastical and military authority. Smith approached one of the privately owned wagons, so the story goes, and ordered several sick men in the wagon out: "Damn them, pull them out!" he shouted. Asking whether they had first sought medical attention from Dr. Sanderson, the men answered that they had not. Smith apparently directed most of his rage at Private Albert Dunham of B Company. Dunham added that he had taken herbal medicine provided by Dr. William McIntire, the assistant surgeon and a Latter-day Saint. They announced that they "would

---

[24]Tyler, *A Concise History*, 153.
[25]George B. Sanderson, Journal, August 31, 1846, 3, University of Utah Library.

leave their bones to bleach on the prairies" before they would take medicine from Sanderson.[26] Infuriated, Smith then threatened to tie a rope around Dunham's neck and drag him behind a wagon for a day if this occurred again. Smith bellowed that he would "cut the throat" of any man who refused medical treatment from the proper authority.

The incredible part of this story comes from Daniel Tyler. One has to accept this narration as apocryphal because the reality of this episode is an obvious absurdity. Tyler maintains that Sergeant Thomas Williams of D Company owned the wagon in question. Smith began his tirade and pulled out his sword (saber) and threatened "to run Williams through if he attempted to allow any more sick to ride in the wagon without his permission."[27] Then, according to Tyler, "Williams braced himself, grasped the small end of his loaded whip and told him if he [Smith] dared to make one move to strike he would level him to the ground."[28] Smith then relented and only inquired as to the sergeant's name. Tyler then related that Smith would respectfully salute Sergeant Williams in future encounters.[29]

This story is just one of Tyler's many fanciful dramas portrayed in his classic but sometimes questionable book published in 1881. Historian John Yurtinus, in his well-researched and documented "A Ram in the Thicket," does not even mention the episode. Some other writers of more recent histories on the battalion simply repeat this episode without questioning the veracity of the event. Yurtinus, however, wrote this in reference to Tyler's scholarship: "Much of this bias against Smith and Sanderson is because Tyler in particular presents a very negative and unsympathetic picture, joining Levi Hancock, David Pettegrew, William Hyde, and others who demanded strict religious obedience. They were often in conflict with Lieutenant Smith, Captain Hunt, Adjutant [Lieutenant] Dykes, and others who generally followed military necessity. Tyler's book reflects his prejudice in this conflict."[30]

---

[26] Bigler, "Extracts from the Journal of Henry W. Bigler," 38.
[27] Tyler, *A Concise History*, 145. [28] Ibid.
[29] Ibid. [30] Yurtinus, "A Ram in the Thicket," 125 n.58.

A CHANGE IN COMMAND

It is incredible that an NCO would deliberately face down an experienced, frontier regular army officer on campaign during war and not be punished. It is almost as unbelievable to think that Smith would draw his saber, but perhaps he did. There are accounts in the frontier and Civil War periods of officers striking men with the flat of their sabers or a riding crop, or threatening instant death by saber or pistol, and in some extreme examples actually carrying out the threat. Though rare, officers sometimes used these methods to motivate their soldiers. Battalion records document on several occasions where men were punished for minor infractions and misdeeds, whether under Smith or later under Cooke. In California, Private John Borrowman was court-martialed on February 26, 1847, for sleeping on guard duty. He received six days' confinement, a fine, and extra duty. At other times, men were tied behind wagons and forced to walk all day for trivial infractions. Even officers, as we will see, would receive stringent punishments for what today would be considered minor offenses.

That Williams owned the wagon and, therefore, had the right to use it as he saw fit is immaterial. He was a soldier and subject to military law and justice. The fact that he purchased a wagon along with others to haul additional baggage was a privilege granted by the commander. Smith could, under the Articles of War, confiscate the property or leave it on the plains of Kansas with little or no recourse from Williams. Smith did none of this. He merely chastised Dunham and Williams for usurping proper military procedures.

Later that evening Smith called all the "orderly" sergeants together and ordered that all sick report to Dr. Sanderson or they would not be allowed to ride in the wagons. They were also to account for their men correctly and truthfully on the company morning reports or daily roll calls. Smith boldly asserted his determination that the battalion would follow established procedure.[31] Over the next several days, some of the sergeants tried to explain to

---

[31] William Hyde, Journal, September 3, 1846, Brigham Young University. Hyde does not record anything about Sergeant Williams and this episode.

Lieutenant Smith that the men wanted to be loyal, but the problem with taking the medicine was based upon their religious faith. On one occasion Smith turned to the adjutant, Lieutenant Dykes, who answered, "that there were no such religious scruples and that the Church authorities themselves took such medicine."[32] This answer by Dykes was just one of many reasons that the men learned to hate this Mormon officer. Dykes's answer was correct in the fact that many church leaders, of course, used mineral medicines, but Brigham Young's most recent pronouncement and counsel to the men was also "a religious scruple" to be followed.

One of the problems Smith faced while serving as an acting commander of the Mormon Battalion was his complete ignorance of Mormonism. Whether Colonel James Allen had learned much about the Mormon faith in the camps in Iowa is doubtful, but he learned enough to earn their respect and support. As for Smith, he probably neither knew nor cared for the Mormons other than the fact that they were soldiers in war. The men obeyed his orders because they had little choice. Smith did not earn the men's respect as Allen had. There were two reasons for this: first, the manner in which he assumed command, and second, his tough, strict leadership style.

On September 5 the battalion camped at a location called Cow Creek, just west of present-day Lyons, Kansas. The Santa Fe Trail was the equivalent of a modern-day major highway and by the 1840s it was a busy and much-traveled route. "No one can form an idea of this road without they travel it. Imagine yourself on a fine turnpike road, and then you can have some idea of this road," wrote Dr. George Sanderson in his journal.[33] Nearly every feature of the landscape had been named, though some names were not too original. In the last few days the battalion had marched past Lost Springs, Diamond Springs, Cottonwood Creek, Running Turkey and Turkey Creeks, the Little Arkansas River, and Little Cow and Cow Creeks. As the men encamped they sighted their first buffalo on the plains.

---

[32]Tyler, *A Concise History*, 145.
[33]George B. Sanderson, Journal, September 1, 1846, 4, University of Utah Library.

A CHANGE IN COMMAND 187

The camp at Cow Creek was close to a significant American historical site, and they undoubtedly had no idea what happened there three hundred years earlier. In 1540, Father Juan de Padilla, a Franciscan missionary, accompanied the Spanish explorer Francisco Vásquez de Coronado during his search for the fabled Seven Cities of Cibola, or the "Seven Cities of Gold." Two years later, Indians known to the Spanish as Quiviras, probably the forefathers of Comanches, near this place attacked and killed Padilla. The land the battalion was crossing was one of inescapable history and heritage.[34]

---

[34] Kimball, *Historic Sites and Markers along the Mormon and Other Great Western Trails*, 195.

CHAPTER NINE

"Tyrants and Oppressors"

*I could scarce refrain from taking my Sword
in hand & riding them of such Tyrants.*
—*John Doyle Lee*

Day after day the Mormon Battalion continued its march across the south-central plains—the "Great American Desert" of U.S. Army explorer Major Stephen Long. Though hardly a desert when compared to other regions, it was nevertheless more arid than what most of the men had ever seen before. Yet there was a certain beauty and attraction to the region. The Cimarron Desert of western Kansas and northeastern New Mexico is actually some of the most scenic and beautiful land in the American West. As they continued, their course was on an obtuse angle from the Rocky Mountains. The eastern slope of the Rockies is a unique natural phenomenon where the gradually rising Great Plains meet the abrupt wall of the towering mountains. As guardians of the western alpine empire, the mountains loom over the low fertile plains, suggesting that trespassing through the granite and sandstone canyons was a perilous passage not to be attempted by the weak and timid.

The native peoples learned through generations to both live in the mountains and respect their rugged danger. Explorers, Spaniards, mountain men, and traders had for several generations traversed these mysterious and forbidding lands at great risk; some did not survive the passage. They gave names to some of the great formations they beheld: the Sangre de Cristo Mountains, Rabbit

Ear Buttes, and Raton Pass were just some of the natural wonders the Mormon soldiers saw from a distance. They crossed just south of the great canyon carved by the Purgatory River in southeast Colorado, though the men believed they were in purgatory themselves. They had left the green, humid climate of the eastern plains and were entering a dry and more desolate region. Dust blinded their eyes, the dry air parched their mouths, and the hot sand scorched their feet as they toiled along under the burning sun. It was like living in an oven.

Parched and exhausted, the men pushed on day after day. Many of the men were sick, sometimes they were hungry, and a few were dying, but the Mormon soldiers and their people pushed on and on, mile after tiresome mile. The camp routine became a mechanical drone of functions: rising, cooking, eating, striking camp, marching, encamping, standing guard duty, and surviving. Some saw the wonder of the land they were crossing. Most saw only the dust and the sagebrush and wondered if Santa Fe and California would be any better. The sick suffered the most, and there was little relief for them. The brethren anointed and blessed each other with the sacred power of the priesthood, but the miracles did not come. The Great Jehovah seemed to have stayed his hand. The blessings of Brother Brigham were lost because of their infidelity in allowing a gentile to assume command when they had the opportunity to place a captain of Israel at their head. A Philistine physician was poisoning them slowly and methodically. Some of the men thought that they had been misled or betrayed. They were in the hands of "Oppressors & Tyrants."

The medical care in the Mormon Battalion has become an obsession in the many histories and receives more attention than it merits. Since so much is written about the topic and its great affect on the morale of the men, one must consider the military and medical qualities surrounding Dr. George Sanderson's practices and the commander's obligation to enforce them. Lieutenant Smith was being neither mean nor malicious in his desire to have the men receive medical treatment through proper authority. Despite all the stories in journals and other histories denouncing George B. Sanderson as "Dr. Death," Smith was simply following established procedure. One has to understand that sickness, disease, and medical service have been a major concern in all military operations from ancient times to the present. Until World War II, there were always more fatalities from disease and natural causes than from actual combat. In the Mexican War, 1,192 men died in battle with another 529 dying later from wounds—a total of 1,721 soldiers killed by enemy action. Yet, 11,155 men died from disease, accidents, or other natural reasons.[1]

To a seasoned veteran of the frontier, medical care was of paramount concern. Yet, because soldiers are not always honest about their actual health status and motivations, a commander had to be careful. Malingerers, slackers, and misfits often used the sick list as a means of shirking duty. Smith had seen this very abuse for years on the frontier. Experienced officers learned to trust their medical staff implicitly—they had to. He demanded that the men follow regulations, without which chaos would reign and the battalion could degenerate and lose much of its combat effectiveness. If the men refused proper and authorized medical care, then they would suffer the consequences and still have to perform their duties.

Dr. Sanderson, at age forty-six, was the ranking battalion surgeon and medical officer. Col. James Allen, the beloved first commander, appointed him. According to the journals and diaries of the Mormon soldiers, Dr. Sanderson was a hated Missourian and a vulgar and profane man. He hated Mormons, or at least professed to. On one occasion, according to Sergeant William Coray, Sanderson impatiently scolded Coray because the infirm were not able to come to sick call: "By God, you bring them here, I know my duty." It is tragic that a medical officer would allow such a terrible relationship to develop, but it did.[2] The men were also forbidden to

---
[1] Bauer, *The Mexican War: 1846–1848*, 397.
[2] William Coray, Journal, September 9, 1846, LDS Archives.

seek treatment from Dr. McIntire or use their own methods without first consulting Dr. Sanderson.

All these facts were not sufficient reason to avoid medical treatment, however. Sanderson's bedside manner gave the men little doubt that he was more of a quack than a physician. He usually prescribed a concoction of calomel and arsenic. Calomel, or mercury chloride, was a medicine used chiefly to deal with constipation, a condition that many doctors thought was a leading cause of abdominal, or stomach disorders.[3]

Some of the men created a clever way to receive the doctor's treatments, but not actually take the medicine, and then be exempt from duty. Private Zadock Judd of E Company described this comical situation: "After as light examination the doctor would give each one a nice little paper containing a dose of calomel. All were treated alike. They were told to take it with water before eating breakfast," but many would simply discard the contents. "[T]he doctor found out the men did not take calomel. After that they had to take it in his presence."[4] According to the men, Sanderson demanded they take the medicine immediately, cursing and castigating his patients. He forced the calomel down the men's throats himself using an "old rusty spoon" as the men claimed.[5] Word spread among the men of Sanderson's notorious methods and many of the sick soon avoided his treatment.

Some even looked upon Sanderson as the butt of jokes or humor. Sergeant William Hyde composed a little ditty about him:

> Our Doc, the wicked swearing fellow
> With Calomel thought to make us mellow
> The boys his poison spurned to take
> Which made him act his father, snake!
> He swore that damned his soul should be
> Or else a change of things he'd see
> To which our feelings did assent
> To have him damned were all content
> His negro boy he whipped outright
> For nought but just to vent his spite

---

[3] See Hall, *Medicine on the Santa Fe Trail*, 64.
[4] Zadock Judd, Autobiography, Utah State University.
[5] Tyler, *A Concise History*, 146.

> Because the sick had not obeyed
> He raved, and like a donkey brayed.
> My mind on him I'd like to free
> But as I'm placed I'll let him be
> Time will show his heart is rotten
> And sure his name will be forgotten.[6]

One of the main issues that caused a rift between Dr. Sanderson and his charges was the teachings of Brigham Young. The Mormon soldiers were faced with a dilemma of choosing between proper military procedure and religious observance. Young and others, namely Private David Pettegrew, Corporal Daniel Tyler, and Sergeants William Coray and William Hyde, protested Dr. Sanderson's methods. The issue was more of policy than personality. It was just one more instance that caused a conflict in the battalion.

Brigham Young had made it clear to the men that they should abstain from mineral medicines if they desired to have the blessing of good health. Church leaders gave their counsel to the men while back at Council Bluffs. In a letter that arrived some time after Dr. Sanderson began his treatments, Young declared, "if you are sick, live by faith, and let the surgeon's medicine alone if you want to live, using only such herbs and mild food as are at your disposal. If you give heed to this counsel, you will prosper; but if not, we cannot be responsible for the consequences."[7]

Coincidentally, this letter arrived on September 17, 1846, the day after Private Alva Phelps of E Company died of some type of congestive ailment. Phelps had for days refused to take Sanderson's concoction and when he finally did, he succumbed a few hours later. Corporal Tyler wrote, "Many boldly expressed the opinion that it was a case of premeditated murder."[8] Private Levi Hancock would later write that "if we obeyed Counsil not one man would die. But, Satan strove against the principle. There appeared to be exertion used in favor of the Devil's ruling altogether."[9]

---

[6]William Hyde, Journal, Brigham Young University Library, 24.
[7]Tyler, *A Concise History*, 146–47; see Wilcox, "The Imperfect Science: Brigham Young on Medical Doctors," 26–36; also, Divett, "Medicine and the Mormons: A Historical Perspective," 16–25.   [8]Tyler, *A Concise History*, 158.
[9]Levi Hancock, Journal, September 16, 1846, LDS Archives.

Why, against all reason, would Dr. Sanderson murder soldiers to whom he was charged to provide medical treatment? Why kill the men of one's own battalion? Was Sanderson's hatred of Mormons that obsessive? It goes against reason that Sanderson was so diabolical. But as A. J. Smith was condemned by the men of the battalion as a tyrant, when, in fact, he was a typical frontier officer, so Dr. Sanderson was a typical frontier doctor, more so than not. Bernard DeVoto wrote, "Sanderson appears to have been a good doctor as doctors went in that, the darkest age of American medicine, and Edwin Bryant [journalist and editor], whose judgement was excellent, spoke of his [Sanderson's] scientific attainments with great respect. But he had no faculty of command or persuasion."[10] Dr. Sanderson's most common medical treatment was based on an assessment of Mormon "malingering" more than illness. Whether Sanderson was qualified or not—whether he used the proper treatments or not—were not the problems. The trouble lay with the men's complete lack of faith in his motives and desire to care for the men. In this regard Sanderson failed. Thus, the antagonism brewed during the first weeks of September.

One of the leading medical authorities of the early nineteenth century was Dr. Benjamin Rush, a friend and colleague of Thomas Jefferson. Dr. Rush edited one of the first American medical volumes that advocated many of the treatments with calomel, quinine, and some sulfur-based drugs that physicians often used. Doctors who employed these practices, along with bloodletting or venesection, were referred to as depletists. "Many of the sick at western military posts and on such western trails as the Santa Fe were treated according to Rush's teachings in this book."[11] Yet, by the 1840s many leading medical experts began to dispel the theories of the depletists, and a slow reaction arose against these rather obsolete treatments. In 1844, Dr. John E. Cooke, brother of Captain Philip St. George Cooke, future commander of the Mormon Battalion, would lose his teaching position at the University of Louisville Medical School for advocating 240 grains of calomel in a daily

---

[10]DeVoto, *Year of Decision*, 325.   [11]Hall, *Medicine on the Santa Fe Trail*, 5–6.

dosage.[12] Historian James McCaffrey wrote concerning medical officers serving under General Taylor: "Doctors in Monterrey [Mexico] substituted sulfate of zinc and myrrh, sometimes accompanied by opium. When the sulfate of zinc also ran short, Dr. John B. Porter reluctantly treated his patients with arsenic."[13] Calomel was a basic medicine in a doctor's arsenal of drugs. "Dr. Nathaniel Chapman, a prominent civilian doctor and the first president of the American Medical Association, favored bleeding the patient every two or three days," wrote James McCaffrey. "Another staple treatment of these ailments was calomel, which Chapman regarded as indispensable."[14] Dr. Sanderson's methods, though now proven harmful and misguided, were typical for his day.

Yet George Sanderson's journal contradicts the impression that many have held for years. Aside from the negative accounts by many of the men about his treatments, one must remember that regardless of what any competent physician prescribed, if it differed from Young's counsel, then the men would have opposed it. The resulting comments and criticisms that circulated through camp would have destroyed the reputation of any medical professional. We now know Dr. Sanderson had a real human side, far different than the devilish "doctor death." Regardless, Sanderson continued to treat the men. On September 11, he recorded, "Our sick improving."[15] Dr. Sanderson saw the potential of the Mormon soldiers, "but I venture to predict when they once get under an officer properly appointed by Genl. Kearny things will be different."[16]

He was a shrewd judge of military matters for a non-professional soldier and recorded, "I must confess I have never seen just such a set of men together in my life. No discipline no subordination nor nothing else. They can be brought to the mark. This Battalion will cost the Government more money in proportion than any Corps they [United States] have, and if not mistaken will render less service." Continuing, Sanderson actually predicted one of the important

---

[12]Ibid., 8; as to the Cooke family, see DeVoto, *Year of Decision*, 238.
[13]McCaffrey, *Army of Manifest Destiny*, 60.   [14]Ibid., 60–61.
[15]George B. Sanderson, Journal, September 11, 1846, 7, University of Utah Library
[16]Ibid., September 29, 1846, 13.

accomplishments that the battalion provided later in California. "The only way or plan the Government can adopt to make them useful is to put them to work building Fortifications," which is exactly what the military did in Los Angeles—constructing Fort Moore.[17]

Throughout his entire journal, there is no criticism of his Mormon charges, no aspersions against any single man or soldier, no bias or prejudice against the Latter-day Saints and their religious faith. There seems to be a tone and sub-theme of understanding and tolerance that is surprising, even for an educated person of this era. On several occasions Dr. Sanderson wrote of the religious attitudes of the Mexican people and there was much familiarity with Roman Catholic observances, which leads one to believe that he was well acquainted with the Catholic Church or was a member himself. His observations are refreshing and poignant.

Interestingly enough, Dr. George Sanderson served with the Mormon Battalion during the entire march to the Pacific and most of its remaining service. He continued to give the men the same medical attention in California that he did on the plains of future Kansas in September 1846. But Sanderson nearly drops from the men's journals and diaries after October 1846. Some sort of modus vivendi may have occurred between him and the men. It would be a stretch to say that the men accepted the doctor; they probably learned to tolerate him.

George Sanderson also captured the rhythm and routine of the march, the heart of the Mormon Battalion story. His words, now revealed in his newly discovered journal, are a new and fresh window to the story.

※ ※ ※

The Mormon Battalion continued across the plains of modern Kansas, the extreme western end of the Oklahoma panhandle, the edge of future Colorado, and into New Mexico. The march was both grueling and exciting for the men. Sergeant Coray recorded that "Numerous herds of buffalow made the plains look quite

---

[17]Ibid., September 20, 1846, 10.

black, as the caravan passed many of our boys gave them chase and succeeded in killing a number."[18] Dr. Sanderson mentioned one of the first buffalo hunts by the men. "I saw during the day some thousands.... There was three killed.... It is a magnificent sight to see a Buffalo Bull die. They are remarkably tenacious of life. They appear to part with it very reluctantly."[19]

The beauty and pageantry of the Great Plains surrounded them as they journeyed on. Under Smith's leadership and direction, the men continued to settle into a camp and march routine. Private James Scott of E Company wrote of the highlights of the normal day crossing the plains to Santa Fe:

> nothing new. just go ahead seems to be the only word, no rest. March, March is the daily task. Day break brings Reveilee sick or well must go either to roll call or it's the Doctor. Next, boys!, get your breakfast, & strike your tents with all possible speed, then left, left all day over the road through dust, over hills, and across valleys, some 12, 13 & 18 miles. Halt, stack arms, pitch tents. run over all creation gathering Buffalo chips or little brush & getting water, draw rations, cook supper, etc; while this is going on, roll call comes on again. by this time the evening chores are finished dark is at hand, attend to evening duties, go to bed & sleep on the rough cold ground with only one blanket & a thin tent shelter from the cold.[20]

The many families and companions made the journey more pleasant for the married, accompanied men, but little is said or written by the other married, unaccompanied men. One cannot help but think that this situation caused perhaps a little envy or jealousy between them. Why should some soldiers have the bliss of marital companionship and families, while others, through no fault of their own, were denied this same benefit? This is one reason why bringing families on a military campaign was poor judgment and against military logic. The most troubling aspect was the distraction that dependent family members brought. It is natural for soldiers to think of family and home. "Have been troubled a good deal to day thinking about home," wrote Dr. Sanderson.[21]

---

[18] William Coray, Journal, September 7, 1846, LDS Archives.
[19] George B. Sanderson, Journal, September 8, 1846, University of Utah Library.
[20] James Scott, Journal, September 26, 1846, LDS Archives.
[21] George B. Sanderson, Journal, September 9, 1846, University of Utah Library.

By mid-September 1846 several important events had occurred in the Mormon Battalion. On September 12, they met some travelers coming up the Santa Fe Trail who turned out to be Latter-day Saints themselves. One was John Brown, the leader of a group of Latter-day Saints famous in Mormon history as the "Mississippi Saints." (This is not the abolitionist John Brown who raided Harpers Ferry, Virginia, in 1859.) These Saints had left their homeland in Mississippi in the early spring of 1846 with the understanding that they would join the main body of the Mormons along the trail west. They arrived at Fort Laramie, actually known as Fort John in 1846, far ahead of Brigham Young, who had decided to establish Winter Quarters on the Missouri. The Mississippi Saints, taking the recommendations of trappers, decided to winter at Fort Pueblo in modern-day Colorado. John Brown and a few companions were on their way home to Mississippi to lead other church members to Winter Quarters when they met the battalion.[22]

Another unique event, which has provided the Mormon Battalion with some national and international fame and inclusion in a major historical record, were the comments and observations of Francis Parkman, one of the great American historians of the nineteenth century. Parkman recorded on September 15 that the Mormon Battalion had encountered five companies of Colonel Sterling Price's 2nd Missouri Mounted Volunteers. Parkman described the large encampment along the Arkansas River:

> These were the Mormon Battalion in the service of the government, together with a considerable number of Missouri volunteers. The Mormons were to be paid off in California, and they were allowed to bring with them their families and property. There was something very striking in the half-military, half-patriarchal appearance of these armed fanatics, thus on their way with their wives and children, to found, it might be, a Mormon empire in California.

The fact that the Mormon Battalion appeared more as a group of pioneers than as a military formation did not escape the discerning eyes of Francis Parkman.[23]

---

[22]Allen and Leonard, *The Story of the Latter-day Saints*, 233–34.

[23]Francis Parkman, *The California and Oregon Trail: Being Sketches of Prairie and Rocky Mountain Life*; reprinted as *The Oregon Trail: Sketches of Prairie and Rocky-Mountain Life*, 402–3.

After making contact with Price's regiment, the Mormon Battalion delivered a load of ammunition that they had been hauling for the Missouri regiment. Price had a large quantity of provisions and supplies in his train, some of which the battalion needed to continue its march to Santa Fe. General Kearny had a few days earlier ordered Smith and the battalion to take the Cimarron route and bypass Bent's Fort.[24] Since Santa Fe was under American control, it was important for Kearny to assemble the entire Army of the West as soon as possible for his planned march to California. This decision, unfortunately, would mean that there would be no opportunity to rest, restock, and resupply the battalion at Bent's Fort, and unless other army provisions came along the trail, they would suffer immensely. Colonel Allen had sent a large amount of supplies forward to Bent's Fort, where he had intended to march. It was imperative to Smith and the battalion that they replenish their shortages.

Lieutenant Smith therefore requested some of the necessary provisions from Colonel Price, who refused. He was not about to provide food and supplies for Mormons, whom he hated. The Mormon presence must have revived emotions from the near–civil war in Missouri in 1838. Smith, therefore, demanded that Price surrender the necessary provisions immediately. Private Henry Bigler's version was that Smith intended to "let loose the Mormons and come down upon them [the Missourians] with his artillery."[25] Whatever the actual events, Price, a volunteer colonel, relented to Andrew Jackson Smith, a lieutenant in the regular army. This is a shining example of military leadership, where a junior officer would confront a senior officer to provide for his men. Fortunately for the Mormon Battalion, both regulars and volunteers looked upon even a regular army lieutenant as a superior to a volunteer colonel, and Smith was able to force the issue.

About this same time, Smith made an obvious and sound military decision for which he has been roundly criticized for over a century and a half. He decided to send some of the women and children

---

[24]Golder, *The March of the Mormon Battalion*, 161.
[25]Bigler, "Extracts from the Journal of Henry W. Bigler," 40.

with an escort of ten soldiers off to Pueblo under the command of Captain Nelson Higgins, commander of D Company. This action directly contradicted one of the conditions that Brigham Young had imposed upon Allen—that the battalion was not to be divided for any reason.[26] Private Levi Hancock, the presiding member of the priesthood, charged his fellow Mormon officers: "I wanted it distinkly understood that it did not agree with my feelings for it was told to us that we must hold together not to devide but it must be done they said and we must take the simerone [Cimarron] rout."[27] Lieutenant Dykes dismissed some of the men's attempts to hold a council on the matter: "there was no time for calling councils, and that President Young did not know our circumstances."[28]

Smith based his decision on a change of orders, the need to conserve valuable supplies, a march across difficult terrain, entering into possible enemy territory and hostile Indian domain, and the opportunity to unburden the battalion of many noncombatants—nine women and over thirty children.[29] It was sound, appropriate, logical, and the right thing to do militarily. It was not a tyrannical measure, but a decision involving vision, experience, leadership, and character. In fact, if he had sent off all of the women and children at this point, including the laundresses, it would have been much the better for operational ability of the battalion. However, it was one of the decisions that would breed contempt for Smith for decades to come. It was one of many such incidents that highlighted the conflicts between prudent military decisions and ecclesiastical authority.

Thus, Captain Higgins, along with an escort of ten soldiers, departed for Bent's Fort and eventually Fort Pueblo with orders to return to the command as soon as practicable.[30] The remaining

---

[26]Tyler, *A Concise History*, 157.
[27]Levi Hancock, Journal, September 15, 1846, LDS Archives.
[28]Tyler, *A Concise History*, 158.   [29]Ricketts, *The Mormon Battalion*, 233–34.
[30]Some sources have Privates John H. Tippets and Thomas Woolsey departing with the Higgins family detachment and joining the battalion later. Tippets did not serve under Higgins, whereas Woolsey overtook the battalion on November 4, 1846, south of Albuquerque. They both accompanied the Willis detachment in November and then made a harrowing winter journey to Winter Quarters. They also joined Brigham Young's pioneer company of 1847, and later helped guide the Mormons at Pueblo to the Great Basin; see Kimball and Knight, *111 Days to Zion*, 27, 43, 137.

noncombatants numbered more than twenty women and perhaps as many as eleven children, some of which included a few young boys or "aides" to the officers. It would be another month before most of the remaining children and most of the women would separate from the battalion.

Writing years later, historian and Mormon leader B. H. Roberts concluded, "Unquestionably, however, the arrangement was in the best interests both of the families and of the Battalion, and accordingly the detachment was made up as proposed, and marched to Pueblo under command of Captain Nelson Higgins."[31]

Nearly a thousand miles away, several hundred men and a few family members were defending themselves against a conglomeration of mob elements and various Illinois county militia who were driving the Mormons out of Nauvoo, their beautiful city. Earlier, Governor Thomas Ford had dispatched a force of ten men and an officer to prevent the depredations committed against the Mormons and citizens of Nauvoo. This squad was completely incapable of guarding a city of thousands against ubiquitous mob parties. Surprisingly, there were also dozens of "new citizens," non-Mormons who had recently purchased property from fleeing Saints at extremely low prices. These "gentiles" manned barricades of wagons, cotton bales, and crates in the streets along with their Mormon allies. The defenders were led primarily by Daniel H. Wells, an old-time settler of the region and recent convert to Mormonism. They also improvised by taking discarded steamboat funnels and making "cannon" out of them. Beginning around September 10, 1846, the "Battle of Nauvoo" was in reality a small affair, but some seven hundred or so armed attackers besieged some two to three hundred defenders for several days. A few were wounded from the attackers deploying a couple of old obsolete cannon and lobbing a few cannon balls down the near-deserted streets, at one time the scene of the energetic activity of a thriving midwestern Mississippi River city. A dozen or more defenders and attackers were wounded and a few others killed, but

---

[31]Roberts, *The Mormon Battalion: Its History and Achievements*, 30.

the battle fizzled eventually as the few remaining Latter-day Saints were forced to cross the river to Iowa by mid-day on September 17, 1846.[32]

The famous Cimarron route, later called a "cutoff"—a nineteenth-century term for shortcut—left the Arkansas River near present-day Ingalls, Kansas. It crossed some sixty miles of mostly dry, barren, and sandy plains until it reached the Cimarron River, hence the name. William Becknell, one of the early merchants and frontiersmen on the new Santa Fe Trail, first used the cutoff in 1822. Becknell made the crossing with pack mules, and it became known as the "dry route" because of the lack of water. The Spanish and Mexicans called it *Jornada del Muerte*: Journey of Death.[33] The battalion would cross through several more Jornada del Muerte passages during their march. (The Spanish were very liberal naming deserts or dry stretches with the most illustrative term possible.)

The cutoff would save the battalion approximately 160 miles in marching distance and perhaps seven to ten days.[34] Time was a critical factor on this march, especially with the battalion's slow rate encumbered with their ox-trains, heavy wagons, and many dependents. The route was sandy and difficult for the wagons and ponderous ox teams to negotiate at times. The ox was the basic source of power for immigrant and trade-good wagons of the early and mid-nineteenth century. Strong, powerful, sturdy, and reliable, the ox could subsist with little feed for some time and could eat some of the worst natural grasses and continue on. But oxen needed water and, like horses, could not survive very long without it. The ox was dependable, but so doggedly slow it is a wonder that the great treks of the West were ever finished. Plodding prodigiously along, even on a good road oxen could make only two miles an hour. Across difficult terrain the rate was worse, perhaps as slow as a mile or less an hour.

---

[32]Roberts, *A Comprehensive History of the Church*, 3: 11–17.

[33]Kimball, *Historical Sites Along the Mormon and Other Great Western Trails*, 199.

[34]It is 830 miles from Independence to Santa Fe via Bent's Fort, but only 660 miles using the Cimarron Cutoff.

"TYRANTS AND OPPRESSORS"

The ox was so essential to the overland caravans was due to its ability to pull the tremendous loads that emigrants and traders required, especially along the road to Santa Fe. The great Santa Fe Trail was not primarily an emigrant trail; it was foremost a commercial route where great caravans of merchandise and trading goods moved back and forth. The powerful oxen were sometimes hitched in four, six, or even ten yoke. A yoke was a pair, arranged together by the heavy hardwood shaped yoke attached to the wagon tongue. Therefore, four yoke of oxen was eight animals. The heavy Santa Fe trading wagons held anywhere from two and one half to five tons of goods. The vehicle itself weighed nearly a half-ton. The best configuration was a wagon with large wheels some six or seven feet in diameter that had huge hubs some eighteen inches in diameter and tires eight inches wide. These wheels were heavy, but their width helped balance the weight through soft sand.[35]

There was no standard military wagon during this era. Tables of organization and equipment allowed regiments a few supply and medical wagons, sometimes called ambulances. The army's logistical needs for extensive campaigns required contracts with civilian firms. These companies employed private wagons that consisted of many various types of freight or immigrant wagons. The vehicles used by the Mormon Battalion were a hodgepodge collection of a few government wagons, contract freight, and privately owned wagons. This proved to be a slight logistical problem because the teams were an assortment of oxen, mules, and horses, which cannot be hitched together. Thus, again the pioneer aspect of the Mormon Battalion was demonstrated in the variety and appearance of the wagon train.

The companies commenced the march across the Cimarron Desert and made fairly good time. Private Henry Standage, E Company, wrote of the desert:

> We traveled 25 miles this day across one of the most dreary deserts that ever man saw, suffering much from the intense heat of the sun and the for the want of water. . . . The teams also suffered much from the sand. I drank

---

[35]DeVoto, *Year of Decision*, 504 n.2.

some water today that the Buffaloes had wallowed in and could not be compared to anything else but Buffalo urine, as a great portion of it was of the same, yet we were glad to get this.[36]

Private Whitworth, a young Englishman, wrote, "We now have the cheering prospect of going 65 miles without water, except what we carry in our canteens, which do not hold more than a quart."[37]

A cloud of dust approaching from the east signaled the arrival of a party pursuing the battalion. After a fast and furious ride of only two weeks from St. Joseph, Missouri, three men drove up in a carriage pulled by a team of horses. Covered with prairie dust and grime were Lieutenant James Pace of E Company and Mormon stalwarts Howard Egan and John D. Lee, who arrived about midday on September 17 with a host of letters for the men, dispatches from the church officials, and the most recent news from the States. The men rejoiced to see their brethren, who were on an errand directly from Brigham Young to receive the men's salaries when they were paid at Santa Fe. Lee saw this task as a secret mission of great importance—secret because they did not want it known that they would be carrying a large amount of cash across the plains along a busy, but dangerous, frontier trail.

Already excited by the importance of starting the march across the Cimarron desert, the men rejoiced at the letters and news that just arrived. "An Express arrived from Fort Leavenworth. Of course every person was anxious to hear some from their wife's and children," wrote Dr. Sanderson, "others from their parents, and some their Sweethearts, and some disappointed not hearing from any body, and others having nobody to hear from." But the drudgery of the march began soon enough: "the mail was opened and each individual received his packages ... we started on our march crossing some of the worst sand hills I ever saw."[38]

Once joined with the battalion, Lee became angry when he

---

[36] Golder, *The March of the Mormon Battalion*, 165–66.
[37] Gracy and Rugeley, "From the Mississippi to the Pacific," 141.
[38] George B. Sanderson, Journal, September 17, 1846, University of Utah Library.

learned that Smith was in command against the direct, but belated, counsel of Brigham Young. John D. Lee immediately called for a halt of the battalion's march so he could confer with the lieutenant, the leading brethren, and the Mormon officers. The officers, of course, refused to make the halt. Lee then sought out Smith and informed him of his confidential mission to collect the men's pay and return it to the church without delay.

Lee pressed the military leaders for the men's expected pay, but Major Jeremiah Cloud, the volunteer paymaster, did not have sufficient funds to make the payments until they reached Santa Fe. Disappointed, Lee commenced causing minor disturbances along the march. Lee had invited Smith to ride in his carriage during the afternoon. He then proceeded to lecture Smith on the rate of march of thirteen miles a day the battalion should make, with the seventh day, or Sabbath being a day of rest.[39] Lee rebuked Smith for the medical care that the men had received at the hands of Dr. Sanderson and specifically addressed the death of Private Alva Phelps. Smith replied that he knew of no abuse of the men at the hands of the surgeon. Lee, in his self-righteous and self-appointed role as an emissary for Brigham Young, chastised Smith further: "When I came up with the Bat. & saw the suffering & oppression of these Soldiers my blood boiled in my veins to such an extent: that I could scarce refrain from taking my Sword in hand & riding them of such Tyrants [meaning Smith and Sanderson]."[40]

Witnessing Lee's actions, Coray recorded, "Lee overtook the Col. [Smith] & commenced at him rough shod, charged him with tyranny & oppression . . . he would cut their cursed throats for them."[41] Lee was out of control and out of mind. Smith, as a gentleman, simply walked away from the situation once the team stopped at a watering hole. Lee wrote of the incident in his journal: "I expected that he would have challenged me for a Duell but instead of that he never resented the first word." On September 20, Lee called for a meeting of the Mormon officers and other leaders at his camp. No one came.[42]

---

[39]Brooks, "Diary of the Mormon Battalion Mission: John D. Lee," 191. [40]Ibid., 192.
[41]William Coray, Journal, September 17, 1846, LDS Archives.
[42]Brooks, "Diary of the Mormon Battalion Mission: John D. Lee," 193.

Meanwhile, that same evening, Captain Hunt called a meeting at a different time and summoned Lee to it. Lee attended and made considerable demands and accusations against the Mormon officers. During this emotional meeting, Lee accused the Mormon officers of betraying their brethren, the church, and Brigham Young. They discussed the possibility of a general mutiny and replacing Smith with a Mormon commander. Hunt accused Lee of undermining his authority. Lee's presence and actions inflamed the men to rebellion: "bro Lee & Egan been stirring up the Bat to revault, that they had no right to council this Bat., that he [Lee] must be put down," said a disgusted Hunt. The situation became so bad that, at one point, Captain Hunt stood and rebuked Lee and threatened to place him under arrest if he did not cease. "The soldiers are now saying if we had a commander to stand up for our rights as Bro (Lee) does we would not suffer and be oppressed as we are."[43] Captain Jesse Hunter summarized the exchange: "Bro Lee has not as much right to be hurt as we have. He came here & assumed the right to dictate to this Bat. & even went so far as to light on our commander & seargon whom we have appointed."[44]

Hunt ended his remarks by saying, "No one has a right to council this but myself & my authority I will exercise in the Name of the Lord & no man shall take it from me."[45] Lee explained that he did not want to assume command of the battalion but had the men's welfare in mind. Some of the Mormon officers felt that Lee was not trying to assert himself over military authority.

Whether all the Mormon officers recognized it or not, Lee was trying to claim some type of authority through his dominating personality. Captains Hunt and Hunter realized it immediately. The military aspect here is that despite church errand or mission, self-righteous indignation or not, Lee had no business interfering with military matters. He was a civilian. With no warrant, commission, or appointment, Lee had no authority to question either Lieutenant Smith's or Captain Hunt's authority, especially in front of the men. Hunt and the others made the mistake of turning the

---

[43]Ibid., 198–99.   [44]Ibid., 198.   [45]Ibid.

issue into a public forum, even if it was just an esoteric exchange among the officers and the newcomers.

Captains Hunt and Hunter deserve some credit and praise for challenging Lee and the others. It is difficult in Mormondom to challenge the authority of those in some type of presiding or recognized position. Lee and Egan were representatives of Brigham Young and the church and therefore carried great weight. Though the captains were correct that Lee had no real authority over them, they were, nevertheless, treading on thin ice because word would certainly return to Brigham Young of the incident. It is for this reason that Hunt took some time at Santa Fe to compose a long epistle to President Young to explain his actions in regards to Lee. Hunt and Hunter were acting as army officers should.

One of the major problems the Mormon Battalion officers and men faced was that they did not know and understand their roles as soldiers in active service. The line between Mormon pioneer and American soldier was too thin in the battalion. Lieutenant Smith met with Lee as a messenger of Brigham Young. When the discussion turned to the criticism of military command policy and a personal attack, Smith excused himself as a gentleman—though he was within his rights to expel Lee from camp and refuse him access to the men, he did not. Hunt and the other Mormon officers felt duty-bound as Latter-day Saints to listen to Lee because he represented Brigham Young. When the meeting became a tirade against military authority, Captain Hunt tried to stop it. Unfortunately, the disease that Lee brought infected the troops and exacerbated the difficulties of the march they were already experiencing. A most serious morale and discipline situation fomented. Soldiers began to challenge the actions and intentions of their leaders.

On September 19, they reached Cimarron Springs, actually known as Wagon Bed Springs, where fifteen years earlier one of the greatest mountain men and fur trappers, Jedediah Strong Smith, died at the hands of Comanche warriors.[46]

The next day, they reached the Cimarron River, in present-day

---

[46] Hafen, *Mountain Men and Fur Traders of the Far West*, 106–7.

Kansas. The river was not really a river at all at this point in its course. It was a wide, dry wash-bed with occasional puddles and runs of water. The men had successfully crossed what was considered a desert of some sixty miles in four days. They would face much longer and more severe deserts in the months to come. For men who were raised in New England, the mid-Atlantic states, or England, the picturesque but austere and arid Southwest was different from any place they had beheld. It could bring both great pleasure and misery.

Crossing the plains and grasslands of Kansas had its human fascinations also. For a Missourian, Dr. Sanderson seems to have had a certain tolerance for the Saints and their religious nature. "I was somewhat amused to day passed two men seated on the grass," wrote the doctor on September 20, 1846, as they were following the Cimarron cutoff. "I thought they was devoutly engaged in prayer or some religious ceremony. Curiosity prompted me to ride up when lo and behold they were playing cards on the wild plains. I apologized for my intrusion and left them."[47]

General Zachary Taylor's army of some 6,640 soldiers arrived north of the 250-year-old city of Monterrey in the northern Mexican state of Nuevo Leon by mid-September 1846. For the first time Taylor was preparing to commit a combined force of regulars and volunteers into battle. Facing the Americans was General Pedro de Ampudía, a Cuban-born, forty-one-year-old governor of this northern state. Ampudía had numerical superiority of some 7,300 troops and the key positions of several dominating hills, fortified behind massive walls and armed with a mixture of large smoothbore siege guns and other assorted artillery. His soldiers, mostly impressed conscripts, manned the narrow streets of this densely populated city with men in nearly every house and on every rooftop. Every street was a narrow avenue that channelized forces into awaiting ambushes.

Taylor had excellent intelligence of the city and the enemy's disposi-

---
[47]George B. Sanderson, Journal, September 20, 1846, University of Utah Library.

tions, due mostly to the services of the Texas Rangers and their forward reconnaissance. Taylor decided to attempt a double envelopment of the city and squeeze the Mexicans to destruction or surrender by the converging pincers. He sent General William Worth and his division of regulars on a wide circling march to the west to attack the Mexican heights at Federación Hill and its dominating fort, El Soldado. Worth attacked the first hill-redoubt on September 21. Meanwhile, Taylor launched another attack from the east against some defensive positions on the eastern fringes of the city itself. The fighting soon fell into a mêlée of horrific urban warfare, with artillery duels at point-blank range as the Americans entered the built-up areas. Thinking that his army was doomed, Taylor ordered most of his forces back out of the city, where they had to again survive the withering Mexican fire through the streets. By the end of the day, Taylor lost 394 men in perhaps the most vicious fighting of the war.

While Taylor licked his wounds on the 22nd, Worth continued his attack on Independencia Hill, another strongly defended ridge. Surprisingly, Ampudía did little to either force his way out and save his army, or counterattack the bruised and battered American army.

On the 23rd Taylor attacked again, this time using his artillery more effectively. With the key outer fortifications taken, the Americans pressed through the city towards the Grand Plaza. The men fought from house to house, breaking through the adobe walls using axes, picks, crowbars, and bayonets. The fighting through the city continued and the streets became slaughter pens for the Americans—hundreds fell. With little ammunition remaining, Lieutenant U. S. Grant, 4th U.S. Infantry, volunteered to return for ammunition. He positioned himself on the flank of his horse away from the enemy and raced down the dangerous streets with one arm around the horse's neck and a leg draped over the saddle.

Worth, ignorant of the latest change of orders, attacked east from his position and basically caused the capitulation of Monterrey. Ampudía, demoralized and shaken, surrendered his exhausted and ruined army to the more exhausted American victors.[48]

Hundreds of miles away, General John Wool, commanding the Army

---

[48]Bauer, *The Mexican War*, 93–101.

of the Center, departed San Antonio, Texas, on September 23, launching his invasion of Chihuahua. He commanded a mixed force of a few regular companies and a large number of volunteers. Wool had a tremendous challenge before him. He would meet Taylor months later deep in the heart of Mexican territory and be on hand for the Battle of Buena Vista.

General Kearny left Santa Fe on September 25, for his march to California with six companies of the 1st Dragoons, some 300 men. Though Colonel Price's 2nd Missouri Mounted Volunteers and the Mormon Battalion were still en route, Kearny left Colonel Doniphan and his 1st Missouri behind at Santa Fe for occupation duty. He also assigned Doniphan the impossible mission of dealing with the elusive Navajo who had been raiding Mexican ranches and cattle herds. Kearny appointed Charles Bent, one of the Bent brothers who founded Bent's Fort, to serve as territorial governor. The campaign to secure New Mexico seemed complete; California was the next prize.

"The name of this river is Semiron," wrote William Coray on September 25, 1846, "because it means lost river in Spanish the reason of the Spaniards calling it so is because of its having no rise nor outlet. It frequently rises 18 inches within a few minutes and without any prospects of rain but the water sinks away in the sand."[49] Such narratives of strange and unusual wonders certainly caught the men's interest. The supreme law of the West is water. Without water there is no life. These men from the East would soon learn this lesson.

The men, especially the NCOs, continued to complain about Dr. Sanderson and his treatments. At various times Smith would call together the "orderly" sergeants, as they were often recorded in the journals, who were in fact, sergeants of the line. (The term orderly meant that their main responsibility that day was administrative duties.) Smith would reprimand them for inaccurate morning reports of the actual status of their platoons and companies. On September 23, Smith told the sergeants in so many words that if

---

[49]William Coray, Journal, September 25, 1846, LDS Archives.

Dr. Sanderson was found negligent in his duties and actually killed a soldier, Smith would hold Sanderson accountable for malfeasance.[50] Just a few days later, Smith again criticized the sergeants for their false reports as they continued to shield the sick men from the duty roster. Smith was also disgusted with the general lack of discipline and failure to follow orders and fulfill assigned duties by the officers and sergeants. Sergeant Coray explained, "the Col. [Smith] threatened to reduce me to the ranks for not communicating his orders to the Capt."[51] Dr. Sanderson observed about this time, "Considerable Sickness but not of a serious character. Lt Smith who commands the Battalion as his patience a good deal tried by the Mormons so very careless about everything."[52]

Though John D. Lee wrote wild and incredibly self-serving accounts in his famous journals, he also had a keen eye for detail and observation. As he accompanied the battalion, he wrote of the camp routine that Lieutenant Smith was trying to instill in this collection of untrained volunteers, especially the changing of the guard:

> 1st Guard mounting is beat at 7, at this call the guard is appointed together in Co's. 5m[minutes] from this call is beat the Adjutant call, when the Adjutant appears before the music [musicians] followed by the quick step march. At this call the several guards march to their posts on the left of the music in double files.... The officers of the guard is posted in the right of the front Rank & the Sergeant of the guard on the right of the rear rank who may be 2nd Lieut. The officer of the day may be the Capt or 1st Lieut & has command of the guard.[53]

When Lee was not writing prose for his journal and recording camp and military routine, he was fomenting rebellion. There was an actual attempt by some of the men to replace Captain Hunt as the senior Mormon officer and bypass the other senior Mormon officers to install Lieutenant Samuel Gully, then serving as battalion quartermaster, in Hunt's place. It is surprising that some of the prominent members of the battalion were actually involved in this

---

[50]Ibid., 284.   [51]William Coray, Journal, September 30, 1846, LDS Archives.
[52]George B. Sanderson, Journal, September 28, 1846, University of Utah Library.
[53]Brooks, "Diary of the Mormon Battalion Mission: John D. Lee," 281–82.

ludicrous episode, among them Lieutenants James Pace and Andrew Lytle, Sergeant William Hyde, and the presiding Mormon authority, Private Levi Hancock.[54]

The scheme failed because of lack of real support to follow through in such a serious and regrettable action. Some were very bitter about the attempt. Sergeant Coray wrote on September 28, "This evening I was informed that a secret influence was used against Capt. Hunt at the same time holding up S. E. Gully as the only fit man to lead this Battalion & that Lee was the head, assisted by [James] Pace, [Levi] Hancock, [Andrew] Lylte and William Hyde." How open this plot became is hard to determine. Few wrote about it. Sergeant Coray, however, concluded, "I must say that I could not suppress thoughts running through my mind but I can keep from writing them."[55] Whatever damage was done to the morale and discipline of the battalion by this incident is impossible to determine. One military principle is apparent. If Lieutenant Smith or Captain Hunt were aware of the matter, they should have banished Lee from the battalion or put him in irons under guard. Lee had clearly violated military law and good order by advocating mutiny. Though a civilian and not directly subject to the Articles of War, Smith would have been justified in taking such action. The punishment for the crime of mutiny for the officers and men of the battalion would have been much more severe—death.

By the end of September 1846, the battalion had passed into modern-day New Mexico. They were less than two hundred miles from Santa Fe and only some two weeks away. The animals were weak but enduring the strain. The climate, terrain, and march exacerbated the condition of the sick men, whereas the healthier men seemed to grow stronger and gain stamina as they progressed. This is one of the natural consequences of conditioning. On September 30, 1846, the battalion reached Carrizo Creek and camped. (Three and a half months later in California, they would encounter a dry wash with an occasional run of water named Carrizo River.) "To day has been one of the hardest marches we have had. On the

---

[54]William Coray, Journal, September 28, 1846, LDS Archives.   [55]Ibid.

men and animals," Dr. Sanderson logged in his journal the same day. "I never saw any thing present a more desolate and barren appearance than the country we have travelled over to day. Much wind and dust in such quantities as to produce almost suffocation. Some of our animals dropped dead and others where left by the road side to die. And what is left look miserable."[56]

On October 2, a soldier, Private William Alexander Follett of B Company, was heard to call Lieutenant Smith a "negro driver," a very derisive insult at the time. Sergeant Coray reported this incident to the commander, who placed Private Follett under arrest. What is striking about this seemingly insignificant story is that a fellow Mormon observed a discipline infraction and reported it to the commander. Sergeant Coray was no admirer of Smith, but he did his duty.[57] The earlier incident involving Sergeant Thomas Williams of D Company, who allegedly defied Smith when he attempted to force sick men from Williams' private wagon, comes to mind. If Smith would place a soldier under guard for making a disrespectful remark, which he did not hear, what would he have done regarding the earlier incident when a sergeant, entrusted with authority over other soldiers, supposedly openly challenged him in public with a whip? It is unthinkable that Smith would have allowed such a serious breach of discipline to go unpunished, when he readily punished much less serious incidents.

General Kearny and his three hundred mounted dragoons made camp at La Joya de Ciboletta, south of Albuquerque on the Rio Grande on the evening of October 2, 1846, when an express arrived from Santa Fe. Captain Philip St. George Cooke recorded an entry on this date in his journal that began one of the greatest leadership challenges and tests of endurance of his fifty-year service in the United States Army. "An express has arrived from Santa Fe; Colonel Price reports his arrival; he confirms the death of [Lieutenant] Colonel Allen of the Mormon Vol-

---
[56]George B. Sanderson, Journal, September 30, 1846, University of Utah Library.
[57]Brooks, "Diary of the Mormon Battalion Mission: John D. Lee," 288–92.

unteers. And now," Cooke wrote with little emotion, "at night, I have been selected to succeed him; which, of course, must turn my face to Santa Fe to-morrow. That is turning a very sharp corner indeed; it is very military; (but it is said to be a manoeuvre not unknown to another profession)."[58]

The glory that Cooke hoped for in Mexico or California was diminishing quickly. The newly conquered people of California were provoked to revolt to gain back their independence. With a small command Captain José María Flores surrounded Lieutenant Archibald Gillespie, U.S. Marine Corps, and his small garrison at Los Angeles and forced its surrender on September 29. A week later, Captain William Mervine, U.S. Navy, landed some four hundred sailors, volunteers, and Marines and marched from San Pedro to retake Los Angeles. He was confronted on October 8, 1846, by Flores and his dashing mounted compadres, who fired away at the dismounted Americans with a small cannon out of range of small-arms fire. When the Americans came close, the Californios would then lasso the cannon with a rope and drag it off to the next firing position. After four dead, ten wounded, and a useless chase across a hot and dry plain, an exasperated Mervine gave it up and determined there must be a better way to reconquer California.[59]

On October 3, the battalion crossed the Canadian or Red River and then reached Ocate Creek near present-day Wooton, New Mexico. Here Lieutenant Smith made perhaps the most important decision as acting commander of the Mormon Battalion. This decision would also have far-reaching and important consequences for a volunteer battalion during the Mexican War. An express dispatch of several dragoons arrived the day before from General Kearny, which he sent out just before he left Santa Fe. Kearny had anticipated the battalion's arrival at Santa Fe for some time. According to Captain Henry Smith Turner, Kearny's acting adjutant, the general thought that the battalion was not far behind the main body of the Army of the West. Writing on August 23, shortly

---

[58]Philip St. George Cooke, *The Conquest of New Mexico and California*, 78; hereafter, Cooke, *Conquest*.   [59]Eisenhower, *So Far from God*, 217–18.

"TYRANTS AND OPPRESSORS" 215

after their arrival in Santa Fe, Turner recorded "the time of starting to [California] depend somewhat upon the success of Captain Allen in raising a Mormon force (of which we know nothing yet) and his arrival here. We suppose him to be within three weeks' march of this place at present."[60] Unfortunately, Kearny's timetable was well behind schedule waiting for the Mormon Battalion. By the time Kearny was ready to leave, he determined to have the battalion discharged if they had not reached Santa Fe by October 10.[61]

Why was it so important to Kearny that the Mormon Battalion reach Santa Fe by October 10th? Kearny was anxious to continue on to California and fulfill the second phase of his campaign. President Polk had ordered Kearny to take California if practicable during 1846. He subdued Santa Fe quickly and more easily than expected. Now the season was growing late and it had been some time since there had been any direct communication from Washington. Kearny may have been concerned about whether his initial operational orders were still valid. Being an aggressive professional in the dark days of earthbound, slow-moving communications, he elected not to wait for a possible cancellation or postponement of his original directives. He would proceed on.[62]

The Mormon Battalion has been called General Kearny's strategic reserve.[63] What does this mean? Was Kearny's mission to take New Mexico and California strategic in nature in fulfilling the national war aims? Absolutely. The battalion was a strategic component of Kearny's operational plans for the invasion and occupation of both New Mexico and California. However, by definition it is difficult to suggest that a mere battalion was a strategic reserve. A strategic reserve, if there truly is such a thing, is something of such colossal power or force that it would tip the balance in a war, not just a campaign. Since the Mexican War was a limited conflict

---

[60]Clarke, *The Original Journals of Henry Smith Turner*, 143.
[61]William Coray, Journal, October 2, 1846, LDS Archives; Tyler, *A Concise History*, 163; William Hyde, Journal, October 3, 1846, Brigham Young University Library; Peterson, "Mormon Battalion Trail Guide," 18.   [62]Clarke, *Stephen Watts Kearny*, 160.
[63]Historian John Yurtinus wrote, "The Mormon Battalion was his [Kearny's] strategic reserve to be held for unexpected problems along the Pacific shore, therefore, Kearney [*sic*] intended to honor his pledge to transport them to new homes in California." Yurtinus, "A Ram in the Thicket," 182.

Second Lieutenant George Stoneman, regular army officer and newly graduated from the United States Military Academy when he joined the Mormon Battalion in October 1846. Shown here later as a Union brigadier general during the Civil War. *Massachusetts Commandery Military Order of the Loyal Legion and the U.S. Army Military History Institute.*

based on resources, the question of strategic reserves never came close to realization. It would be difficult to call anything a strategic reserve in a limited war. The battalion could be more properly referred to as simply a reserve or an operational reserve.

Kearny correctly realized that the battalion had to be near enough to use when necessary. He needed it as a supporting column to his small but very highly trained and experienced force of three hundred regulars of the 1st Dragoons. He had also directed that a mounted company of some eighty Missourians under Captain Thomas Hudson, called the "Laclede Rangers" from St. Louis, accompany the battalion to California. (Hudson's Rangers were unable to procure enough serviceable mounts for the march, so they remained at Santa Fe. Later they would serve under Colonel Doniphan during his march deep into Mexico.)[64]

Kearny had already ordered Colonel Doniphan and his 1st Missouri to Chihuahua to support General John Wool's Army of the Center. Price's 2nd Missouri would serve in New Mexico as an occupation force, along with all the other separate and non-regi-

---

[64]Kearny's Letter Book, 168; the Laclede Rangers were also called the California Rangers, then finally the Chihuahua Rangers. Dawson, *Doniphan's Epic March*, 106.

mental units. If the Mormon Battalion was several weeks behind, then it was useless to support him. He also desired that the battalion bring a supply train to support themselves along the way to California.[65]

There was, however, another extremely important reason for Kearny to have the battalion continue to California. It was based on the promise that the government made to the Mormon people to transport five hundred men to California (the many women and children were probably not part of Kearny's equation). This promise, of course, had no military consequences at all.

Now it was up to Lieutenant Smith to decide how he was going to get a slow-moving, undisciplined, untrained, and heavily burdened battalion of volunteer infantry to Santa Fe through some very difficult and forbidding terrain in just a week's time. The morning of October 3, they marched some six miles to Ocate Creek, where Smith ordered a halt to water the animals and for the men to eat breakfast. The teams were unhitched but kept in harness.

Smith realized that the battalion would never make Santa Fe by October 10 at its present rate of march. He held a commander's call to discuss the problem with the company commanders and the staff officers. Lieutenant Dykes recommended that the battalion be divided into two elements. Fifty of the healthiest and strongest men from each company, 250 total, including the battalion staff, would make a forced march for Santa Fe commencing that afternoon. They would take the best wagons and strongest teams. The remaining "inefficient" men, as they were called, and sick would follow with all the heavy wagons, provisions, and the remaining families. The company commanders would lead their companies in the main body. The rear detachment would be commanded by First Lieutenant George Oman of A Company. All the officers involved concurred with this plan. Smith then put it before all the other company-grade officers, and only four disagreed with the decision: Lieutenants James Pace, Samuel Gully, Andrew Lytle and Lorenzo Clark.[66]

---

[65]Clarke, *Stephen Watts Kearny*, 160–61; Kearny's Letter Book, 168–69.
[66]Brooks, "Diary of the Mormon Battalion Mission: John D. Lee," 288–92.

Quickly, the battalion was organized into the separate elements, through both a volunteer and assignment process. In modern terms this is called task organization, when a commander receives a new mission or mission change and restructures his unit based upon the best organization to accomplish the mission. It is a process that occurs constantly in military units. Many healthy men decided to remain with the slower rear detachment for various reasons, as in the case of Private George Washington Taggart, who wrote, "Capt J Hunter said publicly to His Men that He thought this to be the best move that could be made, but many were opposed to this proceeding, for one I did not feel like volunteering to go on and leave the sick behind consequently I did not go with the first division."[67] Dr. Sanderson showed his lack of compassion as a surgeon and decided to accompany the healthier group; plus he saw this march as a competition of sorts. "We are pushing to see which Command can get to Santa Fe first"; Sanderson meant first from among five companies of Price's mounted regiment also en route to Santa Fe, which was under Lieutenant Colonel David Mitchell.[68] Corporal Daniel Tyler wrote this commentary about Dr. Sanderson, the battalion's chief medical officer departing with the healthy main body: "the fact of Dr. Sanderson leaving the sick behind while he proceeded on with those who were healthy, is a fair indication of the interest he took in attending to the duties of his office."[69] It is difficult to challenge Tyler's assessment.

When the soldiers learned of the reorganization, many were appalled. John D. Lee came to the forefront again to criticize Smith and the Mormon captains for their folly in dividing the battalion against the counsel of the Brethren. The outspoken critics made their noise and complaints; Levi Hancock called the place the Valley of Tears.[70] This was the second division of the battalion, the first being the Higgins family detachment, which had departed September 16, for Fort Pueblo. Sergeant Coray also mentioned

---

[67]George Washington Taggart, Diaries, LDS Archives.
[68]George B. Sanderson, Journal, October 2, 1846, 15, University of Utah Library.
[69]Tyler, *A Concise History*, 163.
[70]Levi Hancock, Journal, October 3, 1846, LDS Archives.

Smith's decision "to take 50 men of each company the capts, 2 Lts, 2 sergts, & 2 corps, & take a forced march to Santa Fe that might claim the right to fitout for California."[71]

Despite the criticism and contempt he has received over the years, Lieutenant Smith, acting commander of the battalion, made the decision to divide the battalion for the forced march to Santa Fe, thereby saving the Mormon Battalion from possible discharge from volunteer service in the United States Army. There is no other way to view this. As unpopular as this division was to some of the men, it was a sound military decision. If Smith would have plodded along with all the slow wagons, ailing men, and families, the history of the battalion might have ended at Santa Fe on October 12, 1846. Fortunately, for posterity, history, and the Mormon Church, Smith decided to make the forced march and keep the deadline, thus enabling the battalion to continue to California.

The main body made excellent time, perhaps a little faster than the normal rate of march that an infantry battalion would be expected to make. It marched twenty more miles the first day and camped near Wagon Mound. This natural landmark is a very distinguishable butte of dark, reddish sandstone that from the north does, indeed, resemble the covered portion of a wagon, thus its name. They soon encountered Mexican settlements, and the men saw the enemy's territory, culture, and people for the first time. Advancing through Apache Canyon, they passed by La Glorieta Pass, a perfectly endowed natural choke point and defensive position. There, in 1862, a ragtag Union army of some 1,350 men would defeat a better-trained and -equipped Confederate army of 1,100 in one of two battles fought in New Mexico during the Civil War.

As the main body of the battalion entered Santa Fe on October 9, two things awaited them: a volley salute led by Colonel Alexander Doniphan, a friend of the Mormons, and Captain Philip St. George Cooke, the newly appointed commander of the Mormon Battalion.

---

[71]William Coray, Journal October 3, 1846, LDS Archives.

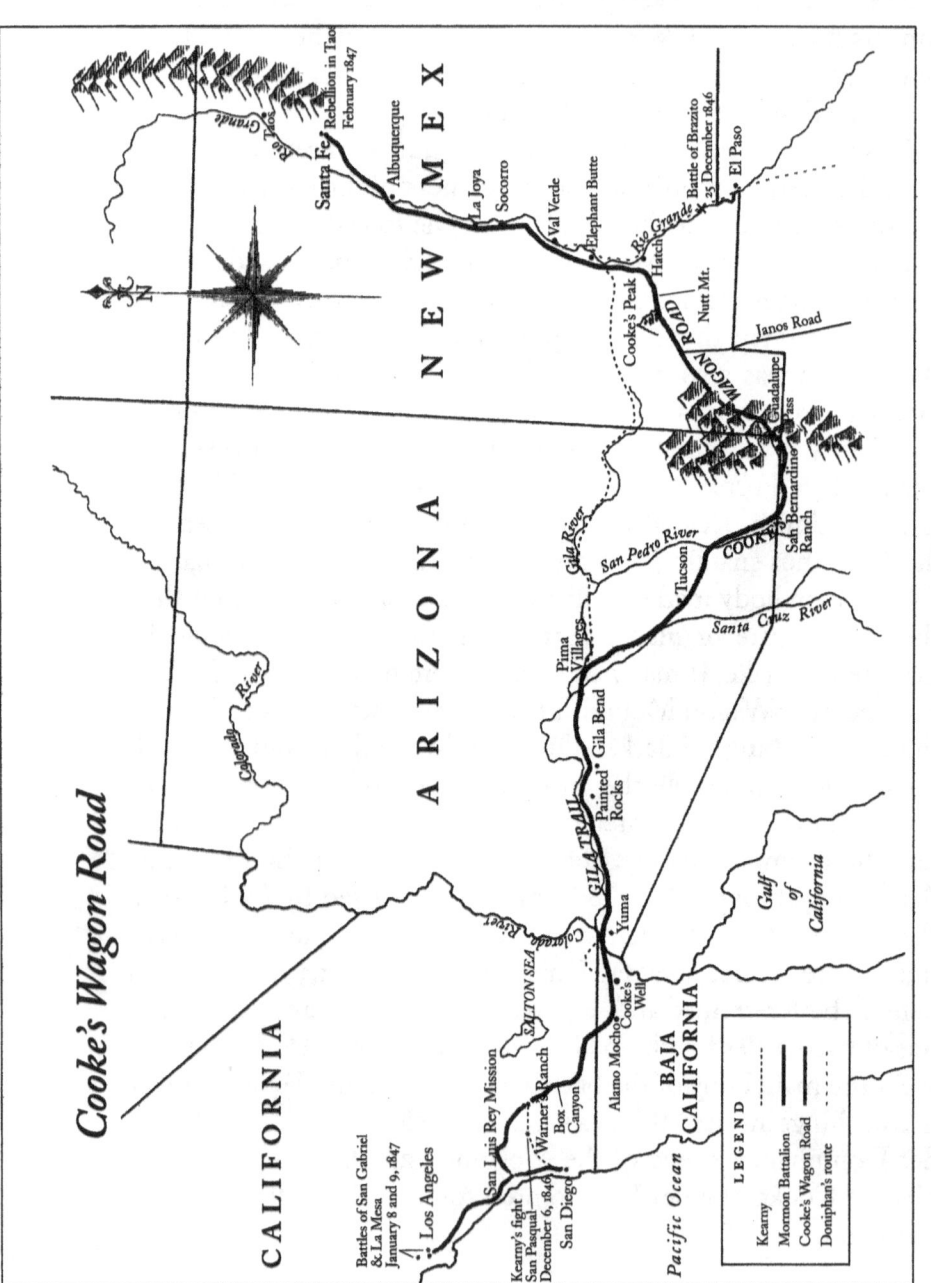

Based on map from *Army of Israel: Mormon Battalion Narratives*, edited by David L. Bigler and Will Bagley (Spokane, Wash.: The Arthur H. Clark Company 2000).

CHAPTER TEN

Cooke in Command

So, every preparation must be pushed,—hurried.
—*Lieutenant Colonel P. St. George Cooke*

Northeast of Santa Fe is the aptly named Apache Canyon. For centuries the Apaches, along with the Arapahos, Southern Cheyenne, Utes, and Navajos, lived on this land. It was their land and the land of their fathers before them. As Kearny and his army approached Santa Fe, their attention was focused not on the native inhabitants of northern New Mexico, but rather on the Mexican forces that were thought to be readying for war.

But Kearny took Santa Fe without a fight. As in all campaigns and wars, rumors outpaced reality: that some 2,000 Mexican regulars were part of an army of 4,000, then an army of 5,000, growing finally to some 6,000 Mexicans who guarded and fortified Apache Canyon. The force that blocked Kearny and the advanced element of the Army of the West was considerably smaller. Governor Manuel Armijo had, in fact, gathered a rather strong force for such a remote area of the Mexican Republic, but it could not have exceeded more than a few hundred men. Though called soldiers, his army was no more than a few regulars and many more raw recruits gathered from small villages for the defense of New Mexico.[1] Under the command of Colonel Manuel Piño, the force grew as Kearny advanced toward Santa Fe. But as Kearny approached,

---
[1] Dawson, *Doniphan's Epic March*, 69.

cooler heads realized that it was perhaps better for all concerned to live under American rule rather than remain a neglected and isolated outpost in the chaotic and tumultuous empire of Mexico. By way of the Santa Fe Trail, American merchants and goods brought life and prosperity to this cattle- and sheep-rich land, where money and manufactured goods were scarce. Quietly, the few hundred defenders questioned their ability to defeat the Norte Americanos.

By the time Kearny entered Apache Canyon, the Mexican resistance had disappeared like a summer cloud. With little fanfare the Army of the West entered Santa Fe, and the Stars and Stripes rose above from the Governor's Palace. In 1610 Spanish explorers and colonists founded La Villa Real de Santa Fé de San Francisco de Assisi, or the 'Royal Village of the Holy Faith of St. Francis of Assisi.' The capital of New Mexico, 236 years old, was now a possession of an invading foreign power. Its some six thousand inhabitants watched with curiosity as the new invaders entered. Some were angry, others joyful. The city was nothing more than a rough, impoverished village straddling a clear, clean mountain creek. Everywhere there were low one-story adobe huts. The majestic sandstone Catholic cathedral stood two blocks east of the Governor's Palace. The streets were dry, dusty passages with open-air markets of goods and abounding in sheep and donkeys. When it rained, the streets turned to rivulets of mud and water. Santa Fe would soon begin to change from a sleepy Mexican city and trading post to a growing mercantile hub of the American Southwest. War and conquest brought the change.

Kearny established American law and order, upheld personal and property rights, and even included the Indian peoples to a degree in the franchise of democracy. He directed Colonel Alexander Doniphan and Willard Preble Hall, one of Doniphan's privates of C Company, 1st Missouri, to write a comprehensive law, or constitution, for the new conquered territory. It became famous in American history as the "Kearny Code," with portions remaining intact for several decades. Doniphan and Hall were lawyers and political rivals in Missouri and at times during the process of writing the document were at odds with each other. Eventually a double-column printed treatise of 115 pages appeared. It incorporated many of the established legal tenets found in the Livingston Code of Louisiana and the Northwest Ordinance, as well as concepts from Mexican and Texan laws and codes. It was printed in both English and Spanish and went into effect in October 1846.[2]

Hall learned by mid-September 1846 that he had been elected from Missouri to the U.S. House of Representatives on the Democratic ticket. Upon his election to Congress, Hall resigned from the 1st Missouri. Assisting Doniphan and Hall was an even more prominent Missourian and Civil War figure, Francis Preston Blair Jr. He was the son of the fiery Frank Sr. and brother to Abraham Lincoln's future postmaster general, Montgomery Blair. Later, Montgomery would serve as a Unionist-Democratic party boss, advisor to Lincoln, congressman, senator, volunteer general, and foe of harsh post-war reconstruction policies in the years to come.[3]

General Kearny arranged military and political affairs quickly, with a fixed determination to hasten on to California. He appointed Charles Bent, one of the brothers Bent from the famous trading post of Bent's Fort, as civil governor of New Mexico. Bent would govern from his own residence in Taos, a few days' ride north from Santa Fe through majestic alpine mountains. Frank Blair became attorney general of the territory. Colonel Doniphan was appointed military and garrison commander at Santa Fe until Colonel Price arrived and relieved him; thereafter, he was to march south to El Paso and Chihuahua to join General John Wool in central Mexico. In the meantime, Doniphan was to control the Navajos and other hostile tribes if necessary.

With most of these arrangements accomplished, Kearny departed on September 25 with six companies (three hundred men) of the 1st Dragoons and Emory's topographical engineer party.[4] (He had

---

[2]Ibid., 84.

[3]The twenty-six-year-old Yale graduate would later be a prominent Missouri leader in the secession crisis and serve as Union "provisional" governor during the Civil War. Clarke, *Stephen Watts Kearny*, 148–49; DeVoto, *Year of Decision*, 335.

[4]William Emory graduated from West Point in 1831 and became a topographical engineer in 1838. He helped survey the U.S.-Mexican border and served as a commissioner for the Gadsden Purchase in 1854. During the Civil War he competently commanded a federal corps in Louisiana and in the Shenandoah Valley.

Philip St. George Cooke. *From Hague, The Road to California: The Search for a Southern Overland Route, 1540–1848. Used by permission of the publisher.*

hoped to have the Mormon Battalion join him to provide him with an infantry component for his command, but the battalion's march to Santa Fe was doggedly slow.) He also appointed the Laclede Rangers from St. Louis to accompany him, but they were unable to find sufficient serviceable remounts, so they were disbanded as a mounted company.[5] By October 6, Kearny was making his way south along the Rio Grande when the famous mountain man and scout Kit Carson and a half-dozen Delaware Indians intercepted him and apprised him of California's conquest by Stockton and pathfinder Frémont. Christopher "Kit" Carson, now a volunteer lieutenant in the California volunteers, having been appointed by a naval officer (an interesting arrangement), had hoped to herald the news of American conquest of California to the nation. But Kearny demanded that Carson return to California with him as guide. The honor of informing Washington of the California prize

---

[5]Ibid., 361.

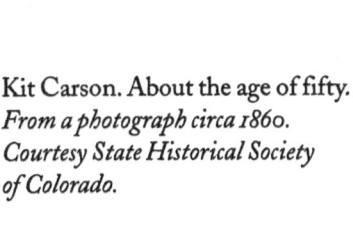
Kit Carson. About the age of fifty. From a photograph circa 1860. Courtesy State Historical Society of Colorado.

was left to another equally skilled mountain man, Thomas Fitzpatrick, who had been guiding Kearny west. (Carson was unaware that a revolt in California was underway and Stockton, Frémont, and Gillespie were scrambling to regain control.) Kearny ordered two hundred of the dragoons back to Santa Fe and left his wagons for the Mormon Battalion to bring forward. Kearny set out for California, riding hard with only an escort of two companies of dragoons, Emory's topographical party, and a couple of mountain howitzers, guided by a disappointed Carson.[6]

Kearny had already made a wise decision to give command of the Mormon Battalion to perhaps his most trusted, accomplished, and proven subordinate, Captain Philip St. George Cooke, 1st U.S. Dragoons.

✳ ✳ ✳

---
[6]Eisenhower, *So Far from God*, 220.

On October 2, 1846, General Kearny wrote General Order No. 33: "Capt. Cooke, 1st Drags. will return to Santa Fe, and assume command of the Battalion of Mormons on its arrival at that place . . . he will conduct [it] to Upper California, following the route now being taken by the Dragoons."[7] The Mormon Battalion had a new commander who was perhaps one of the most celebrated and revered officers of the frontier period. Kearny not only selected Cooke to lead the battalion to California; he had already entrusted Cooke with many other vital assignments in the past. Just weeks before, Captain Cooke had led a twelve-man detail, with the adventurous James Magoffin, to Santa Fe to act as an emissary to negotiate a truce or understanding with Mexican authorities prior to Kearny's arrival. This mission Cooke accomplished with diplomacy and finesse.[8]

Cooke hailed from near Leesburg, Virginia, and was from one of the first families of the Old Dominion. He entered the United States Military Academy at age fourteen in 1823, with special approval from Secretary of War John C. Calhoun. During the admission process a clerical error added the first name of "Philip," and, like U. S. Grant, Cooke took it as an omen and never corrected the mistake.[9] He graduated in 1827 as a second lieutenant of infantry at the age of eighteen, one of the youngest West Point graduates ever. Cooke served in nearly every important campaign, reconnaissance, or major operation of the frontier by the United States Army from the time of his commissioning until the Civil War. His first significant military adventure was with Major Bennet Riley on his overland reconnaissance in 1829 down the Santa Fe

---

[7]Gardner, "The Command and Staff of the Mormon Battalion," 338.

[8]James Magoffin was an enterprising adventurer and businessman on the western frontier and friend to Mexicans and Indians alike. His brother Samuel had married teenage Susan Shelby Magoffin of Kentucky some months before; by this time she was pregnant, but able to record one of the most stirring and vivid accounts of the Santa Fe Trail during the Mexican War. See Susan Shelby Magoffin, *Down the Santa Fe Trail, 1846–47*; DeVoto, *Year of Decision*, 119–20.

[9]See Dumas Malone, *Dictionary of American Biography*, 389; Cadet Hiram Ulysses Grant entered West Point and learned that a mistake had been made by the congressman from Ohio who had appointed him. The congressman assumed Grant's middle name was his mother's maiden name, so he enrolled him as Ulysses Simpson Grant. Grant, for the most part, used this name the rest of his life.

Trail. He served in the Blackhawk War in Illinois in 1832 and the major dragoon expedition of 1834 under Colonel Henry Dodge through Oklahoma. He led his company of dragoons on Kearny's famous Dragoon Reconnaissance of 1845 to South Pass, Santa Fe, and back, a march of over twenty-two hundred miles.

There were few antebellum officers who matched Cooke's years and experience on the frontier. Little did this young eighteen-year-old realize in 1827 that in some thirty years he would publish a two-volume manual for the mounted service, *Cavalry Tactics*, and become the army's leading authority on the mounted service just prior to the Civil War. Cooke had a natural talent and flair for writing. He also published his famous and popular *Scenes and Adventures in the Army* (1857), which was an autobiography of sorts chronicling his frontier service through 1845 with many exciting anecdotal aspects.

P. St. George Cooke, as his signature went, was tall (six feet, four inches) narrow, and lean, with sandy-colored hair and a light complexion. He held the highest traits of a gentleman—he was literally a man of letters, intelligent and well-read. Cooke's family connections alone provided notoriety and fame. His brothers were John Rogers Cooke, a distinguished constitutional lawyer, and Dr. John E. Cooke, as already mentioned, the famous physician and professor at the University of Louisville Medical School. Though not great historical figures, they were well-known and distinguished men in their day.[10]

Cooke was a tough, austere disciplinarian, a rigid task-master, and a thorough planner and campaigner. He was also a harsh but fair officer to his men. Cooke would tolerate no infractions of orders or regulations and had a well-conceived and seasoned vision of military operations and service. Cooke looked at war as more of an adventure than a terrible consequence of humanity. He was determined to follow orders at any cost and brooked no allowance for failure, unprofessionalism, or disobedience. He believed in the standards he enforced and his patriotism was his religion. In 1861

---

[10]For the only complete biography of Cooke, see Young, *The West of Philip St. George Cooke, 1809–1895*.

the sectional crisis consumed the nation and also his family with a son, a nephew, and other family members joining the Confederacy, while Cooke, a Virginian, remained loyal to the Union. The most famous family member in Confederate ranks was James Ewell Brown "Jeb" Stuart, who had married Cooke's daughter Flora. They named their first son, Philip St. George Cooke Stuart, but after Cooke refused to fight for the Confederacy, they renamed the boy after his father. The division and pain in this family caused by the conflict would last for decades.

One of the truly remarkable legacies Cooke left was the many junior officers he led, taught, and mentored. Mentoring is one of the most important responsibilities in the profession of arms. Through Cooke's great ability, the mounted service developed a cohort of cavalry leaders and officers ripe for the Civil War. Among them were "AJ" Smith, George Stoneman (West Point class of 1846, who we will learn more about with the battalion), John Buford (1848, one of the heroes of Gettysburg and perhaps the greatest cavalryman of the war), James Ewell Brown "Jeb" Stuart (1853, the great Confederate cavalryman), and Wesley Merritt (1860, one of the boy wonders of the Civil War).

Cooke departed the day after he received his new orders and command. His bugler traveled with him as an escort, and he left two other dragoons from his company at La Joya, south of Albuquerque, to guard his baggage wagon and personal effects. Arriving at Santa Fe, Cooke immediately went about arranging logistical support for the long and arduous march to the Pacific. Making the march would be a difficult task, preparing for it was just as difficult in many respects. Unless one has served on a long or strenuous military operation, it is difficult to appreciate the tremendous challenge to plan, organize, equip, and maintain such an undertaking. One of Napoleon's maxims was that "an army traveled on its belly." Fortunately for the Mormon Battalion, P. St. George Cooke and the other regular army officers assigned were masters of the art of logistics, foraging, marching across forbidding terrain, managing animals, and maintaining the combat effectiveness of the force.

COOKE IN COMMAND

Except for a few other veteran frontier officers of the 1st Dragoons such as Captains Edmund V. Sumner, Benjamin Moore, and Henry S. Turner, few peers could have succeeded as Cooke did. As for volunteer officers, the only peer was Alexander Doniphan in this respect.

What made matters even more difficult was the terrain that Cooke was about to cross—the great American Southwest. He was to do this with a volunteer battalion, beginning from a base of operations deep in enemy territory, many hundreds of miles from any supply depot, in a land lacking adequate supplies, provisions, animals, and forage. As summarized by historian John Yurtinus, Cooke "would shepherd a quarrelsome, fanatical, and obstinate body of possibly untrustworthy emigrants across an empty desert."[11]

About the only thing in Cooke's favor was the cooler autumn weather, which was actually pleasant for the march across the deserts of the American Southwest. Also, it was unlikely that they would encounter any serious enemy opposition. So, Cooke marshaled all his abilities and resources to prepare the Mormon Battalion for its march to California.

At this point P. St. George Cooke became the heart and soul of the Mormon Battalion. Fortunately for posterity, Cooke kept an invaluable account of events. It is one of the most important primary sources of the history of the Mormon Battalion. Cooke used the journal and transcribed much of it into a report that he delivered to General Kearny in California. This "report" found its way into the Congressional Record and became an official United States government document.[12] Then, Cooke, always wanting to out-do even himself, used his journal and report as the basis of a history published after he retired from active service. He gathered information from other sources concerning events he was not

---

[11] Yurtinus, "A Ram in the Thicket," 183.
[12] See Gardner, "Report of Lieut. Col. St. George Cooke of his March from Santa Fe, New Mexico, to San Diego, Upper California," 15–40, which is also in *House Executive Document* no. 41, 30th Congress, 1st session, 551–63; hereafter, Gardner, "Report."

directly involved in. *The Conquest of New Mexico and California: a Historical and Personal Narrative* was a masterful history published in 1878, a full thirty years after the events transpired. Much of our view of the battalion will be seen through Cooke's worthy and seasoned eyes.

Cooke arrived at Santa Fe on October 7, and immediately made demands on the Quartermaster, Commissary, and Subsistence Departments assigned to support the Army of the West. There was no money or specie available before the arrival of an officer of the paymaster department, which happened to be Major Cloud, traveling with the Mormon Battalion. It was, therefore, difficult to purchase anything. Some merchants and ranchers took credit in advance while awaiting government funds. Cooke worked feverishly to outfit the battalion.

Though Santa Fe was an important trading capital and vast amounts of trade goods, provisions, and animal stock flowed through, without proper authority and acceptable specie—gold or silver coin—it was difficult to purchase and procure supplies and stock. Cooke prepared the wagons and what stock of oxen and beef he could obtain. He also wisely included many packsaddles for the 140 mules he obtained through trade and purchase. These animals, by Cooke's own words, were mostly unserviceable. The Commissary and Quartermaster Departments were overwhelmed and unable to provide complete and quality goods. A mountain of supplies and provisions for the army, including those sent out to support the battalion, was still at Bent's Fort, over two hundred miles away. Between them lay a precarious line of communications through mountains over Raton Pass, vulnerable to raids by Navajos, Apaches, and Mexican guerrillas. With much against him, Cooke was able to assemble enough supplies, provisions, stock, oxen, and pack mules to make a reasonable attempt to reach California.

At this time quartermasters could not or did not use standard issue of rations during a military campaign. They assessed what provisions were available and, using standard quartermaster charts or simple math, divided the amounts by the effective strength and determined the number of days the rations would last or what was required for the campaign. The normal ration was provided from many staples: flour for making bread and biscuits, rice, corn meal, salt pork, jerked beef, desiccated vegetables and fruits, coffee, sugar, whiskey, and the most important ration besides water—stock on the hoof. Though difficult to herd at times and subject to loss, theft, or death, stock was the best source of fresh meat. However, stock also required additional water and feed. There was no standard daily ration for the men, but an assortment of fresh meat, flour, and coffee was considered a reasonable diet. The famous "hardtack" biscuit of the Civil War period was available through the Army Subsistence Department, but probably was not eaten by the Mormon men.[13]

Cooke listed enough rations for sixty days, meaning foodstuffs of flour, beef, and sheep on the hoof. He collected only thirty days' rations—probably all that was allowed—of salt pork, coffee, sugar, and salt.[14] In addition, he acquired twenty-eight beeves and some three hundred head of long-legged sheep called *churros* in Spanish. An experienced frontier officer, Cooke intended to eat the oxen as they gave out. Cooke assessed his mission and the general situation with the experience of a frontier veteran. "Every thing conspired to discourage the extraordinary undertaking of marching this battalion eleven hundred miles," he wrote, "for the much greater part through an unknown wilderness without road or trail, and with a wagon train." Of the Mormon Battalion, he wrote, "It was enlisted too much by families; some were too old,—some feeble, and some too young; it was embarrassed by many woman; it was undisciplined; it was much worn by traveling on foot, and marching from Nauvoo, Illinois; their clothing was very scant." Yet with a voice of optimism he added, "So, every preparation must be pushed."[15]

The two segments of the Mormon Battalion arrived on October 9 and 12, respectively. After nearly sixty days of marching it was a welcome relief for the men to stop, rest, and relax for a few days.

---

[13]Not one of several dozen journals, histories, or accounts that I have read by the battalion veterans mention hardtack. [14]Cooke, *Conquest*, 92. [15]Ibid., 91.

But rest was not entirely possible because of the conditions surrounding them. Many were ill and exhausted, with little or no money to support them, especially the families. It was a comfort, though, to finally take a break from the marches and experience a new city, people, and country.

Generally, the Mormon soldiers were unimpressed by Santa Fe. The land, people, and culture were strange to them. They were indeed in a foreign land. Private Guy Keysor of B Company wrote, "most of the houses have porches the inside of which as also the rooms are whitewashed Doors small, fire places small, & rooms warm & comfortable.... The floor consisting of the ground being cemented to a hard clay & swept clean."[16] Sergeant Coray, the faithful journalist, wrote rather critically, "The Spaniards in Santa Fe are miserly in the extreme and appear much like the lower classes of Germans.... Though there are some well informed genteel Spaniards in Santa Fe who treat strangers with civility, yet, the great mass of them are misers."[17]

The men saw much of the town, and traded and purchased what they could. They attended *fandangos*, a Mexican type of dance and celebration. Private Azariah Smith attended a Catholic mass and concluded, "After the meting I stayed to see the Ladies; some of which looked prety; others looked like destruction."[18] Some thought the Mexican women to be immoral and disgusting, Sergeant Coray, for one, wrote that the "ill manners of the females disgusted me whether it be true or false, I was told that nearly all present were prostitutes."[19] Dr. George Sanderson commented, "I am heartily tired of this place and with all the fatigue and danger before me I would rather proceed on to California than remain here."[20] The days of rest were welcome, but completing the march to California was foremost in every mind.

---

[16]Guy Keysor, Journal, October 13, 1846, Utah State Historical Society.
[17]William Coray, Journal, October 13, 1846, LDS Archives.
[18]Cited in Ricketts, *The Mormon Battalion*, 69.
[19]William Coray, Journal, October 14, 1846, LDS Archives.
[20]George B. Sanderson, Journal, October, 9–19, 1846, University of Utah Library.

COOKE IN COMMAND

Captain Philip St. George Cooke, 1st Dragoons, officially assumed command of the Mormon Battalion on October 13, 1846. He had already determined to reorganize the battalion staff and separate and relieve the sick and afflicted men, sending them to the Mormon settlement at Pueblo. He would then instill some discipline in the ranks. Cooke also became lieutenant colonel of volunteers effective the same day; he retained his rank of captain in the regular army, but not his position in the 1st Dragoons. He immediately reorganized the battalion with official orders that same day. He relieved Lieutenant Samuel Gully as quartermaster officer and appointed Lieutenant Smith in his place and brevet Second Lieutenant George Stoneman as assistant quartermaster officer.[21] Gulley's relief angered many of the men. The relentless John D. Lee and Private Levi Hancock took the dismissal badly. They circulated a petition and delivered it to Colonel Doniphan, who empathized with the men but did nothing. Gulley, therefore, resigned his volunteer commission and returned to the church at Winter Quarters. He would die the next year en route to Utah.[22]

Gulley's relief was never fully explained and Cooke never referred to it directly. He perhaps felt more confident to have a regular army officer of Smith's experience in charge of such a tremendous responsibility. There is evidence that the men felt that Lieutenants Smith and Dykes sought his removal.[23] One must realize that Lieutenant Dykes knew that John D. Lee, Sergeant William Hyde, Hancock, and others attempted to replace Captain Hunt with Gulley earlier as the senior Mormon officer. This in itself would warrant Dykes's advising Smith or Cooke of the affair. The fact that enlisted men and a civilian went to Colonel Doniphan to override Cooke's decision is, in itself, a dangerous precedent. This action was jumping the chain of command and was totally inappropriate in military service. It would soon occur again.

Colonel Cooke continued his assessment of the challenges fac-

---

[21]Tyler's version has the abbreviations "A. C. L." and "A. A. C. L." on page 166. This should have been ACS for "Assistant Commissariat and Subsistence" and AACS, "Acting Assistant Commissariat and Subsistence." Lieutenant Stoneman was a "brevet" second lieutenant because there were no vacancies in the 1st U.S. Dragoons Regiment upon his assignment with the regiment.   [22]Tyler, *A Concise History*, 174–75.   [23]Ibid.

ing him as the new commander of the Mormon Battalion. He wrote, "there was no money to pay them,—or clothing to issue; their mules were utterly broken down; the Quartermaster department was without funds, and its credit bad; and mules were scarce."[24] He had the men examined by competent medical authority to separate the weak and invalid men from the healthy. Cooke, of course, used Dr. Sanderson, the battalion assistant surgeon. Cooke also sought assistance from Dr. Samuel De Camp, senior surgeon of the regular army and department medical officer at Santa Fe.[25] Dr. De Camp requested that Sanderson remain behind at Santa Fe to assist him. George Sanderson declined and remained with his unit, the battalion of Mormons.[26]

Some sixty men were found "inefficient" for service from the medical examinations. Cooke decided to follow Lieutenant Smith's example and send these unhealthy men "to winter at a temporary settlement of the Mormons at Pueblo."[27] Cooke also decided to send all of the women and children with these unhealthy men. He appointed Captain James Brown, commander of C Company, to lead this detachment.

"General Order No. 8, Headquarters Mormon Battalion, Santa Fe October 15, 1846," directed that "Capt. Jas. Brown will take command of the men reported by the assistant Surgeon as incapable, from sickness and debility, of undertaking the present march to California." Cooke's directive also stated, "the laundresses on this march will be accompanied by much suffering and would be a great encumbrance to the expedition." Thus in one sweep of the pen, Cooke ordered all the women and children to Pueblo. He organized the sick detachment, ordering Lieutenant Elam Luddington

---

[24]Cooke, *Conquest*, 91.   [25]Gardner, "Report," 18.
[26]George B. Sanderson, Journal, October, 9–19, 1846, University of Utah Library.
[27]Cooke's journal is preserved in several forms: a U.S. Senate document and reprinted in various other sources: *Journal of the march of the Mormon Battalion of infantry volunteers under the command of Lieut. Col. St. Geo. Cooke, also captain of dragoons, from Santa Fe, New Mexico to San Diego, Cal. (kept by himself by direction of comd'g General Army of the West*, in Sen. Executive Document, no. 2, 31st Congress, special session; also found in Bieber and Bender, eds., "Cooke's Journal of the March of the Mormon Battalion, 1846–1847," in *Exploring Southwestern Trails 1846–1854*; hereafter, the reference is from Bieber's version, and cited as Bieber and Bender, eds., "Journal."

of B Company and several NCOs to accompany Brown. It was to depart on October 17, and the battalion would leave a few days later.[28] Cooke continued with his final preparations for the long march to California. Captain Brown made his preparations for the shorter but also tiresome journey to Pueblo.

The decision to send all the women and children to Pueblo with Captain Brown's detachment caused another fury among some of the men. Fate would have it that many of the husbands with wives sent to Pueblo were healthy. They requested, through their company officers and the adjutant, to be released from duty to accompany their wives and families to Pueblo. Also, some of the officers and NCOs requested that their wives accompany them to California. Initially, these requests were denied based on sound military reasons. Cooke would not have it. Then, as recorded in Cooke's own words, "five wives of officers were reluctantly allowed to accompany the march, but furnished their own transportation."[29]

It was a mistake for Cooke to allow any of the women to continue. Besides the dangers and the possibility of combat, it showed a type of illogical inconsistency. Some saw their wives leave for Pueblo, whereas five men had the opportunity to have their wives continue with the battalion. Perhaps he had his reasons, but it still smelled of favoritism, and some of the men would take issue with the decision later.

Two remarkable and conflicting stories dealing with the division of the battalion at Santa Fe came from Privates John Steele of C Company and John Hess of E Company. Their accounts demonstrate either poor soldiering and professionalism on theirs and Cooke's part, or literary license gone astray. Both of the men had

---

[28]Tyler, *A Concise History*, 166–67.
[29]Cooke, *Conquest*, 91–92. In his "Report" Cooke recorded, "At the earnest request of two captains and three sergeants, their wives were permitted to accompany the expedition," 19. These women were actually wives of both enlisted men and officers in the battalion: Lydia Hunter (who was pregnant), the wife of Captain Jesse Hunter, commander of B Company; Phebe Brown, wife of Sergeant Ebenezer Brown of A Company; Melissa Coray, wife of Sergeant William Coray of B Company; Sophia Tubbs, wife of Private William Tubbs of D Company; Susan Davis, wife of Captain Daniel Davis, commander of D Company; and Davis's son, Daniel Davis Jr., also went along. See Ricketts, *The Mormon Battalion*, 70. There were also several "aides" to officers or adolescents who were still with the battalion.

wives and were healthy, and both mentioned each other as partners in the episode. After complaining through their chain of command and not achieving satisfaction, they determined to approach the senior officers themselves. This is where their stories diverge.

Steele claimed to have marched off with Hess to a saloon, where they found Cooke drinking with many fellow officers. Steel confronted Cooke in front of the other officers and demanded that they not be separated from their wives. "I told him I had a wife there," recorded Steele, "and would like the privilege of either having my wife go to California with me or going back to Bents Fort [actually Pueblo] with her. He spoke very saucy and said he would like to have his wife along with him (but he never had a wife)." Cooke, of course, had a wife, Rachel Hertzog Cooke of Philadelphia. According to Steele, they then marched off together with Steele and Hess keeping stride with the long-legged Cooke. At Colonel Doniphan's quarters, Cooke apparently relented after talking to Doniphan.[30]

Hess's story is that Steele and Hess went to see Colonel Doniphan, the commanding officer of the Santa Fe garrison. Cooke was absent in Hess's version. After a very cold exchange, they were about to leave when Hess made one last attempt to sway Doniphan. "I thought I would venture one more remark, which was, 'Colonel, I suppose you left your wife with her friends, while we are required to leave ours in an enemy's country in care of a lot of sick, demoralized men,'" said Hess. "This seemed to touch a sympathetic cord; he called very sharply, 'Orderly! Orderly!'" He then summoned Lieutenant Dykes, who had not assisted the men in this endeavor at all. Doniphan directed that the men could accompany their wives for Pueblo. This meant a loss of several fit and effective soldiers. Then, according to Hess, Dykes took credit for the change in orders.[31]

This is a most interesting affair. Historian and former military officer Colonel Hamilton Gardner wrote of Steele's version, "I discredit this whole story. Cooke was admittedly a stern disciplinarian

---

[30]Steele, "Extracts from the Journal of John Steele," 11.
[31]Hess, "John W. Hess, with the Mormon Battalion," 51.

COOKE IN COMMAND

in the tradition of the regular army of that time, but his entire military record of 50 years shows no instance of his indulging in an unseemingly quarrel with one of his enlisted men, no matter how rude or undisciplined the latter proved."[32] There is little to add to Colonel Gardner's analysis. Cooke would never have allowed such a scene to occur. On the other hand, Doniphan, being a volunteer officer and sympathetic toward Mormons, probably acted just as Hess described. One must remember that, even for a volunteer officer, Doniphan was different and most unmilitary. He was a tough, courageous, and determined man and natural leader who did not need harsh military discipline to gain the respect of his rough, uncouth Missouri volunteers. Doniphan was reasonable when it came to such situations; Cooke was not and most likely would have arrested both Steele and Hess.

Another change in the battalion staff became necessary when Sergeant Major James Glines was to depart with his family. Cooke selected Private Samuel Ferguson of A Company to replace Glines as battalion sergeant major. Cooke directed other changes due to some of the men wanting to accompany their wives and families to Pueblo. Privates Joel Terrell, David Wilkin, and Jabez Nowland were reduced as corporals or sergeants. Corporals Daniel Tyler and Edward Martin became sergeants in C Company.

There seems to have been a serious morale and leadership problem in C Company. With the departure of Captain Brown, Cooke selected Lieutenant George Rosecrans to assume command of C Company. Rosecrans was the same man who had challenged and criticized Captain Brown at Fort Leavenworth. This was the first of several leadership changes in this unfortunate company.[33]

The Brown sick detachment comprised some eighty-six men, both sick and escorts, some twenty women, and a few children. With a few wagons and twenty days' provisions they departed Sunday morning, October 18, a day later than directed by Cooke.

---

[32]This comment is by the editor, Hamilton Gardner. See Gardner, "Report," 18 n.9.
[33]Cooke's Orders Nos. 9 and 10, dated October 15, 1846; see Tyler, *A Concise History*, 167–68.

Enduring some hardships due to the season, the mountainous route, the number of invalid men, and the few teams and wagons, the detachment reached the Arkansas River just short of Bent's Fort on November 8. Captain Brown secured some sixty days' rations of flour, rice, beans, pork, and other provisions. They reached Pueblo on November 17, 1846, and joined the Higgins detachment and the "Mississippi Saints." En route, Private Milton Smith of C Company died.[34]

Since there was no currency or specie available to American forces in Santa Fe, Major Jeremiah Cloud, the paymaster, paid the men with checks. He tried to pay and cover the expenses of the quartermaster, commissariat, and subsistence departments through this means also. Colonel Doniphan requested that $100,000 in gold and silver be forwarded to cover the expenses of the military occupation in Santa Fe and pay the troops. The gold arrived months later, after most of the units had moved on. In fact, Doniphan's Missourians had already departed Santa Fe on their long campaign through Mexico and did not receive their full pay and entitlements until they were discharged in New Orleans after an entire year's service.[35] The Mormon Battalion was fortunate to receive some pay, even if it was in government checks. The men sent some of their money back to Winter Quarters with Lee, Howard Egan, and former battalion members Samuel Gully and Roswell Stephens.[36] Lee and party would leave Santa Fe the same day as the battalion.

Thus, the Mormon Battalion was spared further antics of the malcontent John Doyle Lee. He would eventually create his own infamy. Thirty years later Lee would be executed in Utah for his involvement in the Mountain Meadows massacre in September 1857. Though becoming the fall guy for many others who were just as guilty, Lee's hands were stained with the innocent blood of over 120 pioneers—men, women, and children. Lee was a strong-willed

---

[34]For an excellent account of the Brown sick detachment, see Bagley and Bigler, *Army of Israel*, 277–332; also, Yurtinus, "A Ram in the Thicket," 264–74.
[35]DeVoto, *Year of Decision*, 419; Dawson, *Doniphan's Epic March*, 187.
[36]Tyler, *A Concise History*, 174.

COOKE IN COMMAND

man, a hardened pioneer, and a zealous champion of the Mormon cause: a true believer and defender of the faith. He was also an egotistical, self-appointed meddler in affairs that did not concern him, and later a cold-blooded murderer. Lee should have been banished from the battalion, as he would be later in Utah.[37]

With the arrangements made to dispatch the unhealthy men and the bulk of the non-combatants to Pueblo, Cooke evaluated the combat effectiveness of his new command. He was shocked by what he saw. The men had not yet received sufficient formal or proper military training. Colonel Allen had conducted some training at Fort Leavenworth. Lieutenant Smith was challenged just to lead them to Santa Fe, let alone drill and train the men. As mentioned, some of the men may have had some previous experience in the militia or in Mormon military organizations, but this hardly constituted realistic and effective training. Few militia officers and units could immediately face battle effectively without very intensive training by professionals. Cooke and the other regulars were the only men who knew their duties and responsibilities in combat. The Latter-day Saint officers and NCOs knew little of soldiering, one reason for the many problems that had arisen thus far. The men were not ready to perform in combat. Cooke recorded his observation: "The battalion have never been drilled, and, though obedient, have little discipline; they exhibit great heedlessness and ignorance, and some obstinacy."[38] Cooke knew that it would take time and effort to train and drill this volunteer battalion to an acceptable standard of combat readiness—something he did not have the luxury to do at present. He had a more pressing matter.

Cooke's mission, as assigned by General Kearny, was to march the battalion to California and bring along the government wagons and property that Kearny left behind in his haste to get to California. He was to follow Kearny's route as much as possible. Another part of Cooke's mission was contained in a written directive by

---

[37]For the most recent treatment of the tragic Mountain Meadows affair, see Bagley, *Blood of the Prophets: Brigham Young and the Massacre at Mountain Meadows*; and the earlier study, Brooks, *The Mountain Meadows Massacre*. See also Brooks, *John D. Lee: Zealot, Pioneer Builder, Scapegoat*.   [38]Cooke, *Conquest*, 92.

Kearny: "to [Lieutenant] Colonel Cooke, assigning to him the task of opening a wagon road to the Pacific."[39] To get the wagons to California, Cooke undoubtedly had to do some road building and exploring to find the best and easiest route. But Cooke's primary mission was not to build a road, it was to get the battalion and wagons to California. In military terminology these additional duties are called implied tasks. To accomplish his mission of marching to California, Cooke had to accomplish many specified and implied tasks, namely to engage in road building at certain points. Cooke therefore assembled what he called "road tools," or enough shovels, picks, crowbars, and so on, to assist in this task. With a battalion of 397 men (Cooke reported 486 men at Santa Fe minus 86 on the sick detachment and the several who resigned) and all the wagons and stock, it would be a difficult proposition.[40] He was to take 25 government wagons: 15 battalion wagons, 3 for each company for supplies and equipment; 6 ox-drawn wagons for the heavy equipment; 4 wagons for the staff and medical corps, and the accompanying paymaster; lastly, 4 or 5 more private wagons for the women and for excess baggage. There were a total of some 30 or 31 wagons. Of course, Cooke's personal baggage, wagon, and two dragoons were waiting at La Joya over a hundred miles south. Mule teams were to pull these wagons, except for the heavy wagons pulled by oxen. Thus, the Mormon Battalion became a caravan of nomads crossing lands of the American Southwest.[41]

Another of Cooke's implied tasks was to find the best route to California. Though he endeavored to follow Kearny's route as much as possible, it was not always practicable for heavy wagons. The only maps of the region available were new commercial maps published in 1846: Tanner's *American Atlas* and Augustus Mitchell's map of Texas, Oregon, and California.[42] These maps were based on two previous expeditions by Frémont and Charles Wilkes. Unfortunately, neither had any real value south of Santa Fe because these expeditions did not penetrate the area that both Kearny and Cooke had to cross. In Cooke's own words, "I discover that the maps are worthless;

---

[39]Ibid., 86.
[41]Ibid., 69.
[40]Bieber and Bender, eds., "Journal," 65 and 67.
[42]Jamison, "The Annotated 1846 Mitchell Map," 49–100.

they can be depended on for nothing."[43] Kearny's decision in June to take Lieutenant William Emory's topographical party with him to complete such a necessary survey was a stroke of brilliance.

Cooke, therefore, recruited some very qualified and experienced guides. They have been often referred to as guides and pilots in many journals and histories, which is accurate, because they did guide and pilot, but herein I will use the military term "scout." When Lieutenant Smith and party overtook the battalion at Council Grove, Philip Thompson, a civilian scout, joined the command at that point. Since they were following the well-known Santa Fe Trail, his services were minimal besides scouting for possible, but unlikely, hostile attacks and looking for water. But now that Cooke was about to cross a very desolate and threatening land, experienced scouts were imperative.

From the early colonial period through the end of the Indian wars, civilian scouts, most often Indians or frontiersmen, were essential to any military campaign. Fortunately for Cooke and the Mormon Battalion, several very experienced but relatively unknown scouts offered their services for hire. Some were either Mexicans or Indians known to us today only as Tasson, Chacon, Francisco, and Appolonius. Little evidence survives concerning these men, other than the fact that they were involved with the battalion as scouts. The main scouts were Pauline (Paulino) Weaver, known as "Old Weaver" in some accounts, Antoine Leroux, Philip Thompson, Jean-Baptiste Charbonneau, and Spanish language interpreter Dr. Stephen Foster. Charbonneau arrived a few days into the march, followed by Leroux, who became the leader of the scouts.[44] Also, congressman-elect Willard Hall, late private of the 1st Missouri

---

[43]Bieber and Bender, eds., "Journal," 107; Goetzmann, *Army Exploration in the American West, 1803–1863*, 127–28.

[44]For the lesser-known scouts there are a few sources: for Philip Thompson, see Brooks, ed., "Diary of the Mormon Battalion Mission: John D. Lee," September 23, 1846. Tyler, *A Concise History*, mentions several of the scouts: Weaver, 233; Francisco, 240; and Talbot, *A Historical Guide to the Mormon Battalion and Butterfield Trail*, 28. Dr. Sanderson refers to Leroux as "our principle Guide" later during the march; see George B. Sanderson, Journal, December 15, 1846, 42, University of Utah Library. It is obvious that Cooke considered him the senior or lead scout also from the many references to and recommendations of Leroux. He was the only scout who had some experience in this area of the Southwest.

Mounted Volunteers, accompanied the battalion and served in an unofficial capacity sometimes as scout, messenger, aide, or as an assistant to Cooke. Weaver and Leroux, and perhaps Thompson, were accomplished frontiersmen and had solid reputations.

Jean-Baptiste Charbonneau was linked, at least by birth, to greatness. He was perhaps the most colorful scout, not only because of his ability and skill, but because of his lineage and education. He was the son of the famous Indian woman and interpreter Sacagawea and the French trader Toussaint Charbonneau. They, including the infant Jean-Baptiste, were members of Lewis and Clark's Corps of Discovery, the military expedition to the Pacific Ocean in 1803–6. Jean-Baptiste was born at Fort Mandan, one of the expedition's winter quarters, where U.S. Army Captain Meriwether Lewis helped deliver the boy.[45]

Stephen Foster, often referred to as Dr. Foster, was the chief interpreter for the remainder of the march. Originally from Maine, Foster graduated from Yale and had practiced medicine in several locations. He was living in Santa Fe when the Mexican War began and served in the Army of the West for seventy-five dollars a month. He offered his services to Cooke and joined as translator and scout.[46]

The scouts' main responsibility was to range ahead of the column looking for any possible danger, finding the best routes and camp sites, and locating the precious lifeblood of the desert: water. Cooke, the dragoon officer, did not have any cavalry assigned to assist him, so he employed his scouts as he would have a patrol of dragoons.[47] Using his scouts, Cooke would lead the battalion to California.

---

[45] Appleman, *Lewis and Clark's Transcontinental Exploration*, 253. Also see Susan Colby, *Sacagawea's Child: The Life and Times of Jean-Baptiste (Pomp) Charbonneau* (Spokane, Wash.: Arthur H. Clark Company, 2005).

[46] Bagley and Bigler, *Army of Israel: Mormon Battalion Narratives*, 147 n.5.

[47] Cooke's bugler accompanied him on his return to Santa Fe to assume command of the battalion, while three dragoons guarded his baggage wagon. These three soldiers were probably later attached to the battalion. Therefore, Cooke had possibly had three mounted, experienced dragoons with him. See Cooke, *Conquest*, 99.

COOKE IN COMMAND

Up to this point the battalion was merely a collection of Mormon men, organized into a military unit and accustomed to certain camp routines. They had been purged of most of the weak and infirm and those unwilling to be divided from their families. The religious character of the battalion had been a hindrance at times, if one evaluates it from a pure military perspective. However, the men had suffered a great deal and still had a tremendous capacity for hardships. They had to a large degree become submissive to military authority. Cooke was correct in stating that they were not disciplined, but it was not the men's fault. It was a failure of leadership and a result of bad timing. There had been no time for Colonel Allen, followed by Lieutenant Smith and now Cooke, to train, drill, and instill discipline in the men. Taking the time to drill and train would have compromised their primary goal of uniting with Kearny. Discipline, drill, and developing combat effectiveness would have to wait, though it was very much on Cooke's mind.

Discipline is an essential quality of any army or military force. Without it there is no power or force to cause men to face the perils of war. It is the glue that keeps a unit together, the twine that binds commander and soldiers as one. Without discipline there is dissension, chaos, and ruin. Discipline has many parts, only one of which is following orders. Another is the ability to perform one's duties under extreme danger. It also causes well-trained soldiers to act and react by drill and training as individuals and also as part of a team such as a company or a battalion. If the order to charge is given, then one charges not as an individual but as a company or battalion without thinking, without questioning, and performing as trained. One of the most important results of rigorous training and good discipline is the ability to overcome one's fears and perform the task at hand. The idea of standing in ranks a hundred yards away from an opposing force and firing point blank into the enemy's ranks is a terrifying proposition at best. To be able to fire, reload, and fire again takes incredible discipline, which is best instilled through rigorous and frequent training. This is the key to conquering one's fears and performing under any situation with total disregard to the enemy's firepower, the surrounding confusion and chaos of battle, the extremes of weather, the difficulty of the terrain, stress, fatigue, sleep deprivation, and the lack of food and nourishment. Discipline is also the power of conducting one's duties during the absence of superiors and the chain of command. All these principles are instilled in the rule of military discipline.

The battalion was about to commence the most challenging and demanding portion of its march. The land became the stage as the men became the players. It is important to have an appreciation of the landscape—the terrain and the deserts they were about to cross. Unless one has actually traveled through this country—New Mexico, Arizona, and southern California—it is difficult to have a feel for the land. Watching western movies, flying above it in an airplane, or even crossing the miles in a car does not give one a full appreciation of the challenge to cross this torturous land on foot. The most important advantage Cooke had was the season. Compared to the average summer temperatures of more than 90 degrees in New Mexico and 100 degrees in Arizona, the late season temperatures would be very moderate and pleasant. With the cooler temperatures, though, came the disadvantage of less monthly rainfall. More precipitation fell during the hot summer months when the heat created frequent thunderstorms. Water would be the greatest concern.

The idea of taking some thirty wagons across eleven hundred miles of such forbidding desert terrain was no light matter. Without adequate maps, Cooke was determined to begin even though he had no real understanding of the route to take. There was, of course, the Old Spanish Trail or New Mexico's El Camino Real, which could be followed for some of the distance, but between present-day Las Cruces, New Mexico, and the San Pedro River in Arizona, there was no generally known passage, especially for wagons. This is not to say that some mountain men and frontiersmen had not been through this land. Of course they had, and Mexicans had built settlements, pueblos, and ranchos, but this information was not readily available to Cooke. So, he was really venturing into the unknown with a slow moving, heavily laden, poorly supplied, and untrained military force. The Mormon Battalion faced tremendous dangers, and the odds against survival and success were real. Only Colonel Alexander Doniphan's campaign through northern Mexico was equal in peril.

Weeks earlier Dr. George Sanderson had made an astute observation concerning marching soldiers long distances across forbidding country, their condition, and their combat effectiveness.

> I think this expedition will satisfy our Government that marching an army to Santa Fe California &c [etc.] is not so easy accomplished as talked about, and that is not all. I feel confident that marching troops such distances breaks them down. They have not the physical force nor mental vigor that they had when they started and of course not efficient for the field if I may use the vulgar term. They are broken down by fatigue. I will speak for my humble self as an individual. I shall return home I have no doubt. satisfied with campaigning on the Prairies.[48]

---

[48] George B. Sanderson, Journal, September 24, 1846, University of Utah Library.

CHAPTER ELEVEN

Cooke's Wagon Road

This march must fail, unless...
—*Lieutenant Colonel P. St. George Cooke*

Jean-Baptiste Charbonneau, hot, dusty, and tired, had been scouting well forward of the battalion looking for precious water. After grazing and resting, Charbonneau's mule became headstrong, and while he tried to saddle it, the ornery animal kicked him and then bolted away. He chased the recalcitrant mule for miles through sagebrush, cactus, and yucca, over hills and draws, until he was so frustrated that he shot the mule with his rifle. Charbonneau collected his saddle, pistols, and gear and walked several miles back to camp.[1] Charbonneau's anecdote gives witness to the challenge, difficulty, and adventure that lay before the Mormon Battalion.

At Santa Fe, once again ignoring the counsel of Brigham Young, the battalion had been divided and another gentile officer had taken command rather than a Mormon officer. Some eighty-six men were en route to Pueblo. Most of the women and children were gone. It was fortunate, however, that the battalion now had the leadership of Lieutenant Colonel Philip St. George Cooke. It is doubtful that Lieutenant Smith would have fared as well as Cooke in leading the battalion across the Southwest.

The religious character of the Mormon Battalion was still the strong pulse of the group. The men joined because Brigham Young

---

[1] Bieber and Bender, eds., "Journal," 110.

and the church had required it of them. If Brigham Young for some reason had changed his mind and sent word to the men at Santa Fe to return to the church, there would had been a mass desertion. M. Guy Bishop, biographer of Private Henry Bigler, wrote,

> Bigler's motives in enlisting were very different from those of most volunteer soldiers. He was not lured by the prospect of adventure, travel, booty, or glory on the field nor even by patriotism. He had joined only because his ecclesiastical leader had requested it. . . . He embarked on this distasteful task [military service] as a religious duty, endured its hardships sustained by a religious consciousness.[2]

The battalion was now facing a difficult and challenging overland journey of nearly eleven hundred miles. It would require all of its strength and will—and Cooke's leadership—to succeed. Training, drilling, and discipline would have to wait. "Our new Commander Cook. Formerly Capt. Cook 1st. Dragoons," wrote George Sanderson, "I think a very good officer."[3]

The first day of march was not a great test in military endurance. They made only six miles to a better grazing area called Agua Fria ('cold water') and camped for the night. There was no fanfare and perhaps few of the remaining American soldiers even took notice of the departure. One unflattering observer was Lieutenant George Rutledge Gibson of the Army of the West, who wrote, "They left without noise or confusion, and I watched them from Fort Marcy as they slowly gained the distance until they were entirely lost to view. . . . The States' have lost nothing by the Mormon emigration, and California gains as little, for the state of Illinois makes a good bargain to get shut of them at any cost."[4] Cooke simply recorded that on "October 19th the battalion was pushed out, by companies, six miles to Agu Frio."[5] Sergeant William Hyde made a more astute observation: "My feelings on leaving Santa Fe were of no ordinary kind. The Battalion had been divided, and thus I had been called to part with many of my brethren whose health

---

[2]Bishop, *Henry William Bigler: Soldier, Gold Miner, Missionary, Chronicler, 1815–1890*, 46.
[3]George B. Sanderson, Journal, October 21, 1846, University of Utah Library.
[4]Cited in Yurtinus, "A Ram in the Thicket," 208. Fort Marcy was named in honor of William Marcy, secretary of war. [5]Cooke, *Conquest*, 92.

was feeble." Hyde then considered what lay ahead: "in the advance of me a long and dreary march before we could reach the shores of the Pacific and time only was to reveal its fatigues and hardships."[6]

With the battalion purged of the sick and most of the dependent families, one would think the march times and distances would improve. This was not the case. The roads, landscape, and especially the sand became difficult obstacles. The terrain from Santa Fe south through areas such as the Rio Grande was extremely hilly and sandy along the La Baja Mesa. Even with fresh stock pulling the heavy wagons they had to travel through sandy river bottoms and over hills, which made the effort very burdensome. It was impossible for the wagons to follow a more direct route, so Cooke had to follow the Old Spanish road. Known as El Camino Real or the Royal Road, it had served as a link between Santa Fe and Chihuahua, Mexico, for over two hundred years. The established route avoided many of the steep hills and mesas. During the more than 200-mile march along the Rio Grande (also called the Rio del Norte), the men often had to double-team wagons and also pull and push the wagons themselves. It was a torturous and painstaking chore at times.

Cooke soon earned the respect of most all of the men. Sergeant Tyler recorded that "We found the judgment of Colonel Cooke in traveling much better than that of Smith, in fact, it was first-class. He never crowded the men unnecessarily."[7] There were, however, some who detested him even from the assumption of his command. Sergeant Coray, for one, wrote, "From the very onset we had taken a dislike to him.... A circumstance occurred this morning which showed how particular the Col. was with us." Coray narrated how Captain Hunter, commander of B Company, had left the battalion without permission to locate a lost mule. When Cooke learned of Hunter's absence, he "ordered him [Hunter] under arrest as soon as he arrived & made him march in rear of his co[mpany] for three days without his sabre."[8] Cooke showed some

---
[6]William Hyde, Journal, October 19, 1846, Brigham Young University Library.
[7]Tyler, *A Concise History*, 184–85
[8]William Coray, Journal, October 20, 1846, LDS Archives.

impartiality in punishing Captain Hunter. Some of the men welcomed this action. An important ingredient found in newly formed militia or volunteer units is the difficulty some men may have in accepting one of their peers as a superior. For Cooke to discipline Hunter, an officer, was seen by many as fair and democratic. It also seemed like a strange or unusual way to reprimand a fellow officer before his company. Normally officers disciplined other officers by a good tongue lashing in private.

The third day from Santa Fe, October 21, Cooke recorded events in a clear, objective, and detached manner. "I ordered a very early reveille and march, to accomplish the twenty-four miles," which he had planned to make that day. "I got the wagons ready before eight o'clock." Then he learned that some of the stock had strayed. He sent out a detail to gather the stock under the officer of the day and the previous night's guard to retrieve the animals. It took an hour to do so. The march began finally and, at one point, Cooke said that it took "an hour and three-quarters before the last wagon passed me." He established a march order by companies where the men followed the company baggage wagons. Describing the road conditions, Cooke recorded, "On this terrible sandy road, down the stream, several oxen fell, and had to be rolled out of the road ... the feet of others [oxen] were bleeding. The last of the command have got into camp at nine P.M.—several wagons not getting nearer than a mile."[9] It was a torturous all-day effort covering the twenty-four miles from San Marcos Arroyo to San Felipe Pueblo, north of Albuquerque. The march strained the teams, the men, and especially the commander.

Cooke showed great exertion in leading his men. His toil was endless. He had to care for the battalion's great logistical requirements, select the best routes, maintain march and camp discipline, and train his novice soldiers in the proper handling and care of animals and equipment. On October 23, he recorded, "This has been a day of hard and unremitting labor to me."[10] A week later Cooke wrote in his journal, "A dumb spirit has possessed all for the last

---

[9]Cooke, *Conquest*, 93–95.   [10]Ibid., 96.

twenty-four hours, and not one in ten of my orders has been understood and obeyed."[11] Later on November 2, near San Marcia, after dealing with many logistical problems and ensuring that his orders were followed, Cooke wrote, "All the vexations and troubles of any other three days of life have not equaled those of the last twenty-four hours. . . . My attention is constantly on the stretch for the smallest things. I have to order, and then see that it is done."[12] This was an amazing statement for a man who had spent some twenty years on the frontier in the rugged regular army serving in some of the most demanding campaigns in frontier history. It also gives us a clue into Cooke's leadership style and the state of discipline in the battalion. Today he would be called a "detail man," or perhaps a "micro manager," because he paid particular attention to every possible detail. He was a rigid enforcer, perhaps because of his personal style, but more likely because the Mormon company officers and NCOs did not know their roles and duties sufficiently so that Cooke could fully trust them. Regardless, Cooke had a very challenging day; he would have many more in the next few weeks.

There was at least one individual who had some select help when it came to chores and making the march. Dr. Sanderson remembered one day, "I got up early this morning and found my servant in obedience to orders had my mules all ready which we did about sun rise." He was referring to a young man named Charles, obviously a black slave. As mentioned, Sanderson census records show that he owned several slaves and some farm property in Missouri. The fact that some of the battalion members owned or brought along slaves is one of the many aspects of the battalion's story not thoroughly investigated by historians.[13]

---

[11] Bieber and Bender, eds., "Journal," 83.
[12] Cooke, *Conquest*, 100.
[13] George B. Sanderson, Journal, October 21 and November 23, 1846, University of Utah Library. An interesting small controversy appears here regarding Dr. Sanderson's property. John D. Lee claimed that fellow Mormon Howard Egan, either out of revenge or in spite against the Missouri doctor, stole some of Sanderson's personal property, a mule and a gold watch. See Bagley and Bigler, *Army of Israel: Mormon Battalion*, 141 n.87. If Sanderson had his watch and mule stolen, two valuable pieces, he probably would have mentioned it in his journal. One must conclude that John Lee was not telling the truth, besides blaming a deed on Howard Egan.

Continuing south past Albuquerque, they made slow but steady progress. The camp and march routine improved. Sergeant Coray recorded, "The Buglers would blow the assembly & the drummers would set immediately & play a Reville, not to exceed 2 minutes in all and if the men were not in the ranks to answer to their names, they were ordered on an extra tour of guard." Guard duty meant an entire night with little sleep, but one would still be expected to march the next day. "Every man was to be in the ranks before the drum ceased... every man must quit all even his breakfast & come in to ranks."[14] Provisions, good water, and the care and management of the animals worried Cooke greatly. Lieutenant George Stoneman was able to trade thirty poor mules for fifteen stronger animals. At Albuquerque, the quartermasters bought corn and other foods as provisions for the men and animals.

Frustration and the lack of military discipline forced Cooke to make important, on-the-spot decisions. He relieved First Sergeant Elijah Elmer of C Company on October 25. According to Cooke, "I reduced to the ranks a first sergeant for failing to form the company at reveille, and giving the excuse that it was not light enough to call his roll."[15] In Elmer's own words, Cooke asked, "Why is not your company out?" Elmer explained that it was too dark to read the roster. Cooke raged, "You God damn fool, consider yourself under arrest."[16] In Cooke's official Order No. 12, Lieutenant Dykes wrote, "Sergeant E. Elmer, of company C, is hereby reduced in the ranks for neglecting, this morning, to form his company while reveille was beating and for telling his Colonel that he did so because he could not see to call the roll." Tyler explained that Elmer actually stopped to lace his shoes, but did not want to tell Cooke the truth. According to Tyler, Elmer was later reinstated.[17]

---

[14] William Coray, Journal, October 23, 1846, LDS Archives. The battalion musicians were fifers and drummers. Cooke had a bugler, who may have been the bugler that Coray referenced. Also, Francis Parkman, the American historian who had met the battalion and Price's Missouri volunteers in September 1846 at the Arkansas River, recorded, "the rolling of the Mormon drums and the clear blast of their trumpets sounded through the mist." Apparently, the Mormon Battalion had a few men who served as buglers, probably of their own design. See Francis Parkman, *The Oregon Trail*, 402–3.

[15] Cooke, *Conquest*, 97.

[16] Yurtinus, "A Ram in the Thicket," 219.

[17] Tyler, *A Concise History*, 179.

Cooke went to great lengths to instruct his men in the proper care of the animals. Like most frontier officers, he was an expert with animals, especially caring for them under adverse conditions. He appointed quartermaster sergeants in each company to be responsible for the animals and teams besides the daily feeding and care of the stock. In the above-mentioned Order No. 12, dated October 25, 1846, Cooke instructed the men on how to harness the oxen and when and how to unharness, graze, and feed all of the animals. He explained how to rotate the animals with fresh stock when they became weak. Cooke also ordered, "The guard must hereafter be kept more strictly at their post. When the guard is stationed, death is the punishment awarded by law to a sentinel who sleeps on his post in time of war, which now exists."[18] Capital punishment was a very serious but common practice in the nineteenth century, especially during war.[19]

The care and feeding of the animals was a constant concern to Cooke. "I called up the captains and gave them a lecture," he wrote on October 28, "on the subject, as to fitting and cleaning collars, shortening harness, etc. and relieving mules, about to become galled; for I have assigned all the mules, giving two extra ones for every team."[20] This type of skill and duty was actually a responsibility of NCOs in the frontier army, though veteran officers learned and knew the practices themselves. Since Cooke did not have the luxury of experienced NCOs, he had to assume many of these responsibilities himself. He instructed the company commanders who, in turn, would hopefully enforce the same standards with their company leaders. Whether some of the Mormon men had experience with pack mules and heavy draft animals is unknown, but it became obvious that whatever experience these men had did not meet with Cooke's standards. Though many Americans had

---

[18]Ibid.

[19]Executing soldiers for desertion and other capital offenses in time of war was a common practice from the War of 1812 through the Mexican War and the Civil War. Though brutal and often remitted, the practice was still used often enough to instill discipline. See Utley, *Frontiersmen in Blue*, 38–49; Linderman, *Embattled Courage: The Experience of Combat in the American Civil War*, 174–76; Bauer, *The Mexican War*, 304–5.

[20]Ibid., 98.

experience on farms and in rural communities with plow horses and mules, and perhaps with oxen or as a teamster, they had not crossed such forbidding terrain where the service of these mules and oxen meant life or death for the soldiers. Again the next day, Cooke complained about the state of the mules: "I have extreme difficulty in having the mules properly cared for; there is great *vis inertia* in such a command."[21]

The new American territory of New Mexico was still in danger of war and pillage, but not by American or Mexican forces. In late October 1846, several thousand sheep were stolen and several herdsmen killed by marauding Navajo Indians at Valencia, just south of Albuquerque. General Kearny had ordered Colonel Doniphan, as military commander, to protect the Mexican ranches and settlements and punish Indian depredations when necessary. This order, however, was a very difficult proposition. Some of the Mexicans determined to guard their flocks and recapture their property by their own means. There were also many rumors that Mexican military forces were heading north from El Paso. One rumor was that seven hundred armed Mexican soldiers were on their way to retake New Mexico. Cooke recorded these Indian troubles and the rumors but concerned himself more with the march of his battalion.[22]

On October 29, at the small Mexican village of La Joya, Cooke reunited with his personal baggage in one wagon and the two dragoons who had guarded them for the last four weeks. For the better part of the way south along the Rio Grande, the march was along rather flat river bottoms and over some hills and sandy reaches at times; segments were choked with willows and other vegetation. South of La Joya they faced the Loma Blanca ('white hill') that many men referred to as sand dunes. They were not sand dunes in the true sense, but merely a steep ridge that meets very close to the river and has a very sandy soil base. The men had to double-team the wagons, and many of the men pulled and pushed the wagons through. It was a trying day of much exertion. All were under

---

[21]Cooke, *Conquest*, 99; *vis inertiæ* is Latin for 'strength of the ignorant.' In Cooke's case he probably meant lack of initiative.   [22]Cooke, *Conquest*, 102.

strain, and Cooke's influence was felt everywhere. A few days later Sergeant Coray exclaimed, "Every man was willing to take 10 days rations on his back if the Col would leave the waggons."[23]

It became necessary for Cooke to make another leadership change in the battalion. Captain Higgins, commander of D Company, had not returned from Pueblo. He had, in fact, arrived at Santa Fe after the battalion's departure, and Colonel Price allowed him and his detail to return to Pueblo—a very gentlemanly gesture for an anti-Mormon. Unaware of this, Cooke issued Order No. 13, dated November 1, 1846, which allowed First Lieutenant George Dykes to resign as adjutant and thanked him for his service. Dykes then assumed temporary command of D Company, replacing Second Lieutenant Cyrus Canfield. Lieutenant Philemon Merrill of B Company became adjutant. Canfield was promoted to first lieutenant in D Company. Dykes was not promoted to the rank of captain, because Higgins was still on the rolls but on detached service.[24]

Even with the change of position, Lieutenant Dykes continued to offend the men. From Fort Leavenworth on, the men viewed Dykes as a scoundrel, dictating commands, ordering long, difficult marches, and taking sides against his brethren over command changes and decisions that arose. Just a few days after his reassignment as company commander, he was on duty as officer of the day when two soldiers refused to salute him and made disrespectful remarks about him. Cooke ordered the men tied to the rear of a wagon, and they ate dust all day long during an eighteen-mile march. Then, the two men, Privates Philander Fletcher and Robert Stewart, both of D Company, had to serve on guard duty that evening. To the men it was a humiliating punishment, and they blamed Dykes. Sergeant Hyde wrote, "The appearance was that he regarded not the lives of his brethren. . . . The present prospect seems to be that indignant feelings are arising in the bosoms of many in the Battalion in reference to the course Lieutenant Dikes is pursuing, which will hardly erase."[25] Hyde naturally had difficul-

---

[23] William Coray, Journal, November 7, 1846, LDS Archives.
[24] Tyler, *A Concise History*, 184.
[25] William Hyde, Journal, November 4, 1846, Brigham Young University Library.

ty separating Dykes, the brother in the church, from Dykes as lieutenant in the army. Cooke's punishment, though tough for the Mormons to accept, was relatively mild.

On November 2, the scouts discovered a note in a post placed by Kearny that read "Mormon Trail," pointing to the southwest. It seemed that the general wanted to ensure the battalion followed the route southward. Fortunately, that same day the experienced scout Antoine Leroux arrived in the battalion's camp, near modern-day Val Verde, New Mexico.[26] (Jean-Baptiste Charbonneau had joined the battalion on October 24.) Kearny had sent Leroux back to guide Cooke forward, attaching him to the battalion. Leroux explained to Cooke that Kearny's route was too difficult for wagons and the land was too dry for so many men and animals. (Also, some Mexican traders had joined with the battalion on November 1, along with their thirty pack mules and other mounts.)[27] He recommended marching farther south some seventy or eighty miles and then heading west some three hundred miles to meet the San Pedro River in modern-day Arizona. None of the scouts had traveled this route before.[28] Cooke accepted Leroux's recommendation.

Antoine Leroux was one of the most traveled and famous mountain men in the West. He had been trapping fur and scouting for nearly thirty years by 1846. He served on one of the largest fur trapping adventures in western history, the William Ashley–Andrew Henry expedition in 1822–23. A hundred fur trappers were to ascend the Missouri River to its headwaters and establish a base of trapping and trading. Misfortune overtook the expedition through Indian attacks—they lost most of their equipment and most of the men never reached the headwaters at all. The entire expedition was a costly failure.[29] Leroux was also very familiar with the Gila River country, and that is why Kearny sent him back to scout for Cooke. However, he had not traveled through the exact area that the bat-

---

[26]Val Verde was the site of Fort Craig and a Confederate victory in February 1862.
[27]George B. Sanderson, Journal, November 1, 1846.
[28]Peterson, "Mormon Battalion Trail Guide," 28.
[29]See Forbes Parkhill, *The Blazed Trail of Antoine Leroux*; Hafen, *Mountain Men and Fur Traders of the Far West*, 81–83.

talion would march, which was farther to the south. Cooke recorded that the scouts estimated it would take at least ninety days to reach California by their proposed route.[30] From this point near Val Verde, the scouts' estimate was off by only two days—an amazing calculation.

Near the battalion Captain John Burgwin of the 1st Dragoons was patrolling and protecting several large caravans of Missouri and Santa Fe traders. Even with war, Mexican and American traders were still on the trail, in this case the Chihuahua Road south of Albuquerque. Rumors from the locals and traders continued to circulate that an armed force of Mexicans was en route to reconquer New Mexico: "[The traders] had received information that a body of Mexicans was marching upon them with a force of seven hundred men," remembered Dr. Sanderson. The traders demanded that Captain Burgwin "march his force to protect them."[31] This rumor probably became fact when Colonel Alexander Doniphan did encounter and defeat a Mexican force north of El Paso weeks later.

They were entering some of the most beautiful but harsh land in the great Southwest. From Val Verde, the Fray Cristobal Mountains rose eastwardly from the river plain with another "Jornada del Muerto" behind it. This route led to Doña Anna and the famous White Sands above El Paso del Norte del Rio Grande. Another small range, the Caballo Mountains, were to the south of the Fray Cristobal on the same side of the river. To the southwest and on the west side of the Rio Grande were San Mateo Mountains, and to the immediate west and a little northwest of Val Verde were the Magdelena Mountains. Directly west of the San Mateo Mountains were the Black Mountains that ran south and joined the Mimbres Mountains, which Kearny and his dragoons had just crossed a few weeks earlier. The Rio Grande was guarded on nearly every side by these small but very rough, barren mountains that rose like sentinels in nearly every direction. One cannot escape the beauty and the majesty of nature that the men of the Mormon Battalion encountered. As beautiful as the scenery was, however, the danger along the march was ever present.

---

[30]Cooke, *Conquest*, 100.   [31]George B. Sanderson, Journal, November 2, 1846.

Private James Hampton of A Company had been on the sick list for several days. On the morning of November 3, Dr. Sanderson released him "as ready for duty, but so far from being well, he died about 2 o'clock in the afternoon of the same day," wrote Tyler.[32] Dr. Sanderson recorded his own account: "about day break this morning we buried a man. This is the second death we have had since we started," the other death being Private Alva Phelps on September 16. "This man died very suddenly indeed. From some affliction of the heart. I think." Whatever Dr. Sanderson's diagnosis and treatment, it was tragic. It could have been his heart, or a number of other causes. There is no record that Sanderson gave him calomel, which he often prescribed.[33]

On this same day just a few hours earlier, Private Abner Chase of D Company, a member of the Brown sick detachment, died along the banks of the Purgatory River over three hundred miles north in modern-day Colorado. The other men who died and have already been mentioned were Privates Samuel Boley and Alva Phelps, as well as Private Norman Sharp of the Higgins detachment, who died on September 28, several days after an accidental, self-inflicted shooting. Private Milton Smith of C Company with the Brown sick detachment passed away on October 28. Of course, Lieutenant Colonel James Allen was the third death in the battalion, which brought the total of the honored dead to eight.

The next morning Hampton was buried in a blanket. Private David Pettegrew wrote these words about his comrade and brother in the faith: "Early this morning at reveille the corpse was borne in silence before the lines; all was silent and we were standing on an elevated point on the banks of the [Rio Grande] river, the occasional ripple of the waters and the barren and desolate land around us made the scenery solemn and produced a feeling of solemnity in almost every bosom."[34] Hampton would not be the last soldier to die.

---

[32]Tyler, *A Concise History*, 186.
[33]George B. Sanderson, Journal, November 4, 1846.
[34]David Pettegrew, Journal, November 4, 1846, Utah State Historical Society.

The operational tempo of the Mexican War had slowed to a crawl. Kearny was making reasonably good time across Arizona, a full month ahead and widening the gap on the slower-moving and heavily burdened Mormon Battalion. Santa Anna was making his way to San Luis Potosi at the head of an untrained and ill-equipped makeshift army of conscripts and peasants to repel Taylor. Within a few weeks Mexicans would select him once again as president of Mexico. Along with the Mexican army, there were over two hundred former American citizens and deserters from Taylor's army marching with Santa Anna. Organized at first as an artillery battery, then designated as the "San Patricio Battalion," these Americans were determined to fight their former countrymen and win appealing land grants and rewards for their treacherous service. Many of the San Patricios were Catholic and Irish and sought to make the best opportunity for themselves away from the rigid American regular army.

In California Commodore John Stockton, John C. Frémont, and the former "Bear-Flaggers" were half-heartedly endeavoring to win back Los Angeles and other key positions from the Mexican Californios. En route by sea, Colonel Jonathan Stevenson and his 1st New York Volunteer Infantry Regiment was coming to reinforce Kearny in California. Colonel Doniphan in New Mexico was piece-mealing his regiment around, chasing and attempting to chastise elusive Navajo raiders.

Meanwhile, President Polk in Washington was furious at the eight-week truce that General Taylor had accepted after his victory at Monterrey in September 1846. Rebuked, Taylor was now making a slow march to the key northern city of Saltillo. Polk and his advisors were miffed by the stubborn Mexican will to fight. The limited war aims that the administration had developed were not working. In spite of the loss of New Mexico, invasions into northern Mexico and, soon to follow, California, Mexico showed no signs of succumbing. American popular support for the war was waning. Polk and his cabinet realized during the dreary autumn months that American forces would have to march to Mexico's door. The war was far from over.

※ ※ ※

Not long after the march commenced along the Rio Grande, Colonel Cooke realized that even more men were unfit for duty. The problem of recruiting unfit men was not a systemic problem peculiar to the Mormon Battalion. A good number of men who joined the army were later found unfit for duty and discharged. The great challenge for Cooke was getting his sick soldiers safely to a place to either be discharged or to recuperate. It also taxed his resources to send rations, wagons, and healthy men to escort and assist the ailing. This, of course, reduced the battalion's combat strength. One soldier who was serving as an escort, Private Thomas Woolsey of E Company, departed with the Higgins detachment at the Arkansas River and returned on November 4. Woolsey also confirmed Cooke's judgment that the Higgins escort party of ten soldiers would winter at Pueblo with the other Saints there.[35]

Cooke could little afford to prolong the decision. Leroux's estimate of ninety days to reach Warner's Ranch in California was well beyond the sixty days of full rations that they had procured upon leaving Santa Fe. Cooke realized that he had to cut the rations to extend what was remaining. Yet his most pressing problem was not rations but dragging sick men along, which was folly.

Reducing the rations seemed a serious situation, according to some of the men. By General Order No. 14, dated November 3, 1846, Cooke ordered that "ten ounces of pork will be issued as the rations, and nine ounces of flour. Fresh meat will be issued at a pound and a half."[36] Some of the men worried about the sanity of making such a long march on the rations that the battalion had available. Private Henry Bigler noted the severe reductions of rations: "I know this much that we were soon put upon three-quarter rations and soon after on half rations."[37] In a more serious and accusatory vain, Sergeant Coray recorded on November 4, "I considered this [the reductions] open abuse. We were only 3 days from settlements where there was plenty of food & mules for sale. Why

---

[35]Bieber and Bender, eds., "Journal," 90.   [36]Tyler, *A Concise History*, 186.
[37]Gudde, *Bigler's Chronicle of the West*, 27.

did not he [Cooke] quiz the guide before it was too late?" Perhaps anticipating the obvious situation of abandoning some of the wagons, Coray criticized Cooke for pursuing his own glory with no regard to the welfare of the men. "Because he wanted to disencumber himself of baggage train," Coray wrote, "and he wanted to make California as soon as possible in order to raise his name in the world by performing a trip with less means and less humanity than any other man. It was well for the old culprit that he had mormons' to deal with. No body else would have borne what we did."[38]

After passing the natural feature later named Elephant Butte, they reached the point where Kearny had departed the Rio Grande for his overland trek to the Gila River. At this place Cooke took action. On November 9, he summarized the situation: "It has now become evident that we cannot go on so, with any prospect of a successful or safe termination to the expedition. The guides say that most of the mules could not be driven loose to California. I have carefully examined them and found that whole teams seem ready to break down." From the precarious condition of the animals, Cooke reported the dismal situation of the battalion itself: "twenty-two men are on the sick report; quite a number have been transported in the wagons ... there are still in the battalion men old, weakly, and trifling; besides all this, the rations are insufficient."[39]

A lesser commander may have aborted the entire mission and returned to Santa Fe or at least abandoned most of the wagons. Cooke continued, "I have determined and ordered fifty-five of the sick and least efficient men shall return to Santa Fe."[40] Surprisingly, some twenty-two men were on the sick list as Cooke mentioned. Thus, nearly two dozen men were willing to brave Dr. Sanderson's treatments, even with all the rumors about him. Sanderson himself logged, "twenty men on sick report ... three cases of measles."[41] Also surprisingly, another thirty men were deemed unfit as the detachment prepared to leave. Either they were acting the game or were fearful to come forward until Cooke ordered the detachment to Pueblo.

---

[38] William Coray, Journal, November 3, 1846, LDS Archives.
[39] Cooke, *Conquest*, 105–6.
[40] Ibid.
[41] George B. Sanderson, Journal, November 9, 1846.

Lieutenant William Wesley Willis of A Company led the detachment to Pueblo. Mrs. Sophia Tubbs with her husband Private William Tubbs joined the group. Four women—Melissa Coray, Lydia Hunter, Susan Davis, and Phebe Brown—and one child—Daniel Davis Jr.—remained, excluding the older boys who were serving as aides. Cooke sent back only one wagon and ox team with Lieutenant Willis. At Santa Fe the detachment received more provisions for their journey to Pueblo. Cooke calculated that he could spare eighteen hundred pounds of flour and other rations with the detachment. With the loss of nearly sixty people in the sick detachment, the projected rations for the remainder of the battalion actually increased by some two weeks.[42]

At this point, Cooke determined to reorganize the battalion. He should not be faulted for a lack of vision in attempting a difficult march with the resources he had available. In an era of limited intelligence-gathering methods and primitive means of transportation, a commander did his best. Adjustments were often required to continue the mission. Cooke realized after nearly three weeks that the existing organization and disposition would not work. He decided, therefore, to discard all unnecessary equipment and leave the last of the ox wagons for the 1st Dragoons to come and recover. The men filled these wagons with excess camp and cooking equipment, pots, pans, and such, and the long upright tent poles. Cooke reorganized the squads or messes with nine men per tent, using their muskets in lieu of the poles. Originally, the excess mules were herded together until used as replacements for a wagon team. Now Cooke had the mule packs, under the direction of the experienced eyes of the Mexican scouts, reorganized and repacked, with each mule carrying sixty to eighty pounds. The remaining spare ten yoke of oxen were packed with loads, as were the extra mules, until it was necessary to use them to relieve the mule teams. Cooke also had the men repack the loads in the wagons to make them lighter and more manageable.

The Willis sick detachment departed the next day, November 10, with fifty-five soldiers, one woman, and one wagon. A few days

---

[42]Cooke, *Conquest*, 105–6.

later three more sick soldiers overtook and joined Willis's party. This detachment, by far, was the worse off and faced the greatest challenges. It was a severe leadership trial for Lieutenant Willis to keep so many sick men moving with so few resources. In several of the journals the men severely criticized Willis for his treatment of the men and his threats.[43] Soon after departing, Privates John Green of C Company, and Elijah Freeman and Richard Carter, both of B Company, died near Socorro within a few days of each other. The Willis detachment finally reached Santa Fe on December 1, and then Private Thomas Woolsey, who had just rejoined the battalion, guided the detachment to Pueblo, departing on the 4th for Pueblo with ten pack mules and eighteen days of provisions. Private Joseph Richards of A Company with Brown's group died at Pueblo on November 21.

After an extremely exhausting trek through the mountains north of Santa Fe, Willis and most of the detachment arrived at Pueblo on December 20, 1846. Twelve soldiers who had lingered far behind remained at a ranch until others returned to bring them in. They struggled into Pueblo on January 15, 1847. One of the twelve left behind was Private William Coleman of A Company, who tried to keep up with the sick men but fell behind and died. It was a severe ordeal, and the harsh words and deeds produced prolonged bitterness among the men through the long winter months.[44] The Mormon Battalion had now lost thirteen soldiers.

Less than 350 men were present for duty out of the some 500 who enlisted at Council Bluffs four months earlier. This did not include the scouts, the dragoons, Major Cloud, Willard Hall, or others. Since its organization, the battalion was now better prepared than ever for actual combat operations. It was free of the old and weak men and most of the dependent families and wives. The battalion had experienced scouts to guide it, and an outstanding frontier officer was in command. Yet, without training and discipline, it still was little more than an organized mass of marching men.

---

[43]See Bagley, *Frontiersman: Abner Blackburn's Narrative*, 45–49; James Allen Scott, Journal, LDS Archives; see also George D. Wilson, cited in Bagley and Bigler, *Army of Israel*, 289–91.
[44]See Yurtinus, "A Ram in a Thicket," 274–91.

Well south of present-day Truth or Consequences, New Mexico, near the small town of Hatch, Colonel Cooke finally decided to leave the established but sandy and difficult Chihuahua Road. On November 13, after only marching a few miles south, Cooke found a note attached to a pole left by Leroux directing him west across the arid tablelands. They left the Rio Grande road and struck out southwest, blazing the wagon road for which he and the battalion would become famous: Cooke's Wagon Road. It was the first time that the Mormon Battalion was actually blazing a new road. To Cooke it was just a practicable decision to follow Kearny's orders to find the most suitable route to bring the battalion and the wagons through. After only fifteen miles they came to a water hole located in a deep crevice of rock at the base of Nutt Mountain. The men called it Foster's Hole, named after the interpreter, Dr. Stephen Foster, who had found it.[45]

Now the battalion was crossing a desert region stretching some 250–300 miles between the Rio Grande and the next major river, the San Pedro River of southeast Arizona. The scouts' ability to find water and to locate the most suitable route over some very trying land was critical. Cooke in his report explained how he employed the scouts to guide and find water:

> Leroux, with five, six or seven others, would get a day in advance, exploring for water, in the best practicable direction; finding a spring or a puddle, (sometimes a hole in nearly inaccessible rocks,) he would send a man back who would meet me, and be the guide. This operation would be repeated until his number was unsafely reduced, when he would await me, or return to take a fresh departure.[46]

This became a leapfrog practice, with scouts taking turns ranging ahead several days and returning to guide the battalion forward. Oftentimes a scout would be several to many days ahead of and separated from the main body. These men, of course, were mounted and had extra horses to accomplish such a difficult and dangerous responsibility.

The battalion continued across the flat and sparse desert land.

---

[45]Bieber and Bender, eds., "Journal," 98–99. [46]Gardner, "Report," 22.

The march was a tiresome routine of breaking camp, marching all day and making camp, sometimes without water. It became routine to take a layover day every few days to rest both man and beast. Cooke and the scouts also had to manage march days in relation to water sources. From Nutt Mountain they headed toward a smaller range of mountains with a very distinctive peak that was the most dominating landmark for miles. The mountains were very steep, rocky, and mostly treeless. Reaching water on November 15, the men rested at the small source of water. The next day they marched thirteen miles to the next water, which they found in what Cooke called a "swampy hole of water near a gap of the mountains." Though water was abundant, "Our men [are] complaining about short rations. They are now getting ten ounces of flour and one half pound of fresh meat." Dr. Sanderson added, "I consider them on about half rations." He was wise enough to explain why "traveling and the pure Atmosphere causes a great desire for food and a good deal of it too. We have about eighty day's rations say half rations to take us through."[47]

Surrounded by cottonwoods and willows, this spring would later bear the commander's name, as Cooke's Spring, as would the mountains he mentioned, Cooke's Range; the dominating peak nearby became Cooke's Peak.[48] Cooke's Spring would also be the site of a stagecoach station on the Butterfield Stage Line from 1858 to 1861, until Indians burned it. The future Butterfield stage would follow Cooke's Wagon Road for hundreds of miles. Cooke and the Mormon Battalion had made its small but important mark on American history.

※ ※ ※

Back in Washington, Polk and party knew that the war was not going as planned. For a few weeks he had contemplated a third major effort to land forces at Vera Cruz and march directly to the capital of Mexico City. Taylor's lethargy at Monterrey proved two things to Polk: first, the

---

[47] George B. Sanderson, Journal, November 16, 1846.
[48] This would be the site of Fort Cummings in 1863–91. Peterson, "Mormon Battalion Trail Guide," 34.

invasion through northern Mexico would not bring Mexico to its knees; second, he could no longer trust Taylor. Polk, conferring with Senator Thomas Hart Benton, one of the few men in Washington whom Polk partially trusted, realized that he had few options for a qualified commander. Polk offered Benton a commission as lieutenant general (three star) to command of the invasion forces, but Congress would not approve anyone to assume the same hallowed rank as George Washington, and Benton would not take command for anything less. Deadlocked, Polk turned to the only man who could actually succeed at such a colossal responsibility: a Whig, General Winfield Scott, a man he dearly detested. With the greatest reluctance, Polk appointed Scott to the new command on November 19, and Scott, gloating somewhat, left the capital on November 23, 1846.

Meanwhile, Santa Anna had deceived everyone again, including Polk, and had assumed control in Mexico. By mid-October 1846, he was in San Luis Potosi organizing another army after General Ampudía's humiliating defeat at Monterrey. It would take some weeks before he was ready to move against General Taylor at Buena Vista.[49]

A few days from Cooke's Range, Peak, and Spring, the Mormon Battalion intercepted the already known Janos (Cooke spelled it Yanos) Road, which connected the abandoned Santa Rita copper mines near present-day Silver City, New Mexico, and Janos in the Mexican state of Sonora. "Copper Mines distance about twenty miles," wrote George Sanderson. "[T]hese mines have not been worked any for the last eight years. The Apache Indians was the cause of their being abandoned."[50]

They continued on November 21 down this road only a mile and a half when Cooke ordered a halt. What happened next is a myth that has creeped into history. Apparently, the men were very concerned that they were marching too much on a southerly course, and taking the Janos Road proved that Cooke was leading them into central Mexico and not on to California. The evening before,

---

[49]Eisenhower, *So Far from God*, 152–53, 161–65.
[50]George B. Sanderson, Journal, November 19, 1846.

Privates Hancock and Pettegrew held prayer vigils with many of their brethren throughout the camp, asking God to help the colonel change his mind. At the halt Cooke realized that the Janos Road would lead too far to the southeast, so he instructed the bugler to "blow to the right," which is an interesting command, since the route of march was always turning back and forth without bugle calls.

Of this incident Cooke simply recorded:

> I marched this morning by the [Janos] road.... But I soon found it leaving level prairie in its first course, and leading over a ridge, twenty-five degrees east of south [bearing 155 degrees]. I had relied on the assertions that Yanos [Janos] was to the south-west.... I had followed the guides in almost every direction but eastward. After proceeding a mile and a half, without any further consultation, I turned short to the right, and directed the march to the hole of water which had been discovered to the south-west.[51]

There are many references of this event in the journals of the men, which universally had Cooke asserting that he did not intend to march into Sonora or Chihuahua. Cooke did not want to fall under the command of General John Wool, commander of the Army of the Center, who was en route from San Antonio to Monterrey to link up with Taylor. When "blow to the right" sounded, Private Pettegrew announced, "God bless the Colonel."[52] According to Private Henry Bigler, the incident was a little less pious. "The Colonel was riding at the head of his command with his pilots, when he made a sudden halt and ordered his men to turn square to the right and swore he would be G_d damned if he was going all around the world to get to California," recorded Bigler.[53]

As happy as the majority was with Cooke's decision, some saw it differently. Dr. Sanderson disagreed with Cooke: "He [a Mexican trader] advised us by all means not to attempt the route West over a country... unknown"—the exact route Cooke eventually followed. Sanderson opposed this decision: "I do not believe his organ of firmness predominates at any rate.... We then launched out on a plain due West never before traveled. This move I do not think

---

[51] Cooke, *Conquest*, 129–30.   [52] Tyler, *A Concise History*, 207.
[53] Gudde, *Bigler's Chronicle of the West*, 28.

prudent for should we fail to find water our enterprise is at an end." He wrote that the more southern direction provided water and "we should probably have a little fighting to do. For my part I would prefer dying on the battle field to perishing in the desert."[54]

To the Mormon men, with their proclivity for religious things, this was divine intervention and became a legend. It seems, however, more of a change of direction to follow the proper route and go to a water hole rather than a matter of divine guidance; nevertheless, to the men it was an inspiring event. The men probably saw Cooke as an instrument in God's hands and an answer to their prayers.

The route the battalion followed over the next few weeks had great consequences to the expansion of the American West. The march would be one reason that vast tracts of land would eventually come under United States control. Dipping down across the modern border between Mexico and the United States, they paralleled the future boundary for some miles before turning back into U.S. territory. The land obtained from Mexico after the war did not include all of southern New Mexico and Arizona. The Treaty of Guadalupe Hildago that settled the war established a line that followed the Gila River in central Arizona directly east across to the Rio Grande near Socorro, New Mexico. Acquiring the land south of this line to the present borders of Arizona and New Mexico was partly the result of the march of the Mormon Battalion. The Gadsden Purchase of 1853 directed the United States to pay Mexico $10 million for this land for a possible railroad route. Cooke's report became part of the Congressional Record and was used by the Franklin Pierce administration as a source when Congress considered the purchase.[55] Through this area, the famous Butterfield Stage line, the San Diego–San Antonio Mail line, gold seekers and

---

[54]George B. Sanderson, Journal, November 21, 1846.
[55]Historian William H. Goetzmann recognized the importance of Cooke's "Report" and the wagon road, as did Lieutenant William Emory at the time. See Goetzmann, *Army Explorations it the American West, 1803–1863*, 141–42.

forty-niners, the Southern Pacific Railroad, and settlements would come. Cooke and the Mormons were the first large group of Americans to pass through this area. Cooke's report provided vital information concerning this territory and was partly instrumental in the government's later interest in obtaining this land, which proved to have a treasure of mineral wealth.[56]

The battalion averaged between sixteen and eighteen miles a day. Cooke allowed a rest day about every four to six days. Pioneer emigrant companies often took rest days, but not always on a standard routine or schedule, whereas the Mormon pioneer companies generally but not always rested on Sunday, their Sabbath. Cooke rested when the men needed it and where there was sufficient water, firewood, and grass for the animals. Though the land was very arid, there was sufficient grass at times for the animals, and the Mexicans had established many ranches in this area. In fact, one of the landmarks the scouts were guiding the battalion toward was San Bernardino, a large abandoned cattle ranch and range that straddles the modern border of Arizona with Mexico.

From the journals and histories, it is very apparent that Cooke had gained the respect and strong regard of most of the men by this point in their long march. There were some who disliked him, such as Sergeants Coray and Hyde, and Levi Hancock, but they recognized his competence as a commander. The weight of Cooke's responsibility grew as the battalion continued across this barren, austere land. Not only was the scouting for water essential, but finding the easiest and most accessible route for the wagons was critical. In late November they passed west of modern-day Deming, New Mexico.

Heading southwest, they crossed a wide, flat plain and made a grueling day's march on November 22. The Mormon Battalion lost all form of march discipline and unit cohesiveness as stragglers limped along for miles. Reaching some small rocky hills called Coyote Mountains, a little water was found, but hardly enough to replenish the men and stock. The men had to use spoons to scoop up water to drink. Approaching this small spring, Dr. Sanderson wrote, "I found

---

[56]Cooke, *Conquest*, 159.

here a poor fellow belonging to the Command with a poor Horse and some fifty Canteens strung round the animals neck and other places full of water going back to meet his thirsty companions."[57] Sanderson added a gloomy prediction and commentary: "a good deal of dissatisfaction among the Mormans and officers of the Battalion. and should we fail to get water to night our campaign is at an end."[58]

When Cooke arrived, he ordered the men away so the mules could have the scarce supply of water. Captain Hunt had some harsh words for him once he learned of Cooke's actions. Though it was unthinkable for a soldier to challenge or rebuke an officer during this era, other officers in private could, with tact and under the proper circumstance, voice concerns to a superior.[59]

Accompanying the battalion was a non-Mormon named Lewis Dent, later an in-law of General and, later, President U. S. Grant. Born in St. Louis in 1822, Lewis Dent was serving as a civilian clerk to Major Cloud, the army's paymaster. He witnessed and recorded some moving observations. In a letter written February 1, 1847, from California to his brother George Wrenshall Dent, he summarized his travels and experiences, and his writings are stirring and poignant. "I saw athletic and vigorous men reduced, by thirst and fatigue, to the imbecility of children," he wrote months later, "their bodies attenuated and feeble; their faces bloated; their eyes sunken; their feet lacerated and bruised, mechanically moving forward, without a murmur and without an object; the latter having been lost sight of in the gloomy contemplation of their present helpless condition."[60]

The march route passed through a saddle between the Coyote Mountains and the higher Little Hatchett Mountains and entered

---

[57]George B. Sanderson, Journal, November 22, 1846, University of Utah Library.
[58]Ibid., November 23.   [59]Tyler, *A Concise History*, 208.
[60]Lewis Dent to George Wrenshall Dent, February 1, 1846, in San Diego, California, originally published in St. Louis in *The Daily Reveille* 4, no. 958 (June 12, 1847): 1–2. Lewis Dent was the older brother of Julia Boggs Dent, who married U. S. Grant in 1848. Another brother, Frederick Tracy Dent, was Grant's roommate at West Point, and they graduated together in 1843. Dent served in Mexico under General Winfield Scott; he was wounded and received two brevet promotions for gallantry. During the Civil War, Colonel Dent served as Grant's aide-de-camp for much of the war.

Playas Valley. Stretching for nearly ten miles on a direct north and south axis, Lake Playas was a dry bed of nothing but tannish, hard-baked dirt. In Cooke's words, "We came in sight of what was apparently a river, but we believed it to be sand. For hours I rode on, approaching it obliquely." Reaching it at dusk he continued, "it was said to be the bottom of a long dry lake or swamp."[61] In his journal Cooke described Lake Playas as flat and polished as marble and the "most extraordinary ground that had ever been seen."[62] Finally the scouts found sufficient water and grass at the west side of the dry lakebed. Late that evening, the stronger men arrived at the water hole at Lake Playas. Others straggled in all night. After refreshing themselves, many of the men returned along the line of march to take water to their comrades. This was the same day on which Charbonneau killed the runaway mule, as described at the beginning of the chapter.

The battalion rested on November 24, and the men and animals took a day to recuperate. After making a forty-mile march in some thirty-six hours and finding little water, Cooke wrote, "these were anxious circumstances, and the responsibility I had taken weighed heavily upon me; their safety and my success seemed both doubtful."[63]

In his *Conquest of New Mexico and California*, Cooke wrote of a fateful tragedy that befell the Apaches at Lake Playas some ten years before the battalion passed through. Here an American named Johnson, along with other Americans and a few Mexican soldiers, parlayed with and then massacred several Apaches and sold their scalps to authorities in Sonora. The Lake Playas killings were a simple foreshadowing of the terrible relations that Americans and the native peoples of the Southwest would endure for the next fifty years.[64]

"These Indians [Apache] are the terror of all the frontier settlements of Sonora and Chihuahua," recorded Dr. Sanderson. As the battalion entered and crossed Apache domain, the men heard the

---

[61]Cooke, *Conquest*, 131–32.
[62]Bieber and Bender, eds., "Journal," 113.
[63]Gardner, "Report," 23.
[64]Cooke, *Conquest*, 135–36.

rumors and legends of Apache warfare and acumen and were concerned. Sanderson wrote, "I am credibly informed that these Indians within twelve years have killed and taken prisoners over twenty thousand Mexicans and destroyed and stolen property amounting to fifteen millions of dollars."[65] Sanderson failed to say who informed him, but many Santa Fe traders, and perhaps Leroux, Charbonneau, and the other battalion scouts, heard of these affairs. Dr. Sanderson wrote several interesting observations at times in his journal. Relative to the Lake Playas massacre a few years earlier, he wrote, "A few weeks ago a party of them [Apache Indians] was induced to enter a [Mexican] Village in Senora by the inhabitants and made drunk and then butchered indiscriminately in the most barbarous manner." The long feud of Mexican and Indian hatred and barbarity was quickly becoming an American problem. Dr. Sanderson summarized, "I do not wish it to be understood that I do not think the Apacha's a bad Indian. I have no doubt they are the most desparate and daring on the continent. But they have had a course pushed towards them."[66]

The Mormon Battalion was about to cross the Continental Divide over the Animas Mountains to the west. Their long march across half the continent had reached an important milestone. The idea of reaching the Pacific Ocean was constantly on the men's minds; it was almost an obsession. Now they were entering the land that drained into the Pacific, yet they were still hundreds of long, hard miles away. Before them lay more mountains, more deserts, many more miles and days of misery, suffering, and thirst—and a Mexican force ready to do battle.

---

[65] George B. Sanderson, Journal, November 17, 1846, University of Utah Library.
[66] Ibid., November 29, 1846.

CHAPTER TWELVE

A Near Battle

... any other company ... would have mutinized.
—*Sergeant William Hyde*

Once again Jean-Baptiste Charbonneau provided the men with an episode of frontier theater. While ascending the Guadalupe Mountains on the border of modern-day New Mexico and Arizona, Dr. Sanderson recorded, "I left Camp very early this morning ... in the company with one of our guides [Charbonneau]. a very enterprising daring fellow." Within just a few minutes Charbonneau had killed a large antelope and "had the skin of[f] and cut up I am confident in five minutes." Continuing their hunt and "passing through the Mountains saw three Grisly Bears a Mother with two Cubs half grown. This man pulls of[f] his coat and hat ties a hanker chief around his head and away he starts up the Mountain to shoot them." Sanderson heard two sharp reports and the echoes of gunfire,

> so quick you would not credit that it was from the same gun. This was one of the most exciting as well as hazardous scenes I ever witnessed. After he shot the first time she [the mother bear] immediately made towards him. He shot the second time and what is almost incredible both the Balls entered the same place.[1]

Colonel Cooke and many of the men also observed this dangerous but entertaining scene. Cooke explained that there "was confused action, one bear falling down, the others rushing about with

---

[1] George B. Sanderson, Journal, November 25, 1846, University of Utah Library.

loud fierce cries ... the mountain fairly echoed." He remembered, "I much feared he was lost, but soon, in his red shirt, he appeared on a rock; he had cried out, in Spanish, for more balls." The cubs scattered before he obtained more ammunition, then the finale: "the bear was rolled down, and butchered before the wagons passed," ending the morning theatrics.[2] It was comic prelude to one of the most difficult challenges the battalion would face. Before them lay the Guadalupe Mountains and miles of desert.

"We all started uppon the march to cross the back bone of North America," recorded Private George Washington Taggart. Though a bit off on his location and basic facts, he remembered, "this chain of Mountains I suppose is called the back bone on account of its being the highest chain of the Rocky Mountains, consequently divides the waters which flows to the Atlantick and Paciffick."[3] The men encountered an extremely rough and rocky range of mountains—a seemingly impregnable obstacle for wagons. The Guadalupe Mountains were a small but rugged range that stood between the battalion and the San Pedro River, still many miles away.

On November 28, 1846, at modern-day Cloverdale Springs, New Mexico, Cooke dispatched his scouts to find the Guadalupe Pass, which followed a rough-hewn old Spanish road that led to San Bernardino, an abandoned cattle ranch, and then to Fronteras, a settlement on the future United States and Mexican border. The battalion camped at the base of the Guadalupe Mountains in the Animas Valley, which lay 5,200 feet above sea level. The Guadalupe peaks rose to an elevation of 6,400 feet, with the western front dropping off like a precipice more than 3,000 feet to the valley floor near modern-day Douglas, Arizona. Covered with cedar, juniper, pine, and the ubiquitous sagebrush, the Guadalupes rose gently, and then very steeply, to the jagged peaks.

The scouts were unable to locate the pass, so Cooke directed Lieutenant George Stoneman to take a detail of men the next day and make a road through the canyons that dropped off several hun-

---

[2]Cooke, *Conquest*, 134–35.
[3]George Washington Taggart, "A Short Sketch of his Travels," December 1, 1846, LDS Archives.

A NEAR BATTLE

dred feet below. The prospect was daunting. Englishman Robert Whitworth lamented, "There is a fearfull steep ravine here, down which our trail goes. It extends for 9 miles, is very Rocky and Steep. Our commander being determined to take waggons through to California, which had never been done before by this route."[4]

It was incredibly arduous, backbreaking work, and after a day the men had only cleared about a mile and a half. On November 30, they emptied the wagons and moved them forward as the work party continued to break rock and dig. All the provisions were packed on the mules and led down. Using ropes, the men lowered the wagons down through the steep, narrow cuts and canyons. The men lost control of one wagon that fell and was dashed to pieces, and then abandoned. Others were damaged and later repaired.

When one thinks of soldiering and war, it may seem rather unusual for soldiers to do such work. Yet history definitely bears numerous examples of soldiers building roads, bridges, dykes, and forts; damming rivers; digging canals; and even changing the courses of rivers. During the Civil War, General Grant tried digging a canal past Vicksburg in 1863; ground soldiers under Benedict Arnold, not sailors, built a flotilla of boats at Lake Champlain during the American Revolution; Hannibal constructed huge rafts on several occasions for his elephants to cross wide rivers; and Alexander the Great built a causeway over a mile long to besiege and capture Tyre.

The men now had to get the wagons over the Guadalupe Mountains. Private Henry Bigler provided this commentary on Cooke's leadership: "I think no other man but Cooke would ever have attempted to cross such a place, but he seemed to have the spirit and energy of a Bonypart."[5] Dr. Sanderson captured the scene: "This day's travel has been one of great interest. the mountains Magnificently grand. This Chain of Mountains. I take to be the grand dividing ridges. Between the waters of the Atlantic and Pacific." He wrote that they camped "on the head waters of a stream that empties itself into the Gulph of California."[6]

---

[4]Gracy and Rugeley, "From the Mississippi to the Pacific: An Englishman in the Mormon Battalion," 149.   [5]Gudde, *Bigler's Chronicle of the West*, 29.
[6]George B. Sanderson, Journal, November 30, 1846, University of Utah Library.

Tragically, just after crossing the Guadalupe Mountains, Dr. Stephen Foster found the pass only a mile away from where they nearly broke themselves making a road. An angry Cooke simply wrote, "my guides are ignorant of this country."[7] This was a tremendous failure on the part of the scouts.

Colonel Cooke recorded in his monthly return for November 1846 that a soldier had deserted. Years later Cooke simply wrote, "Private Allen has disappeared."[8] The soldier was Private John Allen of E Company, who enlisted at Fort Leavenworth and also became a member of the LDS Church at the same time. Sergeant Tyler explained that several men were hunting when Allen failed to return with the others. "John Allen, a worthless fellow," wrote Tyler, "who attached himself to the Church at Fort Leavenworth that he might join the battalion and obtain passage and protection to California. It was thought by some that he deserted."[9] According to George Sanderson, the "Apach[e] Indians took from him his gun and stripped him of everything he wore and sent him on his road," and he nearly died of thirst.[10] If he intended to desert, he certainly botched it, having to return after just four days This is the only desertion recorded in official military documents of the Mormon Battalion.[11]

After crossing down into modern Mexico and reaching the abandoned San Bernardino Ranch, the route eventually turned northwest to intercept the San Pedro River valley in present-day Arizona. Thousands of cattle belonging to Mexican ranches or, more often, from abandoned ranches such as San Bernardino, roamed through the area. Cattle and wild game were plentiful. "We have now meat enough to serve the Command for Ten days," wrote Dr. Sanderson. Most days either the scouts or officers would bring back fresh meat, and some of these hunts had their own stories. Congressman-elect Willard Hall, former private of the 1st Missouri Mounted, and Dr. Sanderson were on one such hunt when,

---

[7]Bieber and Bender, eds., "Journal," 125. See also Cooke, *Conquest*, 135–37.
[8]Cooke, *Conquest*, 138.   [9]Tyler, *A Concise History*, 210.
[10]George B. Sanderson, Journal, December 4, 1846, University of Utah Library.
[11]Tutorow, *The Mexican-American War: An Annotated Bibliography*, 361; Tutorow's material comes mainly from two sources: Edward Mansfield, *The Mexican War: A History of its Origin, 1850*; and Francis Heitman, *Historical Register and Dictionary of the United States Army*.

A NEAR BATTLE

after wounding and chasing a bull several miles, Hall's mule "took into its head to attack the bull and away he ran directly towards the Bull with Hall." As the mule closed on the wounded bull, Hall "threw himself from the mule." Sanderson rode up and finally killed the troublesome animal.[12]

As they marched towards the San Pedro, the battalion intercepted a road first used by Colonel Juan Bautista de Anza in 1775. Colonel Anza led a colony of several dozen families, a few soldiers, and priests to settle in California at San Francisco Bay. Thus, Cooke's wagon road again followed a route used for years. They reached the San Pedro River on December 9 and continued north along the river.[13]

Another circumstance the battalion faced were the predations of the Apache Indians in this harsh land. The Spanish and Mexican ranches were constantly under threat of Apache raids. The men of the battalion learned fully the reputation of this enterprising but brutal band. "The[y] are a wild predatory tribe, frequently making excursions into the villages of New Mexico and Sonora and carrying off Horses, mules, cattle, Sheep, and sometimes Females."[14]

On December 11, while at a halt along the San Pedro, the battalion was harassed by some wild cattle, an event now known in the annals of the Mormon Battalion as the "Battle of the Bulls." Several dozen of these wild animals, no more than a hundred, charged the men at noon-day stop, killing a few mules, jolting a few wagons, injuring a few men, and causing some confusion and chaos. Some of the men proved their mettle and marksmanship by killing a few of the attacking beasts, and thus the "battle" ended when the animals eventually ran off. Lieutenant Stoneman wounded his thumb from an accidental discharge of his firearm.[15]

---

[12]George B. Sanderson, Journal, December 5 and 7, 1846, University of Utah Library.

[13]San Bernardino Ranch is a little known but very historic site in the Old Southwest; Peterson, "Mormon Battalion Trail Guide," 40–41. A few days earlier, a teamster named Elisha Smith died; Tyler, *A Concise History*, 215–16.

[14]Gracy and Rugeley, "From the Mississippi to the Pacific," 149.

[15]There are numerous accounts of this incident. Cooke provided one of the best, as did Tyler; see Cooke, *Conquest*, 145–46; Tyler, *A Concise History*, 218–21; John Yurtinus, "The Battle of the Bulls," 99–108. For an excellent explanation concerning the wild cattle in the area, see David Bigler's foreword in Norma Rickett's *The Mormon Battalion*.

Afterward they marched a few more miles and camped along the San Pedro in the cottonwoods and mesquite. A few days ahead, the Mormon Battalion would face its only true opportunity to engage Mexican forces during its entire service.

General Kearny arrived with his one hundred ragged, nearly starving dragoons at Warner's Ranch on December 2, 1846. He had few horses left; some of the men rode mules in awful condition, and many were dismounted. Advancing forward towards the coast, he was met on December 5 by thirty-five American sailors and mountain men and a couple of field pieces under the command of the ubiquitous Lieutenant Archibald Gillespie, U.S. Marine Corps. Gillespie was Frémont's protégé and late major and adjutant of the "Bear-Flaggers."[16] *Gillespie informed Kearny that about sixty mounted Mexican (Californio) "lancers" under Major Andrés Pico were some ten miles ahead astride Kearny's route of advance. Kearny determined to attack the next day with his force of some 140 men along with Kit Carson and scouts.*

After a heavy rain in the early morning hours, on December 6 Kearny attacked in a valley near a small Indian village called San Pasqual. Descending from a range of ridges of sagebrush, oak brush, and prickly pear cactus chest-high, the dragoons entered the valley. Almost immediately things went wrong for the Americans. Some of the dragoons on better mounts, led by a couple of excited officers, raced pell-mell ahead of the main body. They were soon counter-attacked by the Mexican lancers with devastating effects. Kearny and the main body arrived and found themselves under attack and surrounded by an aggressive foe, well trained for mounted combat. With wet powder, they were unable to fire their muskets effectively. The dragoons, however, eventually repulsed the lancers after a determined fifteen- to twenty-minute skirmish.

Who won this hard-fought but short Battle of San Pasqual? Kearny retained the field, he had freedom of maneuver, and his force was still intact, but battered; thus he earned the victory. But it was costly—Kearny lost eighteen men, some of whom were very promising officers

---

[16]Harlow, *California Conquered*, 181; Kearny had brought two howitzers across the mountains with his party.

and quality NCOs. *Many were wounded, including Kearny himself, with a serious lance wound in the groin. Gillespie had a more dangerous wound in the chest. Spooked from the din of battle, a team of mules dragged a field howitzer off into the Mexican lines. The Mexicans carried away their dead and wounded but did not have nearly as many casualties as Kearny. Another such victory would have cost Kearny his entire force.*

The next day and a few miles later, Kearny found himself blocked by Pico's mounted lancers. Taking advantage of a strong defensive position, Kearny occupied a steep hill. The starving men ate some of their mules, providing the name of the location, "Mule Hill," near modern-day Escondido. In a desperate gamble, Kit Carson, Lt. Edward Beale of the U.S. Navy, and a couple others penetrated the Mexican patrols and lines and escaped barefoot over the thirty miles of rough mountainous terrain to the American lines at San Diego. (They had taken off their boots to make less noise.) A few days later, reinforcements arrived and Kearny and his battered element of the Army of the West entered San Diego.[17]

After following the San Pedro River for some fifty miles, the battalion left the river for Tucson, the next important landmark and settlement, a village of some five hundred inhabitants over thirty miles away. At camp along the San Pedro the evening of December 12, Leroux reported that he learned from Indians that Tucson had a garrison of two hundred men with two pieces of artillery. They also reported that battle was possible. The scouts wisely returned to camp employing separate and circuitous routes to avoid disclosing their return route to camp. The next day, after a march of a few miles, Cooke took a few measures to prepare for the possibility of combat. The men received powder and ball to conduct some practice volleys. Cooke drilled the battalion through the manual of arms and tactics. Though the amount of training and drill the men received is not exactly known, Cooke typically conducted drills in maneuvering and deploying from march column formation to skir-

---

[17]Ibid., 182–88; Eisenhower, *So Far from God*, 221–26.

mishing lines and then to line of battle. This proved to be very discouraging, because the men had not received much training in tactical maneuvers and formations. According to Private Azariah Smith of B Company, the men were "somewhat awkward which made the Colonel swear very much."[18]

Being a realist and not a military opportunist, Cooke sent messages to the Mexican officials in Tucson stating his desire to avoid confrontation and combat. Though Cooke, like most professionals, was willing and perhaps even desirous of the glory and laurels of war, he also recognized the complete futility of engaging in combat in such a remote region for no obvious military or tactical gain. Cooke's mission was to march the battalion to California without delay. To do battle over the small, insignificant village of Tucson was an unrealistic proposition. Unless attacked, there was no tactical or rational basis to engage in combat. The Army of the West was to conquer and occupy New Mexico and California. With the limited troops available, Kearny could not possibly defeat all enemy forces and totally occupy this vast territory. Cooke realized the tactical situation. The Mexican forces in northern Sonora were small and not a serious threat. The Sonorans also seemed to have a general unwillingness to participate directly in military action against the United States.[19]

Following Kearny's example at Santa Fe, Cooke was willing to offer friendship and diplomacy rather than combat.

During the next few days, Cooke marched the battalion slowly but deliberately towards Tucson while he and the Mexican commander, Captain Antonio de Comaduran, played a cat-and-mouse game of messages, ultimatums, and taking each other's scouts and messengers as prisoners. Cooke published orders to the men about honoring Mexican property rights and also wrote a proclamation to the Mexican governor of Sonora, Manuel Gandara, of his peace-

---

[18] Samuel Rogers, Diary, December 13, 1846, Brigham Young University Library; James Pace, Diary, December 13, 1846, Brigham Young University Library; also cited in Bagley and Bigler, *Army of Israel*, 159 n.48.

[19] Cooke, *Conquest*, 152; in Cooke's letter to the governor of Sonora, he acknowledged the fact that Sonora seemed unwilling, unable, and unassisted from the Mexican central government to resist.

ful intentions. Privately, Cooke seemed more concerned at times with the types of cactus he observed than preparing for battle.[20] This could be because Cooke, like most American military professionals, had little respect for the Mexican army.

The Mexican forces that the Mormon Battalion faced have been difficult to assess completely because of the lack of a sufficient historical record. Examining the Mexican army of this era and the small units garrisoned in New Mexico and California specifically, one can draw a few conclusions. The military forces that Mexico employed against the United States Army were inferior in nearly every aspect except in numbers. The Mexican army suffered from abysmal logistical support, poor leaders overall, inadequate training, lack of professionalism, inferior firearms, and poor equipment. Though oftentimes their soldiers were dressed in splendid uniforms of elegant and gaudy design, conveying a sense of discipline and professionalism, the army as a whole was weak and inferior. They carried obsolete muskets that dated back to the 1760s, had virtually no training, and served under severe oppression. They were led by politically groomed and autocratic officers who were poor leaders, ignorant of the art of war, and had little concern for the welfare of the men in the ranks. In battle Mexican soldiers were brave, steadfast, and tough. But they entered battle with almost insurmountable institutional handicaps.[21]

Mexican soldiers of the era were typically either criminals or peasants, pressed or conscripted for terms of up to six years. This was a long term of service by American standards but common in European armies. "Army ranks, moreover, continued to be filled by conscripted vagrants, criminals, and other social malcontents who readily deserted when faced with the prospect of being posted to the far reaches" of the Mexican republic's isolated outposts.[22] Few Mexicans volunteered to fight for country and flag. Within the

---
[20]Ibid., 147–49.
[21]For a complete study of the Mexican army, see DePalo Jr., *The Mexican National Army, 1822–1852*.   [22]Ibid., 75.

Mexican army there was a definite caste system that reflected Mexican society as a whole. Officers were educated and most were from the upper class, though some came from the middle class. They had rudimentary training in the art of war, with their status based more on desire for political or personal gain than for serving the military establishment. There were military schools and academies, but none equal to those in the United States and Europe. While the American military institution copied the French army in tactics, engineering, and professional acumen, the Mexican army copied it for grandeur and appearances.

By the spring of 1846, the Mexican army had more than 28,000 officers and other ranks, over three times larger than the United States Army. At first glance this seems like a strong force for a nation of only seven million people. In examining the army carefully, one learns that nearly 19,000 were *permanentes* or regular army, full-time troops and 10,500 were *activos* or active militia soldiers. These forces were spread over a vast, harsh land at small garrisons called *presidios*.[23] The large size of the Mexican empire, as well as institutional disadvantages, hampered the army from becoming a quality fighting force.

Contemporary accounts explain the quality of the Mexican army. "The Mexicans, as on many other occasions, stood up as well as any troops ever did," wrote Lieutenant U. S. Grant. "The trouble seemed to be the lack of experience among the officers, which led them after a certain time to simply quit, without being particularly whipped, but because they had fought enough."[24] Another commentary on Mexican officers came from a British observer, Charles Bankhead, ambassador to Mexico, who wrote, "The Officers . . . are, as a Corps, the worst perhaps to be found in any part of the world. They are totally ignorant of their duty."[25]

The Mexican army imitated Napoleon's empire in nearly every way: uniforms, organization, tactics, rank and structure, and mili-

---

[23]Ibid., 96.   [24]U. S. Grant, *Personal Memoirs of U. S. Grant*, 1: 169.
[25]McLee and Robinson, *Origins of the Mexican War: A Documentary Source Book*, vol. 2; cited from Great Britain, Foreign Office, Charles Bankhead to Lord Aberdeen, Foreign Secretary, April 29, 1846, Series 50, vol. 196 (Public Record Office, London) #56.

tary courtesy, as did many countries in the decades that followed the Napoleonic era. Unique to North America, the Mexicans developed a beautifully uniformed and aggressively trained arm of mounted cavalry called "lancers." At times and in some battles, they employed these lancer battalions or regiments successfully, but more often than not, they were decimated when opposed by well-deployed and armed infantry. The Mexican people and army also were greatly inspired by the recent and unbelievable success of their kindred Latino leader, Simón Bolivar, who cast off Spanish rule in several South American countries. But the Mexicans failed to develop an equally strong military tradition as Bolivar had.[26]

The muskets used by the Mexican army were similar to the old reliable India-pattern "Brown Bess" of British fame. The Brown Bess was the most common firearm used during the American Revolution. The version carried by Mexican forces was a .75 caliber smoothbore flintlock, which had brass facings or parts called furniture. These firearms were of a design that was nearly a hundred years old; the arms themselves were at least seventy years old. Some units carried more modern but poor European substitutes such as the Prussian Tigre Model 1839 smoothbore musket, some of which were modified with the percussion cap-lock system replacing the flintlock.[27] Rifles carried by a few soldiers in some units were British Baker rifles, which were very similar to the Brown Bess smoothbore musket in style and design. The Baker was a .625 caliber rifled flintlock with a pistol grip stock, had sights front and rear, and was effective up to a few hundred yards. The British Baker rifle also attached a brass-hilted saber bayonet.[28] Cavalrymen carried lances, sabers, and carbines or *tercerolas*.[29]

Mexico had no means to manufacture its own firearms and ordnance for artillery. Gunpowder produced in Mexico was of the most primitive and lowest grade. Mexico had to rely on European imports, namely from Britain, for nearly all of its military supplies.

---

[26]For assessments of the Mexican military, see Eisenhower, *So Far from God*; Bauer, *The Mexican War, 1846–1848*; and McCaffery, *Army of Manifest Destiny*.
[27]Niven, *The Mexican War*, 186–87.
[28]Katcher, *The Mexican-American War, 1846–1848*, 24.
[29]DePalo, *The Mexican National Army*, 97.

By the end of 1846, the supply line was severely curtailed by the American blockade. Most of the Mexican artillery was old Spanish heavy brass, smoothbore pieces, and their main ordnance was solid shot.[30] The antiquated Griveaubal cannon was so old and difficult to employ that many were condemned by ordnance officers, leaving Mexico with only 140 pieces at the beginning of the war.[31]

In the northern states of Chihuahua, Sonora, New Mexico, and Upper California, Mexican forces relied mostly on a mixture of a small cadre of regular troops as a base and assorted militia troops as augmentees. These units were called presidial companies, and were stationed at key presidios, or forts, in the various provinces. There were eight such companies in Texas dispersed throughout the disputed land claimed by Mexico, six in California, three in New Mexico, and others scattered throughout the provinces. Additionally, as William DePalo wrote, "the physical separation of units helped politicize the army by entrenching the personalized leadership of local military commanders," affecting standardized training and professionalism besides army cohesiveness.[32]

Because of the distances, deserts, and terrain, mounted troops, usually riflemen or lancers, filled these companies. Though some were experienced in mounted operations, a cavalry force of riflemen or lancers was at a serious disadvantage against a determined and disciplined infantry unit. Despite Hollywood's best efforts to romanticize the mounted warrior, in reality it is extremely difficult to provide effective and continuous fire while mounted. While some American Indians, Mongolian marauders, and Arab horsemen acquired great skill in mounted warfare, it was always more effective to dismount and fight, unless engaged in very close combat. Lancers were completely useless against mass volley fire. Even the thunderous roar and shock of a cavalry charge could be, and often was, defeated by a strong infantry formation. But at the right point and time in the battle, as the foe's unit cohesion and control began to unravel, a mounted charge could destroy an infantry formation, causing confusion that would lead to a penetration and then a pursuit.

---

[30]Nevin, *The Mexican War*, 186–88.   [31]DePalo, *The Mexican National Army*, 97.
[32]Ibid., 90.

A NEAR BATTLE

The main reason Kearny had difficulty repulsing the lancers at San Pasqual was because rain that morning had dampened his gunpowder. Though suffering heavy casualties, Kearny was still able to defeat the Californio lancers. With all factors being equal—terrain, strength, discipline, firepower, and leadership—infantry will always have the advantage over mounted forces with one exception—the speed of maneuver.

Militarily, Mexico was no real match for the United States, army-to-army, general-to-general, man-to-man. Mexican forces did have the advantage of terrain, climate, and more manpower at certain times and had a shorter logistical trail than the Americans. However, the Mexicans failed to use these advantages wisely. At the beginning of the war, the Mexicans were intoxicated in the belief that their larger regular army and numbers alone would triumph. In fact, most military leaders and observers in Europe expressed the opinion that Mexico would easily defeat and repulse any American army thrown against it.[33]

"We will march, then, to Tucson," wrote Colonel Cooke on December 13, 1846.

> We came not to make war on Sonora, and less still to destroy an important outpost of defense against Indians.... But shall I remind you that the American soldier ever shows justice and kindness to the unarmed and unresisting? The property of individuals you will hold sacred. The people of Sonora are not our enemies.[34]

Cooke had no intention of fighting the Mexicans at Tucson and offered terms. He and some Mexican envoys discussed the situation and all concerned wanted to avoid combat, though each side had its own agenda. According to Cooke, "The terms bound the garrison not to serve against the United States during the present war." He also demanded as tokens of surrender Mexican lances, carbines, and safe passage through Tucson. Captain Comaduran demanded that Cooke march his men on a circuitous route around

---
[33]Millett and Maslowski, *For the Common Defense*, 140.
[34]Tyler, *A Concise History*, 225.

Tucscon, Sonora. By John Russell Bartlett in his Personal Narrative of Explorations, vol. II. Courtesy John Carter Brown Library, Brown University.

A NEAR BATTLE

Tucson, which meant another one hundred miles of marching for his worn and suffering command. Cooke also had no intention in complying with Comaduran's demand. After "a tedious conference of two hours ... the officers departed, assuring me my terms could not be accepted," Cooke recalled. He then determined to march directly to Tucson, come what may.[35]

Mexican forces at Tucson numbered some 200 soldiers according to almost all contemporary accounts. For a village with a population of only 500 inhabitants, this is a very high military population. Obviously if this number is accurate, then some of these men came from surrounding settlements when word arrived of the Americans' approach. Later Dr. Foster, who was held by the Mexicans and had an opportunity to observe their activities, estimated the Tucson garrison strength at 130–150 soldiers.[36] Whatever the Mexican force's number, other factors of firepower, discipline, and leadership were more important.

One speculates whether the Mexicans or the Mormon Battalion would have succeeded in a contest of arms. It is evident that the battalion had nearly every advantage over the Mexicans, despite its many military shortcomings. Historian Clark Johnson wrote that the battalion by this time consisted of "travel-weary, ill-equipped, starving citizens soldiers, who were not physically or mentally seasoned to fight the Tucsonenses."[37] It is true that the battalion men were weak and worn. The battalion left Santa Fe with provisions for sixty days, and by the time it reached Tucson, these provisions should have been nearly gone. Cooke gave some valuable quantities of flour and provisions to the Willis detachment, but, by sending them off, he also reduced his demand significantly. Though the

---

[35] Gardner, "Report," 27.

[36] Ibid; another estimate puts the garrison at fewer than 100 Mexican soldiers. See Clark V. Johnson, "Political Intrigue at Tucson: The Mexican Garrison and the Mormon Battalion," 12. Dr. Sanderson recorded Foster's estimate of 150 Mexican soldiers, some cavalry, and 3 guns (meaning artillery); see George B. Sanderson, Journal, December 13, 1846, University of Utah Library. It is prudent to accept Dr. Stephen Foster's estimate since he was there as an experienced military scout.

[37] Johnson, "Political Intrigue at Tucson: The Mexican Garrison and the Mormon Battalion," 10.

men had been eating a meat-only diet for some time, once they arrived at San Bernardino, they ate much better variety of food. Dr. Sanderson described the diet just the week before approaching Tucson. On December 9, "We found plenty game with Cattle, Antelopes & Deer"; December 10, "We find plenty of fish in the River. We have been and are subsisting on Game"; December 12, "Plenty of Game and Fish."[38] Thus, we see from Dr. Sanderson the battalion was eating well—wild game, beef, and fish.

According to Sergeant Coray, in the few days before reaching Tucson, Cooke's "orders were to kill no more beef cattle till the [December] 9th in consequence of their having so much on hand." Disregarding orders, Coray killed two beef and brought steaks into camp the next day.[39] The basic conclusion is the men were not starving. They were eating plenty of protein, which is the most important source of energy at this time; they also had other protein of wild game and fish. If the men had strength enough to march fifteen to twenty miles each day as they had been, then they also would have had enough strength to fight.

The Mexicans were more accustomed to the land and desert terrain and had become very well adapted to their environment. This would be a strong factor if the engagement was a long campaign across vast distances, where the Mexican's desert skills would had been very important. The Apaches would use the advantage of terrain effectively forty years later, baffling and frustrating several army campaigns until the war of attrition finally defeated these great desert fighters. The battle facing Cooke and Comaduran was not a long or mobile campaign; it would be a one-day small action fight, negating this Mexican advantage.

The pending battle would have been what is called today a movement to contact, which is where the attacking commander has a general or limited idea where the enemy is located but must make contact to develop the situation. Even though Cooke knew where the enemy was, he would still have to maneuver and probe to

---

[38] George B. Sanderson, Journal, December 9–13, 1846, University of Utah Library.
[39] William Coray, Journal, December 4 and 5, 1846, LDS Archives.

A NEAR BATTLE

find the best tactical position to attack: thus, a movement to contact. Cooke held the advantage of superior forces, firearms, firepower, and tactical deployment. An old but still viable principle of offensive war is that an attacking force must have a numerical superiority of three times the defending force. The Mormon Battalion mustered some 350 men against Comaduran's 150 defenders: thus, a little less than the three times rule. Captain Comaduran had two or three brass cannon, which should have been an advantage, but Mexican forces throughout the war demonstrated extreme incompetence in deploying and effectively using artillery. There is little doubt that the Mexicans of Tucson would have employed these pieces any better than their countrymen along the lower Rio Grande. If Comaduran elected to fight in Tucson itself, then it might have been a bloody affair. Again, Cooke's advantage of firepower and forces would have succeeded, but at a cost. The battle would have been limited engagement similar to the one in Monterrey a few months earlier, where the Mexicans were defeated after bloody, urban combat.

One of the most important factors, of course, was leadership. As mentioned, the Mormon Battalion was not properly trained and disciplined for the extreme realities of combat. Cooke knew this and that is why his skill and leadership in battle was imperative as battalion commander. His ability to organize, deploy, and engage the Mexicans would take his utmost ability. He could not rely on his subordinate company commanders for much during a battle. Though they were good and decent men, they were not military professionals and did not have the experience and training to lead effectively. Hopefully, Cooke would have task-organized his battalion, as it is called today, with Lieutenants Smith and Stoneman, West Point graduates, leading multi-company elements of the battalion.

As for Captain Antonio Comaduran, what we do know about him is vague at best. He appears to have been a typical colonial or provincial career officer who acquired the skills of frontier leadership and warfare. He was posted to Tucson in 1818 as a young officer and third in command of the garrison. Eventually, he became captain and commander of Tucson and the surrounding region. Though an officer in the Mexican army, he served more as a police constable or sheriff. The Mexicans were constantly at war with Indians, especially the Apaches, and on occasion defeated them. Comaduran himself met defeat in an Indian ambush in 1848 where he lost fifteen of his men.[40]

The Mexicans at Tucson undoubtedly would have chosen to defend. Lances were seldom effective in the offense and are completely useless in the defense. The only hope Captain Comaduran would have had in defeating the Mormon Battalion's numerical superiority would have been an advantage of superior firearms, which he did not have.

It is reasonable to believe that if the Mormon Battalion had met the Tucson garrison in battle, the battalion would have defeated it and taken the town. But nothing is guaranteed in war, and perhaps some unforeseen factor would have reversed the advantages. There is little doubt, however, that Cooke's leadership and the battalion's superiority in strength and firepower would have triumphed.

Cooke moved the Mormon Battalion forward towards Tucson across a flat desert plain with little water. The men and stock suffered greatly. On December 14, they passed a distillery used to make whiskey where they saw what appeared to be a few Mexican soldiers. Dr. Foster had been missing for a few days when he was exchanged for Captain Comaduran's son, Corporal Joaquín Comaduran, whom Cooke had held as a hostage. Rumors ran through both camps of a great impending battle. Neither wanting battle nor a wide detour, Cooke determined to move directly into Tucson. On December 16, Cooke deployed the battalion for the last miles into Tucson, but soon learned that the Mexican forces under Comaduran had fled. "The Battalion was made ready for engagement," Cooke wrote. "Very soon after, two Mexicans were

---

[40]Johnson, "Political Intrigue at Tucson," 13.

Mission Church of San Xavier del Bac.
From Pacific Railroad Surveys, *Volume VIII.*

met, who gave information that the post had been evacuated, and most of the inhabitants had also left, forced off by the military; that these last had carried off two brass cannon." Later a dozen "well mounted men" escorted Cooke and the men into Tucson, where the men finally received water, rest, and food.[41]

"After a heavy day's march we came to the garrison of Tucson a distance of 16 miles," wrote Sergeant Coray. "We found the town sacked. The troops with nearly all the inhabitants had fled, taking with them their property. Those few who remained entreated us to save the town and preserve their property and we assured them we would do so."[42]

The faithful diarists recorded that the Mexican troops had fled, implying a considerable distance. In reality they had simply moved several miles southwest to nearby San Xavier del Bac Mission, an impressive old Spanish mission rising high above the desert plain

---

[41]Cooke, *Conquest*, 149.   [42]William Coray, Journal, December 15, 1846, LDS Archives.

of chaparral and mesquite.[43] Many of the men were thankful that they were delivered from battle. Private Hancock was one soldier who declared his gratitude to God that Tucson fell without the loss of blood.[44]

According to Private Henry Boyle, "When we arrived here today we were tired, hungry, and thirsty almost beyond endurance."[45] Cooke marched the battalion through the village and bivouacked along an irrigation ditch about a half-mile outside Tucson. Cooke then confiscated some fifteen hundred bushels of wheat from the Mexicans and issued it to the companies and fed the stock. Some of the townspeople visited the camp and traded food and goods.

The next day, December 17, Cooke decided to lead a reconnaissance against the Mexican troops believed to be garrisoned near the mission. Though Cooke had learned from Dr. Foster that the Mexicans had no more than 150 soldiers, rumors flowed that there were actually as many as 200 to 300 hostile troops nearby. Cooke could not ignore this. He asked for 50 volunteers and organized them into three detachments, one under Lieutenant Cyrus Canfield of D Company, one under Lieutenant Robert Clift of C Company, and one under Sergeant William Coray of B Company.

Why Cooke asked for volunteers and organized this unusual reconnaissance is interesting. Perhaps he should have just taken a single company, a cohesive and already organized tactical unit, and led it forward. Instead Cooke took soldiers from different companies and mixed them with other men under leaders with whom they were not accustomed. Dr. Sanderson criticized Cooke's logic here: "having near four hundred men at his command he ought by all means to have taken his whole force to have ensured success." Sanderson provided a more and detailed tactical analysis than Cooke himself. He stated in general terms that the Mexicans had some 150 regulars, probably 200 or so armed citizens, and 3 pieces of artillery. Cooke's hodgepodge, task-organized detachment

---

[43]Johnson, "Political Intrigue in Tucson," 13.
[44]Levi Hancock, Journal, December 16, 1846, LDS Archives.
[45]Henry G. Boyle, Autobiography and Diary, 1: 26, Marriott Library, University of Utah.

moved forward and deployed to conduct a reconnaissance in force to find and engage the enemy if necessary. After marching a few miles through high mesquite with the real possibility of ambush or attack, Cooke decided to abort the reconnaissance and return to Tucson. Yet Sanderson offered an interesting commentary" the "Col. pretended to say he merely went out to protect a detachment of men who was out hunting mules, but this tale with me is no go." Continuing, Sanderson wrote, "I think he began to reflect seriously his hazardous undertaking and wisely called a council of war" and ended the reconnaissance.[46]

Private Standage made a unique but mistaken observation concerning the military situation, laced with a religious anthem: "Surely the Lord is on our side for when we see the advantages the Spaniards [Mexicans] had in this town their numbers being far greater than ours ... in a walled town, well defended against musketry, I am led to exclaim that the Lord God of Israel will save his people in as much as He knoweth the cause of our being here in the United States Service." Though incorrect on the size of the Mexican force, Standage relied upon his faith and thus directed his praise.[47]

Later that evening two sentinels overreacted to some townsfolk returning home and fired their muskets, which alarmed everyone. Quickly, the men formed and deployed in a skirmish line. Cooke sent Lieutenant Stoneman and a company forward to investigate the commotion; they returned reporting that "nothing was discovered."[48]

On December 18, the battalion left Tucson and commenced a seventy-mile, four-day march across a stark waterless desert—an ordeal for the men and animals. Following the Santa Cruz River a few miles until it sank into sandy oblivion, the course headed in a northwest direction towards the next major source of water, the Gila River. The scouts had difficulty finding any sources of water

---

[46]Bieber and Bender, eds., "Journal," 154; George B. Sanderson, Journal, December 17, 1846, University of Utah Library. [47]Golder, *The March of the Mormon Battalion*, 196.
[48]Cooke, *Conquest*, 153–54.

sufficient for all of the men other than a few small pools. At one such pool the animals charged in frantically, muddied the water, and ruined it. By the third day unit cohesiveness and organization had completely disintegrated. Stragglers were scattered miles behind the wagons. "Our Command must have extended for six miles from one extreme to the other," narrated Dr. Sanderson. "If our enemy had known it Fifty of them could have cut us up in detail owing to our being so much scattered."[49] A rather astute observation for a physician.

Some of the stock had died and many, scattered across the desert, were crazed for want of water. Cooke narrated the exertion of the march: "The Battalion had been then marched twenty-six hours of the last thirty-six; they were almost bare-footed." On a personal level, he wrote of the demands that military leaders and commanders face beyond that of normal soldiers: "I have been mounted thirty-two of the last fifty-two hours; and what with midnight conferences, alarms and marches, have had little rest for five days."[50] On and on they drudged past Picacho Peak, a most stunning rock formation that shot straight up into the sky like a cone.[51] At one point Captain Hunter complained about the mules bawling hysterically from the lack of water, whereas Cooke exclaimed, "I don't care a damn about the mules, the men are what I'm thinking of." According to Coray, "I was much pleased at this expression. It was the 1st humane word I had heard from him. Here we were and harsh words would not do in such a time."[52]

The battalion still faced a dire situation; it had overcome this same awful circumstance before. Exactly a month earlier, when crossing the deserts near the Hatchett Mountains, it nearly disintegrated when the line of march became a line of suffering and exhaustion until reaching the water at Lake Playas. Sergeant Hyde wrote this interesting appraisal: "After we were encamped" the

---

[49] George B. Sanderson, Journal, December 19, 1846, University of Utah Library.
[50] Cooke, *Conquest*, 156–57.
[51] At Picacho Peak during the Civil War a very small skirmish of a few Confederates and Union soldiers occurred on April 15, 1862. This was the only engagement in Arizona during the war and the farthest west. See Eppinga, "War's Westernmost Battle," 27–32.
[52] William Coray, Journal, December 19, 1846, LDS Archives.

A NEAR BATTLE

evening of December 20, "the Colonel said that he believed that any other company under like circumstances would have mutinized. But in reference to us, he said that notwithstanding we were worn down, we were ready to obey any orders that might be given." Hyde further explained that had Cooke known the severity of this seventy-mile desert from Tucson to the Gila River, he would have taken the longer route. Some of the men had gone some forty hours or more without water, the animals longer.[53] But water was not the only necessity for survival that the battalion lacked. They were "suffering very much from the want of Shoes," said Dr. Sanderson, who explained that some of the men used "raw hides. Some have their feet wrapped up with blanket and pieces of old cloth."[54]

Finally, on December 21, after marching a few miles, the lead elements sighted cottonwood trees in the distance. It was the Gila River—and salvation. "We were soon gladdened at the sight of the trees of the Gila ... we found it ten miles to its bank. We had struck Gen. Kearny's route, and here went into camp," reported Cooke.[55]

What would become Cooke's Wagon Road was again following known roads in Arizona. The road that Cooke and the men carved out of a wild and trackless desert in New Mexico ended even before they reached the San Pedro. The route that Kearny followed a month earlier is often referred to as the Dragoon Trail. Now the battalion would follow previously established roads to the Pacific, but would have to make some improvements in southern California so its wagons could get through.

After months of mostly salt pork, beef, rations of poor wheat, mutton, and few vegetables, the Mormon Battalion entered the Gila River as if it were the Garden of Eden. "They brought into camp large quantities of corn and corn meal, wheat, and flour, also beans and squashes," wrote Private Henry Bigler.[56] Surrounded by a very

---

[53]William Hyde, Journal, December 20, 1846, Brigham Young University Library; George B. Sanderson, Journal, December 20, 1846, University of Utah Library.
[54]George B. Sanderson, Journal, December 20, 1846, University of Utah Library.
[55]Cooke, *Conquest*, 157–58.
[56]Gudde, *Bigler's Chronicle of the West*, 37.

Village of the Pima Indians, River Gila. *By Seth Eastman.
On deposit in the John Carter Brown Library from the
Museum of the Rhode Island School of Design.*

fruitful and bounteous land, the men encountered a hospitable and thriving people largely unchanged from their ancient past, the Pima Indians. The Pimas were agrarians, not warriors. "They are Savages but they are honest and industrious," explained Sanderson. He said the Pimas were the "happiest [people] to all appearances I have ever seen."[57] No doubt they could fight, if necessary, but they did not conjure up the image of fear and dread that the Apaches and Comanches did.

For once, the men had plenty to eat, and Cooke bought bushels of corn, beans, corn meal, wheat, and other produce. The stock were replenished and soon grew stronger as they marched nearly

---

[57] George B. Sanderson, Journal, December 22, 1846, University of Utah Library. Commenting on the Pimas' fighting acumen, Dr. Sanderson wrote, "They seldom go to war, but when excited to it, are a very troublesome enemy. They use clubs." See George B. Sanderson, Journal, December 23, 1846, University of Utah Library.

due west along the Gila. There are countless journal entries by the men of the good-natured and friendly Pimas.[58] The land, with proper irrigation, produced vast amounts of vegetables, fruits, and wheat. Cooke was so impressed with the land and climate that he recommended to Captain Hunt and others that this would be an ideal place for a future Mormon settlement. Cooke's judgment was correct; Mormons would establish many future colonies in Arizona and become a leading force in its settlement and move to statehood. Battalion veterans would use many of the irrigation techniques they saw along the Gila later in Utah.

A few days along the Gila a scout named Francisco arrived from California bearing dispatches. Cooke learned of the rebellion in California and Kearny's orders to march on with all haste, even though Francisco had left Warner's Ranch before the battle at San Pasqual occurred. The battalion's march was a month ahead of Kearny's expected progress. From Francisco and the Pima Indians, Cooke obtained a few more mules to help with the march.[59]

Christmas Day was not a holiday for the men; they marched eighteen miles and began to cross another desert. This was the desert near the Sierra Estrella Mountains. The passage across this forty-mile stretch occurred where the Gila River made a curve to the north near present-day Gila Bend. It was a barren, forsaken land. The route was either very sandy and difficult to cross for the wagons, or hard-packed, dry clay that proved just as miserable for the men's feet. Though Cooke and good military judgment would not allow a proper Christmas holiday and observance, the men remembered and took note. Sergeant Hyde wrote, "it was rather a strange Christmas to me. My situation with my family in days gone by was called to mind and contrasted with my present situation, at present, on the sandy deserts through which pass the Heli [Gila] and Colorado Rivers."[60] To a soldier, especially in war, Christmas is a difficult day to enjoy when far away from family and home.

---

[58]One will recall that Ira Hayes, a Pima Indian, was one of the Marines who raised the flag in the now famous photograph during the battle for Iwo Jima in February 1945.
[59]Golder, *March of the Mormon Battalion*, 199–200.
[60]William Hyde, Journal, December 25, 1846, Brigham Young University Library.

A few days later, Cooke decided to send forward to California several of his most trusted scouts: Leroux, Charbonneau, and Willard Hall. It appears that Major Jeremiah Cloud of the paymaster department also departed with this party, because later in California, Cloud returned with mules and messages. Cooke needed more animals and provisions to cross the deserts of California to Warner's Ranch. Therefore, he sent these scouts forward to obtain the animals and provisions necessary to finish the march. Pauline Weaver, Dr. Stephen Foster, and a few other scouts remained. Water at this point was no longer a great concern, and food and provisions were adequate, but Cooke was not willing to gamble with the lives of his men. He also considered dividing the battalion and force-marching the strongest and healthiest men on to California, much like Lieutenant Smith had done prior to Santa Fe. There was no sound military reason to do so; therefore he quickly dismissed the idea.[61]

The going along the Gila was easy compared to the arduous trek behind them. There were some difficult and taxing days as they passed through some of most scenic but harsh river land in America. Advancing swiftly, the daily march increased as the stock and men improved. After several days passing through the Pima Indian villages, they met the equally civil and hospitable Maricopa Indians along the Gila River.

New Year's Day 1847 ushered in not only a new year but also a new plan that almost meant disaster for the battalion. Though Cooke had reasonably sufficient provisions for the time being, it was still a diminishing quantity that had to be prudently managed. The road along the Gila was at times very difficult, sandy with occasional ridges to cross. Lieutenant George Stoneman, the acting assistant quartermaster officer, and Cooke developed the novel idea of building a barge of sorts by lashing together two wagons, and shipping the bulk of the provisions by river down to the junction of the Colorado and Gila Rivers about a hundred miles away. Cooke explained:

---

[61] Bieber and Bender, eds., "Journal," 181.

> I am now preparing a boat of the two pontoon wagon-bodies lashed together, end to end, between two dry cottonwood logs; in this I shall put all the baggage I can risk. The river is rapid, and in places three or four feet deep; and here it is one hundred and fifty yards wide. I have determined to send Lieutenant Stoneman in charge; he professes to have had similar experience, and is desirous to undertake it.

Cooke's barge experiment, with over a ton of provisions, including twelve hundred pounds of valuable flour, launched out under Stoneman with a few enlisted men to assist.[62] Dr. George Sanderson predicted, "I begin to fear it may turn out a failure."[63]

Unfortunately, within days Cooke learned that the "experiment" had failed. The heavy-laden wagon-pontoons grounded on sand bars due to the shallowness of the river. Stoneman had the men unload the provisions at different points, which freed the craft, and then continued on. According to one soldier, Cooke was "cross as hell" over the boating fiasco.[64] Young Englishman Robert Whitworth wrote, "Commodore Stoneman came to camp and informed us that boating down the River was no go." Whitmore recorded that Stoneman had left the cargo and brought the empty wagon beds only.[65] "We had in the Boats six day's rations of Pork and flour," wrote Sanderson. "Should we fail to get the provision's the loss will be a very serious one."[66] Cooke then dispatched Dr. Foster and a detail under Corporal William S. Muir of A Company to retrieve the supplies, which were dumped at various points on the banks of the river. Eventually they returned with most of the flour, corn, and some other goods. Unwittingly, they left behind the road tools that Cooke had wisely obtained in Santa Fe to use during the trek. In a few weeks those tools would be sorely needed.

They continued on to the Colorado River, reaching it on January 9, 1847, having camped a mile short of the junction of the two rivers the night before. The land was mostly a flat valley with several rocky ridges cutting into the valley floor. The soil was sandy but

---
[62]Cooke, *Conquest*, 169.
[63]George B. Sanderson, Journal, January 5, 1847, University of Utah Library.
[64]Cited in Yurtinus, "A Ram in the Thicket," 445.
[65]Gracy and Rugeley, "From the Mississippi to the Pacific," 153.
[66]George B. Sanderson, Journal, January 6, 1847, University of Utah Library.

fertile, and with enough water it would prove to be very good farmland. The men again suffered from insufficient rations, long marches across very sandy reaches, and pulling the heavy wagons along. It was a difficult task and many were failing from the exertion. Once more the stock, especially the mules, was failing each day. The beef and sheep that the men were using for rations were in a terrible state. The battalion was on half rations and had been for several days. Sergeant Coray wrote about Cooke, "The Col. cared not for our suffering, as he has plenty. There was only 7 days' half rations and we were more than 15 days from settlements."[67] Though Coray thought Cooke had "plenty," he had half rations like the rest of the men and suffered right along with his men.[68] The "settlements" Coray referred to was Warner's Ranch. Across the Colorado River from the battalion lay California, the object of their long march and trying military service. Only a half-mile-wide ford of the river separated them from the final leg of their journey. The last few months of their military service would be occupation duty in a conquered land. Hungry, near naked and some barefoot, the men approached the river and California. A few pondered over the time and events that had passed before them. Sergeant Coray wrote on January 9, 1847, "It is one year this day since I was in the temple of Nauvoo. I little thought of being here at this time I am certain."[69]

---

[67] William Coray, Journal, January 6, 1847, LDS Archives.
[68] This is reminiscent of the story of Alexander the Great crossing the deserts of southern Iran when his scouts brought him a helmet of water. Standing before his long line of men perishing of thirst, Alexander dumped the precious water into the burning Asian sand.
[69] William Coray, Journal, January 9, 1847, LDS Archives.

CHAPTER THIRTEEN

An Equal March of Infantry

> *... the long, long-looked for great Pacific Ocean appeared plain to our view.... The joy, the cheer that filled our souls.*
> —Sergeant Daniel Tyler

After a grueling eighteen-mile march, 500 men of the 1st Missouri Mounted Volunteers went into camp. Awaiting the rest of his tired regiment, Colonel Alexander Doniphan sat down with some of his men to celebrate Christmas Day 1846 by playing a few hands of cards. Suddenly scouts arrived announcing that a Mexican army was fast approaching. Doniphan stood up, calmly dropped his cards and said they would finish the game later. He then went forth to lead his regiment into battle. It was mid-afternoon when a Mexican force of some 1,300 men, having marched twenty miles from El Paso, prepared to attack the Missourians at an arm of the Rio Grande called Brazito. Under the command of Colonel Antonio Ponce de Leon, the Mexican soldiers from Chihuahua, many of them regulars, deployed to attack.

Momentarily rushed and excited, the Missouri volunteers fell into ranks as Colonel Doniphan coolly formed his defensive plan. He ordered some of his men to lie down and wait until the Mexicans were within a hundred yards before standing, and then to fire with their long-range rifles, devastating at such a short range. A Mexican lancer first rode forward to offer surrender terms to the Americans. He carried a pennant with skull and cross bones, a message of certain death.

An hour later, the Mexicans had an estimated 60 dead, more than 150 wounded, and several cannon captured by Doniphan's regiment. The

Missourians had 7 wounded and no battle deaths. It was an amazing feat. The battle opened when the Mexicans fired and missed ineffectively with their artillery. Colonel de Leon attacked on line with his infantry, who fired several volleys with their archaic "Brown Bess" muskets. Then within close range, Doniphan ordered his prone men to their feet and the regiment opened fire. It was devastating. The Mexican cavalry attacked but was repulsed. Then, Captain John Reid, leading only 14 mounted troops, counter-attacked just as the Mexican line faltered. They drove the Mexicans into retreat and captured several artillery pieces. The battle on Christmas Day 1846 was over and Colonel Alexander Doniphan had his first victory, the battle of Brazito, with his wild and fearless Missouri volunteers.[1]

Meanwhile, Major General Winfield Scott arrived at Camargo on the San Juan River, a tributary of the Rio Grande, on January 3, 1847. General Taylor was 200 miles to the south at Victoria with a reconnaissance force when Scott helped himself to 9,000 soldiers of Taylor's army in the Monterrey area. Scott had already sent Taylor a cryptic note announcing the transfer, but Taylor refused to believe it. No administration or other general, especially a fellow Whig, would be so callous or foolhardy as to take seasoned combat veterans from an army in the field facing Santa Anna's approaching army of more than twice the number! Scott sent Taylor an official order directing the transfer of troops, and the men began the march for the transport boats on the Rio Grande. When Taylor learned of the actual "confiscation" of his army, he was justifiably furious. He would never forgive Scott, despite the fact that President Polk and Secretary of War Marcy had little choice but to approve the transfer if they wanted to defeat Mexico and end the war quickly.

General Kearny arrived at San Diego on December 12, 1846, after his painful march from San Pasqual. There Kearny and brevet Commodore Stockton prepared their combined forces of some 550 men and 6 field pieces for the 140-mile march to capture the small village of Los Angeles. Since Stockton commanded most of the men and was familiar with the area, Kearny served as his "executive." They departed San Diego on December 29, 1846, and arrived near the San Gabriel River some 12

---

[1] Dawson, *Doniphan's Epic March*, III–19.

AN EQUAL MARCH OF INFANTRY

miles east of Los Angeles in early January 1847. José María Flores commanded a force of 500 Californios with 4 old brass cannon and a minimum amount of substandard gunpowder. Flores entrenched his force on a low ridge some six hundred yards west of the river, wisely using the ridge as a very strong defensive position. On January 8, 1847, the thirty-second anniversary of Andrew Jackson's great victory at New Orleans in 1815, the Americans moved across the river under less than effective artillery fire from the Californios and attacked. After a short but fierce battle, the Californios retreated, largely because of the very accurate American artillery that had silenced two of Flores's guns. Each side lost a couple dead and several wounded.

January 9 was another day and another battle, much like Zachary Taylor's dual victories of May 8 and 9, 1846, at Palo Alto and Resaca de la Palma. The second engagement lasted about two hours and was fought on a fertile tableland called La Mesa only a few miles from Los Angeles. Californio cavalry and lancers charged the American forces from vantage points on nearby hills. This time Kearny's powder was not wet, and he formed his troops into Napoleonic squares. The Americans repelled the attackers after an intense skirmish. Surprisingly, both forces had very few casualties. Kearny and Stockton marched into Los Angeles and the military campaign for California was over.[2]

"I believe it to be the most useless of rivers to man," wrote Lieutenant Colonel Cooke of the Colorado River, "so barren, so desolate and difficult, that it has never been explored; running through volcanic mountains and sand deserts, at places through chasms of vertical rock perhaps five thousand feet deep.... It cannot be navigable far."[3] For Cooke, a Virginian, it was difficult to justify the existence of a river unless it was navigable by boats or watered a bounteous land. Though usually a visionary when it came to the West, here was an instance where pessimism reigned. The Colorado was, indeed, never navigable for commercial use, but it was eventually explored and navigated by none other than "Major"

---

[2]Harlow, *California Conquered*, 208–18.   [3]Bieber and Bender, eds., "Journal," 200.

John Wesley Powell in 1869 and again in 1872. The Colorado River flows through some of the most rugged, pristine wilderness on earth and the early settlers had a great challenge ahead of them in exploiting its resources. Conquering the Colorado would take the toil of decades and future generations, but crossing it would require the toil of only two days for the Mormon Battalion.

On January 9, 1847, Cooke sent E Company forward a few miles to act as an advance guard while the other companies approached the junction of the Gila and Colorado rivers. There was no real expectation of contacting an enemy force; it is merely a fundamental military practice to close upon and secure key terrain, and a junction of two major rivers is always key terrain.

The battalion continued the march, but the men were nearly on their knees making it. With all the water and the fruitful land surrounding them, the men were at their closest point to starvation. After all the miles, the months, and the malnutrition, the men had one last great trial to face. "The men are nearly starving for bread...," Sergeant Coray recorded, "great prices are for a morsel. The beef which was the only means for sustenance at this time was of the poorest quality."[4]

In military operations, a river crossing is one of the most difficult and dangerous operations a unit faces. It is difficult because of the physical challenge of getting men, supplies, and equipment—in this case, wagons—across a water obstacle. It is dangerous because a unit's attention and forces are divided; some have crossed, some are crossing, and some are waiting to cross, which makes any unit extremely vulnerable to attack. Masters of the art of war like Napoleon, Cæsar, Alexander the Great, and George Washington all understood the great lessons of amphibious operations. They mastered the task of crossing rivers as though they were mere delays and not obstacles. Fortunately, the Mormon Battalion reached the Colorado River with no expectation of enemy resistance. Therefore, the task at hand was easier but still dangerous for the men and animals. It took an inordinate amount of time for

---

[4]William Coray, Journal, January 8, 1847, LDS Archives.

AN EQUAL MARCH OF INFANTRY

Cooke to get the battalion across the river. The crossing was methodical and deliberate, but extremely slow.

The crossing site was composed of two separate channels and was about a mile wide, including the approaches to the water. The water depth averaged about four feet with a relatively fast current. Fortunately, the pontoon boat that Cooke launched on New Year's Day could now be used to ferry much of the men and equipment across the river, beginning on the morning of January 10. Cooke sent a detail of forty men across the river to burn the thick mesquite underbrush. In the arid west the ubiquitous prickly mesquite is a terrible nuisance to travel through, especially along riverbanks and streams, where it is abundant. The wagons forded across on their own with teams and teamsters. Two mules drowned during the crossing. It was a slow and tedious task of about an hour and a half to make a round trip, which continued all day and through the night. During the crossing, a detail led by Dr. Foster and Corporal Muir returned with about four hundred pounds of the flour from the flotilla debacle.

During the crossing Cooke observed, "I then saw a wagon, the only one of Company C, standing half way across, with mules taken out on a sand bar, and nothing apparently doing." When Captain Davis reported about a half hour later that the wagon was still stuck, Cooke fumed, "I told him they were not trying, that they had the same opportunities as the others ... [and] had got over easily."[5] Sergeant Tyler writing some thirty years later commented, "The wagon which was stuck in the quicksand was released by the worn-out men.... The Colonel charged that it was the inactivity of the men that kept the wagon on the bar."[6]

According to Tyler, Cooke had the opportunity to demonstrate great leadership by "jumping into the river and putting his shoulder to the wheel, thus aiding the half-starved, worn-out men and team." But he did not do so. Cooke was the battalion commander. He knew his place and it was not in the water pushing a wagon, even though he could have, and other leaders throughout time

---

[5] Cooke, *Conquest*, 173–74.   [6] Tyler, *A Concise History*, 241.

have done similar acts. Surprisingly, Tyler later made the following commentary about Cooke: "I esteem Colonel Cooke very highly, and think, perhaps, a less independent and preserving man would have failed in making the journey with wagons."[7]

Finally, before noon on the 11th, the last companies crossed the river. Without much delay, they began a long march across the sandy terrain of the Imperial Desert of California. (The route they followed crossed the modern border into Mexico.) Cooke abandoned two government wagons and dozens of excess mule harnesses as the march began. The animals would be eaten and wagons and other equipment would be abandoned along the road. In the frontier army, experienced officers were more concerned for the welfare of men and animals than keeping excess or heavy equipment. Often, once a difficult passage was made, relief parties were sent back to recover wagons, stores, and other items. Cooke would do this later.

After crossing the Colorado, they marched past the raging fire of mesquite earlier set by the men, and after fifteen miles, finally reached the first well, later known as Cooke's Well. Kearny had dug this well during his march nearly two months earlier. The men found no water when they arrived, only the carcass of a wolf. It was one of the most dreadful days the Mormon Battalion experienced. "The worse prospect for sixty miles ahead," Cooke wrote, "instantly rose to frighten me for the three hundred and sixty nearly worn footmen, who confide all to me."[8] Cooke left another wagon along the road.

Lieutenant George Oman of A Company had earlier been sent forward with a detail to pioneer or improve the road. He and the men dug at the well for some time but reached little water. Then, he commenced digging a new well, which struck water after ten feet, but the sand mixed with the water, making it unsuitable. The men knew there was a washtub belonging to Mrs. Susan Davis, wife of Captain Davis, which could separate the sand from the water. At

---
[7]Ibid.
[8]Cooke, *Conquest*, 175.

first she refused to give up the tub. "Lieutenant Oman reported to me," wrote Cooke, "to my astonishment, that they [the Davises] were unwilling to give up that valuable article!—upon which our lives seemed to depend. I had it taken. . . . I had the tub taken up, and the bottom, which had been bored, knocked out; then it worked better." The men and animals then watered and rested after a struggle of more than eighteen hours.[9] The well eventually failed again. Cooke had a beef slaughtered to feed the weakened men.

Oman soon became the battalion's well digger. Cooke ordered Oman and a detail forward to the next known well called Alamo Mocho. The next day, it took most of the morning to water the animals of three companies, and they pushed out just before noon. The remainder of the unit followed later in the day. Cooke abandoned two more government wagons, leaving only seven of the original twenty-five wagons with which the battalion began their march over nine hundred miles and nearly three months earlier.

The animals were given feed made from a type of mesquite called "tornia" and rested for the night without water. Cooke summarized what they would face the next few days: "I am writing with effort to suppress feeling . . . for a night and two days, in addition to this hard day; and the next hope of water almost three of our average marches still further on; and *behind*, starvation, and failure."[10]

Oman and his men reached Alamo Mocho southeast of modern day Mexicali in Mexico. There were two wells already dug out by Kearny weeks earlier. They had difficulty digging and finding enough suitable water, so Oman dug a third well. The main body arrived on January 13, making thirteen miles that day across a sandy road. It took eight hours to water the animals. Here Cooke considered leaving all of the wagons because of the strain on the animals and the men, and move forward only with provisions packed on mules. He changed his mind, but did decide to leave two more government wagons. Dr. George Sanderson narrated, "Our provisions are getting very scarce. We have only Eight day's half rations of meat, which I hope will take us to the Settlements if our animals

---

[9]Ibid., 176.   [10]Ibid., 177; italics original.

don't entirely fail." Sanderson, having developed a keen eye for the physical qualities a soldier needed to make such a march, added this dire observation: "Our men are beginning to fail."[11]

At Alamo Mocho the trail divided; Kearny had earlier taken the more direct, but difficult, southern route just north of Laguna Salada, or "Salt Lagoon" and the Sierra de Los Cucapas. Cooke elected to take the northern route, which was longer but less taxing.[12] The battalion again was breaking a new trail for wagons.

The next watering hole or well was at Pozo Hondo, west of present-day El Centro in California's Imperial Valley near Plaster City. Instead of Lieutenant Oman, Cooke dispatched Lieutenant Stoneman with Weaver and twenty-five men to Pozo Hondo to prepare the wells. The main body arrived at the wells on January 15, after a grueling two-day march with little water. The march since sunrise that morning was only seven miles, but it commenced after only a few hours of rest. Here they met Major Jeremiah Cloud, the paymaster, returning from San Diego with thirty-three wild and unbroken mules and some cattle. (Major Cloud had gone on to California earlier with Antoine Leroux, Jean-Baptiste Charbonneau, and Willard Hall.) He brought news of Kearny's bloody victory at San Pasqual. Cooke took the news of the deaths of the dragoons very much to heart. He had known many of these men for years and served with them through the worst of conditions, sharing many adventures and dangers together. Since there was plenty of daylight remaining, Cooke marched eleven more miles before stopping.[13] He seemed, at this point, to be overly anxious to make contact with General Kearny. He wanted to be involved in the war, since the war was still raging, according to the messengers. Cooke also knew that to relieve the suffering of the men, he had to make the march across this desert wilderness as soon as possible.

Cooke decided to rest only a couple of hours and then take advantage of the cooler night temperatures to push on to the next source of water. Except for the segments along the San Pedro and

---

[11] George B. Sanderson, Journal, January 13, 1847, University of Utah Library.
[12] Bieber and Bender, eds., "Journal," 208–11.
[13] Ibid., 213–14; George B. Sanderson, Journal, January 15, 1847, University of Utah Library.

AN EQUAL MARCH OF INFANTRY 309

Gila rivers, the entire march from the Rio Grande had been an ordeal of survival against miles, mountains, deserts, and the ability to find water. Water was the overriding factor in all decisions during most of the journey. As for making a night forced march, Cooke issued common-sense directives: "I had a large advance guard and all the guides on duty, telling Weaver not to lose sight of the leading wagon; it was starlight."[14]

The next water was the Carrizo River, which was not a river at all. It was a run of water that after a half-mile sank into the sand. The battalion arrived at the Carrizo after nineteen tough miles on a very hard, rocky road on January 16. Because of the long forced marches and lack of rest and water, dozens of men and animals again straggled for miles. This was a repeat of the marches to Lake Playas in November and to the Gila River north of Tucson in December. Some men filled their canteens and returned along the march route to aid their comrades. The animals had nearly gone mad for water. Dr. Sanderson was one who also suffered: "I have not felt so much fatigued since I have been on this Campaign as I am, at this time."[15]

The next day they moved out and found water at a natural water hole called Palm Springs, then went on a few more miles to Vallecito Creek and Valley. Leaving the Carrizo, the route climbed progressively into a very mountainous area with the high Oriflamme Mountains to the west and the Vallecito Mountains to the east. The mountains were brown and tan colored with reds of clay and sandstone. At Vallecito Cooke ordered a day of rest on January 18. The men and animals desperately needed the rest and water. To Cooke's astonishment, by evening the men were playing music and dancing.[16] They ate the last flour; the coffee and sugar had been devoured for some time.[17] Bread was very important to the men, a staple of diet that offset all the meat and protein they rapaciously

---

[14] Cooke, *Conquest*, 183.
[15] George B. Sanderson, Journal, January 16, 1847, University of Utah Library.
[16] Bieber and Bender, eds., "Journal," 221; the Palm Springs is the not the famous resort city of today.
[17] Cooke, *Conquest*, 186; Vallecito later became a station for the famous Butterfield Stage line and the only station along the stage line that is preserved today as a historic landmark.

devoured. Yet, even with the water, the greenery, and day to rest, they complained. "A good deal of discontent prevails this morning among the officers and men," Dr. Sanderson witnessed around camp. "I must say not without some cause. Many of the Companies are and have been for some time without bread, and all have since we left Santa Fe on short rations of Flour." Soon, hopefully, the rations would improve.[18]

After more than a hundred miles of stark and forbidding desert, at Vallecito they entered a green marshland of plentiful and refreshing water. Though surrounded by desert and ridges of sagebrush, cactus, rocks, and sand, the general terrain was turning a little more green and vegetated. There were willows, marsh grass, oak trees, flowers, and other plants growing in abundance.

Cooke decided to tighten the discipline and march order of the battalion. This was probably due to their close proximity to the California coast and the fact that Kearny had fought an engagement not far from their present location. He sent out a detail working as pioneers with the advance guard, followed by the companies, and then the wagon train.[19]

At Vallecito, Dr. Sanderson made some poignant observations that very candidly prove his insight, his intelligence as a witness and journalist of the Mormon Battalion, and his obvious concern for the welfare of the men; he also shared their misfortune. These journal entries are near the end of his recorded historical account. The condition of the men were readily apparent to his practiced eye: "I have no hesitation in stating the miserable group that was ever seen together officers and men." He recorded the stark reality of his own condition sharing the misery of all the men. "I mean the way of dress. I have no less than six patches of buckskin in my pantaloons, and as many more rents and holes in them. All of the officers in the same predicament. We will see some of the men with their feet and legs wrapped up with old pieces of blankets, some in buckskin & some with raw hide." The men's clothes were nearly rags.[20]

---

[18]George B. Sanderson, Journal, January 18, 1847, University of Utah Library.

[19]In the frontier army, pioneers were today's combat engineers. Oftentimes common soldiers were tasked to perform road clearing, bridge building, and other engineering operations.

[20]George B. Sanderson, Journal, January 18, 1847, University of Utah Library.

Departing early on January 19, the men immediately faced a steep rocky ridge of sagebrush and cactus, which rose at the north end of Vallecito Valley. It was a difficult grade that took hours to climb across. The road through the mountains made a 180-degree turn from heading nearly due west to a course due east. Following the sandy dry creek bed, the route climbed up and up through a narrow defile, now famous in Mormon Battalion folklore as Box Canyon.

Cooke recorded that after receiving a report from his chief scout, "Weaver coolly remarked, 'I believe we are penned up;'. . . I ordered him to find a crossing." Upon reaching Box Canyon, Cooke simply wrote, "I came to the cañon and found it much worse than I had been led to expect; there were many rocks to surmount, but the worst was the narrow pass."[21]

The route followed the dry creek up through the steep cliffs until it became impossible for the wagons to pass through the narrow chasm of rock. Some of the men began to disassemble the wagons as they had at the Guadalupe Mountains, while other men began chipping away at the rock with axes, crowbars, and a few spades. Unfortunately, most of the road tools Cooke had wisely procured in Santa Fe were lost in the pontoon boat fiasco. Two wagons were disassembled and carried over the narrow passage. After much toil, the way was widened so that the other wagons could be pushed and pulled through. There was one twenty-foot wall of rock where the route had to climb up out of the creek bed and pass up over a ridgeline before re-entering the creek bed.

According to Private Henry Standage, "Today we started quite early and traveled about 7 miles through a barren valley when we came to a narrow pass in the rocks, so narrow that we were obliged to break off the rocks, the pass being too narrow to admit a wagon to pass."[22] George Sanderson also recalled, "came to a pass between two mountains very narrow. So narrow it would not allow our Waggons to pass by about fourteen inches." After much labor, "cut the rock's so as to widen" the passage for the wagons.[23] Finally, the

---

[21]Cooke, *Conquest*, 187–88.   [22]Golder, *March of the Mormon Battalion*, 203.
[23]George B. Sanderson, Journal, January 19, 1847, University of Utah Library.

wagons were brought through the canyon and they camped in Blair Valley, a flat plain at the top of the ridge only a few miles farther along the route. There was no water, and the men were exhausted by the end of the day. Dr. Sanderson continued his record: "Upon the whole this has been one of our hard days marches, particularly on the men [who] had to perform so much work on preparing the road and in pulling the Waggon's up the Mountain and letting them down again."[24]

The route headed directly north to Warner's Ranch, the first settlement in southern California. Kearny had reached Warner's Ranch, then turned almost due west and crossed the mountains towards the coast, after which he fought the battle of San Pasqual. Cooke was under orders to follow Kearny to San Diego by whatever route he could get the wagons through. Cooke decided, however, on January 20, to march as quickly and directly as possible to Los Angeles, the most likely place for military action. Cooke rationalized that with Kearny marching from the south, Frémont coming from the north, and the Mormon Battalion closing in from the east, American forces would then encircle and crush the Californios. "It was determined to take the direct road to Los Angeles," wrote Cooke.[25] This was a bold but logical decision.

The route left the San Felipe Valley through Warner's Pass (also known as Cañada Buena) into the San Jose Valley, which was green, fertile, and had plentiful water. The men were still suffering on a diet of beef only. Corporal Muir arrived at camp with news that he had four hundred pounds of flour from the Gila River failure waiting at Vallecito, but he was unable to bring it forward. Cooke sent men back to help with the flour. It was a singular accomplishment by Muir, but something Cooke gave little mention of other than the fact that two soldiers had joined Muir's party without permission. Since their company commander knew they were with Muir, they assumed they had permission. Cooke simply said, "Such things happen among volunteers."[26]

---

[24]Ibid., January 19, 1846, 65.
[25]Cooke, *Conquest*, 189–90.
[26]Ibid., 191.

Jonathan Warner, a Connecticut Yankee, had lived in California since the early 1830s and acquired both respect and, in 1844, a vast ranch from the Mexican authorities. He built his famous adobe ranch house a few miles west of some natural hot springs. His spread encompassed some forty-eight thousand acres. Following the southern route, Warner's Ranch was the first settlement in California able to provide sufficient food and water for travelers—the Sutter's Fort of the south. A few miles to the east was Agua Caliente or 'hot springs,' which is now called Warner Springs.[27]

When the Mormon Battalion arrived on January 21, 1847, they encountered the first house they had seen in California. A simple but truly amazing thing occurred, validating Cooke's ability as a frontiersman. Nearly a month earlier Cooke had dispatched some of his scouts from the Gila River. He told them that he and the battalion would arrive on January 21. Cooke wrote, "It is remarkable that the battalion arrived at Warner's the day that the guides were instructed, December 28th, to meet it [the Battalion] there."[28]

But the gladness of reaching an American settlement was not completely joyful. In the final entry of his journal, Dr. George Sanderson wrote that some Indians a few days earlier "committed an outrage on some Californians. . . . They kept them tied to trees about twenty four hours, and then butchered them in the most inhuman manner. . . . This affair is much to be regretted."[29] Thus ended the remarkable journal of a volunteer assistant surgeon, Dr. George Sanderson, United States Army.

The men enjoyed another day, the 22nd, as a rest day. They ate much, though it was a ration of five pounds of beef per man. A few men traded with Indians for extra food. Some soaked in the hot springs at Agua Caliente. Others just relaxed and wrote in their journals. The most wonderful thing about arriving at Warner's Ranch was that it meant the men had no more deserts to cross. The days now were very pleasant, but the nights were still very cold.

[27]Bieber and Bender, eds., "Journal," 227 n.224.   [28]Cooke, *Conquest*, 191.
[29]George B. Sanderson, Journal, January 21, 1847, University of Utah Library.

After the day of rest, the men made a march of twenty-five miles. The next day it rained and soaked everything, and the march that day covered only four miles along Temecula Creek. On January 25 they resumed the march into the Temecula Valley. When nearing their camp for the night, the Mormon Battalion encountered a very unexpected military force. Deployed across their path were about 150 Indian warriors. Sergeant Coray explained, "Directly we came in sight of the place [the day's camp] and we could plainly see a company of men formed in line of battle. I thought to myself surely we will have to fight now and I knew there could be no better place in the world than the plain which we were then on."[30] The Indians were Temeculas and, though a bit surprised by the advance of the battalion, they had been in the process of burying some 100 tribesmen, having just engaged in a fierce battle against the Californios days earlier. "But we found upon closer examination that it was a body of friendly Indians," Coray added. It did not take long for both sides to realize who they each were, and peace reigned.

Brigham Young had promised that the Mormon Battalion would not see battle if they would be faithful to their religion. According to Sergeant Hyde, "President Young stated at the time of our enlistment that the fighting would all be done up just ahead of us. This we found to be the case both in Santa Fe and throughout New Mexico, as well as in California."[31] Hyde was incorrect in stating the fighting had occurred up ahead in Santa Fe and New Mexico, but there certainly was fighting in California just before they arrived.

In the evening, Cooke received word from General Kearny that he was to bring the battalion to San Diego, as previously ordered. He also learned that the Mexican forces had been defeated and Kearny and Stockton had established American control. The men greeted the news with great happiness. They had no desire to march to Los Angeles or engage in combat, but they were obedient. Cooke, perhaps anxious for a fight, had been training the men

---

[30]William Coray, Journal, January 25, 1847, LDS Archives.
[31]William Hyde, Journal, January 25, 1847, Brigham Young University Library.

in tactics and drill nearly every day once they had left the difficult desert terrain. Though the training was at best inconsistent and not very intensive, it was at least a foundation.

Over the next few days the march turned due west and then southwest into the San Luis Valley along the river. They reached the famous and beautiful San Luis Rey Mission on January 27. It was the most majestic structure the men had seen since the mission at Tucson and the town of Santa Fe. Private Guy Keysor described it: "The buildings porches, & railings being of beautiful white gives the edifice a degree of splendour that the traveler's eye seldom meets with in these western wilds."[32] The men were very impressed with this mission, and other missions they would see in California. However, these Catholic missions were, in fact, in a state of disrepair due to the secularization laws; Mexico had disenfranchised the Catholic Church and its missions and confiscated much of its property in Mexico and, specifically, California.[33]

Just a mile past the mission, the men climbed a bluff, where to their lasting memories they beheld the Pacific Ocean. Their long, grueling ordeal and proud march of some 1,900 miles was almost at an end. The ocean was the greatest symbol of their accomplishment. Cooke expressed his own poignant feelings: "I caught my first sight of the ocean, as smooth as a mirror, and reflecting the full blaze of the declining sun; from these sparkling green hill-tops it seemed that the lower world had turned to impalpable dazzling light."[34] Private Henry Boyle wrote, "I never Shall be able to express my feelings at this enraptured moment. When our colums were halted every eye was turned toward its placid Surface every heart beat with muttered pleasure evry Soul was full of thankfulness, evry tongue was Silend, we all felt too ful to give shape to our feelings by any expression."[35]

Sergeant Tyler added his thoughts: "one mile below the mission, we ascended a bluff; when the long, long-looked for great Pacific Ocean appeared plain to our view, only about three miles distant.

---

[32] Guy Keysor, Journal, January 27, 1847, Utah State Historical Society.
[33] Harlow, *California Conquered*, 26–27.   [34] Cooke, *Conquest*, 195.
[35] Henry Boyle, Diary, January 27, 1847, Marriott Library, University of Utah.

The joy, the cheer that filled our souls, none but worn-out pilgrims nearing a haven of rest can imagine."[36]

After this stunning, unforgettable experience, the battalion continued their march southward to San Diego. Kearny had sent a guide to lead them in. They were also ordered to herd along cattle, which they would need. At this time thousands of cattle roamed about the beautiful green hillsides, free and wild, and Cooke sent several men to round up the stock. They camped at an abandoned ranch, Agua Hedondia, meaning 'dirty' or 'nasty water,' a few miles south of modern-day Carlsbad. That night the men slept to the cacophony of a powerful sound—the sonorous magic of the crashing waves on the beach. Private Robert Bliss of B Company wrote the next day, "Last night was kept awake by the roaring of the sea; but this morning put forward on our journey again over hills and through valleys beautiful indeed."[37]

The next day the march continued from Agua Hedondia, paralleling the ocean only a few miles away. The route joined the El Camino Real, the Royal Road, which they followed the rest of the day. "Traveling in sight of the ocean, the clear bright sunshine, with mildness of the atmosphere, combined to increase the enjoyment of the scene before us," exclaimed Sergeant Tyler. "We no longer suffered from the monotonous hardships of the deserts and cold atmosphere of the snow-capped mountains."[38] Because the men had marched every day since their rest at Warner's Ranch on January 22, Cooke ordered a halt at midday after fifteen tiresome miles. The next day, January 29, 1847, would bring the battalion to San Diego some sixteen miles away and the end of their march.

After a few miles Cooke turned off the main road and marched over a high mesa, through Soledad Valley, and down the road to San Diego. As they drew closer to the bay, the men could see the masts of American sailing vessels—warships—at anchor. This was a strange sight for men who had just crossed half the continent.

---
[36]Tyler, *A Concise History*, 252.
[37]Bliss, "The Journal of Robert S. Bliss, with the Mormon Battalion," 67–96, 85.
[38]Tyler, *A Concise History*, 253.

AN EQUAL MARCH OF INFANTRY 317

The ships were a symbol of American power and might. After the trackless miles of sand and desert, to see great sailing ships with masts and rigging pricking the rich blue sky from the blue-green bay was a vision of majesty and security.

Kearny had ordered Cooke to encamp the battalion at the old San Diego Mission about five miles due east of the small village of San Diego and the nearby port. The mission was situated on a plain on the bluffs surrounded by orchards and gardens. The companies arrived just before dusk. It was a dramatic moment—both the great day and great march ended together. After beginning their epic march on July 21, 1846, at Council Bluffs, the Mormon Battalion had made a military march of some nineteen hundred miles. The importance of the march did not escape Cooke, a professional career officer and an amateur historian. Cooke would write a few days later, "history may be searched in vain for an equal march of infantry."[39]

"The crowning satisfaction of all to us was that we had succeeded in making the great national highway across the American desert, nearly filled our mission," wrote Sergeant Daniel Tyler in a fitting commentary of the end of the march, "and hoped soon to join our families and the Saints, for whom, as well as our country, we were living martyrs."[40]

Late in the evening, Lieutenant Colonel Philip St. George Cooke, commander, Mormon Battalion, reported to Brigadier General Stephen Watts Kearny, commander, Army of the West. In a truly memorable and inspiring natural setting, Cooke recorded, "The evening of this day of the march, I rode down, by moonlight, and reported to the General in San Diego."[41]

---

[39] Bieber and Bender, eds., "Journal," 239.
[40] Tyler, *A Concise History*, 253.
[41] Cooke, *Conquest*, 196.

CHAPTER FOURTEEN

Occupying California

*If brought into action they would
prove themselves as good men.*
—*Dr. John S. Griffin*

The new American governor of New Mexico, Charles Bent, was one of the most important American traders in the West. With his brother William, he was a founder and namesake for Bent's Fort. In the early morning hours of January 19, 1847, Governor Bent was awakened by dozens of men at the door of his comfortable Spanish-style home in Taos, seventy miles north of Santa Fe. Mexican revolutionaries and Indian allies led by Pablo Montoya and Tomás Romero entered Bent's home, and within minutes Bent was reeling with several arrows in his body and other wounds. His wife and children narrowly escaped by breaking holes in the adobe walls, crawling from room to room and fleeing. Bent, wounded severely, had no such luck. He was later found scalped, believed to be alive at the time, and then beheaded.

Leading a quick campaign to end the revolt, Colonel Sterling Price, the commander of the American military forces in New Mexico, defeated the revolutionaries twice in skirmishes, with dozens of dead and wounded. By February 4, 1847, time was running out for the rebels, who were cornered in two large pyramid-like buildings. For three days Price fired on and pounded the rebels, first at the church in town, and then in the large structures at ever-closer ranges. Finally, realizing their hopelessness, the rebels surrendered. They had lost some 150 killed in just a few days. American losses were 7 dead, though 40 more later died of wounds, *including Captain John Burgwin, 1st Dragoons. Weeks later seven ringleaders met their fate at the end of a rope.*[1]

When the Mormon Battalion arrived in California, the men were unaware of the great firestorm they had entered. Instead of conflict between the U.S. and Mexican forces, they found a near-civil war existing between factions of American military leadership. General Kearny was by rank and authority the senior military commander and wartime governor of California. He had orders from President Polk and even carried the official documents so stipulating. But that did not matter to two men who ignored Kearny to the point of treason and went about creating the California they envisioned. In their Cæsar-like, self-anointed way, brevet Commodore Robert Stockton and Lieutenant Colonel John Charles Frémont (recently commissioned in a line regiment) challenged Kearny's military authority to govern California as a new possession of the United States. Seldom in American history has there been such open and blatant opposition to legal authority by those professing to maintain that same authority.[2]

Months earlier Frémont had been scolded by Commodore Sloat, who demanded to know by what authority Frémont and the "Bear-Flaggers" could declare independence one minute as a separate republic and then assume to be part of the United States the next, all as a whim on the air. Frémont boasted with his typical bravado, "I had acted solely on my own responsibility, and without any expressed authority from the [United States] Government to justify hostilities."[3]

---

[1] Eisenhower, *So Far from God*, 233–40.
[2] Frémont had been acting as a volunteer lieutenant colonel, though he had no official commission from the president. However, unknown to him until November 1846, he had been appointed a lieutenant colonel in July of the newly formed Regiment of Mounted Riflemen, which was fighting in Mexico without him. Frémont owed his promotion to his father-in-law, Senator Benton, who wrangled a commission out of Polk. Frémont, now a lieutenant colonel in the regular army and no longer with the Corps of Topographical Engineers, would never serve a day with his new regiment. See Chaffin, *Pathfinder: John Charles Frémont and the Course of American Empire*, 344, 346. For older but classic accounts of Frémont's life, see Nevins, *Frémont: Pathmarker of the West*, 294; Harlow, *California Conquered*, 222.
[3] Chaffin, *Pathfinder: John Charles Frémont*, 343.

OCCUPYING CALIFORNIA

Kearny arrived at San Diego in mid-December 1846 severely wounded and leading a starving and exhausted command of fewer than a hundred dragoons, a dozen of whom were also wounded. Stockton commanded several hundred U.S. Marines and sailors who had already participated in several land operations. Frémont led several hundred "volunteers" who, at this point, were more loyal to him than to anyone else, or for that matter, to the United States. Kearny did not have the military forces available to directly confront Stockton and Frémont if their dispute escalated into an open conflict. On January 17, 1847, Kearny wrote to the adjutant general in Washington,

> It will be seen by the Presidt. & Secty of War, that I am not recognized in my official capacity, either by Com. Stockton or Lieut. Col Fremont, both of whom refuse to obey my orders or instructions from the President, and as I have no Troops in the country under my authority, excepting a few Dragoons, I have no power of enforcing them.[4]

Kearny wisely awaited the arrival of the one military organization that he knew would follow him without hesitation: Cooke's Mormon Battalion.[5]

Frémont seemed to be suffering from an intoxicating view of his own glory and self-importance. In part influenced by Stockton's absolute arrogance, Frémont had completely lost touch with reality. His self-importance was increased when he obtained the surrender articles from the Californio leaders. After making a lethargic march from Santa Barbara to support Kearny and Stockton in early January 1847, Frémont met with the defeated Californios after the battles of San Gabriel and La Mesa. He wrangled from them a truce and treaty that at least ended the hostilities, but solved nothing for the long term. He basked in the glory as the self-anointed, true conqueror of California and saw himself as a California version of Sam Houston, giving birth to a new republic. If he could not have the glory of creating a new republic, he would settle for military command and civil governorship of California invested on him by Stockton, the senior American official on the scene until Kearny arrived. Stockton, standing back and dispensing

---

[4] Kearny's Letter Book, 186.   [5] Chaffin, *Pathfinder: John Charles Frémont*, 371–72.

authority and law as if from Mt. Olympus, thought himself above the pettiness that ruled Frémont and displaced Kearny. Stockton gave Frémont his unauthorized sanction as governor of California on January 16, 1847. The very next day Frémont met Kearny in a heated confrontation during which Frémont produced a letter of his authority and claim to military and civil control of California. Kearny cautioned Frémont to rescind the letter and his claim. Kearny recounted his high regard for Frémont's familial connection with Senator Thomas Hart Benton, but the obstinate Frémont dismissed Kearny's charity and the affair escalated.[6]

Meanwhile, unknown to Kearny and Stockton, on January 22 Commodore W. Branford Shubrick, Stockton's replacement, arrived at Monterey. Ironically, Stockton departed by ship the same day from San Diego for a cruise south along the Mexican coast, leaving the remainder of the Pacific Squadron in various ports in California. By the time Stockton returned weeks later, Shubrick was in command, and had joined with Kearny and supported his governorship and legal authority to command all American forces in California.[7]

The Mormon Battalion was now in occupation duty of a conquered foreign land. Yet, until the additional forces and official instructions that Kearny needed arrived, he and his dragoons, Cooke, and the Mormon soldiers teetered on a threat of civil war and rebellion for several months. To guard against another Mexican-Californio revolt, something possible but unlikely, the battalion was quartered and stationed at various key places between Los Angeles and San Diego. A more likely threat of confrontation came from Frémont and his capricious and foolhardy claims. Here again, Kearny deployed the battalion to best support his goal to gain control as governor of California. First, however, after some six months in service and enduring an arduous march, the men would now learn how to be soldiers and receive the training they so desperately needed.[8]

---

[6]Ibid., 369–70.   [7]Bauer, *The Mexican War*, 195.   [8]Harlow, *California Conquered*, 256.

OCCUPYING CALIFORNIA 323

"The mission of San Diego is beautifully situated on a gentle elevation of table land," wrote Sergeant Nathaniel Jones of D Company. "The building is about fourteen rods in front and is a little over a one story high. The walls are unburnt brick and white-washed outside and in. The building is covered with concave tile." He continued. "The square here was nearly the west end in the rear of the church. The rooms are dark and damp with brick floors. There are two beautiful vineyards on the flat in front of the building."[9] As soon as the men began cleaning the damp, dusty, and insect-infested mission, C and K Companies of the 1st U.S. Dragoons moved in and took over the best spots. Thus, regulars over volunteers.[10] The men rested from their footsore march, but they were still suffering from a poor diet exclusively comprised of meat, and at times that was still not sufficient. Even in bounteous California the army logistical system had not established an efficient process to acquire and feed its troops properly. The Mormon soldiers were also wearing nothing more than rags and were in a pitiful state.

While the men were resting, cleaning, and doing other such chores, Colonel Cooke wrote his congratulatory order, dated January 30, 1847:

> The lieutenant-colonel commanding congratulates the battalion on their safe arrival on the shore of the Pacific Ocean and the conclusion of their march of over two thousand miles. History may be searched in vain for an equal march of infantry. Nine-tenths of it has been through a wilderness where nothing but savages and wild beasts are found, or deserts where, for want of water, there is no living creature.

Cooke described in some detail their successes and the obstacles involved; then he ended with a most curious but fitting complement for volunteers by a regular army officer: "Thus, volunteers, you have exhibited some high essential qualities of veterans."[11] Cooke later read the order.

---

[9] Jones, ed., "Extracts from the Life Sketch of Nathaniel V. Jones," 12–13.
[10] Golder, *March of the Mormon Battalion*, 206.
[11] Bieber and Bender, eds., "Journal," 238–40.

Historian Jack Bauer wrote, "While the dispassionate historian may eschew such verbal fireworks, the Mormon march was clearly one of the most notable accomplishments of a war in which American soldiers made some of military history's more illustrious marches. Cooke's accomplishment ranks with those of Kearny, Doniphan and Wool."[12]

The battalion's march, as Cooke wrote, was unequaled in severity and difficulty, but not just in miles alone. It was a monumental feat, a test of will, stamina, and loyalty—rarely equaled in American history but it was not the longest march in world or American military history, as has often been asserted.

In many of the histories and published material about the Mormon Battalion, the idea germinated that it made the longest march in *military history*. After comparing the battalion's march to other military marches from ancient through modern times, Mormon historian B. H. Roberts wrote shortly after World War I:

> . . . since the Battalion's march has not been equaled by any march of infantry in the World's Great War, nor in ancient times, it is not likely now, owing to the new methods for the transportation of troops that have been developed more, that the Mormon Battalion's march across more than half of the north American continent will ever be equaled. It will stand as the world's record for a march of infantry.[13]

Whether B. H. Roberts started this claim is not important, but through the years it has gained a foothold in the myths and legends of the battalion. More recent writers have narrowed the scope of the claim, asserting that the march was the longest by *infantry* in American military history. Some historians and groups still hold to this claim.[14]

---

[12]Bauer, *The Mexican War*, 139.

[13]Roberts, *The Mormon Battalion: Its History and Achievements*, 4.

[14]Robert O. Day claims, "their march to California still holds the record as the longest march ever made by U.S.infantry"; see *The Mormon Battalion: The Lord's Faithful*, x. Dan Talbot stated that it was "the longest military march in history" (*A Historical Guide to the Mormon Battalion Trail*, 2). Truman Madsen wrote the battalion made the "longest sustained infantry march in history (two thousand miles) from Iowa to San Diego" (*Defender of the Faith: The B. H. Roberts Story*, 305). William E. Barrett wrote, "The march of the Mormon Battalion is often called the greatest march of infantry in the history of the world" (*The Restored Church*, 239).

OCCUPYING CALIFORNIA 325

As with all events, reality is often different from the perpetuated history. The battalion's march pales in comparison to other much longer marches. The actual distance traveled is a point of controversy—some put it at 2,000 miles and others suggest higher estimates of 2,200 miles or more. Most experts put the battalion's march at roughly 1,900 miles.[15]

In 1966 two writers for *National Geographic* boarded a land-rover jeep and followed the route that Alexander the Great marched twenty-three centuries ago. By the time the odometer stopped counting, including air and water miles and horseback trails over mountain passes, they had traveled some 25,000 miles.[16] Whether these determined journalists followed Alexander's exact route is open to debate, but by any standard Alexander made the longest march of infantry in world history—a distance of at least 22,000 miles. Some may deride Alexander's march and conquests because it encompassed at least a decade (though he made many long marches in a few months' time during those ten years) or that it was a combined army of cavalry and infantry and other troops. He made one forced march of 2,500 miles in less than a year from modern-day western Egypt, through Palestine, Iraq, and Iran, and into Afghanistan.

As part of Napoleon's invasion of Russia in 1812, some of his army began the campaign from Spain, several hundred miles away from Napoleon's base of operations in Germany. Most of the army came from the Rhine River valley and marched over 1,000 miles each way, enduring the bitter weather of the Russian steppes and brutal Cossack raids. In 1934–35 Chinese communist forces marched some 6,000 miles during what is now called the "The Long March." The distance marched by the Mormon Battalion was not the longest march of infantry in military history.

---

[15] Stanley B. Kimball has done some of the most extensive research on the Mormon and other historical trails. He has settled on 1,850 miles, the distance from Council Bluffs, Iowa, to San Diego. See Kimball, *Historic Sites and Markers along the Mormon and other Great Western Trails*, 181. See also Urwin, *The United States Infantry*, 72. Urwin credits the Mormon Battalion with marching 1,125 miles from Santa Fe to San Diego and also mentions the distance of 600 miles from Fort Leavenworth to Santa Fe, via the Cimarron Cutoff. With some 150 miles from Council Bluffs to Fort Leavenworth, this totals 1,875 miles.

[16] Schrieder and Schrieder, "In the Footsteps of Alexander the Great," 1.

The battalion's route was also not the longest march of infantry in American military history. In 1857 President James Buchanan dispatched an armed force to Utah to quell an alleged civil rebellion by Mormon leaders and install new territorial officials. This episode is now called the Utah Expedition or Utah War. After the Mormon militia and the winter season had stopped Colonel Albert Sidney Johnston's army from entering the Valley of the Great Salt Lake in 1857, General Winfield Scott sent reinforcements the next year. Eight companies of the 6th U.S. Infantry marched from Fort Leavenworth to Fort Bridger, where they learned that the Utah conflict had been resolved. The 6th Infantry then received orders to continue its march to the Pacific. After a two-week rest this regiment began its march to Pacific Coast forts, a total march of more than 2,200 miles.[17] General Scott also ordered several companies of the 7th Infantry from Fort Belknap, Texas, and Fort Arbuckle, Arkansas, to join the columns forming at Fort Leavenworth. These regiments marched 400 and 600 miles, respectively, to Fort Leavenworth, and then as regimental units continued all the way to Camp Floyd, Utah Territory, another 1,200 miles or more. So, the 6th Infantry made a longer march than the Mormon Battalion, and the 7th Infantry's march at least equaled it.[18]

Even Cooke, in his laudatory remarks praising the battalion's long march, recorded his estimate of 1,125 miles as the distance from Santa Fe to San Diego. He wrote in his report, "If I had continued on the most direct route to San Diego the distance would have been rather under 1100 miles. (about 1800 miles from Independence, Missouri by Santa Fe)." Thus Cooke confirmed the distance from Fort Leavenworth (basically the same distance as Independence, Missouri) to San Diego. Adding the 150 miles to Council Bluffs, Iowa, the total route of the march was about 1,950 miles.[19]

It would be wonderful to state that the Mormon Battalion made

---

[17]Gallagher, *Fighting for the Confederacy: The Personal Recollections of General Edward Porter Alexander*, 10–13; Coakley, *The Role of Federal Military Forces in Domestic Disorders: 1789–1878*, 218.
[18]Coakley, *The Role of Federal Military Forces in Domestic Disorders*, 209.
[19]Gardner, "Report," 33–34.

the longest march of infantry in American history, but the facts do not sustain this claim. The criteria needed to establish and prove this "longest military march" myth are not as important as other aspects of the battalion's service. As Cooke stated, "an equal march of infantry" also means that it was perhaps unequaled in endurance, perseverance, and difficulty. There are more significant achievements to consider and honor than the distance in miles measured by an odometer.

General Kearny left for Monterey soon after Cooke and the Mormon Battalion arrived, leaving Cooke in command of all the troops loyal to Kearny. The controversy with Frémont and Stockton was still a steaming hot problem. With the battalion's arrival and other reinforcements soon to arrive, Kearny decided to visit American consul Thomas Larkin to try to settle the impasse with Stockton, while Frémont stewed at Los Angeles. To better deploy forces loyal to Kearny, he ordered Cooke to the Mission San Luis Rey, near present-day Oceanside in northern San Diego County, through which the battalion had just passed a few days earlier when entering California. The dragoons in San Diego would accompany them to San Luis Rey. Cooke, upon receiving his orders, wrote this interesting commentary of the military situation in California: "Lieut. Colonel Cooke was thus left in the command of the only troops in California that had been mustered into the service of the United States; a few dragoons, and a battalion of volunteers, which up to that time had never had opportunity to receive regular instruction in arms."[20]

The battalion left San Diego on February 1, with the dragoons leading the way, following the route these mounted soldiers had used a few weeks earlier. It was inland from the battalion's route along the coast. They passed "Mule Hill," where the besieged Kearny and dragoons ate mule flesh awaiting reinforcements from Stockton, and where Kit Carson and others made their heroic pas-

---

[20]Cooke, *Conquest*, 277–78.

sage and evasion through enemy lines. They also saw the fertile San Pasqual Valley where the small but vicious battle had taken place on December 6, 1846, and where many dragoons were killed. After an easy march, they arrived at San Luis Rey on February 3. The next day Cooke read and published his congratulatory order.

Now, for the first time the men received training and drill for the purpose they were recruited, the purpose they served, the purpose they made the long march to California—to be soldiers in volunteer service of the United States Army. Regardless of Cooke's great leadership in getting the battalion intact to California, and the many services he performed for his men, there were those who still regarded him as evil and a tyrant.

Private Levi Hancock wrote of Cooke a few days before reaching San Diego, "in fact he [Cooke] is a miserable creature and often curses and dams the soldiers He is as mean as I ever saw a man [Lieutenant A. J.] Smith who led us is a gentleman to him—he is a small low lived cuss." Wrote Hancock, "The Devil I believe would hate his oppression towards any body and would let him have no power in his kingdom and would let him no authority over any body he [Cooke] sometimes will say that this Battalion is a mob and he sees it sticking out more and more every day and would be glad to have some one say something to take exceptions."[21] Some of the men felt as Hancock did about Cooke, but most of them respected his ability and some even admired him. Private John Riser of D Company later wrote,

> From the commencement of this march until we arrived in California . . . hardships and privations by long marches without water and scanty food, which only the most robust could endure. Had it not been for the cool headedness and sagacity of our stern commander . . . we must have all perished before reaching our destination. There is no doubt in my mind but that Colonel Cooke was one of the ablest officers then in the Army to undertake such an enterprise with such scanty supplies at his command . . . he appreciated our services to the cause that he was engaged in and which he expressed to the battalion.[22]

---

[21]Levi Hancock, Journal, January 26, 1847, LDS Archives.
[22]Cited in Ricketts, *The Mormon Battalion*, 121.

OCCUPYING CALIFORNIA 329

Hancock and the other Cooke detractors had another cause for their criticism: religion. It may be easy to judge that Privates Levi Hancock and David "Father" Pettegrew and Sergeants William Hyde, William Coray, Daniel Tyler, and others were trying to undermine the military authority and discipline in the battalion. This was certainly not their intent, but it may have been the result at times. They were trying to merely live their religion and follow the directives given by Brigham Young. Hancock, for one, was very altruistic about his motives behind the spiritual matters of the men. Tyler praised Hancock's service:

> Brother Hancock was very zealous, and did his best to influence the men to live their religion taught under every circumstance. He was really deserving much credit for the zeal and diligence he manifested in his missionary work among his brethren, but it was very apparent that some of the [Mormon] officers regarded his action as officious, and entertained a feeling of jealously towards him on that account.[23]

Now that the long march was over, the desire to have regular, established worship services on Sundays became an important part of the men's routine. As soon as Sunday worship commenced, another issue arose that caused conflict. Captain Jefferson Hunt felt that it was his right to preside over the services, whereas Levi Hancock, the presiding ecclesiastical authority, claimed that by virtue of his position in the Mormon priesthood, he should preside. Hunt had received permission from Cooke to hold the meetings and organize the programs and even select the speakers. Hancock, Pettegrew, and others balked at the idea.

On February 14, the men held the first organized service with Lieutenant Dykes and Hunt delivering sermons. Lieutenant James Pace wrote that Hunt's sermon "was all a combustible of wind & but little matter or a greait cry & but little wool."[24] Hancock called for meetings and then announced that sacred religious ordinances were to be performed to prove their devotion to God. Soon many of the men were performing washings and anointings, which are

---

[23] Tyler, *A Concise History*, 266.
[24] James Pace, Journal, February 14, 1847, Brigham Young University Library.

sacred rites or observances of cleansing using water and anointing with olive oil, some of many ordinances performed in the Nauvoo Temple and then later in other temples in Utah.[25] Sergeant Coray probably articulated the internal conflict for spiritual leadership best: "This variance had existed a long time between the parties, the fact of it was bro. Levi thought he had the most authority and the Capts. thought they had the most authority and so it went."[26] One historian wrote, "If such a revival was led by Levi Hancock, it probably meant that the military Captains had not satisfactorily performed their chores and that the men were willing to turn to other leaders."[27]

The root problem lay not with the men, their religious attitudes, and the spiritual leaders, nor with the Mormon and regular army officers, but with the situation itself. Organizing a military unit from one religion for the purpose of fulfilling a particular program of a church that was not aligned with national war aims or given proper military practice and discipline caused the conflict. It is natural for a division or conflict of authority to arise, regardless of the religion of the troops. The conflict over authority and religion ceased only when the battalion was discharged, and the men later broke into factions based on their sides in the controversy.

At San Luis Rey on February 5, Cooke finished his "report" and forwarded it to Kearny by courier. Considering the handwritten method of preparing reports under Spartan conditions, Cooke produced an incredibly well-written and authoritative document that covers twelve printed pages in the House of Representatives record. In longhand it was much longer. Whether he began this report during the march is not known, but he finished it within a week of the journey's termination.[28]

Beginning on February 8, the men trained nearly every day for

---

[25] Allen and Leonard, *The Story of the Latter-day Saints*, 169; Campbell, *Establishing Zion: The Mormon Church in the American West, 1847–1869*, 168–70.
[26] William Coray, Journal, February 15, 1847, LDS Archives.
[27] Yurtinus, "A Ram in the Thicket," 540.   [28] Gardner, "Report," 15–40.

several weeks. Cooke delegated the training to Lieutenant George Stoneman. This was his first real opportunity at training soldiers since his graduation from West Point the previous year. Stoneman first trained and drilled the company officers and the NCOs in their commands and movements in the morning. Then, in the afternoon the company officers would instruct and lead the men by squads of ten soldiers through the manual of arms. The initial training was apparently done without firearms until the men became accustomed to the movements by squads, platoons, companies, and then, by battalion. This method of training is the building-block method that the military still uses today. Training begins with the most basic unit and builds up through larger units and more complex drills. The training and drill progressed well for the most part, though there were a few bumps along the way.

"Commenced to learn the drill," wrote Sergeant Hyde.

> The Colonel and Lieutenant Stoneman commenced at 9 A.M. drilling the commissioned and non-commissioned officers. The drill was kept up one hour after which the different companies were divided into squads and drilled one hour in the forenoon and one hour in the afternoon, by their respective officers I had a company [squad] of 10 allotted to me. This drill was kept up from day to day during our stay at the mission.[29]

During this time of training, Cooke tried to instill better discipline in the ranks. He established a strict daily schedule. Private Robert S. Bliss of B Company recorded,

> Nothing very interesting takes place from day to day only camp duties & those are first Revillee a little after daylight when we have to parade & answer to our names then sweeping our rooms & breakfast next our parade ground all about our quarters is cleaned and drained of the ground at 10 O clock one hour's drill then Dinner Call at 3 O clock 1 hour drill at 5 O clock Parade & Inspection of arms then supper at 8 O clock Tattoo or roll call then we have a chance to sleep till daylight.[30]

Writing in the narrative form about himself, "Lieut.-colonel Cooke immediately commenced a thorough practical instruction of the battalion in tactics; the absence of books made it a difficult

---

[29]William Hyde, Journal, February 8, 1847, Brigham Young University Library.
[30]Bliss, "Journal of Robert S. Bliss," 86.

and laborious task,—teaching and drilling officers half the day, and superintending, in the other half," Cooke concluded, taking a bit of pride in the accomplishment. "But all were in earnest, and in a very few weeks the complete Battalion exercises were mastered."[31]

While drilling A Company one day, Cooke became so angry he simply quit and walked off the parade field. The next day, March 8, Cooke relieved four NCOs because of their inability to execute the drills properly. Finally, on March 13, after more than a month of training, the men drilled with firearms, attaining the necessary level of proficiency for combat operations. Their training and drilling as an entire battalion had come to an end.

One commentary on the Mormon Battalion's combat readiness came from an unusual and independent observer. Dr. John S. Griffin, Kearny's surgeon, observed B Company later in San Diego:

> The Californians have no great ideas of their [the Mormons'] soldier like qualities and in action would not dread them much—this arises in a great measure from their dress—carriage &c—which is as unlike any soldier—as any thing could possibly be—yet I think if brought into action they would prove themselves good men—as I am told they are generally fine shots and they drill—tolerably well—they are bear-footed and almost naked.[32]

Griffin was a seasoned surgeon with the 1st Dragoons, and he knew something of soldiering.[33] Drill and training was one thing, instilling discipline was another.

On February 25, 1847, a court martial was convened, the first such held in the Mormon Battalion. Private John Borrowman of B Company fell asleep on guard duty and was sentenced to six days' confinement and a fine of $3. Also, the court convicted Privates Isaac Peck, John Mowry, and Ebenzer Harmon, all of C Company, for stealing and butchering an Indian's cow and sentenced them to ten days' confinement and a fine of $2.50 each.

---

[31]Cooke, *Conquest*, 280.
[32]Ames, "A Doctor comes to California: The Diary of John S. Griffin, Assistant Surgeon with Kearny's Dragoons, 1846–47," 54.
[33]Dwight L. Clarke, Kearny's biographer, credits Griffin with six years' service on the plains with the frontier army. See Clarke, *Stephen Watts Kearny: Soldier of the West*, 112.

When Cooke learned of the sentence recommended by the court martial against Borrowman, he was livid. Cooke wrote,

> The sentence of the court in the case of Private John Borrowman is excessively lenient, and the court probably considered mitigating circumstances which should only have been done in recommending the prisoner to mercy. That the prisoner was brought before a Battalion court martial, instead of a general court martial, whose power of inflicting punishment extended, for this crime, to the life of the criminal, was the exercise of great leniency on the part of the commanding officer, and it will not be repeated. Proceedings, therefore, in this case, are disapproved, and the sentence is remitted.[34]

For Cooke, the penalty for sleeping on guard duty during war was death. This is not to say that he wanted Borrowman shot or hanged, but he certainly thought the sentence given was extremely lenient. The commanding officer at any level has great power to punish severely, lessen the punishment, or completely dismiss charges. The court martial or board is not the final authority in the military judicial system—the court simply makes a recommendation. It is always the commander or, more properly defined, the convening authority, who has final say in judicial matters. Courts martial are serious matters, but they are not always negative and often end with more mercy than many civil judicial actions.[35] This would not be the last court martial in the battalion, but relative to the rest of the army, it had few discipline problems that required such formal measures.

Cooke was the commander, but he could not enforce all the standards all the time by himself. The officers and NCOs of any unit are the force that supports the commander and accomplishes his directives and orders. One of the only officers in the battalion to consistently enforce strict discipline was Lieutenant George Dykes, the former adjutant and now the acting commander of D Company. Dykes, as well as Lieutenant "AJ" Smith and Dr. Sanderson, have been roundly criticized in many of the journals

---

[34] Tyler, *A Concise History*, 268.
[35] The basic law governing military proceedings at that time was the Articles of War, which have been revised many times and now is the Uniform Code of Military Justice or UCMJ.

and histories for decades. Sergeant Tyler was a driving force in establishing a historical bias against Dykes.

John Yurtinus wrote this appraisal of Dykes when the battalion was marching to Santa Fe: "Daniel Tyler blamed George P. Dykes for the long marches in hot weather and throughout his book leaves a very unfavorable impression of the Adjutant." Some of the men hated Dykes because he seemed arrogant and aloof. Also, he later decided to leave the LDS Church, which further damaged his reputation with the veterans and his fellow Latter-day Saints in Utah. He joined the Reorganized Church of Jesus Christ of Latter Day Saints, one of several groups that also claimed to be the original church founded by Joseph Smith. Dykes then commenced a spirited campaign to gain converts among the Utah Saints that criticized his former church. This was enough to discredit his service in the eyes of many. Yet militarily, Dykes served well as battalion adjutant and as company commander. He was one of the few Mormon officers who really learned the profession of arms during his short term of military service.[36]

One of the difficult situations in the unit was the relationship the Mormon officers had with the men. They seemed to desire to be both officers and leaders, and also brothers in the church simultaneously. This was—and is—a very difficult proposition. Due to the unique nature of the battalion's composition, this situation was a great challenge for the men, especially the officers. One day these officers would cease being officers with authority and become ordinary Saints again. As mentioned, some of the decisions and actions by the Mormon officers were held against them for years. Military decisions were often seen as a religious persecution to the enlisted men, who were convinced of their victimization.

Because of the lack of quality provisions, Cooke cut the rations on March 17, which to the men was a cruel and inhumane measure. In a land of great plenty such as California, this decision caused much concern among the men. "Great talk through the Battalion of refusing to do duty until more food is furnished as the country abounds in beef and a plenty of rations at San Diego," wrote Private Standage.

---

[36]Yurtinus, "A Ram in the Thicket," 68 n.38.

"Several of Co. D put under guard and [Private William B.] Maxwell put in the stocks for refusing to drill."[37] The men had been suffering from a poor diet of mostly beef for some time and the men were justified to complain, but not to disobey orders. On February 14, Cooke sent Lieutenant George Oman to Warner's Ranch to procure flour and beans for the men. Also, on February 26, six wagons full of bolted or sifted flour, soap, sugar, coffee, and many other items arrived from San Diego. Cooke also sent Lieutenant Samuel Thompson and a detail of ten men back across the desert to the Colorado River to retrieve the wagons and supplies abandoned there. Yet, to some of the men, these provisions were still not enough, and they took issue with Cooke's seemingly harsh decision.[38]

The record is silent as to the complete situation Cooke faced. The resupply of six wagons may seem sufficient, but if one considers the amount of food necessary to feed 350 men three times a day—six wagonloads of food would not last long. In the winter, even in sunny California, fresh produce was not always available. Kearny was responsible not only for the battalion but his dragoons, several hundred American sailors and marines, and perhaps many of the local populace whose livelihoods were disrupted by the occupation. There is a great deal to consider in logistics.

Lieutenant George Dykes, commanding D Company, was responsible for the provisions that give rise to the battalion's problems. The refusal of D Company to perform their duty became a threat against his authority; Dykes charged some men with insubordination. Cooke reduced Sergeant Nathaniel V. Jones and Corporal Lewis Lane in rank on March 18 for complaining about the rations and refusing to drill until they were fed better.[39] Of the situation, Jones wrote, "He [Dykes] carried false reports to the Colonel and through his false reports broke me of office, which he had purposed on doing from the first, and he bragged of it."[40] It is impossible to determine the truth of this incident.

This illustrates an important military principle. In a contest of

---
[37]Golder, *March of the Mormon Battalion*, 213.
[38]James Pace, Journal, Feb. 28, 1847, Brigham Young University Library.
[39]Tyler, *A Concise History*, 272.
[40]Jones, "Extracts from the Life Sketch of Nathaniel V. Jones," 13.

opinions or accusations between an officer or NCO against a subordinate, it is nearly always inevitable that the superior officer will triumph. That is military law and order, unless there is overwhelming evidence that the officer is either mistaken or lying. The military is a not a democracy, and as difficult as it is for many who have never served in the military to understand this concept, this is the only way that an army can operate. The opposite is chaos. Officers and NCOs rule supreme and their orders and testimony carry great weight. The other edge of the sword is the opportunity for abuse. A superior who falsely accuses a subordinate, using power and position to justify his actions, has no integrity. Though he may immediately succeed, he actually fails because he loses the respect of the common soldier, who will follow his orders but not respect him as a leader. Officers and NCOs carry a tremendous responsibility as leaders.

Discipline in any military unit is the bedrock of unit cohesion and effectiveness. Discipline infractions chip away at the rock of unit integrity. The American army in the Mexican War experienced many serious discipline problems by both regulars and volunteers—the Mormon Battalion had surprisingly few. The most important ingredient preventing discipline problems rests on the most important principle of military art: leadership.

"From some of the bitterest experiences suffered during the Mexican War," historian Joseph E. Chance wrote, "it was found that the success of a volunteer regiment depended, to a large degree, on the competence of its officers. Many volunteer regiments whose ranks were filled with first-rate men, failed in Mexico simply because they had elected unqualified officers."[41] There is no doubt that much of the credit for the battalion's lack of serious discipline problems was a direct result of Cooke's stern leadership. There are numerous examples of discipline problems elsewhere that shock the soul.

A company of the 1st New York Volunteers lost fifty-five men, about half of the company, to desertion before it even embarked by ship for Mexico. While at port in Valparaiso, Chile, twenty-nine men deserted from the 1st New York, whose regiment later served

---

[41]Chance, *Jefferson Davis' Mexican War Regiment*, 12.

under Kearny in California.[42] In a North Carolina regiment, the men mutinied against the commander and attacked him. He, in turn, killed one man and wounded two others in self-defense. Then some twenty-five officers of the regiment demanded this same commander's resignation, and when it did not come, two officers resigned themselves rather than serve under him.[43] In Pittsburgh, before leaving for Mexico, Private George W. Fenner of the 1st Pennsylvania Volunteer Infantry murdered a teenager. Later, in New Orleans, soldiers from D Company of the regiment destroyed a liquor store, stole chickens, geese, and turkeys from farmers, and threatened their commander, Captain Joseph Hill, who resigned and left the army in fear for his life.[44]

One of the worst vices that all armies faced in war was excessive drinking, which of course plagued units during the Mexican War. On September 7, 1846, during the march to Monterrey, Mexico, five companies of the 1st Georgia Volunteer Infantry broke into a huge fistfight after a drinking spree where "firearms and bayonets and swords were freely used." It took the entire 4th Illinois to subdue the rioters, but not before two Illinois men were killed, four wounded, and two officers stabbed with bayonets.[45]

Perhaps the most heinous of all Mexican War incidents occurred about the time of the Battle of Monterrey in September 1846. To avenge the death of a fellow comrade, soldiers from the 1st Arkansas Cavalry Regiment murdered some twenty to thirty Mexican citizens—men, women, and children. This was a war crime that went unpunished. This same regiment later served with less than distinction at the Battle of Buena Vista. Joseph Chance wrote, "This regiment, in fact, compiled its fighting record mostly against the women, children, and old men of Mexico. Its officers equated war with [street] fighting and reasoned that since they were good brawlers, they must also be good warriors."[46]

---

[42]McCaffery, *Army of Manifest Destiny*, 48.
[43]Ibid., 116–17.
[44]Hackenburg, *Pennsylvania in the War with Mexico*, 8 and 13.
[45]McCaffery, *Army of Manifest Destiny*, 118–19.
[46]Chance, *Jefferson Davis' Mexican War Regiment*, 115.

The regiments of the regular army had superior training and discipline for the most part, but even they experienced some very serious incidents. Captain Braxton Bragg, artilleryman and hero of so many battles in Mexico, was lying on his cot when one of his soldiers rolled an eight-inch shell under it and lit the fuse. The cot, his belongings and tent went up in a terrific explosion. The dazed Bragg walked out miraculously unscathed.[47]

The infamous Saint Patrick's or "San Patricio" Battalion of Mexican artillery was perhaps the greatest symbol of poor discipline during the war. Made up of mostly regulars and a few volunteers who had deserted from the United States Army, the battalion fought in several battles against American forces. This was treason of the highest order and, as the war ended, dozens received their just rewards at the end of a rope.[48]

Not all volunteer regiments and units achieved these types of records. Jefferson Davis's "Mississippi Rifles" performed brilliantly in several battles and had very few discipline problems or desertions. Doniphan's and Price's Missouri regiments, though hard-cut and rough, also served admirably while facing extremely difficult challenges. With adequate training and proper leadership, volunteer regiments performed as well as the regulars in battle. Compared to most regiments and battalions, the Mormon Battalion had a remarkably clean record.

In mid-February 1847, General Zachary Taylor was to fight his last and perhaps greatest battle of the war. General Santa Anna had finally arrived with his army of 15,000 a few miles south of a small ranch settlement called Buena Vista. He began the march northward with 23,000 men, but lost thousands of soldiers along away to thirst, starvation, and straggling. Taylor's army of some 4,750 consisted of mostly new, untested volunteers and a few hundred regular dragoons and artillerymen. On February 22, Santa Anna advanced north through the narrow, deep canyons and steep mountains and attacked with divisions in column along the main road called the "narrows," while another wing of his

---

[47]McCaffery, *Army of Manifest Destiny*, 92.   [48]See Miller, *The Shamrock and the Sword.*

OCCUPYING CALIFORNIA 339

army maneuvered across the plateau, which was a large flat plain cut through with deep gullies and steep ridges to the base of the mountains. But Santa Anna did a poor job coordinating his forces, and the Americans easily repulsed the half-hearted attacks. The next day would be a different matter.

Santa Anna attacked simultaneously in an aggressive, brutal, two-pronged assault. By 9 A.M., the Americans still held the road to the west and had cut hundreds of Mexicans down. But on the American left flank one infantry and two cavalry regiments were thrown back with many casualties as the Mexicans were enveloping the flank. When Taylor arrived on the field about this same time, an alarmed General John Wool said, "General, we are whipped!" Looking out across the battlefield, Taylor replied, "That is for me to determine." Immediately, he ordered Colonel Jefferson Davis's "Mississippi Rifles" forward to head off the determined Mexican attack. The Mexican attack was stopped and then repulsed. A Mexican cavalry attack tried to succeed where the infantry divisions failed, but they were punished by Captain Braxton Bragg's artillery. Another unsupported Mexican attack later in the day nearly broke the American lines but was again checked by artillery. As the sun set, the battle died down and Santa Anna, claiming a great victory, withdrew during the night. Reinforcements arrived in the late evening to bolster Taylor's mauled, but still intact, army. It was Taylor's greatest moment.[49]

On February 28, 1847, Colonel Alexander Doniphan and his most unorthodox 1st Missouri Mounted Volunteers met a Mexican force in Chihuahua under the command of Brigadier General Pedro García Conde. The Mexican commander had developed a masterful defensive plan with his force of 1,200 cavalry, 1,500 infantry, and over 100 artillerymen. He selected a plateau near the Sacramento River, which the main road crossed after coming over a sixty-foot bluff. He placed three batteries of artillery across the road and positioned his infantry in strong entrenchments parallel to the road. Then Conde deployed his cavalry forward for reconnaissance and security. It was a well-developed defensive position.

Doniphan arrived with less than 1,000 men and saw the trap that was set for him, but he was too clever to fall for it. Perhaps he was too

---

[49] Eisenhower, *So Far from God*, 178–91; Bauer, *The Mexican War*, 208–18.

unconventional to not think of an alternative. He decided to sweep wide around to the west, off the main road. After much hard labor, the men and animals dragged the three hundred wagons of Santa Fe trader goods up over the steep embankments and cliffs through gullies and cuts. He then arranged the wagons in four parallel columns and placed his infantry and the artillery under Major Meriwether Lewis Clark between the columns of wagons and moved forward with his own mounted Missourians leading the way. By the time Conde realized what had happened, it was too late. Conde threw his cavalry at the Americans, but Doniphan's artillery drove them off. Doniphan attacked the southern flank of the fortified positions by first blasting it with his artillery and then charging with infantry. The Missourians captured all of the Mexican artillery and trains, killed 300, wounded another 300, but lost only two Americans dead and seven wounded. It was an amazing and glorious victory by an exceptional and unconventional man with his Missouri volunteers.[50]

The Kearny-Frémont fracas was on hold until February 13, when, to Kearny's delight, Colonel Richard B. Mason, his good friend and comrade of more than two decades, arrived at San Francisco. Now commander of the 1st Dragoons after Kearny's promotion, Mason lay near death aboard ship. Kearny joined his ailing friend, who had dispatches from General Scott confirming that Kearny was indeed military commander and civil governor of California. Scott wrote that the "senior officer of land forces" was to be governor.[51] The unusual thing about Colonel Mason's dispatch was that he, Mason, was actually to serve as governor—because Kearny was being recalled for duty in the proposed invasion of Mexico, once California was subdued with no threat of re-invasion by Mexican forces. Since Kearny was in the midst of a wrestling match with Frémont and Stockton for control of California, Kearny stayed on longer and Mason assisted him.

With full confidence, Stephen W. Kearny, brigadier general and

---

[50]Dawson, *Doniphan's Epic March*, 142–57; Eisenhower, *So Far from God*, 244–47.
[51]Clarke, *Stephen Watts Kearny*, 277; Harlow, *California Conquered*, 250–51.

civil governor, drew his pen and wrote a proclamation and "joint" circular of March 1, 1847, establishing a proper government and outlining military authority. Kearny had also been appointed commander of the newly established Tenth Military Department of the United States and organized his forces accordingly. Kearny divided California into military districts with Cooke commanding the Southern Military District from Santa Barbara to San Diego. Mason, if he lived, would command the Northern Military District from Monterey. Cooke would command his battalion, C Company, 1st Dragoons, and Frémont's California Battalion of Volunteers once the Pathfinder subordinated himself to both Kearny and Cooke. Meanwhile, "governor" Frémont was in Los Angeles organizing his government with no knowledge of these recent events.

On March 2, Commodore James Biddle arrived at Monterey to take command of the Pacific Squadron from Shubrick, who had replaced Stockton, who in turn had assumed command from Sloat.[52] Three days later, Colonel Jonathan Stevenson and three companies of the 1st New York Volunteer Infantry Regiment arrived at San Francisco.[53] Kearny had been long awaiting this reg-

---

[52] One wonders what chaos was occurring at the Navy Department. In less than eight months, the Pacific Squadron had witnessed four separate commanders, which confused all present: the naval officers and sailors, the commodores themselves, the army officers, the American settlers, and especially the Mexican-Californios. Also, there were only four brigadier generals in the regular army during the war, but the navy seems to have had dozens of commodores of equal rank floating about. See Harlow, *California Conquered*, 252.

[53] Clarke, *Stephen Watts Kearny*, 291–92. There has been confusion for years about the 1st New York Volunteers, appearing as the "7th" in many accounts and histories. The story behind this mystery is that the 1st and 7th New York Volunteer Regiments were the same regiment. The state of New York originally recruited and organized seven regiments of volunteers in the summer of 1846. Stevenson's regiment became the 7th New York Volunteer Infantry Regiment and was the first to ship out. Eventually, after Stevenson's departure, there were only enough volunteers of the remaining six regiments to fill one complete regiment, which was designated as the 1st New York. However, on February 28, 1848, the War Department redesignated Stevenson's 7th New York Volunteer Regiment as the 1st New York, since it mustered and departed first; and Colonel William B. Burnett's 1st New York was redesignated as the 2nd New York Volunteer Regiment. Official documents reprinted over the years perpetuate this designation error. To confuse things even further, these were volunteer regiments organized and often manned by men of the state militia. The New York militia had hundreds of companies and dozens of regiments, the most famous of which was the "Dandy" 7th New York Regiment consisting of gentlemen and elites of the upper classes in New York City. This regiment never served during the Mexican War. The 2nd New York Volunteer Infantry fought under Scott in central Mexico. See Tutorow, *The Mexican War: An Annotated Bibliography*, 360; see Biggs, *Conquer and Colonize: Stevenson's Regiment and California*, 1977, 48 n.10.

iment as reinforcements. They sailed in the fall of 1846 from New York City, making the long cruise in about five months. The other companies, a total of ten, arrived within days aboard other ships. Kearny was now official governor and commander of California, and had some 500 New York and 350 Mormon volunteers, 60 Regular army dragoons, and hundreds of American sailors and marines under his command. Frémont was finally foiled—yet he was too foolish to realize it.

※ ※ ※

General Winfield Scott, on March 9, 1847, was poised for one of the largest amphibious operations in military history before the great invasions of World War II. Nearly 12,000 combat soldiers, 41 ships, 65 "surf boats" (used as a type of landing craft), dozens of small gunboats, dozens of artillery pieces from field howitzers to siege guns, and mountains of supplies and provisions assembled off the coast of Vera Cruz, Mexico. Scott deserves much of the credit, but not all. The quartermaster general, Colonel Thomas S. Jessup left his department in Washington and, from New Orleans, orchestrated the enormous logistical challenge with coolness and efficiency. There were many problems, but Scott and Jessup did the best they could and succeeded beyond reasonable expectations. The U.S. Navy's Commodore David E. Conner, unlike Stockton in California, gave Scott his complete support in every possible way. What unfolded was a truly "joint" operation of the first magnitude.

Scott's plan was to deploy the small gunboats some one hundred yards from shore to provide covering fire for the invasion forces. The larger ships would fire from longer ranges with their larger caliber guns. The surf boats were specially designed by Scott himself, some forty feet long, four feet deep, and capable of carrying some seventy combat troops with sailors manning the oars. They were designed for shallow water but deep enough to withstand the surf. The invasion force was organized into three divisions, two regular and a volunteer division.

Facing the American invasion were the well-established, ancient Vera Cruz fortifications, consisting of several forts with high walls that circled the city. There were some 135 artillery pieces, heavy siege guns, and hundreds of troops under General Juan Morales. The invasion had enormous potential for many casualties and defeat. By mid-afternoon on March 9, the first wave of several dozen boats rolled across the surf and hit the beach. The men ran to cover. Thousands more followed during the remainder of the afternoon.

Surprisingly, not one Mexican cannon or gun challenged the Americans as they landed ashore: a great military mistake. By nightfall nearly 12,000 men were safely on the beach. On March 22, after his offer of surrender was rejected, Scott commenced the bombardment of Vera Cruz with his land and sea guns. Three days later General Morales surrendered the city. Scott was now ready to launch his march to capture Mexico City and end the war.[54]

Kearny's circular arrived at San Luis Rey on March 14. Cooke was happy with the vindication of his mentor and friend. The particulars of the circular outlined the military organization that Cooke was to establish, one of which dealt with Frémont's men. The California volunteers were to be officially inducted into the United States Army as volunteers, superseding Stockton's unofficial actions of a few months earlier, and then be immediately discharged from the service completely. Frémont would command the California Battalion under Cooke's control. Cooke sent a courier to ascertain the status of his forces and their disposition. Frémont basically blew Cooke off. He refused to muster his battalion again into federal service, since he had already done so with Stockton. He also refused to disband them or to turn over government cannon and ordnance to Cooke. The situation would get nastier.

Cooke also ordered B Company under Captain Jesse Hunter to San Diego to relieve the dragoons there. Sergeant Hyde wrote, "orders were read in the evening, notifying Company B that they were to be ready the next morning to take up a line of march for San Diego to take charge of that place."[55] B Company arrived at the old mission in San Diego on March 17. Thus, the Mormon Battalion was divided again as it continued to serve as occupation forces.

---
[54]Eisenhower, *So Far from God*, 253–65.
[55]William Hyde, Journal, March 14, 1847, Brigham Young University Library.

CHAPTER FIFTEEN

"You Are Discharged"

We had already served our enemies one year.
—Sergeant William Hyde

"We now have all we want to Eat for the first time since we left Santa fee & spend our time more happy amidts the various scenes here," wrote Private Robert Bliss of B Company, the day after his company arrived in San Diego.[1] After the dragoons left San Diego in late March 1847, Captain Jesse Hunter, commanding B Company, became the senior ranking officer in this beautiful, small coastal town. Hunter's company had less than eighty soldiers by this time because of all the losses from the sick detachments. He ordered a detail of eighteen men, initially under Sergeant William Hyde, to man a small fort, or redoubt, with seventeen artillery pieces on a hill above the town.[2] (One wonders who would employ the guns during a battle, since Hyde and his men had no artillery training whatsoever.)

Because of the Kearny-Frémont fracas and the Californio revolt, tensions and rumors were high. Hunter kept the men on alert with loaded muskets much of the time and drilled them often to ensure they were always ready for action. One rumor in late April had fifteen hundred Mexicans marching north from Sonora to retake California. For the most part, the men of B Company settled into a routine that helped them endure the loneliness and boredom.

---

[1] Bliss, "The Journal of Robert S. Bliss," 89.
[2] William Hyde, Journal, March 18, 1847, Brigham Young University Library; this entry is a summarization of three months, because the next date is June 22, 1847.

With better food and more leisure time, the men did great good in San Diego. Many men hired themselves out to the local populace to do various things. They dug wells, built a brick kiln and made bricks, constructed a school and a courthouse, opened a blacksmith shop and a tannery, produced leather goods, did carpentry work, and many other commercial enterprises—all for hire, of course. Some men even became involved with local affairs. Lieutenant Robert Clift served as *alcalde* in San Diego, similar to a mayor or justice of the peace.[3] It was Clift who directed that the men build the courthouse and school. Except for not being with their families and the main body of the Saints, the men were doing very well. Yet fate would also bring tragedy.

Lydia Hunter, wife of Captain Hunter, one of four women who made the entire trek, gave birth to a boy, Diego, on April 13, 1847. But because of complications, she died two weeks later. It was a great loss to her husband and to the morale and happiness of B Company and the many friends she left behind. The new baby boy would never know his mother, an unfortunate and common occurrence in those days. She was buried near the beach at Point Loma.[4]

There were other deaths in the battalion. Private Albert Dunham of B Company died on May 11 in Pueblo, Colorado, after a three-day bout with an illness and without Dr. Sanderson's treatments. (It was Dunham who was involved in the incident on the trail in Kansas where Sergeant Thomas Williams allegedly faced down Lieutenant Smith. Williams had departed with his wife at Santa Fe with the Brown sick detachment.) More men died over the next few weeks, mostly those among the sick men in Pueblo.

---

[3]Jonathan Stevenson to Richard Mason, June 28, 1847, Los Angeles, 10th Military Department Records, National Archives.
[4]Bliss, "The Journal of Robert Bliss," 91; Yurtinus, "Ram in the Thicket," 549. Some writers have made the claim that Diego Hunter was the first Anglo-American born in California. With an American population of nearly one thousand by the time the war started, it is rather improbable to make this claim. If one says that he was the first American birth once California became a United States possession in January 1847, it would be more possible, but still highly unlikely considering the population. See Ricketts, *The Mormon Battalion*, 8. Dr. John S. Griffin, General Kearny's surgeon, wrote, "This was the first American woman who ever bore a child in San Diego." This claim is still doubtful but more plausible than for all of California. See Ames, ed., "A Doctor comes to California," April 27, 1847.

Private John Perkins of C Company died January 19, 1847; Private James Scott of E Company died February 5; on February 25, Private Melcher Oyler passed away and Private Eli Dodson died March 21, both of A Company; D Company's Corporal Arnold Stevens died March 26; Private Mervin Blanchard of A Company died April 10; and Private David Smith of E Company succumbed March 23 at San Luis Rey.[5] The roll of the dead was now at twenty-one.

With the extra time and money, some men found the opportunity to make mischief. Captain Hunter, just weeks after his wife's passing, became drunk, along with Lieutenants Ruel Barrus and Robert Clift, the future *alcalde*.[6] Writing of the matter, Private Thomas Dunn said,

> There has been many such things happen in the character of our officers, which is degrading to their profession . . . for to them [the officers] we looked for better things. I have not penned anything against them before, because I have hoped and looked for better conduct and example, but I have looked in vain.[7]

Regardless of some of their less-than-saintly conduct, the men of B Company gained the respect and high regard of the local Mexican populace and many of the Americans in San Diego. Though still dressed in rags and mostly barefoot, they proved to be industrious and honorable. Religious prejudice, however, had accompanied the battalion to California. Private Bigler wrote,

> Some of the leading men of the place told us that when they heard that a set of Mormon soldiers were coming to San Diego, they had a great notion to pack up and leave the place, for they had been told that the Mormons would steal everything they could lay their hands on. Not only that, but their women would be in danger of being insulted by them.[8]

But after months of service, attitudes changed. Dr. John S. Griffin wrote, "the prejudice against the Mormons here seems to be wearing off . . . they are extremely industrious—they have been engaged

---

[5] Daniel Tyler claimed that Smith died from Dr. George Sanderson's treatments; see Tyler, *A Concise History*, 274.
[6] Thomas Dunn, Journal, May 12, 1847, Utah State Historical Society.
[7] Ibid., May 16, 1847.
[8] Gudde, *Bigler's Chronicle of the West*, 60.

while here in digging wells, plastering houses, and seem anxious and ready to work."[9]

By the first of July 1847, the men of B Company were anxious for only one thing: to end their military service and return to their families out on the Great Plains. With only a couple of weeks of service left, they had to endure as best they could. "At daylight five pieces of artillery were fired from our fort to welcome in the birthday of American Independence," wrote one soldier, "after which we marched in order down into town and gave our officers a hearty salute of musketry, also cheering the whole town. This seemed to take so well with the citizens that they brought out all the wine and brandy we wished to drink and a great deal more."[10] Perhaps to help them forget their loneliness, some celebrated a little too much on the 4th of July, with a number of the men going on a drunken spree. This same day, Captain Hunter announced that B Company was to march north to Los Angeles to be discharged. Their days in the Mormon Battalion were numbered.

In early April 1847, the weather and time was ripe for the advanced party of Latter-day Saints under Brigham Young to begin the long trek to future Utah. After a long and bitter winter on both sides of the Missouri River, the Saints were anxious and ready. Selecting 144 tough, strong, and faithful men, Young organized his party into groups of ten and appointed a captain over each. Yet, dissension in ranks added three women and two children to go along while one man dropped out. Harriet Decker Young, the wife of Brigham Young's brother, refused to be left behind without her husband: either she went or he would remain behind. Young relented and two other women were added to make it "proper" for women to travel with so many men. Additionally, the two children of one of the women joined the party. Among the group were Privates John H. Tippets and Thomas Woolsey, still members of the Mormon Battalion who had just made a harrowing winter trek from Pueblo to Winter Quarters to join the Saints.

---

[9] Ames, "A Doctor Comes to California," 54.
[10] Bigler, "Extract from the Journal of Henry W. Bigler," 61.

"YOU ARE DISCHARGED"

It was a confusing start on April 4, with Heber Kimball moving his wagon and a small group west towards the Elkhorn River. Others followed. Then, the April general conference of the church occurred, and they all returned to attend. Again they moved out. Many returned several more times to get more food, more ox teams, and other things. It would be at least a week before the party was truly organized and actually under way—it was the first trickle of the rushing torrent to come.

Moving overland from Vera Cruz towards Mexico City, General Scott faced his first major action. Captain Robert E. Lee, Corps of Engineers, conducted what is called today a "leader's recon" well forward of and circled around almost behind the Mexican forces at a place called Cerro Gordo ('Fat Mountain'). On April 15, Lee informed Scott how they could out-maneuver and defeat the Mexicans. Scott only had 8,500 men and was in a very vulnerable position, but it was an attack that he knew he had to make. Santa Anna, fresh from his self proclaimed "victory" at Buena Vista, had once again, against many odds, scraped together another army of some 12,000 to 15,000 men and 43 pieces of artillery. He held a very strong position on high terrain that dominated the National Highway between Vera Cruz and Mexico City, the same route the Spaniard Hernando Cortez had taken three centuries earlier in the conquest of the Aztecs. He placed three batteries of artillery forward on three hills that commanded the highway. Yet, Lee's plan was to swing the bulk of the army, two of three divisions, to the north, then west, and attack Santa Anna from his flank and rear along a difficult but passable trail.

Once again, maneuver, leadership, and American artillery carried the day. With a forward deployment that ended in a small battle on April 17, the main attack occurred the next day. After a bloody contest climbing and fighting for every inch up Cerro Gordo, including bayonet charges and counter-charges by the Mexicans, American forces finally took the heights. It was a costly victory, for though it was brilliantly planned, the execution broke down at times. Scott's army was bruised but not broken, and he was determined to continue on to Mexico City.[11]

✳ ✳ ✳

---
[11] Eisenhower, *So Far from God*, 278–83.

Aware that Frémont's loyalty was in question, and also of the significance of Los Angeles as a key military possession, Cooke departed San Luis Rey with the other four companies of the Mormon Battalion on March 19, en route to Los Angeles. Cooke left behind at San Luis Rey a group of thirty men from all the companies, most of whom were sick. Lieutenant George Oman was in charge of these men, while Lieutenant Stoneman, now commanding C Company, 1st Dragoons, was in overall command there.[12] To replace Stoneman as acting assistant commissary and subsistence officer, Cooke chose Lieutenant Robert Clift and sent him to San Diego to work directly with Major Thomas Swords of the quartermaster department. The day after reaching Los Angeles on March 23, the battalion bivouacked south of the town for a week, and then moved north of the pueblo. East of Los Angeles on the San Gabriel River plain Frémont's unruly and testy California volunteers camped. At this time Frémont was on a mad dash north to Monterey to see Kearny, now that events had turned against him. The entire situation was extremely sensitive and dangerous because Frémont refused to face the realities of proper authority and changing circumstances.

During the restless months of March and April 1847, Frémont's California Battalion of some two hundred men saw themselves as the true military force and conquerors of California. Following Frémont's reckless lead and Stockton's arrogance, these California volunteers ignored Kearny and Cooke's authority. The day after reaching Los Angeles, Cooke rode out on March 24 to the California Battalion's camp and met with Captain Richard Owens, the officer in command and "secretary of state" in Frémont's government. Cooke observed the men in camp and inventoried their artillery and other ordnance. Two of the pieces were the howitzers the dragoons had brought from Fort Leavenworth. He requested that Owens and his men submit to his authority, whereby they could be properly mustered into United States service and then be immediately discharged.

---

[12]It was obvious that Cooke had great trust in Lieutenant Oman, the battalion well-digger. Cooke sent him to Warner's ranch after provisions, and now left him in charge at San Luis Rey.

"YOU ARE DISCHARGED"

Cooke tried fervently to persuade Owens to relinquish command:

> I very coolly and in perfect temper, exhausted every information, every argument, every appeal to his patriotism,—every motive in this distant land, for obedience and union amidst enemies; pointed out the disastrous consequences likely to ensue to public interests and to persons, by this treasonable course. In vain; he had received Frémont's orders to obey none other, and nothing more would he do.... The President of the United States, in person, would fail to get the artillery, or be obeyed by Captain Owens with his Battalion, until Lieutenant-colonel Fremont gave the permission![13]

Perplexed, Cooke departed and returned to his headquarters.

After Cooke's failure to obtain the California volunteers' obedience, Colonel Richard Mason tried himself in late April 1847. By this time Frémont was back from Monterey after having another disagreeable interview with General Kearny. Mason and Frémont had a very violent argument when Colonel Mason tried to secure the artillery from him. In his normal impetuous manner, Frémont challenged Mason to a duel. Mason, the challenged, had the right to choose the type of weapons, and selected shotguns loaded with buckshot. Kearny had to intervene to stop this madness. "After some difficulty, he [Mason] finally succeeded in discharging Frémont's men and taking ten pieces of cannon held by them, which were immediately brought to Los Angeles and turned over to Colonel Cooke," recorded Tyler.[14]

In his report Cooke wrote, "The general's orders are not obeyed? ... to be refused to them [ordnance and artillery] by this Lieut. Colonel Frémont and in defiance of the orders of his general? I denounce this treason or this mutiny."[15] The situation continued to brew over the next few weeks and was a major reason that a fort was constructed on terrain that controlled the entire pueblo of Los Angeles—and overlooked some very beautiful country.

"This is indeed a beautiful country if the inhabitants were good and as beautiful it would be a Paradise in reality," wrote Private

---

[13]Cooke, *Conquest*, 291–92.   [14]Tyler, *A Concise History*, 275.
[15]Clarke, *Stephen Watts Kearny: Soldier of the West*, 303.

Henry Boyle of C Company.[16] California was a wonderful, garden-like land and the men were happy to be there, away from the rugged deserts they had just crossed. Though the men had a relatively comfortable existence, they knew that their time in volunteer service was growing short, increasing their loneliness for their families. That may explain why the men sometimes behaved badly by getting drunk and consorting with local women. If there is anything that is common throughout military history, it is the poor behavior of soldiers when bored or idle. Leadership has been the key to this problem since ancient times, and the Mormon Battalion in California was in the midst of a leadership crisis.

Captain Hunt spoke before his brethren on March 30, relating the circumstances of his turning the command over to Lieutenant Smith on the plains in Kansas. Whether all the men accepted his actions or not, at least they heard his explanation. Soon Hunt's subordinates would be his peers again. This particular event, the change in command, would trouble some of the men for many years to come. It was just a matter of a few weeks before their service was over, and they were growing restless.[17]

As all soldiers, they missed their families dearly, even more so because they had no idea where their families were, either in camps along the Missouri River, or making the long trek across the plains to California, the Great Basin, or some other unknown destination. The anxiety this situation caused was painful. "My thoughts go to my family continuly," wrote Private Robert Bliss while at San Luis Rey, "how they fare are they well and contended are they looking for the time to meet me in the fall with as much anxiety I do them often Dream of home & its Pleasant fireside but wake only to hear the Bugle sound or Drums beat for Duty."[18]

Now that military action against the Mexicans was over, in California, the men thought their service was no longer necessary. "On

---

[16]Quoted in Yurtinus, "Ram in the Thicket," 565.

[17]Golder, *The March of the Mormon Battalion*, 216. In a modern context, National Guard and Reserve members at times command and supervise soldiers who are their peers, or in some cases their employers during the week on drill weekends. It is a very strange and unusual working and leadership relationship that reservists have faced for years, normally with success.   [18]Bliss, "The Journal of Robert Bliss with the Mormon Battalion," 87.

"YOU ARE DISCHARGED"

the 6th [April]," according to Sergeant Tyler, "a petition for discharge of the Battalion was gotten up and signed by most of the soldiers, on the ground that peace was declared in California and their services could be dispensed with, allowing them to return and aid their outcast families."[19] Another soldier added, "It [the petition] was signed by a majority of the Battalion present, though the most part of our officers went strongly against it." The Mormon officers knew full well that Kearny and Cooke would never endorse a petition; the army is not a democracy and does not act on petitions, so they refused to forward it. There were some officers who did favor it: Captain Daniel Davis and Lieutenants James Pace, Andrew Lytle, and Samuel Thompson.[20] This was an interesting drama in military history—volunteers sending a petition around to terminate their military service.

At Los Angeles the men of the four companies continued to drill and perform the normal duties and details expected of soldiers. They were becoming more expert in drill and tactics, but some of the officers still had difficulty performing the commands. "This day was spent in camp until 4 P.M. when the Senior Cap (Hunt) called a dress parade. Many were the mistakes made by the Cap's awkwardness," remarked Private Henry Standage.[21] Lieutenant Pace wrote that Hunt "presented himself before the Battalion as Coln [colonel] but soon shoad to evry observing Eye that he was not a Commander [of] the Parade to his shame."[22] Just days later though, on April 12, Colonel Mason, soon to take Kearny's place as military governor of California, inspected the battalion's drill. "Today Col. Mason of the regiment of first dragoons gave us the praise of being the best volunteers of any he had ever seen in the manual of arms," wrote Private Nathaniel Jones.[23] There is little doubt that after the intense training the Mormon Battalion received at San Luis Rey, it was now fully prepared and effective for combat. Soon, a few of the men would see blood in an actual fight.

---

[19] Tyler, *A Concise History*, 275.
[20] Jones, "Extracts from the Life Sketch of Nathaniel V. Jones," 14.
[21] Golder, *The March of the Mormon Battalion*, 216.
[22] James Pace, Diary, April 4, 1847, Brigham Young University Library.
[23] Jones, "Extracts from the Life Sketch of Nathaniel V. Jones," 15.

Cooke, as commander of the Southern Military District, realized the importance of certain key points and routes in southern California. Of course, the most important route was the El Camino Real, which linked all the missions along the coastal plain. Also of great military importance was the Old Spanish Trail, which ran east from Los Angeles to the San Bernardino area, and then crossed the San Bernardino Mountains via Cajon Pass to the high mountain terrain of the Mojave Desert and thence into modern-day Nevada and Utah. The key point to safeguard was Cajon Pass, about forty miles east of Los Angeles. The incessant warfare between first the Spanish and then the Mexicans against the local Indian peoples continued to rage. It was a limited but gruesome war of raids, ambushes, retaliatory attacks, and wholesale murder on both sides. With the United States in control, it was now an American problem. Unwisely, and perhaps sometimes unjustifiably, Americans were quicker to side with the Californios than the native peoples. Cooke therefore determined to protect the local ranchers and secure this critical pass.

"The Dragoon[s] under Lieut. Stoneman returned today having killed 4 Indians. The Indians had been committing depredations on the Spaniards and taking life," recorded Private Standage.[24] Cooke had sent out Stoneman's company to catch and punish a group of marauding Indians for crimes they had committed earlier. On April 11, Cooke ordered C Company, under the command of Lieutenant George Rosecrans, on a specific mission to guard Cajon Pass and protect private property, especially that of an American named Isaac Williams, who owned a large ranch in the area. On the April 22, Lieutenant James Pace relieved C Company with a platoon-sized detachment consisting of twenty-seven men from each of the four companies at Los Angeles.

On May 8, Cooke issued the following order: "Lieutenant Thompson, with twenty men of the Mormon Battalion, rationed for three days, will march immediately to a rancho, within six miles

---

[24]Golder, *The March of the Mormon Battalion*, 215.

"YOU ARE DISCHARGED"

of the foot of the mountain and use every effort to destroy the hostile Indians reported to be in the vicinity."[25] A few days later Lieutenant Thompson returned to report that he had encountered the hostile Indians in a fight near Williams's ranch.

Private Jones narrated the action:

> On the 9th [May], at the mouth of the canyon, we separated, eight of us went up on the mountain to cut off their escape in that way. We attacked them in the head of the canyon. We killed six of them. How many there were in the first place I do not know but there were some [who] escaped certain. We returned to camp just before night. There were two men wounded, one in the face and one in the thigh, though not dangerous.

Jones wrote of the tragic affair after the action, "The Spaniards [Mexicans serving as scouts] used the Indians very brutally, scalped them and cut off their ears and nose before we knew what they were about or we would have prevented them."[26]

The two Mormon soldiers who were slightly wounded were Private Benjamin Mayfield of A Company, with the thigh wound, and Private George Chapin of E Company, wounded below one of his eyes. This was the only fighting that any members of the Mormon Battalion experienced during their military service. It was not combat; it was more of a police or posse action. Thompson and his platoon were out chasing and fighting Indians who had robbed and murdered some Mexicans.[27]

Cooke sent out other patrols to guard the pass and other locations, but this was the only incident of any serious nature. The unrest and excitement of war in California was mostly over and was being replaced with a shaky but peaceful occupation.

The men's service in Los Angeles was very different from that which B Company experienced in San Diego. Instead of working on private and community projects for hire, the four companies began building a United States military garrison in Los Angeles.

---
[25]Tyler, *A Concise History*, 281.
[26]Jones, "Extracts from the Life Sketch of Nathaniel V. Jones," 16–17.
[27]Tyler, *A Concise History*, 281.

With the perceived threat posed by Frémont's seemingly intractable attitude and the possibility of another Mexican-Californio uprising, Cooke decided to build a fort on a hill just north of the central plaza of Los Angeles.

The idea to build the fort occurred about the same time as the strongest rumor and the most excitement went forth concerning Frémont's volunteers attacking the Mormon Battalion. Writing about the night of April 25, Private Standage recorded, "Last night we were called up and ordered to load and fix bayonets, as the Col [Cooke] had sent word that an attack might be expected from Col. Fremont's men before day." The Mormon men lay with their muskets loaded during a sleepless night. "They [the California volunteers] have been using all possible means to prejudice the Spaniards and Indians against us by telling them we would take their wives & thereby rousing an excitement through the country," Standage continued.[28] Surprisingly, the Mormons received assistance from an unexpected source.

Many historians of the battalion have highlighted the idea that the California volunteers were Missourians, and thus were at odds with the Mormons. Some of these American settlers may have been from Missouri, but probably not all. But the opportunity for clashes was always present—Los Angeles had a number of saloons and brothels in town where the soldiers visited, especially Frémont's men. The few dragoons garrisoned in town defended the Mormon men saying, "Mormon boys.... Stand back; you are religious men, and we are not; we will take all of your fights into our hands.... You shall not be imposed upon by them."[29] The rumors concerning the Mormons soon died, as most rumors do, but the emotion and attitudes were still real.

Measures were needed to insure proper military authority. "Head Quarters S[outhern]. M[ilitary]. District, Los Angeles, April 24, 1847," went Order No. 9 from Cooke.

> The Mormon Battalion will erect a small fort on the eminence which commands the town of Los Angeles. Company A will encamp on the ground

---

[28]Golder, *The March of the Mormon Battalion*, 219.
[29]Tyler, *A Concise History of the Mormon Battalion*, 280.

to-morrow forenoon. The whole company will be employed in the diligent prosecution of the labors for one week.... The hours of labor will be from half past six o'clock until 12 o'clock, and from 1 o'clock until 6 o'clock.... Lieutenant [J. W.] Davidson, First Dragoons, will trace to-morrow on the sight selected, his plan, which has been approved of, a fort.

Work began on April 25 and lasted for several weeks with all the companies rotating through the weekly work plan.[30] There was a very serious tactical reason to build a fort in Los Angeles, but it was also a clever stroke by Cooke to keep the men busy and their minds occupied.[31] Mormon soldiers were, for the most part, far better behaved than their non-Mormon counterparts.

In Los Angeles the nearly three hundred Mormon soldiers commenced putting their religious affairs back in place, because many were alarmed at the behavior of some of the brethren. "In the afternoon the seanry of drunkeness was lamentable," recorded Lieutenant James Pace on March 25, shortly after the four companies arrived at Los Angeles. Some of the men went on a drinking spree beginning March 23 and lasting through the 25th. "The screams & yells of drunken Mormons would of disgraced the wild Indian mutch moor a Laterday Saint," continued Pace.[32] Reports came from San Luis Rey that some of the men were consorting with Mexican and Indian women.[33] Something had to be done, and the Mormon officers were not stepping in to curb this behavior. Therefore, the religious leaders put on the mantle.

On April 18, many of the men organized themselves into an ecclesiastical group within the Mormon church and priesthood, called the Quorum of Seventy. Most of the men held the Mormon priesthood and had wide experience in officiating and administering in their faith. Private Stephen St. John of E Company was selected to serve as the president of the quorum. In Mormon practice, the Quorum of Seventy was a body of seventy men, each

---

[30]Ibid., 279.
[31]Harlow, *California Conquered*, 270. Kearny and Cooke, having received some evidence and many reports that the Mexican government was sending an invasion force to recapture California, took some necessary but limited precautions. Building stockades or forts for long encampments is a fundamental military principle.
[32]James Pace, Diary, March 25, 1847, Brigham Young University Library.
[33]Levi Hancock, Journal, April 18, 1847, LDS Archives.

ordained as a "seventy," which is another separate position in the priesthood along with elder, deacon, priest, and so on. The quorum is presided over by seven presidents, with one serving as senior president.

"This morning I met with the 70s as before appointed," wrote Private Standage.

> Singing and remarks by Pres. St. John on the evils arising in the Battalion, to wit: drunkenness, swearing and intercourse with squaws &c. . . . Pres. St. John voted in as Senior President of the Quorum and James Pace, Andrew Lytle, Daniel Browett, [Jonathan] Holmes, Frederic[k] Faursney [Fauney], [Jeremiah] Willey, to be his Councillors, a Quorum being organized.

Perhaps the most symbolic event that occurred as a result of this organization was a religious disciplinary action. Standage continued, "John Allen's case taken into consideration and he [was] cut off from the Church, Adjourned sine die."[34]

This was an official action by ordained members of the church and their decision was binding: John Allen was no longer a member of the Church of Jesus Christ of Latter-day Saints. With this example, some hoped that the immoral behavior of some of the men would cease. It was believed that these actions—excommunicating Allen and establishing priesthood administration outside of the military chain of command—would empower the church leaders. The Quorum was "resolved to use all possible means in righteousness to stop Drunkeness [w]horedoms & evry other abominable practice."[35]

This represented a shift in the power base among the men. Historian John Yurtinus wrote, "The power conflict between the highest religious authority and the military leadership [Mormon officers] which had been festering for months produced a definite transfer of power from the military to the religious leaders at Los Angeles."[36] One of the important causes of the shift in informal authority was the Mormon soldiers' loss of confidence in their brother officers. Private Standage painted a very poignant picture:

---

[34]Golder, *The March of the Mormon Battalion*, 217–18.
[35]James Pace, Diary, April 18, 1847, Brigham Young University Library.
[36]Yurtinus, "Ram in the Thicket," 580.

"The fact is if our Battalion Officers who profess to be our brethren would act as fathers to us we could have easier times but they seek to please the Gentiles and to gain favor at our expense."[37]

With formal religious structure now organized among the men, Mormon priesthood leadership now became prominent in the men's affairs. Religious authority would become critical the last few weeks of the Mormon Battalion's service while the specter of re-enlistment hovered over them.

General Winfield Scott's army of some ten thousand was now disintegrating before his very eyes. It could not have come at a more precarious time and place. He was now deep in enemy country and over a hundred miles from his base of operations, connected by a long and tenuous lifeline behind him. Some three thousand troops, nearly all of his volunteers from seven regiments, were leaving the army because their one-year term of service was soon to expire. In an official letter Scott wrote, "The general-in-chief regrets to learn . . . that, in all probability, not one man in ten of those regiments will be inclined to volunteer for [the duration of] the war. This pre-determination offers, in his opinion, no ground for reproach, considering the long, arduous, faithful, and gallant services of these corps."[38] The campaign to march on and capture Mexico City to end the war came to an abrupt halt.

Scott now had only some seven thousand soldiers, mostly regulars, to continue the campaign. Meanwhile, the undaunted Santa Anna and his countrymen were in Mexico City forming yet another army to throw at the Americans.

Scott knew his army was vulnerable, but he continued his march on to Puebla, which was a better place to wait for reinforcements. The aged Arthur Wellesley, duke of Wellington and victor of Waterloo, pronounced Scott's doom. "Scott is lost!" he wrote from England. "He has been carried away by successes! He can't take the [Mexico] city, and he can't fall back on his bases."[39] For Scott, wait he would; give up, never.

---
[37]Golder, *The March of the Mormon Battalion*, 219.
[38]Eisenhower, *So Far from God*, 296.   [39]Ibid., 298.

※ ※ ※

General Kearny returned to Los Angeles in early May 1847. He was satisfied that California was now under American control, and that strong and efficient government was in place. The Frémont threat was over, though in Kearny's mind he was yet to pay for his foolish insubordination. Following orders from the president, Kearny was ready to return to the United States, and the best and quickest route was overland. Before leaving he decided to make a quick tour of the American garrisons in California to hopefully persuade some of the volunteers, especially men in the Mormon Battalion, to re-enlist. He still did not trust some of the American settlers because of their vain attempt to support Frémont. Kearny was also concerned that California was still vulnerable to Mexican revolt. American military occupation forces numbered just over 1,000 men at this time, according to Kearny's muster reports: 88 men of the 1st Dragoons; 107 men of a battery of the 3rd U.S. Artillery; Colonel Stevenson's 550 1st New York Volunteers; and 314 men of the Mormon Battalion.[40] If the Mormons volunteered for another year, it would ensure California's security. Thus, Kearny desired to have the Mormon men re-enlist.

Kearny's attitudes about the Mormons as a people and a religion were very interesting, considering how much he had relied upon their support and loyalty during the crisis with Frémont. "The General and I have just had a talk about the Mormons," wrote Captain Henry S. Turner, Kearny's adjutant, adding that the general

> having been long stationed in the West is [a] high authority relating to this most objectionable community to my present knowledge of them. He says they are a very sinning people but that they have also been much sinned against. His impression is that if let alone they will gradually slide back into an ordinary condition, that persecution has kept them together.[41]

Kearny's wisdom here was astounding: once settled in Utah and after decades of growth and prosperity, the Mormons did gradually slide, or assimilate with the rest of the country.

---

[40]Kearny's Letter Book, 221. Ricketts and others provide other totals. See Ricketts, *The Mormon Battalion*, 278–80. [41]Quoted in Clarke, *Stephen Watts Kearny*, 304.

Captain Hunt was the first to inquire about re-enlisting the battalion, as early as March 17, in a letter to Captain Turner. Since California would require skilled artisans and mechanics to develop industry, community services, and local business, Hunt suggested that he return to Council Bluffs under government expense and recruit more men to come to California to establish these services. Of course, his recommendation was rejected, but the need for men to re-enlist had already occurred to Kearny.[42] Kearny, Stevenson, and Cooke had difficulty seeing how California could remain secure without the battalion's service for another year. The men of Colonel Stevenson's 1st New York Regiment had enlisted precisely for the opportunity to come to California and then remain there as settlers.[43]

Kearny was under the impression that the original intent of the Mormons was to settle in California when he sent Captain James Allen to their camps in June 1846. Now, the Mormon men were consumed with the idea of returning east to meet their fellow Mormons moving west or rejoin loved ones in the camps in Iowa. The fact that Brigham Young and the advance party were trekking to Utah was unknown to both Kearny and the battalion men in May 1847, but they knew that with the coming of spring the Saints would be underway. Some of the men were favorably impressed with California to the point that they had already determined to settle there. With the church leaders gaining more influence within the battalion, the idea of rejoining their people became the highest priority. The petition that the men circulated in early April to be released from active service was strong evidence of the men's great desire to return to their families; fortunately, the Mormon officers did not forward this petition to Cooke or anyone else. Nevertheless, Kearny and Stevenson would have a difficult challenge finding volunteers among the Mormons willing to re-enlist.

---

[42] Captain Jefferson Hunt to Captain Henry S. Turner, San Luis Rey, March 17, 1847, 10th Military Department, National Archives.

[43] The New York Volunteers were authorized travel at government expense to California, but according to Colonel Stevenson in a letter to Secretary of War William Marcy, "it must be explicitly understood that they [the volunteers] may be discharged without a claim for returning home." See Biggs, *Conquer and Colonize*, 30.

Beginning on May 8, General Kearny conducted an inspection tour at Los Angeles, which continued over the next few days, and included the four companies of the battalion. He praised their mastery and efficiency in drill and tactics. He spoke of the need to maintain a strong military force in California. According to Tyler, Kearny "remarked to an officer, that history might be searched in vain for an infantry march equal to that performed by the Battalion, all circumstances considered, and added: 'Bonaparte crossed the Alps, but these men have crossed a continent.'"[44]

"After inspection the Gen caused them to be placed in close order and made some few remarks to the Battalion," wrote Private Standage, "thanking them for their good behavior &c. Also endeavoring to persuade the single men to re-enlist."[45] Writing on May 10, Private Jones recorded,

> This morning the Battalion was paraded for General Kearney and Stevenson to inspect. He made a great many remarks concerning us in the highest terms... he promised to represent our conduct to the President and in the halls of congress and give us the justice that we merited. He promised us some clothing and advised us to re-enlist into the service for twelve months, and many other things.[46]

Kearny, Cooke, and Stevenson used clothing and uniforms as incentives to convince the nearly naked men to re-enlist, a play that did not work as they hoped. The men considered their options, but for the most part they were determined to return east.

By May 14, Kearny was ready to leave Los Angeles, head north to Sutter's Fort, then proceed overland to Fort Leavenworth. Captain Hunt sent a letter with Kearny's party to Brigham Young explaining the state of mind among his Mormon brethren. "I have," wrote Hunt, "... done the best I knew and used every endeavor to console the men and make the burdens laid on them by the officers of the regular army light as I could. But every good intention was construed into evil. Of all characters I was most vile."[47] Hunt very

---

[44] Tyler, *A Concise History*, 281–82. There is little doubt that Tyler used Cooke's line in the beginning of this statement, but Kearny probably said the latter comment.
[45] Golder, *The March of the Mormon Battalion*, 222.
[46] Jones, "Extracts from the Life Sketch of Nathaniel V. Jones," 17.
[47] Cited in Carter, *Our Pioneer Heritage*, 11: 355–37.

much wanted the men to re-enlist with the possibility of him officially assuming command as a volunteer lieutenant colonel. He would spearhead the re-enlistment effort.

The attitude among most of the men was such that they had no desire to serve a day longer than their one-year service obligation. They were homesick for family and friends, and they were ready to leave. No inducements, short of another call from Brigham Young, would entice most of them to re-enlist. The religious leaders strongly encouraged the men to return to the main body of the Saints, where their numbers and strength were needed. There came to be almost a face-off between those who desired discharge and the few Mormon officers who desired the men to re-enlist. Tensions and personalities clashed at times. Through May and June the problem of re-enlistment festered.

In late June, Colonel Stevenson made a last attempt to get the entire battalion to re-enlist. There were several inducements offered the men over the next few days: new uniforms of Stevenson's regiment, eighteen cents a day for working on the fort in addition to their regular pay as soldiers, and the opportunity for Mormons to serve in the highest ranks within the battalion.[48] The ad hoc organization of a battalion at this time in military service provided that a lieutenant colonel commanded four companies or more and a major anything less. With a strength of a little more than three hundred men, the battalion should have been reorganized into three companies. Colonel Mason, now governor and commander of the 10th Military Department, directed that each volunteer company had to have at least sixty-four men, so in order to fill out a five-company battalion, the entire strength of the present battalion would have to re-enlist.

One soldier wrote insightfully regarding the re-enlistment debate: "Our officers are becoming more and more like men, giving us as many privileges as they can conveniently. They have not been more than half as strict for a few days past," wrote Private Standage on June 27. "In fact they seem to realize that their power as military

---

[48]See R. B. Mason to J. D. Stevenson, Monterey, June 5, 1847, 10th Military Department Records, National Archives; J. D. Stevenson to R. B. Mason, June 16, 1847, Los Angeles, Mormon Battalion Papers, National Archives.

commanders will soon be gone and that their influence will go too." He continued, "In as much as they know that there are men in this battalion who stand as high and much higher in the Priesthood, therefore it seems as though they wished to restore that confidence in some measure which they well know has departed during the last 12 months."[49]

On June 22, Colonel Stevenson was in to San Diego to re-enlist B Company. There he offered his pitch, which met with some success. According to Private Robert Bliss, Stevenson "Gave us the praise of being the best company in the Southern Division [District] of California; the most Inteligent & correct Soldiers Said we were universally esteemed & respected by the Inhabitants & in Short we had done more for California than any other people & gave us an invitasion to [en]List again for 6 months."[50] After a few days, some twenty or so decided to re-enlist, and Captain Jesse Hunter, Sergeant William Hyde, and others of B Company returned with Colonel Stevenson to Los Angeles to assist the efforts there.[51]

In Los Angeles the re-enlistment efforts and discussions turned into a real democratic process. During the last days of June, meetings and gatherings were held. Sometimes Stevenson spoke; at other times Hunt addressed the men, then men such as Private Hancock, Sergeant Hyde, and Captain Hunter expressed their opinions. It was almost a comic situation, with the last vestiges of military protocol crumbling. Again, the promises and inducements were offered. "He [Stevenson] also promised us in case the Battalion should enlist again that we should be privileged to elect our own Lieut.-Col. and less the Battalion only our own Major and all others below," wrote Private Standage. "We were also promised to be discharged in Feb. next with one year's pay."[52]

Stevenson addressed the men in Los Angeles on June 29. He again laid out the necessity of having a strong military force in California, lauded the battalion's service, and reminded the men of the

---

[49]Golder, *The March of the Mormon Battalion*, 229–30.
[50]Bliss, "The Journal of Robert S. Bliss, with the Mormon Battalion," 96.
[51]Thomas Dunn, Journal, June 22, 1847, Utah State Historical Society; William Hyde, Journal, June 22 and 24, 1847, Brigham Young University Library.
[52]Golder, *The March of the Mormon Battalion*, 230.

"YOU ARE DISCHARGED"

advantages and offers available should they re-enlist. He remarked, "Your term of service will soon close. It is of the utmost importance that troops be kept here until others can be transported." Voicing a serious but possible alternative, he added, "I have the right to press you into the service for six months longer, if deemed necessary, and have no doubt but I would be sustained in so doing.... I have decided not to press you to serve longer. I am required to make a strong effort to raise at least one company, and the entire Battalion if possible." He then mentioned the lieutenant colonelcy being given to a Mormon elected by the men, sympathized that their families were in a precarious situation, and ended with a call of patriotism.[53]

Later in the day, Hunt spoke, as did several others, both for and against re-enlisting. Perhaps the most interesting comments came from Sergeant William Hyde, who initially espoused the re-enlistment effort, but then opposed it: "But with me, his [Stevenson's] arguments had no effect further than it greeved me to see some of our officers seeking after power and filthy lucre at the bitter expense of their brethren. My conclusions were if Captain Hunt and others wanted power, they should have claimed it at the death of Colonel Allen at time it was their right to claim it." Hyde continued, "But now, for us to enter service for another year for the purpose of gratifying the selfish feelings of any man or set of men, was entirely repugnant to my feelings. We had already served our enemies one year and offered our lives as a sacrifice to save the people of God." Hyde wrote that, "Several speeches were made by Captain Hunt and others in favor of our re-enlistment," and then there was a silence for a while. "It fell to my lot to be the first to break the silence," and he rose up and spoke: "let others do as they may, God being my helper, I shall return to my family and to headquarters [of the church]. I was followed by Father Pettigrew and Brother Daniel Tyler and others" who more or less took the same position. After the day's efforts only a dozen or so men from the four companies in Los Angeles were willing to re-enlist.[54]

The men took more time to discuss the opportunities that fur-

---
[53] Tyler, *A Concise History*, 293–94.
[54] William Hyde, Journal, June 29, 1847, Brigham Young University Library.

ther military service would provide, but the religious leaders were completely against it. The debate that had begun in April continued until July. Eventually, some eighty-two men re-enlisted under Captain Daniel C. Davis, the former commander of E Company. They were called officially the "Mormon Volunteers," because they were only of company strength.

The men should not be condemned for their decision not to fully support the re-enlistment efforts. They had joined for one year's service; they had left their families in a wilderness; they had marched some nineteen hundred miles across some of the most forbidding land in America; they had suffered privations that few soldiers in history have faced; they had served their time honorably. Now it was time to return to their families. If General Scott could lose three thousand volunteers at the threshold of victory at the very gates of Mexico City, then Colonels Mason and Stevenson could occupy a subdued California without the service of the Mormon Battalion.

Through the dirt and dust and burning sun of central Mexico, nearly one thousand shaggy, nasty-looking men in worn, thread-bare rags marched through Saltillo and camped a few miles from the battlefield of Buena Vista. Colonel Alexander Doniphan and his 1st Missouri Mounted Volunteers proudly joined the fellow Americans of General John Wool's army on May 22, 1847. Their long campaign to invade and conquer Chihuahua was finally over. By mid-June the regiment was in New Orleans, receiving its first pay in nearly a year and being discharged from volunteer service. By groups they made their way up the Mississippi River to their homes in Missouri. Arriving at St. Louis on the anniversary of their enlistment at Fort Leavenworth, Doniphan's men were swept into the great celebration of their glorious year's service. Colonel Doniphan's 1st Regiment of Missouri Mounted Volunteers made one of the most incredible military marches in American history—some three thousand miles, led by an exceptional citizen-soldier.[55]

Out on the plains of what would become eastern Wyoming, the pioneer company under Brigham Young reached Fort Laramie, called Fort John

---

[55]Dawson, *Doniphan's Epic March*, 184–93.

at that time, on June 1, 1847. To their surprise they met an unusual group. Some twenty or so fellow Mormons had been at the fort for two weeks awaiting Young's advance company. They were some of the "Mississippi Saints," who were ahead of the main body the year before and wintered in Pueblo along with more than a hundred soldiers and family members of the Mormon Battalion. Young decided to send an escort party south to Pueblo to bring the more than two hundred Mormons living there back up the trail, and then direct them to follow on behind his advance party. Privates John Tippets and Thomas Woolsey would guide the group.

A few days earlier, Brigham Young, often referred to as the "Lion of the Lord," had delivered a scorching lecture chastising his advance party for their meanness, swearing, laziness, cruelty to animals, and generally wicked ways. He called them to repent or he would leave them in the wilderness; he would no longer tolerate their unsaintly behavior. The party was now more than halfway to its final destination, the Valley of the Great Salt Lake.

"His conduct in California has been such that I shall be compelled on arriving in Missouri to arrest him and send him under charges to report to you." Thus did General Kearny write in August 1847 concerning Frémont to Brigadier General Roger Jones, adjutant general, in Washington.[56] Earlier in May, Kearny was ready to leave California and turn command over to Colonel Richard Mason. Kearny selected a detail of fifteen Mormon soldiers to escort him and his party back east. A number of senior officers would accompany Kearny, including Major Thomas Swords of the Quartermaster Department, Kearny's adjutant Captain Henry Turner, Dr. George Sanderson, Congressman-elect Willard Hall of the Mormon Battalion, and Lieutenant Colonel John C. Frémont and many of his comrades.

One other officer would accompany Kearny overland to Fort Leavenworth. Cooke wrote years later,

> The time of service of the Mormon Battalion expired in July, and the acceptance of the resignation of its Lieutenant-colonel commanding hav-

---

[56]Clarke, *Stephen Watts Kearny: Soldier of the West*, 316.

ing been earnestly urged by him [Cooke himself], in order that he might also return by this opportunity, it was accepted by General Kearny, May 13, and he embarked, next day, with him and his suit, on the *Lexington* at San Pedro for Monterey.[57]

With Cooke's departure, the Mormon Battalion had lost its finest and most capable commander; the heart and soul of the battalion was now gone. The men would never forget the man who led them across the Southwest over a difficult march and had made them an effective fighting unit. Nearly ten years later, the former sergeant major of the battalion, James Ferguson, wrote of Cooke's comradeship, and also of Lieutenants A. J. Smith and George Stoneman:

> We had made many friends. Lieutenants Smith and Stoneman parted us with regret. . . . And our brave Colonel he was rigid in his discipline, and often cross and exacting. But beneath it all, he had a kind, manly heart, and while sometimes he would curse us to our face, he would defend us as his own honor in our absence.[58]

On May 14, 1847, Cooke embarked with Kearny, three of the battalion escorts, and others aboard the *Lexington* at San Pedro. The other Mormon escorts rode overland under the command of Lieutenant William Tecumseh Sherman, of C Company, 3rd U.S. Artillery Regiment. Sherman, who was destined to become one of the greatest Union generals during the Civil War, had arrived in California with Colonel Mason and Stevenson's New York volunteers.

Lieutenant Colonel Philip St. George Cooke, with his resignation as commander of the Mormon Battalion, resigned also from the volunteer service and became a captain again in the regular army subject to being reassigned back to the 1st Dragoons. Unknown to him at the time, Cooke had been promoted to major in the 2nd U.S. Dragoons on February 16, 1847, and also received a brevet promotion to lieutenant colonel. The promotion was recommended by President Polk and approved by Congress for gal-

---

[57]Cooke, *Conquest*, 305.
[58]Tyler, *A Concise History of the Mormon Battalion*, 368.

James Ferguson, c. 1860.
From Orson F. Whitney,
History of Utah, *1:622.*

lant war service on February 20, 1847. He relinquished command of the Southern Military District to Colonel Stevenson. Command of the battalion was not officially given to any officer by orders, though in all the official correspondence and records after May 13, Captain Jefferson Hunt assumed the role as acting commander. Stevenson exercised operational control over the battalion as commander of the Southern Military District.[59]

Kearny's escort of 15 Mormon soldiers and the rest of the party with some 170 mounts left Sutter's Fort in mid-June and proceeded at very quick pace eastward. They soon reached the camps of the Donner tragedy a few months earlier. In this location along Truckee Creek, some forty people perished from the misfortune of their prolonged trek and the deep snows they encountered near the sum-

---

[59] On June 5, 1847, Colonel Richard Mason, commander of the 10th Military Department, wrote Captain Jefferson Hunt, "Captain, I am very desirous, in the present Condition of affairs in California, to have the Battalion under your Command Continue in service for another term of twelve months, unless sooner discharged. . . . [addressed] Capt Jefferson Hunt, Comdg Mormon Battalion, Pueblo de los Angeles." Letters, 10th Military Department, National Archives.

mit of the Sierra Nevada. Kearny's party had the unpleasant task of burying the remains of the dead, some of whom were victims to cannibalism. They burned the cabins because of the stench and filth, and perhaps also due to evidence of the hideous and gruesome deeds they beheld.[60]

Frémont and his men normally traveled and camped separately from the others. Following the well-known California Trail, they crossed the Nevada deserts at a fast pace and continued for several weeks, following the Humboldt River and then the Snake River to Fort Hall. They reached South Pass on the same day, July 24, 1847, that Brigham Young and the last group of the advance pioneer company entered the Great Basin. They missed Young's party by only a couple of weeks. Along the Oregon Trail they encountered thousands of people—men, women, and children—going west, many of whom were Mormons following Young's advance party. The migration of 1847 was just one of many waves of emigrants, waves that would swell in the coming years.

Kearny arrived at Fort Leavenworth on August 22, traveling the nineteen hundred miles in about two months at a rate of over thirty miles a day. Immediately upon arriving at Fort Leavenworth, Kearny had Frémont arrested.[61] The court martial took place in Washington that fall and Frémont was found guilty of insubordination, mutiny, and disobedience. He was cashiered from the service, but President Polk remitted the sentence. Frémont, with his usual impetuous and foolish flair, made a great scene of resigning his commission and eventually returned west to California with his family. He conducted a couple of minor explorations, served in the United States Senate representing the new state of California, and was the first presidential nominee of the new Republican Party in 1856. During the Civil War his service was abysmal as a Union general. Frémont died in near-poverty years later with his loving wife, Jesse, at his side.[62]

---

[60]Jones, "Extracts from the Life Sketch of Nathaniel V. Jones," 19; for the best account of the Donner–Reed Party, see Stewart, *Ordeal by Hunger: The Story of the Donner Party*.
[61]Clarke, *Stephen Watts Kearny: Soldier of the West*, 335.

Private "John Allen," wrote Private Henry Standage,

> ...had been in the calaboose some several weeks for desertion of his post as a picket guard. He did not belong to the Church. Was cut off by a Quorum of 70s. at this place for drunkness, swearing and many other vices. He was baptized on our road to Santa Fe. Joined the Battalion at Fort Leavenworth and never was a Mormon.... His sentence is to have half of his hair shaved and to be drummed out of town.

One of course would wonder how Standage considered Allen not a Mormon, though he was baptized as a member as any other Mormon. Some weeks later Allen was apprehended and imprisoned, but soon afterwards dug through the adobe wall to escape and was never heard of again.[63] This was the last formal discipline proceeding before the battalion's discharge.

The soldiers had only two things on their minds the last few weeks of their service: to return to their families and how to do it. Through the end of June and early July the men bought horses, mules, saddles, and provisions and learned of the best routes to return east. Some word had arrived of battles and victories in Mexico but nothing of the church and their families. "All hands were now busy making preparations to leave," wrote Private Bigler on July 4 in San Diego, "for their homes where ever that was whether on Bear River, California, or Vancovers Islands up the British possessions for the truth is we do not know where President Young and the Church is!"[64] Colonel Stevenson also dedicated Fort Moore in Los Angeles in honor of Captain Benjamin Moore, 1st Dragoons, killed at San Pasqual.

With B Company's arrival in Los Angeles on July 15, the Mormon Battalion was once again united for the first time in four months. The next day was the one-year anniversary of their mustering at Council Bluffs. It had been a long year, nearly two thousand miles from their starting point, with hundreds of miles marching back and forth through California. Over twenty men

---

[62]Frémont had been commissioned a lieutenant colonel in the new Regiment of Mounted Riflemen in the summer of 1846, though he never served with the "Brave Rifles" regiment. Allan Nevins's biography is very generous to Frémont. See Nevins, *Frémont: Pathmarker of the West*. [63]Golder, *The March of the Mormon Battalion*, 225.
[64]Gudde, *Bigler's Chronicle of the West*, 57 n.19.

Twenty-four-year-old Ruel Barrus was a second lieutenant in Company B. This photo was taken in Los Angeles, 1847. *Courtesy International Society, Daughters of Utah Pioneers.*

had died; a third of the original battalion and most of the camp-followers had departed through a long and lonely winter; and now, after such an eventful and challenging year, their service had come to an end. There was little ceremony and formality; all that was necessary was the words.

Newly promoted Captain Andrew Jackson Smith, 1st Dragoons, walked out to where the battalion had formed by companies, "then marched down between the lines [ranks] in one direction and back between the next lines, then in a low voice said: 'You are discharged,'" narrated Private Azariah Smith. "This was all there was of the ceremony of mustering out of service," wrote Smith, "this veteran corps of martyrs to the cause of their country and religion. None of the men regretted the Lieutenant's brevity; in fact, it rather pleased them."[65]

Thus ended the service of the Mormon Battalion—the only religious unit in American military history.

---

[65] Cited in Golder, *The March of the Mormon Battalion*, 236.

Epilogue

I was still imbued with military service.
—*Private John Riser*

With the Mormon Battalion discharged, the men determined what they would do next. For several days they organized themselves into various parties and groups to return east to their families. For many it took another year before they left. Some even decided to stay in California for the season to work and earn more money, or to possibly settle there permanently.[1]

About eighty men re-enlisted for six more months, and since the new unit was only company strength, it was officially called the Mormon Volunteers and served in San Diego under the command of Captain Daniel C. Davis. Private John Riser of the former C Company recalled, "I was still imbued with military service. I again enlisted with eighty others into service of the same."[2] Unlike the battalion men, the Mormon Volunteers were immediately issued uniforms, according to Colonel Stevenson: "They uniformed themselves from head to toe in the uniform of my regiment."[3] This uniform was not the standard army issue uniform of the day, neither the sky blue pattern or the summer cotton duck, but a New York militia version. It was "very neat and serviceable; pantaloons

---

[1] Other writers devote entire chapters to the return trips and adventures of the men. See Ricketts, *The Mormon Battalion*; see also Bagley and Bigler, *The Army of Israel: The Mormon Battalion Narratives*.

[2] Cited in Ricketts, *The Mormon Battalion*, 261.

[3] Charles Hughes, ed., "A Military View of San Diego in 1847: Four Letters from Colonel Jonathan D. Stevenson to Governor Richard B. Mason," 41.

of dark, mixed grey, with scarlet strip or cord up the seam of the leg, blue coats with scarlet trimmings." Stevenson had enough additional uniforms to supply his men and the Mormon Volunteers.[4] The fact the Mormon Volunteers received uniforms has caused some confusion over the years about whether the Mormon Battalion men did, in fact, wear uniforms: the battalion did not; the volunteers did.

The volunteers were officially mustered into service on July 20, 1847, four days after the Mormon Battalion's discharge by none other than Captain A. J. Smith. Their service through March 14, 1848, was uneventful; they performed occupation duties in San Diego. Two of their number died: Sergeant Lafayette Frost, originally of A Company, died September 8, and Private Neal Donald, of C Company, died November 5, 1847. These were the last deaths of soldiers who had enlisted with the Mormon Battalion. Other battalion veterans died returning to Utah, or in Iowa after their discharge. The roll of honor of those who died while in active service in either the Mormon Battalion or Mormon Volunteers ended with twenty-two names.

Much could be and has been said about the Mormon Battalion's contributions to California history and settlement, the opening of the West, and the roads and trails the men used in their travels. The battalion's involvement in the phenomenon of manifest destiny is important. The battalion's most commonly cited accomplishments are Cooke's Wagon Road, a future route for the Butterfield Stage Line and one of the routes the gold-rush "Forty-niners" traveled; the Gadsden Purchase of 1853; and the community projects in San Diego and the construction of Fort Moore in Los Angeles.

The epic of march and the very fact that the battalion endured such a grueling journey is central to the story, just as is the march of Xenophon and his Greek soldiers, or even in literary tales such as *Moby Dick* or *The Adventures of Huck Finn*, where the journey itself

---

[4]Francis D. Clark, *Stevenson's Regiment in California, 1846–1848*, reprinted as *The New York Volunteers in California*, 14.

becomes the story. The battalion's route was critical to American history because just seven years later, the Untied States was willing to pay Mexico millions of dollars for the Gadsden Purchase to fill in that nice little portion along the border south of the Gila River. If it were not for Cooke's report and Lieutenant William Emory's survey and others' support, the importance of the region would not have been recognized and the purchase would not have taken place.

Yet, the Mormon Battalion's long journey and its service in California are only a part of its impact on American, western, and LDS history. The fact that battalion veteran Henry Bigler and others were present and recorded when James Marshall found gold on January 24, 1848, helped establish the actual day of the find. Though some of the battalion veterans worked and earned riches in the gold fields, most of them finished their contracted labor to build Sutter's grist mill and other projects—the reason the men were working there in the first place. The route the men carved through Carson Pass and down the Carson River in the Sierra Nevada would become a thoroughfare for the great rush of 1849. Their eastbound route would lead tens of thousands of westbound travelers in one year.[5] (In the 1990s officials named a mountain peak near Carson Pass after Melissa Coray, the wife of Sergeant William Coray.)

The many other histories written about the battalion members and their later lives and their pioneering adventures in Utah and in the West are too voluminous to describe here. Some of the men used their military experience later in the Utah while serving in the territorial militia. Battalion Sergeant Major James Ferguson served in several high positions in the Nauvoo Legion in Utah, as did a few others.[6] Some served against their former commander,

---

[5]Gudde, *Bigler's Chronicle of the West*, narrates Bigler and other Mormons' involvement in the discovery of gold. Kenneth Owens, *Gold Rush Saints: California Mormons and the Great Rush for Riches*, documents many of the former battalion members' activities in the mines and exploring trails through the Sierra Nevada Mountains.

[6]At least one battalion soldier served in the Civil War in the eastern armies. Private Henry Wells Jackson of D Company served in the Army of the Potomac and died at Chesapeake General Hospital in Washington, D.C., on May 28, 1863. Whether he died of wounds or disease is unknown, but it was just weeks after the major battle of Chancellorsville, Confederate General Robert E. Lee's greatest victory. See Larson, *A Database of the Mormon Battalion*, 145.

Colonel P. St. George Cooke, who was in command of the 2nd U.S. Dragoons during the Utah Expedition of 1857–58. Private Lot Smith of E Company and of the Volunteers served as a major in the Nauvoo Legion and later led raiding parties against the U.S. Army during the Utah War. Just a few years later Major Smith commanded a squadron of mounted Utah militia mustered in federal service for a short time in Utah and Wyoming during the Civil War. He eventually lost his life in Arizona at the hands of hostile Indians. Battalion service was a core and defining experience in the lives of the men, and "[i]t is from this episode," wrote historian Richard Roberts, "that the military experience gained by these veterans became a base on which the militia force was built upon in Utah."[7]

The men became pioneer and Mormon heroes over the next few decades. Their service and exploits have been retold for generations from the pulpit, at firesides, and in print. In 1855, Brigham Young and the church held a special reunion for the men in the Social Hall in Great Salt Lake City. It was there that Young used, perhaps for the first time, the phrase often associated with the Mormon Battalion: "A Ram in the Thicket." He captured the Biblical symbolism of God giving Abraham a ram to sacrifice in lieu of his son, Isaac. The Mormon Battalion was, in many ways, the "ram" that offered itself to financially save the Mormon people.

The 1855 reunion, which in many ways served as a forum for Young's anti-government tendencies during the church's conflict with federal authority, was followed by other events, celebrations, and even annual reunions that continued for decades. The Saints saw the veterans as martyrs for their cause. Many legends with unsophisticated rationale arose touting, for example, the ratio of Mormons who served in the battalion as opposed to volunteers from other states or religious groups. The "longest march" theory arose in around the turn of the nineteenth century and was validated by Mormon historian and general authority B. H. Roberts in his 1919 *The Mormon Battalion: Its History and Achievements*. During

---

[7]Roberts, *Legacy: The History of the Utah National Guard from the Nauvoo Legion Era to Enduring Freedom*, 5.

EPILOGUE

the Mormon-federal government conflict of the 1850s, the prevention theory supposedly purported by Senator Thomas H. Benton—that U.S. Army and state militia were to prevent the Saints from leaving the United States and/or destroy them if they failed to raise the battalion—was an example of the emotional tirades that raised the Mormon soldiers up as martyrs of a powerful and sometimes evil and vicious United States.

As the years went by and the battalion ranks thinned, reunions, banquets, and socials were even more pronounced and important, showcasing group photographs, medallions, and other memorabilia. In 1927 the state of Utah dedicated a Mormon Battalion Monument on the capitol grounds, built from private donations. Books, poems, songs, and other literary items appeared. Eventually the LDS Church would build a Mormon Battalion Visitors Center in "old town" San Diego to honor and portray to the public the men's military service. However, the center is actually more of a missionary proselyting tool than an actual historical venue.

There are numerous towns, settlements, and other public features named after battalion veterans, men and women, in Utah and Arizona. Davis County in Utah is named after Captain Daniel C. Davis. The towns of Huntsville, Layton, Hanksville, Hyde Park, Hatch, Hinckley, Huntington, and Draper, just to name a few, are named after battalion veterans.[8] The military lineage and honor of the battalion has an obtuse connection with the modern Utah Army National Guard, who adopted in the late 1990s a shoulder sleeve patch depicting a hatless soldier reminiscent of the Mormon Battalion statue on the Utah state capitol grounds.

Aside from the many benefits the LDS Church received from the men's service already addressed, there were other tangible results that occurred after their discharge in California. Church officials in Utah purchased a large tract of land at modern-day Ogden from trader and rancher Miles Goodyear from some of the men's salaries received upon mustering out. Thus one of the largest cities and most successful settlements in the pioneer era of Utah was

---

[8]Bagley and Bigler, *The Army of Israel: The Mormon Battalion Narratives*, 446.

obtained through battalion salaries used by church authorities towards the purchase.

One of the downsides of the men's year-long absence was the unfortunate lack of care and assistance that some of the wives and families received. It is important to realize that during the winter of 1846–47, in the camps in Iowa and modern Nebraska, Brigham Young and the leaders had their hands full feeding and caring for thousands of Saints, and they all generally suffered together. Some Mormons had more means and were better prepared than others. The families of the battalion men felt neglected in many cases.[9]

A catch-word, sometimes over-trivialized, has made its way into Mormon culture and expression: that these battalion veterans are to be held in "honored remembrance." There is nothing wrong with honor and remembrance, as long as the praise is not overdone and superfluous. Heritage groups and family associations continue to locate the headstones and remains of each battalion participant and enshrine them with a new monument recognizing their service and connection. This is a noble venture. Yet, as is often the case, ordinary people in the time line of history can become mythic characters, and lose all their blemishes and warts in the process. Thus an incredible level of praise and near hero-worship, especially in Mormon culture honoring the "blessed pioneers," cover the enshrined ancestors with a façade of perfection and glory that makes it difficult to understand the real stories and characters. These ancestor and family groups, societies, and battalion associations carry on the march of the battalion through time, sometimes with little real thought or understanding of its actual significance and history.

The honor and remembrance at times does a disservice to the battalion's true nature and significance. Just as the battalion was unique as a religious unit, its very uniqueness leads to the continual inclusion of post discharge and non-military stories and connections. Few military organizations in history are burdened with this zealous appendage—always including additional narration regard-

---

[9]Ibid., 422–27.

EPILOGUE

ing what occurred to the men after their military service. These discharged men did not depart individually, as do most veterans, into the next stage of their lives. Due to the geography of where they were, the challenges of economy and resources, and their intense religious ties, they formed various groups that took separate and sometimes very extended journeys back to their families and the Saints. This non-military appendage to the battalion's history has become almost as important to some as their year's volunteer military service. The inclusion of this post-battalion history has caused the members of this unique military unit to be painted as pioneers and not soldiers. It has thereby overshadowed the true dimensions of martial service and campaigning for political objectives and morphed the story into a pioneer-based faith-promoting fable. When the men were discharged on July 16, 1847, in Los Angeles, the Mormon Battalion story ended.

The overriding interpretation of the battalion's "pioneer" drama continues in books, dramas, videos, documentaries, and Sunday school lessons. Yet, aside from all the events, the accomplishments, the long and arduous march, the pioneer piousness and other military topics, the Mormon Battalion's supreme significance was its unique character as a religious military unit in a nation that does not tolerate such mixing.

As for the non-Mormon regular officers who appeared in this story, some of their later service has been mentioned. Philip St. George Cooke's service of more than fifty years was honorable and important. During the Civil War he ran afoul of the younger and less experienced Major General George McClellan and was eventually removed from field command and relegated to staff positions. He retired from the army in 1873 and devoted his energies to writing his memoirs and several other well-received books about his service and adventures. Cooke died in 1895, one of the most accomplished frontier army officers in American history.

Both Andrew Jackson Smith and George Stoneman had much

more combat service during the Civil War than Cooke. Smith died in 1897 in St. Louis at the age of eighty-two. George Stoneman commanded the Cavalry Corps of the Army of the Potomac and led a disappointing cavalry raid behind enemy lines during the Chancellorsville campaign in 1863. He was relieved and sent to the Western Theater, where his uneven service under Generals Grant and Sherman was at times either superb or lacking. He commanded both cavalry and infantry corps. In 1864, Stoneman was captured by Confederate forces and soon afterwards exchanged. He returned to active service and ended the war as a major general, and retired from the army in 1871 due to a disability. He was elected governor of California in 1883 on the Democratic ticket. George Stoneman died in 1894 at age seventy-two.

The man who was the heart and soul of the Army of the West and responsible for bringing more territory under the United States flag than any other soldier in American history, General Stephen Watts Kearny, unfortunately met death soon after the Mexican War at the relatively young age of fifty-four. After testifying at Frémont's court martial and receiving much public criticism from Frémont's political allies, he served as military governor in Mexico, where he contracted yellow fever. Returning to Jefferson Barracks in St. Louis, he assumed command of the 6th Military Department late in the summer 1848. He died October 31, just weeks after his wife Mary delivered a new baby boy: Stephen Watts Kearny Jr. General Kearny was perhaps the greatest frontier soldier of the antebellum army.

The Mexican War, the stage upon which the drama of the Mormon Battalion was performed, continued after the battalion's discharge. General Scott's invasion of central Mexico culminated with the capture of Mexico City in September 1847 and ended Mexico's military effort. The last battles of Churabusco, Contreras, Monte del Rey, and the final assault on Chapultepec Castle became the great final victories of an amazing string of American triumphs rarely surpassed in American military history. The aged duke of Wellington criticized Scott's invasion in the spring of 1847,

EPILOGUE 381

but by the end of the year, the victor of Waterloo called Scott's achievement one of the greatest campaigns in history. As the final battles were being fought, Nicholas Trist, Polk's agent of peace, was in Mexico, and after the capitulation, negotiated a treaty with the Mexican officials. Through the Treaty of Guadalupe Hildago, the United States gained much of the land that it had conquered, comprising today's California, Nevada, Utah, Arizona, New Mexico, and western Colorado. It also settled the Texas boundary issue at the Rio Grande—one of the issues that caused of the war. Yet, the United States paid Mexico some $15 million for these territories that it already occupied. Few victors in history have made such concessions.

The Mormon Battalion never saw combat during the Mexican War. It served honorably for one year and then was discharged in California. There are many reasons why historians and students of military history or the Mexican War have ignored or neglected to study the Mormon Battalion with any relish or thoroughness, and often omit it in their studies. The fact that it did not fight is perhaps the most obvious reason; perhaps the difficulty of dealing with the complex culture, theology, and related dimensions of the Mormon faith has discouraged a serious military study. Of course, the battalion served as part of General Kearny's Army of the West, which has been often seen as a sideshow of the war, though it was through this campaign that Polk's true goals of national expansion materialized.[10]

The Mormon Battalion is actually an important subject for American and military history, as has been demonstrated. Its service provides some outstanding and rare features unique in military—especially American military—history. It is the only unit that has mustered in federal service with a religious designation; it was organized for religious purposes and not so much for patriotic zeal. Government (military) authorities approached a religious

---

[10]Eisenhower, *So far from God*, 195.

leader, not a recognized government entity, to extend the call of enlistment, and a religious leader chose the leaders instead of allowing the time-honored tradition of the men electing their own leaders. Some of the salary and entitlements were returned to the church body for use, whereas other funds went to support the men's families. To add to this unusual and distinctly rare historical situation, many of the soldiers' families were themselves on the march, crossing a wilderness during an exodus caused by religious intolerance to a new and forbidding homeland. This is an amazing set of circumstances—unique, distinct, and significant in American history.

Though plagued with internal strife and much fraternal bitterness, overall the men served admirably and had few serious discipline problems compared to many units of the era. Most of the battalion's commanding officers were from the regular, professional army, following a policy of the U.S. government that regulars command the Mormon volunteers. This was rare during the Mexican War—most officers in volunteer units were volunteers themselves. There was discord with the battalion's commissioned assistant surgeon, which unfortunately has been exacerbated in journals and accounts. The men were unaccustomed to strident military methods and practice, but when eventually trained in California, they were prepared for combat.

But the real accomplishment of the battalion is not found in a legend and tradition claimed a record in miles marched. This truly remarkable and enduring march that crossed the land, the deserts and mountains, despite the hardships and the difficulty of the cutting a road through tortuous terrain for wagons and ox teams. The faithfulness of Cooke and his men were evident when General Kearny needed an armed force to challenge John C. Frémont's disobedience and establish United States control over a large and remote territory.[11] The leadership of regular army officers provided the discipline, competence, and resourcefulness to convince a distrusting religious sect to enlist men to serve an ungrateful nation;

---

[11]Chaffin, *Pathfinder: John Charles Frémont*, 371–72.

to complete an arduous trek across a trackless wilderness; and to ensure American sovereignty in a distant new land. Without James Allen, Andrew Jackson Smith, George Stoneman, and especially Philip St. George Cooke, the Mormon Battalion legacy could have possibly resulted in failure or misfortune. One must also recognize the devotion, humility, faithfulness, and sacrifice of these selfless Mormon men, their families, and the far-sightedness of Brigham Young, the father of the Mormon Battalion.

War in itself is at the opposite spectrum of most religious-minded people. People who are immersed in spiritual qualities of charity, benevolence, and peaceful pacifism may seem unsuitable for combat. However, sometimes religious people make the best soldiers. World history is replete with religious-political wars and armies, usually bent on destroying other religious armies. From the Crusades to the Thirty Years' War, from the Yom Kippur War to the numerous holy wars, religion and religious military units are common in the world experience—but not in the United States military experience.

The Mexican War, as most wars, could have been avoided with more clear and astute statesmanship. If Polk had not been so determined to gain New Mexico and California, first by threats and concessions and then by graduated pressure, the war might have been avoided. Through patience and growing American settlement, the United States might have gained these territories eventually, but Polk and most Americans were not patient. Polk's poor choice of John Slidell to lead the American diplomatic effort doomed the process from the beginning. Mexican leaders ignored the realities of America's expansionism and the obvious fact that Mexico could not hope to prevent America's westward movement to the Pacific. Mexico refused to accept Texas's self-determination by not acknowledging its independence and autonomy. Still considering Texas as Mexican territory, it wrongly misjudged Texas and American unity, which rendered the diplomatic opportunities nearly void, especially when Mexican governments came and went with the changing seasons. The Mexicans, therefore, could have negotiated for the best possible concession available and thus avoid war. Yet the players on both sides were often misguided, visionless, and lost in their own myopic view. Pride and other weak human emotions entered and war occurred.[12]

The Mormon Battalion, fortunately, did not experience the brutality of combat; none of its soldiers was killed in hostile action. Brigham Young's promise that the battalion would not meet and engage the enemy came to pass. The men of the Mormon Battalion, along with the actual combatants, both American and Mexican, served their countries as they should have and as their countrymen expected—with courage, honor, and sacrifice, many paying the ultimate price.

---

[12]Pletcher, *The Diplomacy of Annexation*, 597–601.

APPENDIX A

Army Pay Scale 1846*

Rank	Officers	Infantry/ Artillery	Dragoons/ Engineers
Major General	200		
Brigadier General	104		
Colonel		75	90
Lieutenant Colonel		75	
Major		50	60
Captain		40	50
1st Lieutenant		30	33.33⅓
2nd Lieutenant		25	33.33⅓
Sergeant Major		17	17
1st Sergeant		16	16
Sergeant		13	13
Corporal		9	9
Private		7	8
Principal Musician		17	
Musician		8	
Bugler		9	
Surgeon	60		
Asst. Surgeon	50		
Hospital Steward	16		
Hospital Matron	6		

*A Compendium of the Pay for the Army from 1785 to 1888 (Washington: Government Printing Office, 1888), 8-51.

APPENDIX B

Mormon Battalion Command and Staff

Battalion Commanders
Lt. Col. James Allen
July 16, 1846–August 23, 1846

Capt Jefferson Hunt (Acting Commander)
August 24–30, 1846

1st Lt Andrew Jackson Smith (Acting Commander)
August 30, 1846–October 13, 1846

Lt. Col. Philip St. George Cooke
October 13, 1846–May 13, 1847

Capt Jefferson Hunt (Acting Commander)
May 13, 1847–July 16, 1847*

Battalion Staff
Adjutant
1st Lt. George P. Dykes
July 16, 1846–November 1, 1846

2nd Lt. Philemon Merrill
November 1, 1846–July 16, 1847

---

*Lieutenant Colonel James Allen to Brigadier General R. Jones, August 12, 1846, Fort Leavenworth, with attached "Names of the Officers of the Mormon Battalion of Volunteers," National Archives, microfilm copy 139, Utah State Historical Society. Other lists claim the ranks of 3rd lieutenant and 3rd and 4th sergeants, ranks that did not exist. See Tyler, *A Concise History*, 118–125. Subsequent authors have continued such errors; see also Ricketts, *The Mormon Battalion*, 20–28.

Quartermaster Officer
2nd Lt. Samuel Gully
August 6, 1846–October 15, 1846 (resigned commission)

1st Lt. Andrew Jackson Smith, 1st US Dragoons
October 15, 1846–July 16, 1847
(serving also with 1st U.S. Dragoons in California)

Assistant Quartermaster Officer
2nd Lt. George Stoneman, 1st U.S. Dragoons
October 15, 1846–March 15, 1847

Quartermaster Sergeant
Sgt. Sebert Shelton
July 16, 1846–August 6, 1846

Sgt. Reddick Allred
February 11, 1847–July 16, 1847

Assistant Surgeons
Dr. George B. Sanderson, Volunteer Medical Corps
August 1, 1846–May 13, 1847

Dr. William McIntire, Contract Surgeon
July 16, 1846–July 16, 1847 (discharged while en route to Utah)

Battalion Sergeants Major
Sergeant Major James Glines
July 16, 1846–October 15, 1846

Sergeant Major James Ferguson
October 15, 1846–July 16, 1847

Battalion Scouts
Pauline Weaver
Antoine Leroux
Philip F. Thompson
Jean-Baptiste Charbonneau
Willard Hall
Dr. Stephen Foster
Appolonius
Chacon
Francisco
Tasson

Mormon Battalion Command and Staff

Company Commanders

A Company
Capt. Jefferson Hunt
July 16, 1846–
July 16, 1847

B Company
Capt. Jesse Hunter
July 16, 1846–
July 16, 1847

C Company
Capt. James Brown
July 16, 1846–
October 18, 1846*

1st Lt. George Rosecrans
October 18, 1846–
July 16, 1847

D Company
Capt. Nelson Higgins
July 16, 1846–
September 16, 1846*

1st Lt. George Dykes
November 1, 1846–
July 16, 1847

E Company
Capt. Daniel Davis
July 16, 1846–
July 16, 1847

Company Officers

A Company
1st Lt. George Oman
2nd Lt. Lorenzo Clark
2nd Lt. William Willis*

B Company
1st Lt. Elam Luddington
2nd Lt. Ruel Barrus
2nd Lt. Philemon Merrill

C Company
1st Lt. George Rosecrans (Acting Commander, see above)
2nd Lt. Samuel Thompson
2nd Lt. Robert Clift

D Company
1st Lt. George Dykes (Acting Commander, see above)
2nd Lt. Sylvester Hulett
2nd Lt. Cyrus Canfield

E Company
1st Lt. James Pace
2nd Lt. Andrew Lytle
2nd Lt. Samuel Gully (resigned October 18, 1846)*

---
* Pueblo Detachments

Non-Commissioned Officers

A Company	B Company	C Company	D Company	E Company
1st Sgt. Phineas Wright (reduced to Pvt., March 9, 1847)	1st Sgt. William Coray	1st Sgt. Orson Adams (Pueblo Detachment October 18, 1846)	1st Sgt. Nathaniel Jones (reduced to Pvt., February 18, 1847)	1st Sgt. Edmund Brown
Sgt. Ebenezer Brown	Sgt. William Hyde	Sgt. Elijah Elmer (promoted 1st Sgt., October 18, 1846)	Sgt. Luther Tuttle (promoted, 1st Sgt., February 18, 1847)	Sgt. Richard Brazier
Sgt. Reddick Allred (Battalion Staff, February 11, 1847)	Sgt. Albert Smith	Sgt. Joel Terrell (Pueblo Detachment, October 15, 1846)	Sgt. Thomas Williams	Sgt. Ebenezer Hanks
Sgt. Alexander McCord	Sgt. David Wilkin	Sgt. Alpheus Haws (Pueblo Detachment, October 15, 1846)	Sgt. Daniel Browett	
Cpl. Gilbert Hunt	Cpl. David Rainey	Cpl. Jabez Nowlin	Cpl. Arnold Stephens	Cpl. Stephen St. John
Cpl. Lafayette Frost	Cpl. Thomas Dunn	Cpl. Alexander Brown	Cpl. John Buchannan	Cpl. John Binley
Cpl. Thomas Weir (reduced to Pvt., March 9, 1847)	Cpl. John Chase	Cpl. Edward Martin (promoted Sgt., October 15, 1846)	Cpl. William Coons	Cpl. Roswell Stephens
Cpl. William Muir (promoted 1st Sgt. March 9, 1847)	Cpl. Edward Wilcox	Cpl. Daniel Tyler (promoted Sgt., October 15, 1846)	Cpl. Lewis Lane (reduced to Pvt., February 18, 1847)	Cpl. James Scott
	Alexander Horace (promoted Cpl., March 8, 1847)			

Bibliography

Primary Sources

Archives of the Church of Jesus Christ of Latter-day Saints, Salt Lake City, Utah

Boyle, Henry G. Reminiscences and Diaries, 1846–1888; also see Autobiography and diary of.
Henry Boyle. Special Collections, Marriott Library, University of Utah.
Bullock, Thomas. Journal, Photocopy.
Clayton, William. Journal.
Coray, William. Journal, entries by date in Journal History, microfilm.
Hancock, Levi. Journals 1846–47.
Journal History, The Church of Jesus Christ of Latter-day Saints.
Pettegrew, David. "A History of David Pettegrew." LDS Archives and Utah State Historical Society.
Pixton, Robert. "The Life of Robert Pixton."
Richards, Willard. Journal.
Scott, James. Diaries, 1846.
Taggart, George Washington. "A short sketch of His travels with the Church of Jesus Christ of Latter day Saints on their journey from the City of Joseph."
Taylor, John. Journal.
Young, Brigham, Papers and Collection.
Journal History of The Church of Jesus Christ of Latter-day Saints.
Manuscript History of The Church of Jesus Christ of Latter-day Saints.

Other Manuscript Collections

Allen, James Jr. Cadet Records, Cadet #575, class 1829, United States Military Academy.
Dent, Lewis. Letter to George Wrenshall Dent, February 1, 1847, San Diego,

California, printed in the St. Louis *The Daily Reveille* 4, no. 958, June 12, 1847, and the St. Louis *The Weekly Reveille* 12, no. 29, June 19, 1847; reprinted in *Nauvoo Journal: Dedicated to Church History and Biography, 1830–1857* vol. 11, no. 1, Spring 1999.

Dunn, Thomas. Journal of Thomas Dunn, 1846–1849, Typescript, Utah State Historical Society.

Hyde, William. Private Journal of William Hyde, Brigham Young University Library.

Judd, Zadock. Autobiography of Zadock Knapp Judd (1827–1907), typescript, Brigham Young University and Utah State University Libraries.

Kearny, Stephen Watts. *Diary and Letter Book, 1846–47*. Missouri Historical Society, St. Louis, Missouri. See von Sachsen-Altenburg, Hans, *Winning the West: General Stephen Watts Kearny's Letter Book, 1846–1847*, under Secondary Sources.

Keysor, Guy M. Papers, Utah State Historical Society.

Pace, James. Diary of James Pace, 1811–1888, Brigham Young University Library.

Rogers, Samuel H. Reminiscences and Diary, 1841–1886, Brigham Young University Library.

Sanderson, Henry W. Diary of Henry Weeks Sanderson, Brigham Young University Library.

Sanderson, George B. Journal, 1846–47, Special Collections, Marriott Library, University of Utah.

Steele, John. Diary of John Steele, 1846–1898, Brigham Young University Library.

Tippets, John Henry. Journal, Utah State University Library. Records in the National Archives, Washington, D.C. "Mexican War Correspondence." House Executive Document #60 (30–1) vol. 7, 1848, Serial 520.

Record Group 94, Records of the United States Army Adjutant General's Office: Mormon Battalion Papers and Muster Rolls, Microfilm, M565, 567. Letters Received (Main Series) 1822–1860, Micro Film, M-567, 319.

Record Group 98, Records of United States Army Commands: 10th Military Department (California, 1846–1851). Letters Received and Sent, Micro Film, M-210.

Government Publications

Act of the Second Congress of the United States, Statute I, Chapter 28, May 2, 1792, *The Public*

Journal of the March of the Mormon Battalion of infantry volunteers under the command of Lieut. Col. P. St. Geo. Cooke, also captain of dragoons, from Santa Fe, New Mexico to San Diego, Cal. (kept by himself by direction of the comd'g General Army of the West). Senate Executive Document, no. 2, 31st Congress, Special Session; reprinted in Cooke, Philip St. George, William Henry Chase Whiting, and François Xavier Aubry. *Exploring Southwestern Trails, 1846–1854*, ed. by Ralph P. Bieber in collaboration with Averam B. Bender. Philadelphia: Porcupine Press, 1974.

A Map and Report of Lieut. Allen and H. B. Schoolcraft's visit to the Northwest Indians in 1832, April 12, 1834; 23d Congress [Doc. No. 323], House of Representatives, 1st Session, transmitted from the War Department.

Statutes at Large of the United States of America. Boston: Charles C. Little and James Brown 1845.

Report of Lieut. Col. P. St. George Cooke of his March from Santa Fe, New Mexico, to San Diego, Upper California, House Executive Document no. 41, 30th Congress, 1st Session, 551–63.

Published Autobiographies, Memoirs, Diaries, and Edited Accounts

Ames, George Walcott Jr. "A Doctor comes to California. The Diary of John S. Griffin, Assistant Surgeon with Kearny's Dragoons, 1846–47." *California Historical Society Quarterly* 22 (September and December 1942): 193–224, 333–38.

Bagley, Will. *Frontiersman: Abner Blackburn's Narratives*. Salt Lake City: University of Utah Press, 1992.

Barton, Noel R., and Myron W. McIntyre. *Christopher Layton*. Christopher Layton Family Organization, 1966.

Bigler, Henry W. "Extracts from the Journal of Henry W. Bigler." *Utah State Historical Quarterly* 5, no.2 (April 1932): 35–64.

Bliss, Robert. "The Journal of Robert S. Bliss, with the Mormon Battalion." *Utah Historical Quarterly* 4, no. 3 (July 1931): 67–96.

Brooks, Juanita, ed. *On the Mormon Frontier: The Diary of Hosea Stout, 1844–1861.* 2 vols. Salt Lake City: University of Utah Press, 1964.

———. "Diary of the Mormon Battalion Mission: John D. Lee," *New Mexico Historical Review* 42, nos. 2–3 (July and October 1967): 281–332.

Clark, Francis D. *Stevenson's Regiment in California, 1846–1848*. New York: George S. Evans & Co. 1882. Reprinted as *The New York Volunteers in California*. Glorietta, New Mexico: Rio Grande Press, 1970.

Clarke, Dwight. *The Original Journals of Henry Smith Turner: With Stephen Watts Kearny to New Mexico and California 1846–1847*. Norman: University of Oklahoma Press, 1966.

Cooke, Philip St. George. *The Conquest of New Mexico and California*. New York: G. P. Putnam's Sons, 1878. Reprinted, New York: Arno Press, 1976.

Edwards, Frank S. *A Campaign in New Mexico with Colonel Doniphan*. Philadelphia: Carey and Hart, 1847.

Gallagher, Gary W. *Fighting for the Confederacy: The Personal Recollections of General Edward Porter Alexander.* Chapel Hills: University of North Carolina Press, 1989.

Golder, Frank A. *The March of the Mormon Battalion, From Council Bluffs to California: Taken from the Journal of Henry Standage.* New York: The Century Co., 1928.

Gracy, David B., II, and Helen J. H. Rugeley, "From the Mississippi to the Pacific: An Englishman in the Mormon Battalion," *Arizona and the West: A Quarterly Journal of History* 7, no. 2 (Summer 1965): 127–60.

Grant, Ulysses S. *Personal Memoirs of U. S. Grant.* 2 vols. New York: Webster and Company, 1885.

Gudde, Erwin G., ed. *Bigler's Chronicle of the West: The Conquest of California, Discovery of Gold, and Mormon Settlement as Reflected in Henry William Bigler's Diaries.* Berkeley: University of California Press, 1962.

Hess, John W. "John W. Hess, with the Mormon Battalion." *Utah Historical Quarterly* 6 (April 1933): 47–55.

Jones, Rebecca M., ed. "Extracts from the Life Sketch of Nathaniel V. Jones." *Utah Historical Quarterly* 4, no. 1 (January 1931): 2–23.

Magoffin, Susan Shelby. *Down the Santa Fe Trail, 1846–47.* New Haven: Yale University Press, 1926.

Moulton, Gary E. *The Journals of the Lewis and Clark Expedition.* 13 volumes. Lincoln: University of Nebraska Press, 1986–2002.

Pratt, Parly P. *Autobiography of Parley Parker Pratt.* Salt Lake City: Deseret Book, 1938.

Quaife, Milo Milton. *Diary of James K. Polk during his Presidency, 1845 to 1848.* 4 vols. Chicago: A. C. McClurg & Co., 1910.

Von Sachsen-Altenburg, Hans. *Winning the West: General Stephen Watts Kearny's Letter Book, 1846–47.* Boonville, Mo.: Petitanoui Publications, 1998.

Smith, Joseph Jr. *History of the Church of Jesus Christ of Latter-day Saints.* 7 vols. Salt Lake City: Deseret Book, 1978.

Steele, John. "Extracts from the Journal of John Steele," *Utah Historical Quarterly* 6, no. 1 (1933): 3–23.

Tyler, Daniel. *A Concise History of the Mormon Battalion in the Mexican War 1846–1848.* 1st printing, 1881; 4th printing, Glorietta, New Mexico: Rio Grande Press, 1980.

Secondary Sources

Books
Allen, James B., and Glen M. Leonard. *The Story of the Latter-day Saints.* Salt Lake City: Deseret Book, 1986.

BIBLIOGRAPHY

Allie, Stephen J. *All He Could Carry: U.S. Army Infantry Equipment, 1839–1910*. Leavenworth, Kans.: Fort Leavenworth Historical Society, 1991.

Appleman, Roy E. *Lewis and Clark's Transcontinental Exploration*. Washington, D.C.: Department of Interior, 1975.

Arrington, Leonard J. *Brigham Young: American Moses*. Chicago: University of Illinois Press, 1986.

Bagley, Will. *Blood of the Prophets: Brigham Young and the Massacre at Mountain Meadows*. Norman: University of Oklahoma Press, 2002.

——, and David L. Bigler. *Army of Israel: Mormon Battalion Narrative*. Spokane, Washington: Arthur H. Clark Co., 2000.

Barrett, William E. *The Restored Church*. Salt Lake City: Deseret Book, 1973.

Bauer, K. Jack. *The Mexican War*. Lincoln: University of Nebraska Press, 1974; paperback edition, Bison Books, 1992.

Bieber, Ralph P., and Averam B. Bender, eds. *Exploring Southwestern Trails 1846–1854*. Philadelphia: Porcupine Press, 1974.

Biggs, Donald C. *Conquer and Colonize: Stevenson's Regiment and California*. San Rafael, Calif.: Presidio Press, 1977.

Bishop, M. Guy. *Henry William Bigler: Soldier, Gold Miner. Missionary, Chronicler, 1815–1890*. Logan: Utah State University Press, 1998.

Brooks, Juanita. *John Doyle Lee: Zealot, Pioneer Builder, Scapegoat*. Salt Lake City: Howe Brothers, 1984.

Bushman, Richard L. *Joseph Smith and the Beginnings of Mormonism*. Urbana: University of Illinois Press, 1984.

Campbell, Eugene E. *Establishing Zion: The Mormon Church in the American West, 1847–1869*. Salt Lake City: Signature Books, 1988.

Carter, Kate B. *Our Pioneer Heritage*. 17 vols. Salt Lake City: Daughters of the Utah Pioneers, 1968.

Chaffin, Tom. *Pathfinder: John Charles Frémont and the Course of American Empire*. New York: Hill and Wang. 2002.

Chalfant, William Y. *Dangerous Passage: The Santa Fe Trail and the Mexican War*. Norman: University of Oklahoma Press, 1994.

Chance, Joseph E. *Jefferson Davis's Mexican War Regiment*. Oxford: University of Mississippi Press, 1991.

Clarke, Dwight L. *Stephen Watts Kearny: Soldier of the West*. Norman: University of Oklahoma Press, 1961.

Coakley, Robert W. *The Role of Federal Military Forces in Domestic Disorders: 1789–1878*. Washington D.C.: Center of Military History, 1988.

Coffman, Edward M. *The Old Army: A Portrait of the American Army in Peacetime, 1784–1898*. New York: Oxford University Press, 1986.

Crawford, Mark. *Encyclopedia of the Mexican–American War*. Santa Barbara, California: ABC-CLIO, 1999.

Dawson, Joseph C. III. *Doniphan's Epic March: The 1st Missouri Volunteers in the Mexican War*. Lawrence: University of Kansas Press, 1999.

Day, Robert O. *The Mormon Battalion: The Lord's Faithful*. Oviedo, Fl.: Day to Day, 1997.

DePalo, William A. *The Mexican National Army: 1822–1855*. College Station: Texas A&M Press, 1997.

DeVoto, Benard. *The Year of Decision: 1846*. Boston: Houghton Mifflin Co., 1984.

Doubler, Michael D. *I Am the Guard: A History of the Army National Guard, 1636–2000*. Washington, D.C.: Government Printing Office. 2001.

Edwards, Frank S. *A Campaign in New Mexico with Colonel Doniphan*. Philadelphia: Carey and Hart, 1847. Reprint, Ann Arbor, Mich.: University Microfilms, 1966.

Eisenhower, John S. D. *So Far from God: The U.S. War with Mexico, 1846–1848*. New York: Doubleday, 1989.

Faust, Patricia L., ed. *Historical Times Illustrated Encyclopedia of the Civil War*. New York: Harper and Row, 1986.

Frazier, Donald S. *The United States and Mexico at War: Nineteenth-Century Expansionism and Conflict*. New York: Macmillan, 1998.

Furniss, Norman F. *The Mormon Conflict, 1850–1859*. New Haven: Yale University Press, 1960.

Gillet, Mary C. *Army Historical Series: The Army Medical Department: 1818–1865*. Washington, D. C.: United States Army Center of Military History, 1987.

Gluckman, Arcadi. *Identifying Old U.S. Muskets, Rifles and Carbines*. Harrisburg, Penn.: Stackpole Books, 1965.

Goetzmann, William H. *Army Exploration in the American West, 1803–1863*. Austin: Texas State Historical Association, 1959.

Hackenburg, Randy W. *Pennsylvania in the War with Mexico: The Volunteer Regiments*. Shippensburg: White Mane Publishing, 1992.

Hafen, LeRoy R. *Mountain Men and Fur Traders of the Far West*. Lincoln: University of Nebraska Press, 1982.

Hall, Thomas B., M.D. *Medicine on the Santa Fe Trail*. Arrow Rock, Mo.: Arrow Rock, 1987.

Harlow, Neal. *California Conquered: The Annexation of a Mexican Province, 1846–1850*. Los Angeles: University of California Press, 1982.

Hassler, Warren W. Jr. *With Shield and Sword: American Military Affairs, Colonial Times to the Present*. Ames: Iowa State University Press, 1982.

Heitman, Francis B. *Historical Register and Dictionary of the United States Army from its Organization, September 29, 1789, to March 2, 1903*. Washington, D.C.: Government Printing Office, 1903; reprinted, Urbana: University of Illinois Press, 1965, 2 vols.

Hill, Donna. *Joseph Smith: The First Mormon*. Salt Lake City: Signature Books, 1977.

Howe, David Walker. *The Political Culture of the American Whigs*. Chicago: University of Chicago Press, 1979.
Johnson, Clark V., ed. *Mormon Redress Petitions: Documents of the 1833–1838 Missouri Conflict*. Provo, Utah: Bookcraft, 1992.
Katcher, Philip. *The Mexican–American War, 1846–1847*. Oxford, U.K.: Osprey Publishing, 1998.
Kimball, Stanley B. *Historic Sites and Markers Along the Mormon and Other Great Western Trails*. Chicago: University of Illinois Press, 1988.
———, and Hal Knight. *111 Days to Zion*. Salt Lake City: Deseret News, 1978.
———. "The Mormon Battalion on the Santa Fe Trail in 1846." Santa Fe: U.S. Department of Interior, 1996.
Larson, Carl V. *A Database of the Mormon Battalion: An Identification of the Original Members of the Mormon Battalion*. Salt Lake City: Mormon Battalion, Inc., 1997.
———, and Shirley N. Maynes. *Women of the Mormon Battalion*. Providence, Utah: Watkins Printing, 1995.
Launius, Roger D. *Alexander William Doniphan: Portrait of a Missouri Moderate*. Columbia: University of Missouri Press, 1997.
———, and John E. Hallwas, eds. *Kingdom on the Mississippi Revisited: Nauvoo in Mormon History*. Urbana: University of Illinois Press, 1996.
LeSueur, Stephen C. *The 1838 Mormon War in Missouri*. Columbia: University of Missouri Press, 1987.
Leonard, Glen M. *Nauvoo: A Place of Peace, A People of Promise*. Salt Lake City: Deseret Books, 2002.
Linderman, Gerald E. *Embattled Courage: The Experience of Combat in the American Civil War*. New York: The Free Press, 1987.
Lord, Walter. *A Time to Stand*. New York: Pocket Books, 1963.
Madsen, Carol. *Journey to Zion: Voices from the Mormon Trail*. Salt Lake City: Deseret Books, 1997.
Madsen, Truman G. *Defender of the Faith: The B. H. Roberts Story*. Salt Lake City: Bookcraft, 1980.
Mahon, John K. *History of the Militia and the National Guard*. New York: Macmillan, 1983.
Malone, Dumas. *Dictionary of American Biography*. New York: Charles Scribner's & Sons, 1935.
McLee, Ward, and J. Cordell Robinson. *Origins of the Mexican War: A Documentary Source Book*. Salisbury, NC: Documetary Publications, 1982.
Meyer, Michael C., and William H. Beezley, eds. *The Oxford History of Mexico*. Oxford, U.K.: Oxford University Press, 2000.
McGaffrey, James M. *Army of Manifest Destiny: The American Soldier in the Mexican War, 1846–1848*. New York: New York University Press, 1992.

McPherson, James M. *Battle Cry of Freedom: The Civil War Era.* New York: Oxford University Press, 1988.

Miller, Robert Ryal. *The Shamrock and the Sword: The Saint Patrick's Battalion in the U.S.–Mexican War.* Norman: University of Oklahoma Press, 1989.

Millett, Allan R., and Peter Maslowski. *For the Common Defense: A Military History of the United States of America.* Rev. ed., New York: Free Press, 1994.

Moore, Robert J. Jr., and Michael Haynes. *Lewis & Clark: Tailor Made, Trail Worn: Army Life, Clothing, and Weapons of the Corps of Discovery.* Helena, Mont.: Farcountry Press, 2003.

Nevin, David. *The Mexican War.* Alexandria, Va.: Time Life Books, 1978.

Nevins, Allan. *Frémont: Pathmarker of the West.* Lincoln: University of Nebraska Press, 1992.

Norton, Herman A. *Struggling for Recognition: The United States Army Chaplaincy, 1791–1865.* 2 vols. Washington, D.C.: Office of the Chief of Chaplains, 1977.

Oaks, Dallin H., and Marvin S. Hill. *Carthage Conspiracy: The Trial of the Accused Assassins of Joseph Smith.* Urbana: University of Illinois Press, 1979.

Owens, Kenneth N. *Gold Rush Saints: California Mormons and the Great Rush for Riches.* Spokane, Wash.: Arthur H. Clark Co., 2004.

Parkhill, Forbes. *The Blazed Trail of Antoine Leroux.* Los Angeles: Westernlore Press, 1965.

Parkman, Francis. *The California and Oregon Trail: Being Sketches of Prairie and Rocky Mountain Life.* New York: George P. Putnam, 1849. Reprinted as *The Oregon Trail: Sketches of Prairie and Rocky-Mountain Life.* Ill. Ed. Boston: Little, Brown and Co., 1892.

Paxton, W. M. *Annals of Platte County, Missouri.* Kansas City, Mo.: Hudson-Kimberly Publishing, 1897.

Pletcher, David M. *The Diplomacy of Annexation: Texas, Oregon and the Mexican War.* Columbia: University of Missouri Press, 1973.

Prucha, Francis. *The Sword of the Republic: U.S. Army on the Frontier, 1783–1846.* London: Macmillan, 1969.

Quinn, D. Michael. *The Mormon Hierarchy: Origins of Power.* Salt Lake City: Signature Books, 1994.

———. *The Mormon Hierarchy: Extension of Power.* Salt Lake City: Signature Books, 1997.

Reilly, Robert M. *United States Martial Flintlocks.* Lincoln, RI: Andrew Mowbray, Inc., 1965.

Rich, Richard C. *Ensign to the Nations: A History of the LDS Church from 1846 to 1972.* Salt Lake City: Bookcraft, 1975.

Richardson, James S. *A Compilation of Messages and Papers of the Presidents.* 8 vols Washington: Bureau of National Literature, 1911.

Ricketts, Norma. *Melissa's Journey with the Mormon Battalion: The Western*

Odyssey of Melissa Burton Coray, 1846–1848. Salt Lake City: International Society Daughters Utah Pioneers, 1994.

———. *The Mormon Battalion: U.S. Army of the West, 1846–1848*. Logan: Utah State University Press, 1996.

Roberts, B. H. *The Mormon Battalion: Its History and Achievements*. Salt Lake City: Deseret News, 1919.

———. *A Comprehensive History of the Church of Jesus Christ of Latter-day Saints*. 6 vols. Provo, Utah: Brigham Young University Press, 1965.

Roberts, Richard C. *Legacy: The History of the Utah National Guard from the Nauvoo Legion Era to Enduring Freedom*. Salt Lake City: National Guard Association of Utah, 2003.

Robinson, Cecil, trans. and ed. *The View from Chapultepec: Mexican Writers on the Mexican–American War*. Tucson: University of Arizona Press, 1989.

Schlesinger, Arthur M. *The Age of Jackson*. New York: Little Brown & Co. 1945.

Schroeder, John H. *Mr. Polk's War: American Opposition and Dissent, 1846–1848*. Madison: University of Wisconsin Press, 1973.

Sellers, Charles. *James K. Polk, Continentalist, 1843–1846*. Princeton: Princeton University Press 1966.

Shalhope, Robert E. *Sterling Price: Portrait of a Southerner*. Columbia: University of Missouri Press, 1971.

Smith, George Winston, ed. *The Chronicles of the Gringos: The U.S. Army in the Mexican War, 1846–1848: Accounts of Eyewitnesses and Combatants*. Albuquerque: University of New Mexico Press, 1968.

Smith, Justin. *The War with Mexico*. 2 vols. New York: Macmillan Co., 1919.

Sonne, Conway B. *Saints on the Seas: A Maritime History of Mormon Migration, 1830–1890*. Salt Lake City: University of Utah Press, 1983.

Stegner, Wallace. *The Gathering of Zion: The Story of the Mormon Trail*. Salt lake City: Westwater Press, 1981; reprint, New York: McGraw Hill, 1964.

Stewart, George. *Ordeal by Hunger: The Story of the Donner Party*. Boston: Houghton Mifflin, 1936; recent reprinting, 1988.

Talbot, Dan. *A Historical Guide to the Mormon Battalion and Butterfield Trail*. Tucson: Westernlore Press, 1992.

Tutorow, Norman E. *The Mexican–American War, An Annotated Bibliography*. Westport, Conn.: Greenwood Press, 1981.

Udall, Pauline. *Captain Jefferson Hunt of the Mormon Battalion*. Salt Lake City: Nicholas G. Morgan Sr. Foundation, 1958.

Urwin, Gregory J. W. *The United States Infantry: An Illustrated History, 1775–1918*. New York: Sterling Press, 1991.

Utley, Robert. *Frontiersmen in Blue: The United States Army and the Indian, 1848–1865*. Lincoln: University of Nebraska Press, 1967; reprint, Bison Book, 1981.

von Sachsen-Altenburg, Hans. *Winning the West: General Stephen Watts Kearny's Letter Book, 1846–1847.* Booneville, Mo.: Pekitancui Publications, 1998.

Weigley, Russell F. *History of the United States Army.* New York: Macmillan Co., 1967.

Wert, Jeffry D. *Gettysburg: Day Three.* New York: Simon and Schuster, 2001.

Wiggins, David. *The Rise of the Allens: Two Soldiers and the Master of Terrace Hill.* Mount Horeb, Wisc.: Historical Midwest Books. 2002.

Wilentz, Sean, ed. *Major Problems in the Early Republic 1787–1848: Documents and Essays.* Lexington, Mass.: D. C. Heath and Company, 1992.

Winders, Richard Bruce. *Mr. Polk's Army: The American Military Experience in the Mexican War.* College Station: Texas A & M University Press, 1997.

———. *Crisis in the Southwest: The United States, Mexico and the Struggle over Texas.* Wilmington, Delaware: Scholarly Resources, Inc., 2002.

Young, Otis E. *The West of Philip St. George Cooke, 1809–1895.* Glendale, Calif.: Arthur H. Clark Co., 1955.

Zobell, Albert L. *Sentinel of the East: A Biography of Thomas L. Kane.* Salt Lake City: Nicholas G. Morgan, 1965.

Articles

Archer, Christon. "Fashioning a New Nation," in Michael C. Meyer and William H. Beezley, eds. *The Oxford History of Mexico.* Oxford, U.K.: Oxford University Press, 2000.

Balance, Jim. "Stevenson's Regiment: First Regiment of New York Volunteers," *California National Guard's 150th Anniversary, 1849–1999.* California National Guard Pamphlet, 1999.

Baugh, Alexander L. "The Haun's Mill Massacre and the Extermination Order of Missouri Governor Lilburn W. Boggs." *Religious Studies Center Newsletter* 12, no. 1 (September 1997): 1–5.

———. "The Battle between Mormon and Missouri Militia at Crooked River." *Regional Studies in Latter-day Saint History: Missouri,* ed., Arnold K. Garr and Clark V. Johnson. Provo: Brigham Young University, 1994.

Black, Susan Easton. "The Mormon Battalion: Conflict Between Religious and Military Authority." *Southern California Quarterly* 74, no. 4 (Winter 1992): 313–28.

Campbell, Eugene E. "Authority Conflicts in the Mormon Battalion." *BYU Studies* 8, no. 2 (Winter 1968): 27–142.

Christiansen, Larry D. "The Struggle for Power in the Mormon Battalion." *Dialogue: A Journal of Mormon Thought* 26, no. 4 (Winter 1993): 51–69.

Davis, David Brion. "Nativist Reform and the Fear of Subversive Conspiracies," in Sean Wilentz, ed., *Major Problems in the Early Republic 1787–1848: Documents and Essays.* Lexington, Mass.: D. C. Heath and Company, 1992.

BIBLIOGRAPHY

Divett, Robert T. "Medicine and the Mormons: A Historical Perspective." *Dialogue: A Journal of Mormon Thought* 12 (Fall 1979): 16–25.

Eppinga, Jane. "War's Westernmost Battle." *America's Civil War* 6, no. 3 (July 1993): 27–32.

Gardner, Hamilton. "The Nauvoo Legion, 1840–1845: A Unique Military Organization." *Journal of the Illinois State Historical Society* 54, no. 2 (Summer 1961): 181–97.

———. "The Command and Staff of the Mormon Battalion in the Mexican War." *Utah Historical Quarterly* 20, no. 4 (1952): 331–51.

———. "Report of Lieut. Col. P. St. George Cooke of his March from Santa Fe, New Mexico, to San Diego, Upper California." *Utah Historical Quarterly* 22 (January 1954): 15–40.

Gibson, Harry W. "Frontier Arms of the Mormons." *Utah Historical Quarterly* 42, no. 1 (Winter 1974): 4–26.

Hughes, Charles, ed. "A Military View of San Diego in 1847: Four Letters from Colonel Jonathan D. Stevenson to Governor Richard B. Mason." *Journal of San Diego History* (Summer 1974): 33–43.

Hussey, John A. "The Origin of the Gillespie Mission." *California Historical Society Quarterly* 19, no. 1 (1940): 43–58.

Jamison, Max W. "The Annotated 1846 Mitchell Map: Francis Moore Jr.'s Chronicle of the Mormon Exodus, the Mexican War, the Gold Rush, and Texas." *Nauvoo Journal: Dedicated to Church History and Biography 1830–1857* 11, no. 1 (Spring 1999): 49–100.

Johnson, Clark V. "Political Intrigue at Tucson: The Mexican Garrison and the Mormon Battalion." *The Nauvoo Journal* 9, no. 2 (Fall 1997): 10–15.

Luce, W. Ray. "The Mormon Battalion: A Historical Accident." *Utah Historical Quarterly* 42 (Winter 1974): 27–38.

Miles, Edwin. "Fifty-Four Forty or Fight—An American Political Legend," *Mississippi Valley Historical Review* 44 (September 1957): 291–301.

Richards, Paul C. "Missouri Persecutions: Petitions for Redress." *BYU Studies*, 13, no. 4 (1973): 520–37.

Saunders, Richard L. "Officers and Arms: The 1843 General Return of the Nauvoo Legion's Second Cohort." *BYU Studies* 35, no. 2 (1995): 138–51.

Schrieder, Helen and Frank. "In the Footsteps of Alexander the Great." *National Geographic* 133 (January 1968): 1–65.

Van Orden, Bruce. "Causes and Consequences: Conflict in Jackson County." *Regional Studies in Latter-day Saint Church History: Missouri*, Arnold K. Garr, ed. Provo: Brigham Young University, 1994.

———. "The March of the Mormon Battalion in its Greater American Historical Setting." *Regional Studies in Latter-day Saint Church History: Arizona*. Brigham Young University Department of Church History and Religion, 1989.

Vazuez, Josefina. "War and Peace with the United States," in Michael C. Meyer and William H. Beezley, eds. *The Oxford History of Mexico*. Oxford, U.K.: Oxford University Press, 2000.

Wilcox, Linda P. "The Imperfect Science: Brigham Young on Medical Doctors." *Dialogue: A Journal of Mormon Thought* 12 (Fall 1979): 26–36.

Yurtinus, John. "'Here is One Man Who Will Not Go, Dam'um': Recruiting the Mormon Battalion in Iowa Territory." *BYU Studies* no. 4 (Fall 1981): 475–87.

———. "The Battle of the Bulls." *Military History of Texas and the Southwest* 14 (1977): 99–108.

Unpublished Works

Baugh, Alexander L. "A Call to Arms: The 1838 Mormon Defense of Northern Missouri." Ph.D. dissertation, Brigham Young University, 1996.

Peterson, Charles S., John F. Yurtinus, David E. Atkinson, and A. Kent Powell. "Mormon Battalion Trail Guide." Utah State Historical Society, 1972.

Sanders, Sandy M. "In the 1846, During the War with Mexico, was President Polk's Decision to Employ a Battalion of Mormons a Military or Political Decision?" Master's Thesis, U.S. Army Command and General Staff College, Fort Leavenworth, Kansas, 1994.

Yurtinus, John Frank. "A Ram in the Thicket: The Mormon Battalion in the Mexican War." Ph.D. dissertation, Brigham Young University, 1975.

Index

Aberdeen, Lord: 41
Adams, Orson: 390
Agua Caliente: 313
Agua Fria: 248
Alamo Mocho: 307, 308
Allen, Ben Franklin: 119
Allen, James: 9, 12, 34, 85, 99, 100, 115, 122, 123, 125, 128, 129, 133, 142, 145, 151, 154, 156, 159, 170, 172, 174, 176, 180, 181, 186, 191, 199, 213, 215, 239, 258, 361, 383, 387; addresses the Mormons, 120, 121; allows concessions to Mormon Battalion, 136, 137, 138, 139; appoints Dr. Sanderson, 150; appoints staff of Mormon Battalion, 135-136; bio. of, 117, 118, 119, 120; death of, 11, 169, 171; meets with B. Young, 126, 127; photo of, 116
Allen, John: 144, 146, 276, 358, 371
Allred, Reddick: 388, 390
Almonte, Juan N: 46
Ampudía, Pedro de: 208, 209, 266
Animas Mountains: 272
Animas Valley: 274
Apache Canyon: 221, 222
Apaches: 42, 230, 266, 271, 272, 277, 290, 296
Appolonius (scout): 241, 388
Arkansas River: 202, 238
Armijo, Manuel: 221
Army of Occupation: 37
Army of the West: 8, 9, 10, 25, 29, 33, 69, 76, 98, 120, 140, 148, 158, 159, 164, 177, 199, 214, 221, 230, 242, 280, 380, 381; enters Santa Fe, 166, 222
Army, United States: 86; and militia, 82; artillery in, 91; desertion in, 87, 90; firearms of, 93, 94, 95; general history of, 83, 84; methods of fighting, 92; officer corps of, 86; punishments in, 90; strength of, 1840s, 82
Articles of War: 86, 176, 185, 212
Artillery: 91
Ashley–Henry expedition: 256
Atchinson, David: 58

Backenstos, Jacob B: 110
Bagley, Will: 33
Bancroft, George: 68
Bankhead, Charles: 282
Barrus, Ruel: 347, 372, 389
Battle of the Bulls: 277
Battles. See Brazito, Buena Vista, Cerro Gordo, Churubusco, Contreras, Crooked River, La Mesa, Molino del Rey, Monterrey, Palo Alto, Resaca de la Palma, Sacramento, San Jacinto, San Pasqual, Vera Cruz
Bauer, Jack: 48, 324
Beale, Edward: 279
Bear Flag revolt: 9, 132, 147, 320
Becknell, William: 202
Beddome, William: 145, 150
Bell, William H: 152
Bellevue: 138

Bennett, John C: 62
Benson, Alfred O: 73
Benson, Ezra T: 128
Bent, Charles: 12, 210, 223, 319
Bent, William: 14, 319
Benton, Thomas Hart: 77, 112, 113, 266, 320, 322, 377
Bent's Fort: 9, 10, 103, 148, 158, 199, 200, 223, 230, 238, 319, 236
Biddle, James: 341
Bigler, David: 33
Bigler, Henry: 109, 127, 134, 199, 248, 260, 267, 275, 295, 347, 371, 375
Binley, John: 390
Bishop, M. Guy: 248
Black Mountains: 257
Blackburn, Abner: 143
Blackhawk War: 227
Blair, Francis Preston, Jr: 223
Blair, Montgomery: 223
Blair Valley: 312
Blanchard, Mervin: 347
Bliss, Robert S: 316, 331, 345, 352, 364
Boggs, Lilburn: 58, 59
Boley, Samuel: 10, 143, 258
Bolivar, Simón: 283
Borrowman, John: 185, 332, 333
Box Canyon: 311
Boyle, Henry: 292, 315, 352
Bragg, Braxton: 91, 338, 339
Brannan, Samuel: 8, 10, 70, 71, 73, 75, 147
Bravo, Nicolas: 10
Brazier, Richard: 390
Brazito, battle of: 13, 174, 301, 302
Brooklyn (ship): 8, 10, 70, 147
Browett, Daniel: 390
Brown Bess (gun): 283, 302
Brown, Alexander: 390
Brown, Ebenezer: 235, 390
Brown, Edmund: 390
Brown, James: 12, 13, 138, 167-168, 169, 234, 235, 237, 238, 258, 263, 389; photo of, 168
Brown, John: 198
Brown, Phebe: 235, 262

Bryant, Edwin: 194
Buchanan, James: 41, 326
Buchanan, Robert C: 116
Buchannan, John: 390
Buena Vista: 266; battle of, 14, 210, 337, 338
Buffalo: 197
Buford, John: 228
Burgwin, John H: 146, 257, 320
Butterfield Stage Line: 265, 268, 309, 374

Caballo Mountains: 257
Cajon Pass: 15, 354
Calhoun, John C: 118, 226
California: 68, 73, 77, 78, 132; invasion of planned, 66, 67, 69, 73, 74
California Trail: 370
California volunteers: 116, 147, 164-166, 224, 259, 278, 320, 321, 341, 343, 350, 351, 356
Calling Forth Act: 83
Calomel: 195, 258
Camargo, Mexico: 10, 132, 302
Camp Floyd: 326
Canadian or Red River: 214
Canfield, Cyrus: 167, 255, 292, 389
Carrizo Creek: 212
Carrizo River: 309
Carson, Christopher "Kit": 11, 12, 224, 278, 279, 327; photo of: 225
Carson Pass: 375
Carter, Richard: 263
Carthage, Ill: 61
Castro, José: 164
Cavalry: 91. See also Dragoons
Cerro Gordo, battle of: 15, 349
Chacon (scout): 241, 388
Chance, Joseph: 337
Chapin, George: 355
Chapman, Dr. Nathaniel: 195
Charbonneau, Jean-Baptiste: 241, 247, 256, 272, 273, 298, 308, 388; bio of, 242
Charbonneau, Toussaint: 242
Chase, Abner: 258
Chase, John: 390

INDEX   405

Chihuahua: 66, 210, 216
Chihuahua Road: 257, 264
Church of Jesus Christ of Latter-day Saints: 56. See also Mormons
Churubusco, battle of: 16
Cimarron Desert: 189, 203
Cimarron River: 202, 207, 208, 210
Cimarron Springs: 207
"Circular to the Mormons": 9
Clark, Lorenzo: 389
Clark, Meriwether Lewis: 107, 340
Clark, William: 107, 122
Clay, Henry: 39
Clift, Robert: 167, 292, 346, 347, 350, 389
Cloud, Jeremiah H: 11, 177, 178, 180, 205, 230, 238, 270, 298, 308
Cloverdale Springs: 274
Coahuila: 42
Coleman, William: 263
Colorado River: 13, 14, 298, 300, 303, 304, 305, 335
Comaduran, Antonio de: 280, 285, 288, 289, 290
Comaduran, Joaquín: 290
Comanches: 182, 296
Conde, Pedro García: 339, 340
Conner, David E: 68, 342
Contreras, battle of: 16
Cooke's Peak: 265
Cooke's Range: 265
Cooke's Spring: 265
Cooke's Wagon Road: 13, 295, 374; beginning of, 264; importance of, 268-269; used by Butterfield stage line, 265, 268
Cooke's Well: 306
Cooke, Dr. John E: 194, 227
Cooke, John Rogers: 227
Cooke, Philip St. George: 10, 12, 13, 14, 15, 25, 34, 36, 85, 105, 118, 146, 148, 180, 185, 194, 213, 214, 229, 230, 247, 248, 274, 354, 376, 387; and confrontation at Tucson, 287-291; appointed commander of Mormon Battalion, 225-226; assumes command, 233, 234; bio. of, 226, 227, 228; comments on Colorado River, 303; conflict over women w/ Battalion, 236; congratulates Battalion, 323; departs Calif. and Mormon Battalion, 367-369; evaluates Battalion, 239, 240; evaluations of by Battalion men, 249, 328; later career of, 379; orders building of Ft. Moore, 356; photo of: 86, 224; prepare's Battalion for combat, 279; records events, 250, 251, 261, 271, 273-274, 298, 307, 311, 327; reorganizes Battalion, 260-263; reports to Kearny in Calif., 317; visits California Battalion's camp, 350, 351; writes report, 330
Cooke, Rachel Hertzog: 236
Coons, William: 390
Coray, Melissa: 136, 235, 262, 375
Coray, William: 35, 169, 191, 193, 196, 205, 210, 211, 212, 213, 232, 235, 249, 252, 255, 260, 261, 269, 288, 291, 300, 304, 314, 329, 330, 390
Coronado, Francisco Vásquez de: 187
Corps of Engineers: 90
Corpus Christi: 46, 47
Cortez, Hernando: 349
Cottonwood Creek: 186
Council Bluffs, Iowa: 16, 109, 120, 121, 122, 128, 130, 172
Council Grove: 11, 173, 174, 176, 177, 241
Cow Creek: 186, 187
Coyote Mountains: 269
Crooked River, battle of: 62
Cross, Truman: 38
Custer, George Armstrong: 175

Davidson, J. W: 357
Davis, Capt: 305
Davis, Daniel C: 138, 178, 235, 353, 366, 373, 377, 389
Davis, Daniel, Jr: 235, 262
Davis, Jefferson: 31, 91, 118, 338
Davis, Susan: 235, 262, 306
de Anza, Juan Bautista: 277
De Camp, Dr. Samuel : 234

de Leon, Antonio Ponce: 301, 302
Delaware Indians: 224
Dent, George Wrenshall: 270
Dent, Julia Boggs: 145
Dent, Lewis: 36, 145, 270
DePalo, William: 284
DeVoto, Bernard: 103, 104, 173, 194
Diamond Springs: 186
Disease: 88, 89
Dodge, Henry: 103, 227
Dodson, Eli: 347
Doña Anna: 257
Donald, Neal: 374
Doniphan, Alexander: 9, 12, 13, 14, 15, 31, 58, 99, 107, 108, 174, 216, 222, 223, 229, 233, 236, 237, 238, 254, 257, 259, 301, 302, 339, 340, 366; bio of, 106
Donner tragedy: 369, 370
Dragoon Trail: 13, 295
Dragoons: 37, 38, 69, 91, 103, 104, 105, 115, 119, 174, 216, 223, 227, 233, 257, 332, 340, 350, 356, 360, 368, 371, 376. See also Cavalry
Duncan, John: 91
Dunham, Albert: 183, 184, 185, 346
Dunn, Thomas: 347, 390
Dykes, George P.: 11, 13, 136, 159, 167, 171, 178, 180, 184, 186, 200, 217, 236, 256, 329, 333, 335, 387, 389; appraisal of: 334; negative view of: 255

Edwards, Frank: 53
Edwards, John: 99, 105, 111
Egan, Howard: 175, 204, 206, 207, 238, 251
Eisenhower, John S. D: 29
El Camino Real (California): 316, 354
El Camino Real (New Mexico): 244, 249
Elephant Butte: 261
Elkhorn River: 14, 349
Elmer, Elijah: 252, 390
Emory, William: 107, 223, 225, 241, 375

Far West, Missouri: 59
Fenner, George W: 337

Ferguson, James: 368, 375, 388; photo of, 369
Ferguson, Samuel: 237
"Fifty-four Forty or Fight": 39
Firearms: 152-154
1st Missouri Volunteers: 105, 106, 108, 148, 216, 242, 276, 301, 302, 339, 366
Fitzpatrick, Thomas: 225
Fletcher, Philander: 255
Flores, José María: 214, 303
Follett, William Alexander: 213
Ford, Thomas: 61, 110, 112, 201
Fort Atkinson: 105
Fort Brady: 118
Fort Bridger: 326
Fort Crawford: 105
Fort Des Moines: 119, 120
Fort Hall: 370
Fort Laramie (Fort John): 198, 366
Fort Leavenworth: 8, 9, 10, 11, 15, 16, 69, 76, 77, 79, 101, 103, 104, 105, 108, 109, 129, 143, 144, 145, 146, 148, 149, 150, 151, 152, 155, 156, 157, 158, 159, 161, 167, 169, 170, 172, 177, 237, 326, 350, 370; arrival of Mormon Battalion at, 145; location of, 101
Fort Leavenworth Road: 161
Fort Marcy: 248
Fort Moore: 15, 196, 371, 374; building of, 356-357
Fort Pueblo: 198, 200, 218. See also Pueblo, Colo
Fort Scott Road: 161
Foster's Hole: 264
Foster, Dr. Stephen: 241, 264, 276, 287, 292, 298, 299, 305, 388; bio. of, 242
Francisco (scout): 241, 297, 388
Fray Cristobal Mountains: 257
Freeman, Elijah: 263
Frémont, John Charles: 9, 10, 16, 116, 132, 147-148, 164-166, 224, 225, 240, 259, 278, 312, 320, 322, 327, 341, 356, 360, 367, 370; conflict with others in California, 321, 340, 343, 345, 350, 351

INDEX   407

Fronteras: 274
Frost, Lafayette: 374, 390

Gadsden Purchase: 268, 374, 375
Gaines, Edmund: 68
Gallatin, Missouri: 58
Gandara, Manuel: 280
Garden Grove: 130
Gardner, Hamilton: 236, 237
Gardner, Kansas: 161
Garnett, Richard B: 109
Gibson, George Rutledge: 248
Gila River: 13, 14, 256, 261, 268, 293, 295, 297, 298, 304, 309, 375
Gillespie, Archibald: 12, 214, 225, 278, 279
Gillet, Mary C: 89
Glines, James H: 136, 159, 171, 237, 388
Gold discovery: 375
Golder, Frank Alfred: 32
Goliad: 43
Goodyear, Miles: 377
Grand River: 128
Grant, Jedediah M: 113
Grant, Ulysses S: 30, 36, 93, 98, 145, 209, 226, 270, 282
Great Basin: 77
Green, John: 263
Griffin, Dr. John S: 332, 347
Guadalupe Mountains: 13, 273, 274, 275, 276, 311
Guadalupe Pass: 274, 276
Gully, Samuel: 156, 157, 169, 171, 172, 212, 217, 233, 238, 388, 389

Hall, Willard Preble: 146, 222, 223, 242, 276, 277, 298, 308, 367, 388
Hampton, James: 258
Hancock County, Ill: 60
Hancock, Levi W: 35, 157, 158, 184, 193, 200, 212, 218, 233, 267, 269, 292, 328, 329, 330, 364
Hanks, Ebenzer: 390
Hardee, William: 38
Harmon, Ebenzer: 332

Harrison, William Henry: 45
Hatchett Mountains: 294
Haun's Mill: 59, 134
Haws, Alpheus: 390
Heitman, Francis: 151
Hendricks, Drusilla: 134
Hendricks, William: 134
Herrera, José Joaquín de: 48
Hess, John: 235, 236, 237
Higgins, Nelson: 11, 128, 138, 167, 178, 200, 201, 218, 255, 389
Higgins detachment: 238, 258, 260
Hill, Joseph: 337
Hitchcock, Ethan Allen: 98
Horace, Alexander: 390
Hosea, Stout: 54
Hudson, Thomas: 216
Hughes, George W: 116
Hulett, Sylvester: 389
Humboldt River: 370
Hunt, Celia: 136
Hunt, Gilbert: 390
Hunt, Jefferson: 15, 136, 138, 161, 163, 168, 169, 173, 175, 178, 179, 180, 183, 184, 206, 207, 211, 233, 270, 297, 329, 352, 353, 361, 362, 365, 369, 387, 389; explores taking command of Battalion, 176
Hunt, Matilda: 136
Hunter, Jesse: 138, 206, 207, 218, 235, 249, 250, 294, 343, 345, 346, 347, 364, 389
Hunter, Lydia: 235, 262, 346
Huntington, William: 120
Hurricane Point: 167
Hyde, Orson: 155
Hyde, William: 140, 149, 166, 169, 184, 192, 193, 212, 233, 248, 249, 255, 269, 273, 294, 297, 314, 329, 331, 343, 345, 364, 365, 390

Imperial Desert: 306
Imperial Valley: 308
Independence, Missouri: 56, 102, 104
Indians: 189, 221, 314, 355, 376; lands of, 182; Mormon Battalion and, 15, 355
Infantry: 92

Irish Brigade: 135

Jackson County, Missouri: 56, 57
Jackson, Andrew: 44, 65, 72, 73
Jackson, Henry Wells: 375
Jackson, Thomas: 30
Jalapa, Mexico: 15
Janos Road: 266, 267
Jefferson, Thomas: 84
Jefferson Barracks: 105, 174
Jessup, Thomas S: 342
Johnson, Clark: 287
Johnston, Albert Sidney: 118, 326
Johnston, Joseph E: 118
Jones, Nathaniel V: 323, 335, 353, 355, 390
Jones, Roger: 116, 173, 174, 367
Judd, Zadock: 130, 192

Kane, Dr. Elisha Kent: 72
Kane, John: 72
Kane, Thomas L: 71, 129, 141
Kansas City: 104
Kearney: 100
Kearny, Stephen Watts: 8-16, 25, 29, 31, 34, 68, 69, 73, 74, 77, 102, 104, 115, 116, 119, 120, 136, 147, 159, 162, 164, 172, 174, 175, 180, 199, 210, 213, 214, 215, 216, 221, 223, 224, 225, 226, 229, 241, 254, 256, 257, 259, 278, 279, 285, 302, 303, 308, 312, 314, 316, 317, 320, 327, 337, 360, 361, 362, 370; bio of, 103; conflict with Frémont and Stockton, 320-322, 340, 345, 351, 367; death of, 380; directed to muster Mormon volunteers, 108; establishes government in California, 341; organizes troops, 105, 107; takes Santa Fe, 221
Kearny Code: 222, 223
Kendall, Amos: 8, 72, 73, 74, 77
Keysor, Guy: 232, 315
Kimball, Heber C: 126, 128, 129, 349
Kimball, Stanley B: 325
Kirtland, Ohio: 56, 58

La Baja Mesa: 249

La Joya de Ciboletta: 213, 254
La Mesa, battle of: 14, 303
LaClede Rangers: 107, 216, 224
Laguna Salada: 308
Lake Playas: 271, 272, 294
Lancers: 283, 285
Lane, Lewis: 335, 390
Larkin, Thomas: 164-166, 327
Laundresses: 136
Layton, Christopher: 155
Lee, John D: 175, 189, 207, 211, 218, 233, 238, 239, 251; criticizes Mormons with Battalion: 206, 211-212; objects to Smith's command: 205
Lee, Robert E: 30, 118, 349
Leesburg, Virginia: 226
Leroux, Antoine: 241, 260, 264, 272, 298, 308, 388; bio. of: 256
Lewis, Meriwether: 107, 122, 154
Lewis and Clark: 101, 242
Lexington (ship): 368
Little Arkansas River: 186
Little Cow Creek: 186
Little Hatchett Mountains: 270
Little, Jesse C: 7, 8, 9, 71, 72, 155; and meetings with Pres. Polk, 72-79; meets with B. Young, 129, 130
Loma Blanca: 254
Long, Stephen: 189
Longstreet, James: 30
Los Angeles: 12, 14, 214, 302, 351, 353, 360, 374; work of the Mormon Battalion in, 355-357
Lost Springs: 186
Luddington, Elam: 234, 389
Lyons, Kansas: 186
Lytle, Andrew: 212, 217, 353, 389

Magdelena Mountains: 257
Magoffin, James: 10, 226
Magoffin, Susan Shelby: 226
Manifest destiny: 66
Marcy, William: 8, 66, 68, 69, 74, 78, 108, 111, 302

INDEX

Maricopas: 298
Marshall, James: 16, 375
Martin, Edward: 237, 390
Martin, Jesse: 109
Mason, Richard B: 15, 340, 341, 351, 353, 363, 366, 367, 368
Matamoros: 8
Maxwell, William B: 335
Mayfield, Benjamin: 355
Mazatlán, Mexico: 68
McCaffrey, James: 195
McClellan, George: 30, 379
McCord, Alexander: 390
McIntire, Dr. William: 136, 145, 150, 151, 183, 192, 388
Meade, George: 30
Meadows, Mountain: 175-176
Medical practices and treatment: 88, 89, 190-196
Merrill, Philemon: 13, 255, 387, 389
Merritt, Wesley: 228
Mervine, William: 214
Mexican army: evaluation of, 281-285
Mexican revolution: 41-42
Mexican War: 25, 27, 81; and Texas, 42, 43, 44; artillery in, 91; assessment of, 383-384; continuation after the battalion's discharge, 380; battle tactics of, 96; firearms used in, 93, 94, 95, 152-154; increase in army size during, 67; medical science during, 88, 89; military practices during, 81-100; popular attitude toward, 53-54; progress of, 131-132, 147-148, 164, 208-210, 213-214, 259, 265-266, 278-279, 301-303, 319-320, 338-340, 342-343, 349, 359, 366; recruitment for, 30, 52-53; religion and, 31; summary of, 29-32; uniforms used during, 95
Mexico City: 7, 14; capture of: 359
Military Road: 161
Militia: 67, 68, 82, 84, 99; legislation concerning, 83
Mimbres Mountains: 257

Mississippi Rifles: 338, 339
Mississippi Saints: 198, 238, 367
Mitchell, Augustus: 240
Mojave Desert: 354
Molino del Rey, battle of: 16
Monroe Doctrine: 53
Monterey, Calif: 9, 10, 68, 132, 147
Monterrey, battle of: 11, 208-209, 337
Montoya, Pablo: 319
Moore, Benjamin: 15, 229, 371
Morales, Juan: 342, 343
Mormon Battalion: 108; arrival at Ft. Leavenworth, 145; assessment of, 381-383; authorized by Marcy, 108; Brigham Young instructs, 140; builds Ft. Moore, 355-357; chronology of, 7-16; clothing of, 96, 133, 154, 155; command of, 85, 115-117, 171-181; command of assumed by Cooke, 225-226, 233; conflict with Sterling Price, 199; confrontation at Tucson, 285-293; consumption of alcohol by, 144-145, 157, 347, 348; contributions of to California history, 374-375; deployed in California, 322; description of by Parkman, 198; detachment of sent to Pueblo, 234, 235, 237, 238; discipline and, 243, 336; divided by Smith: 199-200; divided in California: 343; drill and training of: 158, 331, 332, 353; encamp in San Diego, 317; families with, 136, 182, 197, 199-200, 234, 235; fight with Indians, 355; firearms issued to, 152-154; first march by, 143-145; harassed by wild cattle, 277; historical sources re, 32-33, 35; illness in, and second detachment of, 260-263; length of march by, 324-327; loses Cooke as commander, 368; march rate of, 163; medical care of, 190-196; military purpose of, 81; misdeeds by members of, 143, 357; organization of, 9, 99; origin of, 69, 74, 76, 78; pay received by, 238; purpose of to LDS church, 156; rations for, 231; recruitment of, 120, 125-

129, 130-131, 133-134, 136, 139; re-enlistment by members of, 360-366; religion vs. military conflict, 207, 330, 334; religious character of, 157, 247-248; reunion for, 1855, 112, 113, 376; rosters of, 145; scouts with, 241, 242; service in Los Angeles, 355-357; summary of, 26-29; uniqueness of in American military service, 134-135
Mormon Trail: 9, 115
Mormon Volunteers: 16, 373, 374
Mormons: attitude toward the war, 54; attitude toward US, 1846, 109-110; impressed with Allen, 117; in Missouri, 56-59, 62; interest in California, 77; migration of from Illinois: 8, 9, 14, 16, 122; persecutions against, 56, 57; pioneer party migrates to Utah, 348, 349, 366-367; plan to move west, 70; source for volunteers in Army of the West, 8, 9; supposed conspiracy against by U.S. govt, 110-114
Mount Pisgah: 9, 109, 115, 117, 120, 123, 128, 129, 130
Mountain Meadows: 238
Mounted Riflemen: 91, 96
Mowry, John: 332
Muir, William: 299, 312, 390
Mule Hill: 279, 327

Napoleon: 325
Nauvoo Legion: 34, 60, 61, 62, 375, 376
Nauvoo, Ill: 7, 11, 59, 61, 70, 129, 201, 202
Navajos: 223, 230, 254
Nevin, David: 89
New Mexico: 44, 66, 69, 104, 210, 216, 219, 221, 222, 319
New York Volunteers: 99, 259, 336, 341, 360, 361, 368
Nowland, Jabez: 237
Nowlin, Jabez: 390
Nueces River: 30, 38, 44, 47
Nutt Mountain: 264, 265

Ocate Creek: 214, 217
Olathe, Kansas: 161
Old Spanish Trail: 244, 354
Oman, George: 306, 307, 308, 335, 350, 389
Oregon: 8, 9, 39, 40, 41, 45, 69, 75
Oregon Trail: 69, 96, 370
Oregon-California Trail: 102
Oriflamme Mountains: 309
Owens, Richard: 350
Oxen: 202, 203
Oyler, Melcher: 347

Pace, James: 159, 171, 172, 175, 204, 212, 217, 329, 353, 354, 357, 389
Pacific Squadron: 322, 341
Padilla, Fr. Juan de: 187
Palm Springs: 309
Palo Alto, battle of: 8, 73, 303
Panic of 1837: 58
Paredes, Mariano: 7, 48
Parkman, Francis: 198
Patten, David W: 62
Peck, Isaac: 332
Perkins, John: 347
Pettegrew, David: 157, 184, 193, 258, 267, 329
Phelps, Alva: 142, 193, 205, 258
Phelps, Margaret: 142
Picacho Peak: 294
Pico, Andrés: 278
Pico, Pío: 164
Pierce, Franklin: 268
Pimas: 296, 297, 298
Piño, Manuel: 221
Pitt, William: 141
Pixton, Robert: 130
Platte River: 122
Platte River Road: 102
Playas Valley: 271
Pletcher, David: 48
Point Loma: 346
Polk, James: 7, 8, 9, 30, 31, 39, 41, 45, 46, 47, 48, 51, 52, 66, 67, 68, 69, 77, 78, 99, 105, 108, 110, 112, 115, 116, 130, 173, 215, 259, 266,

302, 320, 370; character of: 73-74; supposed persecution of Mormons by: 111
Polk, Leonidas: 118
Polygamy: 60
Pony Express: 102
Porter, Dr. John B: 195
Potawatomi lands: 123, 125
Powell, John Wesley: 304
Pozo Hondo: 308
Pratt, Orson: 16, 125
Pratt, Parley P: 155
Price, Sterling: 14, 148, 175, 179, 180, 198, 210, 213, 223, 255, 319; bio. of, 148-149; denies supplies to Mormon Battalion, 199
Prince, William: 109
Pueblo, Colo: 10, 11, 12, 13, 137, 201, 233, 234, 235, 238, 239, 247, 255, 261, 262, 263, 346; Mormons sent to, 200. See also Fort Pueblo
Purgatory River: 190, 258

Quorum of Seventy: 357
Quorum of the Twelve Apostles: 7, 110, 120

Rabbit Ear Buttes: 189
Rainey, David: 390
Raton Pass: 190, 230
Rawson, Daniel: 129
Republic of California: 132
Republic of Texas: 44
Resaca de la Palma, battle of: 8, 73, 303
Revolutionary War: 84
Rich, Russell C: 175
Richards, Joseph: 263
Richards, Willard: 126, 128, 129, 134
Ricketts, Norma B: 33
Riley, Bennet: 226
Ringgold, Sam: 91
Rio Grande: 30, 38, 44, 47, 104, 132, 224, 249, 261, 264
Riser, John: 328, 373
Roberts, B. H: 110, 201, 324, 376

Roberts, Richard: 376
Robinson, Cecil: 42
Romero, Tomás: 319
Rosecrans, George: 167, 237, 354, 389
Running Turkey Creek: 186
Rush, Dr. Benjamin: 194

Sacagawea: 242
Sacramento, battle of: 14, 174, 339
St. Joseph, Missouri: 102, 104, 144
St. Louis: 129
San Bernardino Mountains: 354
San Bernardino Ranch: 276, 277
San Antonio: 44, 68
San Diego: 13, 14, 279, 302, 316, 323, 345, 346, 373, 374
San Diego Mission: 317
San Diego–San Antonio Mail line: 268
San Felipe Pueblo: 250
San Felipe Valley: 312
San Francisco: 70
San Gabriel River: 14, 302
San Jacinto, battle of (1836): 43, 44
San Jose Valley: 312
San Juan River: 302
San Luis Potosi: 266
San Luis Rey Mission: 14, 315, 327, 328, 330, 343, 347, 350, 352, 353, 357
San Luis Valley: 315
San Marcos Arroyo: 250
San Mateo Mountains: 257
San Pasqual: 302, 308, 312, 328; battle of, 13, 15, 278, 285, 297, 371
San Patricio Battalion: 259, 338
San Pedro River: 13, 274, 277, 279, 308
San Pedro River: 256
San Xavier del Bac: 291; sketch of: 291
Sanderson, Ellen Johnson: 152
Sanderson, Dr. George: 11, 89, 150-152, 171, 172, 177, 178, 181, 182, 183, 185, 186, 197, 204, 208, 210, 211, 213, 218, 232, 234, 245, 248, 251, 257, 258, 261, 265, 266, 267, 269, 271, 272, 273, 275, 276, 277, 288, 292, 293, 294, 295, 299, 307, 308, 310, 311, 312, 313,

333, 346, 367, 388; journal of, 35, 145, 152, 195; medical care of Battalion by, 190-196, 205; Mormon hostility towards, 184
Sanderson, Henry: 143
Sangre de Cristo Mountains: 189
Santa Anna, Antonio López de: 10, 14, 15, 43, 44, 48, 164, 259, 266, 302, 338, 339, 349
Santa Cruz River: 293
Santa Fe: 8, 10, 11, 12, 69, 73, 120, 146, 176, 181, 215, 230, 235, 238, 263; description of, 232; taken by Kearny, 221
Santa Fe Trail: 9, 11, 102, 103, 104, 108, 161, 162, 166, 176, 177, 182, 186, 190, 198, 203, 222, 241; Cimarron route of, 202
Sarpy, Peter A: 138
Schoolcraft, Henry: 118
Scott, James: 197, 347, 390
Scott, Winfield: 13, 14, 16, 31, 65, 66, 67-68, 92, 266, 302, 326, 340, 342, 349, 359
2nd Missouri Volunteers: 108, 148, 161, 179, 198, 199, 216
2nd U.S. Dragoons: 25
Sharp, Norman: 258
Shawnee Indian scouts: 107
Shelton, Sebert C: 136, 156, 169, 388
Sherman, William Tecumseh: 368
Shubrick, W. Branford: 322, 341
Sierra de Los Cucapas: 308
Sierra Estrella Mountains: 297
Slavery: 52
Slidell, John: 7, 8, 46, 47, 48, 383
Sloat, John D: 10, 68, 132, 147, 341
Smith, Albert: 390
Smith, Andrew Jackson: 11, 12, 15, 34, 85, 171, 173, 174, 182, 184, 190, 194, 197, 199, 210, 211, 213, 214, 217, 219, 228, 239, 328, 333, 346, 352, 368, 372, 374, 379, 380, 387, 388, 390; bio. of: 175; conflict with J. D. Lee, 205, 207; conflicts with Mormons, 183-186; photo of, 85; temporary command of Mormon Battalion, 172, 176, 177, 178, 179, 180, 181

Smith, Azariah: 232, 280, 372
Smith, David: 347
Smith, Elisha: 277
Smith, Hyrum: 59, 61, 128
Smith, Jedediah Strong: 207
Smith, Joseph: 34, 56, 57, 58, 59, 60, 63, 68, 128, 145, 148-149; and Alexander Doniphan, 106, 107; assasination of, 61
Smith, Lot: 376
Smith, Milton: 238, 258
Smith, Samuel: 175
Snake River: 370
Snow, Erastus: 16
Socorro: 268
Soledad Valley: 316
Sonoma: 132
South Pass: 370
Southern Pacific Railroad: 269
St. John, Stephen: 357, 390
Standage, Henry: 35, 203, 293, 311, 353, 354, 356, 358, 362, 371
Steele, John: 54, 128, 144, 149, 235, 236, 237
Stephens (Stevens), Arnold: 347, 390
Stephens, Roswell: 238, 390
Stevenson, Jonathan: 15, 259, 341, 363, 364, 366, 369, 371, 373, 374
Stewart, Robert: 255
Stockton, John: 259
Stockton, Robert F: 10, 14, 147, 164-166, 224, 225, 302, 303, 314, 320, 321, 322, 327, 340, 341, 343, 350
Stoneman, George: 14, 85, 146, 216, 228, 233, 252, 274, 277, 293, 298, 299, 308, 331, 350, 354, 368, 379, 380, 388
Stout, Hosea: 127
Stuart, James Ewell Brown "Jeb": 228
Sumner, Edmund V: 105, 229
Swords, Thomas: 350, 367

Taggart, George Washington: 143, 156, 274
Taos: 14, 223
Tasson (scout): 241, 388
Taylor, John: 128, 129, 155

INDEX 413

Taylor, Zachary: 7, 8, 10, 14, 30, 31, 37, 38, 46, 47, 51, 67, 68, 73, 98, 104, 131, 195, 208, 209, 259, 265, 302, 303, 338
Temecula Creek: 314
Temeculas: 314
Terrell, Joel: 237, 390
Texas; boundary controversy concerning, 7; gains statehood, 45; Republic of, 44, 45; role in Mexican War, 39, 42, 43, 44, 49
Texas Rangers: 209
Thompson, Philip: 174, 241, 388
Thompson, Samuel: 15, 335, 353, 354, 355, 389
Thornton, Seth: 8, 37, 38, 51
Tippets, John H: 131, 157, 200, 348, 367
Torrejón, Anastasio: 37
Treaty of Guadalupe Hildago: 16, 29, 268, 381
Trist, Nicholas: 15, 16, 381
Truth or Consequences: 264
Tubbs, Sophia: 235, 262
Tubbs, William: 235, 262
Tucson: 13, 279, 280, 285; painting of, 286
Turkey Creek: 186
Turner, Henry S: 152, 214, 215, 229, 360, 361, 367
Tuttle, Luther: 390
Twiggs, David: 68
Tyler, Daniel: 35, 121, 131, 175, 180, 181, 184, 193, 218, 237, 249, 252, 276, 305, 306, 315, 316, 317, 329, 334, 351, 353, 390. See also United States Military Academy
Tyler, John: 7, 45, 46

Uniform Militia Act: 83
United States Military Academy: 31, 84, 85, 90, 98, 118, 174, 216
Utah Expedition: 25
Utah War: 326, 376

Val Verde: 256, 257
Valencia: 254
Vallecito Creek: 309, 310, 311, 312

Vallecito Mountains: 309
Van Buren, Martin: 39, 59
Vancouver Island: 41
Vera Cruz: 10, 48, 265; battle of, 342, 343
Volunteer regiments: 67, 96, 99
Vose, Josiah: 98

Wagon Bed Springs: 207
Wakarusa River: 166
Walaroosa, Kan: 11
War of 1812: 83
Warner Springs: 313
Warner's Ranch: 14, 260, 278, 297, 298, 300, 312, 313, 316, 335
Warner, Jonathan: 313
Washington, George: 82, 83
Weaver, Pauline: 241, 298, 308, 311, 388
Weir, Thomas: 390
Wellesley, Arthur: 359
Wells, Daniel H: 201
West Point. See United States Military Academy
Wharton, Clifton: 148, 172, 173, 180
Whigs: 52
White Sands: 257
Whitworth, Robert: 145-147, 150-151, 163-164, 204, 275, 299
Wiggins, David: 119
Wilcox, Edward: 390
Wilkes, Charles: 240
Wilkin, David: 237, 390
Williams, Isaac: 15, 354, 355
Williams, Thomas: 184, 185, 213, 346, 390
Willis, William Wesley: 13, 262, 389
Willis sick detachment: 262, 263
Winter Quarters: 12, 14, 198, 200, 233, 238
Woodruff, Wilford: 120, 122
Wool, John: 11, 15, 68, 209, 216, 223, 267
Woolsey, Thomas: 200, 260, 263, 348, 367
Wooton, N.M: 214
Worden, Kansas: 162
Worth, William: 16, 209
Wright, Phineas: 390

Yell, Archibald: 73
Yellow fever: 89
Young, Brigham: 7, 9, 14, 16, 59, 69-70, 71, 73, 77, 109, 120, 122, 123, 125, 129, 131, 138, 139, 155, 156, 157, 173, 175, 176, 179, 180, 183, 186, 200, 204, 207, 247, 314, 329, 348, 361, 362, 363, 366, 367, 370, 371, 376, 378, 383; assumes leadership of Mormon Church, 61; attitude towards U.S. govt., 112; instructions to Battalion members, 140, 141; meets with James Allen, 126, 127; notified of Allen's death, 172; recruits Mormon Battalion, 114, 121; teachings re medicine, 193

Yurtinus, John: 33, 113, 138, 184, 229, 334

*History May Be Searched in Vain:
A Military History of the Mormon Battalion*
by Sherman L. Fleek
has been produced in two editions:
a trade edition of 750 copies
bound in blue linen-finish cloth,
and a collector's edition of 55 copies,
bound in bonded leather, signed,
and numbered, of which 50 are for sale.
The book is set in Caslon Old Style type,
and was designed by Ariane C. Smith.

www.ingramcontent.com/pod-product-compliance
Lightning Source LLC
Chambersburg PA
CBHW020940230426
43666CB00005B/98